THE
CLASSICAL
TRADITION
IN WESTERN
ART

Benjamin Rowland, Jr.

HARVARD UNIVERSITY PRESS
Cambridge, Massachusetts
1963

THE CLASSICAL TRADITION IN WESTERN ART

Distributed in Great Britain by Oxford University Press, London

Library of Congress Catalog Card Number 63–17211

Printed in the United States of America

To my
Teachers, Colleagues, and Friends
Who share a love of the
Classical Tradition

PREFACE

I CANNOT claim, like Gibbon, to have been inspired to pursue this history of the vicissitudes of the classical ideal while seated amidst the ruins of the Capitoline listening to friars "singing vespers in the temple of Jupiter." It was, however, during a year in Rome, devoted primarily to investigating the Greco-Roman background of the art of Gandhara, that the spell of the enduring classical style began to affect me more and more powerfully, its history and strength anything but a "decline and fall." My wanderings in Italy and in Romanesque and Gothic France impelled me to organize a course on the classical tradition given in the General Education program of Harvard University. Out of this series of lectures, presented a number of times in the last years, this book has emerged.

Everyone who has approached the subject of the classical tradition is eternally indebted to the pioneers in this study: Aby Warburg, Erwin Panofsky, and Ernst Gombrich. In tracing many phases of this development it is hardly possible to do more than paraphrase their definitive studies of the renewal of antiquity. I am further indebted to Ernst Gombrich for his advice and counsel during a summer of research at the Warburg Institute in London. I must thank him and the members of the staff of the Warburg Institute for their courtesy and the extending of every facility in this ideal scholar's library.

Although the title of this book may suggest a comparison with Gilbert Highet's *The Classical Tradition in Western Literature,* I have not, beyond the borrowing of this title, sought to emulate Professor Highet's complete and erudite coverage of the entire field. As an introduction to the theme of the persistence of the classical ideal in art I have thought it more inviting to the student and general reader to discuss only a few representative works in the many different periods covered in the text. Obviously many artists and many works that have no less fascination for this study have had to be omitted. Although it is impossible to separate style from iconography in dealing with a subject of this type, I have sought to present the various transformations of the classical primarily from the point of view of style with less emphasis on the iconographical apparatus examined in such masterful fashion by Professor Panofsky in his many works on renascences in Western art.

It has always been my belief that the value of a book of this type hangs on the quality of the illustrations. Every effort has been made to obtain the best possible prints. I have taken many photographs myself in an effort to present just the right interpretation and proper angle of the subject to be discussed. In this connection I must thank Dr. Ernest Nash and his associates in the Fototeca di Architettura e Topografia dell' Italia Antica for their tireless assistance in finding prints of many objects otherwise unobtainable. I owe a special debt of gratitude to the photographic establishment of Lucchesi in Rome and to the ladies of the Cambridge Camera for their painstaking efforts in producing the best prints from my negatives. To the many museums and private collections that have generously given permission to reproduce their works of art, a word of thanks. Anyone who writes a book in the field of Fine Arts at Harvard must express his special gratitude to Louise Lucas, Mary Ward, and Rose Marie Mitten of the library of the Fogg Art Museum for their unfailing help in solving many tedious problems of bibliography and reference.

My special thanks are due to the Bollingen Foundation and the American Council of Learned Societies for grants which made possible two summers of research in Europe.

Cornelius Vermeule, himself engaged in writing a work on the theme of the classical tradition, has been extremely generous in his advice from repeated readings of the manuscript. For their reading of the work and their many valuable suggestions I must also thank my colleagues, Sydney Freedberg and Frederick Deknatel of Harvard University. Joachim Gaehde of Brandeis University must be remembered here, too, for his advice on the chapters on medieval art. Ida Treat Bergeret has been extremely kind in her criticism of the style of various chapters and for persuading me to adopt the present title of the book. I owe a special debt of gratitude to Laura de Lucia, for many years my *maestra* in Italian, for her assistance in the translation of many Italian passages. I should also like to thank Elizabeth B. Weissbach of The Winsor School for help in Latin translations. I hope that these and other friends who have helped me will consider themselves included in the dedication of this book. To my wife goes a special acknowledgment for her many valuable and creative suggestions for the writing of the text, her typing a great part of the manuscript, and, what is most important of all, her unfailing encouragement in bringing this work into being.

Cambridge, Massachusetts   Benjamin Rowland, Jr.
1 June 1963

CONTENTS

CONTENTS

CONTENTS

CONTENTS

ILLUSTRATIONS

ILLUSTRATIONS

ILLUSTRATIONS

THE
CLASSICAL
TRADITION
IN WESTERN
ART

To thy house
Comes Pericles. Receive the friend of him
Whose horses started from the Parthenon
To traverse seas and neigh upon our strand.

—W. S. Landor, "To Julius Hare," II, 13–16

— I —

Introduction

He who beholds the skies of Italy
Sees ancient Rome reflected, sees beyond,
Into more glorious Hellas, nurse of gods
And godlike men.   —Landor *

THE purpose of this book is to provide an introduction to art through the understanding and love of our common Western heritage from Greece and Rome: the exaltation of the beauty and nobility of man in sculpture and painting. This ennoblement of the human being as the most intrinsically perfect form imaginable for the revelation of the emotions and passions, tender and strong, happy and sad, that illumine and darken man's mind, stems from the Greeks' selection of the human shape as the embodiment of the unknowable beauty of the gods. The vicissitudes that have accompanied this momentous Hellenic choice through later centuries constitutes in itself a history of Western art and taste.

Many avenues lead us to what is called an appreciation of art through the analysis of form, content, technique, and historical association. My interpretation might be defined as a humanistic introduction to art, since there is implicit in the subject, the classical tradition, the premise of the accepted beauty of the human form and the no less moving beauty of everything that it reflects. The peculiar perfection and ideality achieved by the antique have so haunted the Western mind that in some periods their imitation has been no less important than the imitation of nature. The never-ending opportunities for the reordering of nature on the basis of the kind of generalized perfection first realized in Greece of the fifth century B.C. have provided inspiration for artists of every subsequent period. Critics of many different times have referred to the antique as a second nature, because the classical prototypes were so refined away

* Walter Savage Landor, "To Shelley"

1

from everything transitory and materially inconsequential that they achieved a kind of formal idealization, based on nature but portraying a nature so enhanced as worthy of imitation as nature herself.

The abstraction of reality in classical art, especially in its archaic phase, has an appeal to the modern eye and mind, a subjective interpretation conditioned by the taste of our time that we can perhaps regard as a translation into terms of Winckelmann's note: "To those who know and study the works of the Greeks, their masterpieces reveal not only nature in its greatest beauty, but something more than that; namely, certain ideal beauties of nature which, as an old commentator of Plato teaches us, exist only in the intellect." [1]

Athough the reaction of a modern student first experiencing a work of the classical period cannot be the same passionate romantic recognition of ultimate beauty that shook the souls of Goethe, Shelley, and Byron, or moved a Hildebert in the twelfth century, or a Michelangelo in the sixteenth, the enduring intrinsic values of form that abide in a Greek masterpiece will, in a different way, move anyone with the least aesthetic sensibility to descry there something of an order and regulated canon of beauty that, in its perfection, has always remained apart from time and change: to discern like Keats "a shadow of magnitude." [2]

The classical in art or literature means first of all the attainment of an order and balance that are lacking in the confusion and complexity of our own lives. It presents a perfection in the reconciliation of the real and the ideal, the personal and impersonal, which makes for something rational, self-contained, and lucid. This equilibrium and impartiality offer a security that has drawn men to identify themselves with this classical ideal in all later periods. In a specific way the kind of self-contained, rational presentation found in the perfection of form and structure in Greek art and Greek tragedy has offered the solution of problems of artistic expression to men of many later ages. This is a perfection that has enchanted and directed the mind of Western man for millenniums, for the ideal achieved by the Greeks of the Great Period has in its completely satisfying rightness of artistic statement become a standard and accepted norm of beauty. In art this norm is based on the beauty of man as a symbol of divinity and human perfection and order. The Greeks were the first to make the human figure the focal point of artistic interest and expression (figure 1).

The complete detachment of the images of Greek gods and goddesses,

2

their compelling serenity and angelic perfection of body, make them appropriately superhuman: as emblems of living perfection they present in their ideality a second, superior race in marble and bronze that impels to admiration and emulation. This rarefied norm is the result of a refining process, in which every distracting blemish of accidental reality is removed, to leave as a kind of core a pristine symbol of humanity in its final, intrinsic shape.

It has become almost a fixed convention in all writing on the Greek spirit since the days of Winckelmann to laud the ideality of Hellenic life and art, its moderation, calm, and stupendous grandeur. Indeed, the idea of everything Greek as a veritable synonym of the self-contained and rational had become firmly fixed in the intellectual concept of the ancient world as early as the seventeenth century in the perfect balance and restraint of emotion in the polished lines of Corneille and the stately architectural calm of Poussin's compositions. The famous motto before Apollo's oracle at Delphi, "Nothing in excess," was something the Greeks aspired to, but certainly did not exemplify to the last man, nor in art to the last statue. The childish behavior of the heroes of the Iliad and the raucous humor of the Greek comedy present a somewhat different picture of Hellenic civilization. The unedifying barbarity of divine behavior in the myths, the treacheries and atrocities of war in the epics and on earth are quite at variance with the notion of all-pervading moderation. Greek life and conduct in the days of Pericles and of Socrates were not invariable models of decorum. The subjects of many Greek vase paintings are enough to inform us that the Greeks were as much given to excesses of one kind or another as any people on earth. If the Greeks had left us conceptions of humanity which in their nobility and heroic grandeur, their perfect balance of the real and the abstract surpassed anything ever made by human hands, it is because these noble embodiments of human perfection and vitality were what the Greeks aspired to, not what they were. These works of art were reflections of a world that philosophers and artists dreamed of, and not of the Greek world as it was in actuality. Like all public monuments of any age they had the intended function of exalting the beholder to aspire in pride and patriotism to emulate the titanic beauty of form and spirit that the gods and heroes in marble personified.

Our conception of Greek art has become so fixed in the conventions established by the writers in the eighteenth century and their successors that we find it impossible to think of ancient sculpture except in terms of a kind of petrified nobility of pose and expression. The notion of the Greek ideal concocted in the last three centuries, although totally different from the original conception of that ideal, is nonetheless important, because it was on this heightened interpretation of Hellenic art as all balance and serenity that the whole structure of the imitation of the classical tradition was built.

The story of the mutations of classical ideals in later periods of Western art is not simply an account of imitation or slavish copying; it is an examination of how this basic Western heritage, the classical ideal, was used as a continuing source of the most vital and original kind of creation, in which classical forms and subject matter served only as a point of departure for new, creative ideation. One reason for the immortality of the classical ideal is at once its perfection and its adaptability for the solution of artistic problems in every age and circumstance. And this is because since its first perfection it has been so much a part of man in the Western world.

Certain moments of history have witnessed a deliberate return to antiquity for political reasons: such was the thirteenth-century imitation of Augustan models as an artistic reënforcement for the imperial policy of Frederick II, or the espousal of classical ideals by the French revolutionaries and, later, the Roman taste of Napoleon's Empire. These phenomena are an integral part of the life story of the classical tradition, which stimulated a momentary acceleration of the pulse-beat of a life-stream that had always coursed, although sometimes almost imperceptibly, through the veins of Western humanity.

When the father of modern art history, Johann Winckelmann, wrote in 1755, "To take the ancient models is our only way to become great, yes, unsurpassable if we can," [3] he was expressing one of the last and most fervent appeals for a return to the paradigm of antique art to build anew. The influence of Winckelmann, alas, may be seen only in the sterile attempt to copy rather than understand the classical ideal in the neoclassic period of the eighteenth and nineteenth centuries. It stands as only one of many such turns to the past throughout the centuries that generally were marked by a far more original and creative inspiration from the antique.

One of the most famous and influential statements about Greek art is the observation by Winckelmann that "the most prominent general characteristic of the Greek masterpiece is a noble simplicity and quiet grandeur in pose as well as in expression." [4] This definition of the serene and self-contained nature of Greek art had a profound effect on the interpretation of antiquity throughout the nineteenth century, notably on the impassioned writing on Greece by the Sage of Weimar.

Although this picture of the Greek world as a civilization controlled, balanced, restrained, perfect in harmony and proportion in all things, may not agree with the real nature of Greek society in its violent and passionate aspect, more Dionysian than Apollonian, the fact remains that the greatest Greek contribution to our civilization was, together with the understanding of man, a substitution of rational experience for reliance on supernatural forces of fear and magic, such as had governed the ancient Oriental empires of Egypt and Mesopotamia. A world intelligible in terms of finite experience rather than unknown powers separated the Greeks from the nonrational cultures of the East. Such a conception based on reason made man the master and center of a finite and understandable world. Such a world view inevitably produced an art that was finite, simple, concrete, expressing itself in forms that in their order and tangibility reflected an imaginative personal expression impossible in the absoute societies of the ancient East. It is obvious that the very limitation of Greek art in subject and technique could, and often did, lead to a sterile copying of models, however perfect, by later artists lacking the imagination of the Hellenic creators. We shall be concerned in later chapters with an exploration only of the imaginative use of the classical heritage by men who learned from the antique best to express themselves and their times.

The modern world is linked by many avenues to the worlds of Greece and Rome, and much that is an accepted part of our lives in law, in finance, in our speech and usages is our inheritance from these complex civilizations that have never lost their hold on Western culture. The literature and art of the ancient period have never really died out or atrophied: they have always been at hand to kindle the minds of those who seek their inspiration. They have provided an enrichment without which Western civilization would be thin and materialistic.

Although for some of the more passionate devotees of Hellenism, like Goethe, Christ and Mary seem scarcely to exist, the part played by Christianity in the preservation of the classical tradition cannot be overlooked in a consideration of this survival. The relation between the writings of

the Christian theologians and the pagan classics is one aspect of the preservation of Greek and Roman learning in the Middle Ages. In art the
demands of the Christian religion provided new uses for the forms and techniques of the artists of the dying world of paganism. The classical vocabulary in the plastic arts became enormously enlarged and enriched with
its adaptation to provide the pictorial iconography of Christianity.
Throughout the centuries following the death of the gods in the Late
Antique Period, the persistence of the classical language of expression in
art owes its survival to its new role in the service of the Christian religion.

Every succeeding culture has understood and interpreted the classical
Greek tradition according to its own needs. This process can be traced
through every period in the evolution of Western man and his art. For
the visitor attuned to their spell the gods still seem present in the long blue
alleys of the sky over the Acropolis, in the groves at Olympia, and on the
barren height of Delphi, exerting an invisible enchantment over their
old Attic home. And so they did for centuries in the mind of Western
man—whether as daimons or poetic fantasies, as symbols of a lost day,
exiled at last by Heine to Hyperborean realms. The power that the gods
exerted magically over the poetic and artistic imagination more than
compensated for their loss of an official cult. No ancient devotee was
more conscious of their enduring magic and mystery than the Neoplatonists of fifteenth-century Italy; none adored them more fervently than
the mad Hölderlin. They lived again as dazzling phantoms in the Walpurgisnacht of Goethe's *Faust,* and Stefan George sought to conjure the
gods to a new life. In art, as in philosophy and literature, the Olympians
have had many lives. In them, as of old, man continued to recognize his
own image; the shattered fragments of the images of the gods beckoned
to a perfection once achieved and ever attainable anew. If classical art
seems a tyranny, it was bondage elected by men of poetic vision in every
age and only rejected in those times when any discipline however salutary
looms as an imposition on what is described as freedom of expression.

Although the rigorous dependence on the antique required by the
French Academy of the seventeenth century or the endless drawing from
the cast prescribed in the dusty routine of nineteenth-century studios
turned the lessons of the ancients to drudgery, in the eye and mind of men
like Poussin or Ingres or Picasso, the true discernment of the hidden
order and pagan sensuality of classical art provided a springboard for
soaring flight.

6

This book is not intended to be a history of plagiarism—to pinpoint the very models Michelangelo or David copied in their works—but to indicate how the creative imaginative use of such prototypes led to compositions both original and grand and inevitably appropriate to the mentality of the time.

— 2 —

The Greek Ideal

Zeus caused a russet cloud to draw nigh to them and rained on them abundant
gold, while grey-eyed Athena herself bestowed upon them every art, so that they
surpassed all mortal men by their deftness of hand, and along the roads rose works
of art like unto beings that lived and moved; and great was their fame.

—Pindar *

THE Greeks of the Great Period, the age of Pericles, were, like no other
people before or since, absorbed in the study of themselves, the study of
man and his relations to the world of space and matter, as well as to the
world of myths, which no philosopher and no scientist had succeeded in
explaining away. Perhaps the greatest Greek contribution was the bringing of order and conscious thought into life, the explaining of phenomena
by natural events rather than by supernatural intervention; that is, understanding nature in intelligible rather than supernatural terms. According to Anaxagoras it was Mind that brought order out of chaos.[1]

In such a world of reason and factual finite experience art is a world
of forms, a world to be kept small, clear, orderly, statuesque, and tangible. The chief concern of Greek art and thought was more order than expansion, a point of view that to a certain extent led to a sacrifice of that
variety and fluidity defined under the heading of romantic.

The kind of limitation the Greeks set themselves is exemplified in the
Athens of Pericles and his ideal of refinement without extravagance,
knowledge without effeminacy, and harmonious expression of all the
powers that make up the beauty and worth of human nature (figure 2).
This was something attainable in the atmosphere of freedom provided in
Athens, where, as Pericles said, we live exactly as we please. The result
was an individuality and expression, impossible in the despotisms of the
Oriental world. As has already been noted, the actual Greeks of the fifth

* Pindar, *Tenth Olympian Ode*

8

century were violent, impulsive, and shrewd. Neither all art nor all life was completely chaste and calm. The Dionysian element of Greek life was all frenzy and wild passion; the scream of the maenads often drowned out the serene measures of Apollo's lyre. In the Athenian noon of Pericles the Acropolis (figure 3) probably presented a garish collection of statues, slabs, and monuments, touched with brilliant colors. The deceptive magic of time has removed the gaudy accessories of this ancient hill, so that we see only the marble husk of the Parthenon, isolated in majestic simplicity (figure 4). In spite of these seemingly unclassical incongruities there was an underlying exemplification of the restraint, composure, and poise of the classical ideal.

The three great Greek tragedians—Aeschylus, Sophocles, and Euripides—very closely parallel the sculptured forms of Greek art. Aeschylus creates men and women of colossal stature dominated by their fate and by their gods; Euripides creates men and women as they really are, appeals to the emotions, and cultivates rhetorical sophistication; Sophocles stands between these two as the Periclean period is situated between the ages of Cimon and Alcibiades; he himself tells us that he alone created men as they should be drawn. His characters are true to life, true to type, self-consistent. They move by acts of will, distinct and intelligible; these are real men and women raised to heroic stature, actuated by motives of the highest nobility and dedicated to justice. They show the same elimination of baser motives, baser instincts, low, petty, and ridiculous instincts, as the Parthenon sculptures reveal an elimination of all extraneous superficial detail, so that they, like the Sophoclean characters, stand out as clarified models of heroic human nature.

Too much can probably be made of the facile comparisons between Greek sculpture and the works of the Greek dramatists, but this much can be said, that the tragedies of Sophocles are classic in the same way as the sculpture of Phidias. The dramatist and the sculptor are endeavoring to create *human* beings—the emphasis is intentional—as they really ought to be—as models of spiritual beauty and moral integrity, a harmony of the divine and the mortal. The sculptor does this by the superior beauty with which he carves the working of the soul in a visible form. The vast army in stone created by Greek sculptors, forming as it were a second superior population, was an eternal and astonishing reminder to posterity of the wealth of the nation, and to humanity of its highest capabilities and highest nobility.

9

The culture of the age of Pericles rested on the belief in the all-embracing perfection of the state, the State of Attica and City of Athens, to whose good the citizens were to subordinate their individual interests and devote their lives in war and peace alike. The whole spirit of the age glorified the greatness of Athens. It was Pericles' ambition that Athens should be the capital of Hellas, at once the strongest and the most beautiful city in the Greek world.

Whether or not the democratic ideals of Pericles coincide with modern notions of democracy is beside the point. The fact remains that they suited the Greeks of the fifth century, and the harmony between state and citizens was such as to produce a harmony between intellect and emotion in the individual. It remains that this type of society made for the creation of a kind of art specially suited to its own needs.

The keynote of the classic age is that man is the measure of all things: the chorus in *Antigone* sings, "Many things are strange and nothing is stranger than man." [2] Herein is a reflection of the regard for the marvelous and not ordinary quality of the human being and the human mind. This was a completely anthropomorphic society; not only did the Greeks make gods like men, but also men like gods. There was no form of human experience or natural force that was not represented by an anthropomorphic metaphor. Greek art is a synthesis of all things related to man in the cosmos. As Heraclitus said, "When opposites unite, the loveliest harmony is born from the most different elements." [3] "On the shield [of Achilles]," Homer tells us, "the divine armorer, Hephaistos, wrought the earth, the sea, and the heavens, the rounded moon and the tireless sun; also, he set there all the stars that crown the firmament. He graved thereon also the gods and deities of rivers and springs, the life of man in war and peace." [4] This is the cosmos of the Greeks and the inexhaustible subject matter of their art.

The perfection of the Greek ideal, the works of the fifth century B.C. and their robust forebears of the Archaic period, only exerted a sporadic influence on later revivals of the Hellenic taste. After the age of Hadrian, these earlier works of Greek art are largely forgotten, lost in the turmoil and destruction of the centuries of barbarism that overwhelmed Greece and her eastern provinces. Byzantine art as well as the revivals of the antique in Carolingian, Romanesque, and Gothic times were based on the tradition of Roman or, at best, Greek art translated into Latin forms. Until the nineteenth century, the classical tradition was based on the later

Greek art of the Hellenistic period and the further developments out of this style in Rome that provided inspiration for countless generations of artists in the Western world. At the very foundations of all later classical taste were the monuments first discovered and admired with such fervor by men of the fifteenth and sixteenth centuries in Italy. The vicissitudes of this classical taste will be the subject of this book; its creative nurturing of artists, our theme.

— 3 —

The Archaic Period

He gave man speech, and speech created thought,
Which is the measure of the universe;
And science struck the thrones of earth and heaven,
Which shook, but fell not; and the harmonious mind
Poured itself forth in all-prophetic song.

And human hands first mimicked and then mocked,
With moulded limbs more lovely than its own,
The human form, till marble grew divine;
And mothers, gazing, drank the love men see
Reflected in their race, behold, and perish.

—Shelley *

THE term Greek art describes the entire evolution of Hellenic sculpture and painting from the seventh century B.C. until the final absorption of Greece and her culture into the Roman world. It will be useful, therefore, to devote a few pages to an analysis of selected examples of Greek art from the Archaic through the Hellenistic periods in order to illustrate the specific character of the works in a number of successive styles that became norms for the emulation of later generations.

What we call the Greek ideal is perhaps nowhere more nobly embodied than in the type of Apollo, a Hellenic creation that developed over a period of centuries to attain its final perfection in the fifth century. It was inevitable that Apollo, the god of law, of rational order and light, should be conceived in the loveliest shape the Greek mind could imagine: a beautiful man. In the creation of this concept the body is made to conform to certain laws of proportion and to partake of the abstract divine beauty of mathematics in order to create a deity calm, contained, and clear as day, qualities appropriate to a god of light and measured justice.

* Percy Bysshe Shelley, "Prometheus Unbound"

12

The earliest Apollos or *Kouroi* of the seventh and sixth centuries B.C. are imbued with a ritual stiffness; they are formalized and rigid, but in their clarity and ideality they look forward to the final humanistic solution of the problem. The development is in the direction of a smoother coördination of the various shapes comprising the bodily frame, shapes which to a degree still remain formalized, but become beautiful in their coördination and organic articulation. The final Greek attainment of perfection and beauty in the presentation of the ideal human form is achieved between 480 and 400 B.C. This perfection is a complete revelation of the Greeks' passionate pleasure in the beauty of the human body displayed in the heightened sensuality of perception that went into the making of these images. In part this delight in the beauty of the intrinsic naked body follows that religious dedication and love which gave athletics and the cult of physical perfection a solemnity and rapture that we have not experienced since.

Typical of the earliest Greek sculpture is the statue of an Apollo or Kouros in the Metropolitan Museum of Art which is dated in the sixth century B.C. (figure 5a). The youth stands in a rigidly frontal position with arms pressed close to the sides and one foot advanced to ensure a firm stance. The resemblance of such images to Egyptian prototypes was noted by Diodorus of Sicily, who stated that the Pythian Apollo of Samos "resembled Egyptian works with his arms stretched stiffly down his sides and his legs separated by a stride." The passage from Diodorus explaining the Egyptian method for arriving at the proper proportions for statues states that the sculptors began by "dividing the structure of the entire body into twenty-one parts and one-fourth in addition; they express in this way the complete figure in its symmetrical proportions." [1] This is a type of canon based not on actual physical proportions of real human beings but on the employment of an entirely abstract or mathematical modulus calculated to produce an appropriately abstract or mathematical perfection in the image. The Greek Kouroi are, however, completely original conceptions; instead of the entirely frozen rigidity of Egyptian figures, the Kouroi are imbued with a feeling of pent-up vitality that expresses itself in the tension of the clenched fists and the implication of movement in the striding legs. These statues in the untrammeled abstraction of the bodily form, denoting at the same time an aliveness and throbbing virility, are the "perfect expression of ideal youthful manhood, conceived by the aristocratic Hellenic society of archaic times." [2] A feeling of youthful manly strength is implied in a nonrealistic fashion, by the athletic ideal of proportion with massive shoulders tapering to a wasplike waist, in the litheness of the form, and an emphasis on muscular strength in the linear conventions symbolizing the tautly stretched tendons of the frame; in other words, this athletic vigor and pulsating physical life are presented in essentially abstract terms.

The head of the archaic Apollo is a cubic mass, to which the features are attached in such a way that the eyes and mouth are only drawn on the unpenetrated solid surface (figure 5b). The size of the eyes is exaggerated, as though by this device to enhance the ghostly, luminous quality of the mask. Every feature is a sort of hieroglyph that spells "eye," "nose," and "ear." The hair is a repetition of knob-like whorls; the ears, formalized volutes. This is the product of a period when the whole cosmos was reduced to a system of geometric proportion; seemingly, the head is itself a reflection of such a world-view, an exercise in simplified geometric forms ideographically suggesting a concept without direct contact with nature.

The torso of this early Apollo statue is a very significant detail, because it shows that the treatment of the anatomy is entirely abstract or, one might say, decorative, in the way in which the muscles of the abdomen are rendered only by a series of incised lines, more like surface ornament than any really organic definition of the body's structure. This patternized symbolical conception of the body is typical of the ideographic approach of the Archaic period. It is the first step toward a style which maintains a balance between this kind of simplified formality and a suggestion of the real anatomical mechanism as well—the wonderful realization of organic perfection of the classic ideal of the fifth century B.C.

— 4 —

The Transitional Period

Now glorious Leto's child goes up with the sound
Of his hollowed harp to Pytho's rocky ground.
His raiment is breathing of heaven, sweet melodies thrill
With dirling note to the touch of his golden quill;
And thence to Olympus, swift as thought, he towers,
To the house of Zeus, and joins the assembled powers.*

THE thirty years between 480 and 450 B.C. are often referred to as the Transitional period, because the style of these decades is marked by a change from the rigor and convention of the Archaic to the freedom and finality of classic expression achieved in the Great Period of 450 to 400 B.C. Some of the most beautiful realizations of the Greek ideal in sculpture are found in the works of the Transitional period, among them the noble embodiment of Apollo in the great figure in the west pediment of the temple of Zeus at Olympia (figure 6).

The subject of this great statue, Apollo, was more than the master musician delighting Olympus with his golden lyre and more than the unerring archer destroying the monsters of pestilence and darkness. He was not so much the sun god, properly speaking, but a god of light whose true radiance is the illumination of darkness and ignorance. The divine will or law was revealed through his oracle at Delphi, which had among its precepts, Know thyself, and Everything in moderation. Apollo's light is the light of reason and, above all, he is the bestower of that law and order that separate civilization from barbarism. It is in this role that Apollo looms in the pediment at Olympia. He manifests himself as the arbiter of conflict between the civilized world and barbarism enacted in the struggle between centaurs and lapiths that fills the composition on either side of the towering god. He rises above the carnage to reprove the

* *Second Homeric Hymn*

15

bestial fury of the centaurs in a gesture of sovereign authority that embodies the Greek ideal: calm, pitiless, confident in the power of his radiant physical beauty.

With the sculpture of Olympia the gods take on an imperturbable majesty united with a generalized perfection of form that makes them truly larger than life. The figure of Apollo has a majestic rigidity that in many respects still represents the formalized additive approach of the Archaic. But the bodies, like that of Apollo, reveal an at once pliant and organic articulation that is far different from the abstract geometric anatomy of an archaic Kouros. The hair, carved in a cap of wavy ridges culminating in a wreath of spiraling curls that frame the face (figure 7), the still rather formal almond eyes, and the rather flat decorative figuration of the abdominal muscles are all elements reminiscent of the archaic approach. But the new, completely organic articulation of the body and its parts creates an illusion of physical life and breathing vitality within an abstract framework. At the same time one feels that what we describe as the archaic character of this style enhances the godlike authority of the great columnar form. It is obvious that such an impression of superhuman beauty and power recedes in proportion as the very limitations which create this illusion are replaced in later periods by a more particular realism that reduces divinity to humanity.

The Apollo of Olympia looms as one of those superhuman beings, celestial powers, not men, who move in the terrible tragedies of Aeschylus. In the Olympia pediment, as in the doom that overtakes Orestes and Agamemnon, the divine Apollo stands in the full majesty of his power among struggling men, guiding their struggles and their fate. The figure of the god of radiance and reason, stern and terrible, is a symbol of that exaltation of the period of triumph after the Persian wars. Symbolically representing the restoration of order disturbed by the intrusion of the outrageous barbarians, he appears in the shape already close to the grandeur of Phidias, but still marked by a tension and the air of an heroic protector appropriate to this hour.

A bronze counterpart of the great Apollo at Olympia is the famous Chatsworth head, formerly in the possession of the Dukes of Devonshire and now deposited in the British Museum (figure 8). This wonderful work of art was originally part of a cult statue which unfortunately was smashed to pieces by the peasants who discovered it at Tamassos in Cyprus in 1836. Like no other surviving fragment this noble head of

Apollo reveals the consummate craftsmanship of the great bronze images of the early fifth century. To an even greater degree than the Olympian Apollo this head has a kind of regal serenity and aloofness, and at the same time a severity that reminds one of the formula of archaic art. What differentiates this metal head from its marble counterpart is the softness and delicacy in the modeling of the features and facial planes, and at the same time the rather more pictorial richness in the treatment of the cluster of ringlets which enframe the face like a halo. This softness and richness of definition were specifically conditioned by the greater possibilities for such treatment in a piece of sculpture that was molded, rather than carved in marble. As in the head of the Apollo at Olympia, the calm and nobility of this countenance is achieved by the classic technique of elimination, that is, the omission of all irregularities and accidents of conformation such as appear in an actual human face. The face of this god is presented as a simplified mask, in which the underlying structure, although completely organic from an anatomical point of view, is reduced to a kind of ideal mask composed of smooth interlocking and sharply differentiated surfaces. The awe-inspiring serenity and radiance of the divine face are mitigated somewhat by the contrast of the soft enframement of the curls. The cap of hair is still composed according to the archaic principle of the separate representation of each individual curl and the definition of the wavy locks flowing from the brow in a series of individually incised lines, which in themselves make up a light rhythmic design which again serves to relieve the awful solemnity of the features. Like the great statue at Olympia it would be hard to imagine a more perfect embodiment of Apollo as the deity who, more than any other, personified the Greek ideal of reason and order and the light which separates the civilized man from the darkness of barbarism. This is the god who personifies at once wisdom and the passionless search for truth, the lord of wise council who inspired his oracle at Delphi and moved both Pindar and Herodotus by his divine wisdom.

The same severe style represented by the static and serene form of the Apollo in the pediment of Olympia received an active embodiment in one of the most famous statues of classical antiquity, the Discobolus of Myron (figure 9). This sculptor was active in the first half of the fifth century, and his art, like that of the Olympia pediments, is in every way a transition from the style of the Archaic period to the final perfection of the age of Phidias. The original of the Discus-thrower was in bronze; and of the

17

existing copies in marble the most perfect is that formerly in the Lance-lotti Collection, now in the Museo delle Terme in Rome. This magnificent realization of athletic action represents the discus-thrower in a split second of inaction before he brings his arm forward to hurl the discus on its course. It has a wonderful suggestion of both imminent dynamic action and repose. This suggestion of the possibility of movement and tensely contained energy is achieved by the composition of the figure: the suggestion of dynamic movement implied in the zigzag directions of torso and legs is completely contained within the boundary of the enclosing curves, bracketed by the elliptical curves of the arms. The thrust and counterthrust of body and limbs and the winglike sweep of the extended right arm at once provide a linear pattern of organization and variety, and convey the feeling of pent-up energy and exploding vigor. In its mathematical balance and clarity of pattern and structure the statue meets the Greek ideal of intelligibility and variety.

In this, one of the earliest realizations of the Greek athletic ideal portrayed in action, there is a more marked, emphatic definition of muscular structure than in the essentially motionless image at Olympia. The magnificent body is comprised of individually modeled muscles, and each one of these muscles is perhaps more strained than would be demanded by the effort of the athlete's throw. But this exaggeration makes the entire muscular structure completely legible. This somewhat additive approach in the rendering of the bodily form lacks the completely organic and fluid articulation of the separate parts of the body that was achieved in the art of Phidias and his followers. The rendering of the hair as a cap of many separately recorded ringlets is another echo of the archaic technique. But in its entirety the statue is a definite milestone in that progression from the particular to the general, which marks the development of Greek sculpture toward its final perfection in the carvings of the Parthenon. As a summation of the intrinsic beauty of the male body in harmonious and balanced equilibrium and the depiction of the lithe action and pulsating vitality of the human form the Discobolus has never been surpassed.

— 5 —

The Great Period

Pheidias! either God came to earth from Heaven to show thee his likeness or thou didst find a way to see God.

—Philip *

As the French painter Ingres wrote, "There was once on the earth a little corner of land where, under the most beautiful skies . . . the arts and letters bathed nature in a second light for all earth's peoples and for all generations to come." [1] This is the famous hellenophile's dream of the golden noon of Athenian greatness under Pericles, that brief moment in time's cycle when the promise of perfection of the earliest productions of Greek art reached a consummation. This perfection was made possible in part by technical advances in the craft of stonecarving and in part by the atmosphere of freedom provided for individuality of expression in the Athenian democracy. The overpowering nobility and pristine beauty of the human form presented by the artists of the age of Pericles is the result of the Hellenic conception of the gods as beings human in form but superhuman as models of beauty, immortal and yet fallible to human ills, at once titanic protectors as controllers of all cosmic forces and avengers of evil deeds. The peculiar heroic ideal of fifth-century Greek art is a combination and synthesis of forms and forces preëxistent in earlier periods. It is also a repudiation of these earlier modes: it retains something of the self-imposed formality of archaic art but it is no longer an additive collection of parts nor geometric in proportion; it is realistic but never specific in its realism, so that unlike, for example, an ancient Egyptian portrait, it has no relation to an individual's superficial appearance.

Among the sculptors of the Great Period, Polyclitus is generally ranked second only to the great Phidias. He was the leading sculptor in the school of Argos. Accounts by ancient writers tell that, although versatile in sub-

* Philip, "On Pheidias' Statue of the Olympian Zeus," *The Greek Anthology*

19

ject matter, his fame rested chiefly on his statues of athletes. Although no original work by Polyclitus has survived, a number of later copies of his sculptures both Greek and Roman give an idea of his style. A particularly fine example is the Spear-bearer or Doryphoros in the Museo Nazionale at Naples (figure 10).

Both Greek and Roman critics assert that Polyclitus was actuated by a desire for perfection in proportion, the creation of human figures, which in their harmonious relation of the parts to the whole would excel or improve the accidental and varied beauty of individual human beings. Although his canon or system of measurement is sometimes described as consisting merely of a ratio of seven heads to the total height of the body, it was obviously a more complete and complicated approach than this simple ratio would indicate. It was a humanistic and mathematical harmony of proportion based on the relation of each part of the body to all the other parts and to the whole.[2]

The masterpieces of Polyclitus were destined to exercise an enduring influence in all later periods when the classical ideal was venerated as an infallible source of inspiration. This admiration was occasioned not only by the intrinsic beauty of his forms but also by the persistent legend that this beauty presented a kind of special, infallible formula through the sculptor's employment of a scientific, mathematical approach to the problem of perfect proportion in the human body. As Galen relates,

Chrisippos holds beauty to consist in the proportions not of the elements but of the parts, that is to say, of finger to finger and of all the fingers to the palm and wrist, and of these to the forearm, and of the forearm to the upper arm, and of all the parts to each other, as they are set forth in the Canon on Polykleitos.[3]

Here is one of the earliest expressions in Greek art of the idea that beauty and ideality in sculptural representation should be characterized by an intellectual and mathematical, rather than purely sensual structure. In such a system based on mathematical measurement the moduli or numbers and the system of proportions were to be used only for the underlying structure of the image.

This canon is something quite different from the system of measurement followed in the Archaic period, which was based on an a priori division of the entire stature of the figure into a fixed number of numerical units in much the same way as the archaic concept of the cosmos was fitted into a preconceived geometric scheme. Polyclitus' efforts to create a norm of beauty parallels the direction of the philosophy and science of his time in its attempt to simplify the complexity of all experience and phenomena into easily comprehensible and concrete terms.

In the Polyclitan ideal of the nude male body the weight is on the left leg and the right arm is flexed while the right leg and left arm are relaxed, so that the statue achieves a wonderful balance in weight and tension and a suggestion of lithe activation. The head and the torso and muscular divisions of chest and abdomen all have a square-cut cubic shape collectively suggesting a stocky ideal of beauty. This repetition of solid shapes that comprise the body in itself imposes an abstract harmony on the statue and is an approach far removed from the literal copying of a model. The representation of the parts of the body and their interrelation is anatomically correct—some Polyclitan statues even show the veins beneath the skin—but carving reduces the surface to a succession of smooth and softly interlocking planes without the least suggestion of texture, so that we recognize the abstraction and are never disturbed by any attempt to imitate literally flesh and blood in marble or bronze.

The most famous name in the Great Period is that of Phidias, who was director of works for Pericles and responsible for the completion of the Parthenon with its sculpture, as well as the author of some of the most famed statues of antiquity. The divine beauty of images by Phidias is based not on those preconceived systems of geometric measurement which prevailed in the Archaic period but on preconceived concepts of what human loveliness should be to evoke the awesome beauty of the gods. The creation of the plastic illusion of divinity belonged to the genius of Phidias who attained a perfection in a religious image parallel to Polyclitus' devising of a perfectly balanced portrayal of a man. Phidias worked by imagination rather than imitation or reliance on a canon. A legend recalls that Phidias himself stated that his famous statue of Zeus at Olympia, one of the Seven Wonders of the World, was patterned on the lines of Homer,

So spake the son of Kronos and nodded his dark brow, and the ambrosial locks waved from the king's undying head; and he made great Olympus quake.[4]

Phidias' masterpiece was the colossal image of gold and ivory that was the object of devotion in the shrine of the Father of the Gods in the Olympian grove. Although this great image has long since disappeared, a noble head of Zeus in the Museum of Fine Arts, Boston, gives us some idea of its appearance and of what is meant by the Phidian style (figure 11). This work is a Greek copy of the fourth century B.C. and was found at Mysola, near Halicarnassus, which once had a sanctuary dedicated to Zeus. This image of the great god who "scatters the clouds and stirs the depths of the sea" is first of all a generalization intended not as a likeness of any specific person but as a symbolic embodiment of the wisdom and awesome grandeur of the ruler of Olympus. Pagan and even Christian critics who saw the statue at Olympia before it was destroyed realized that Phidias reached his own perfection by his own sense of the divine. To the people it was the very image of Zeus himself revealed; to the philosopher it perfectly represented the form in which Zeus would appear if he chose to manifest himself to mortal eyes.

To gain an idea of what the original and the copy in Boston tried to set forth it is well to bear in mind what Zeus himself personified in the ancient pagan religion. Zeus is a very old deity, at once a sky god and cosmic force, who held supremacy in sky and earth and sea. He was regarded as a divinity of right and inexorable justice, whose anger sent men to death in tempestuous retribution or to dark doom. He is at once the personification of luminous day and the magic engineer of weather in his control of thunder and life-giving rain. As the immortal father of all he is the quickening force that works in the seed in the earth and in the womb. As the ritual addressed to his sacred oak in the grove at Dodona proclaimed, "Zeus was and is and ever shall be, oh great Zeus: earth gives forth fruits, therefore call on Mother-Earth." [5]

Directed to the expression of this concept of supernatural majesty and power, the head of Zeus presents a concept, not of any specific individual, but of the ideal beauty of humanity in general. Such a conception begins with the articulation of the muscular and bony architecture of the head in abstract fashion. This is not the abstraction of an archaic head in which the features are so many hieroglyphs additively combined in a cubic mass, but an abstraction based on the refinement of the artist's knowledge of human features reduced to an absolute permanent beauty. In this it is the expression of a period when man was the true center and measure of the universe.

The features and the head as a whole are carved in sharp contours and smoothed convex surfaces, a technique that imposes abstraction on the conception. There is no indication of texture such as would characterize an individualized portrait. The precision and hardness with which the

face is carved give it more the character of an ideal mask than a naturalistic rendering of a real countenance. All superficial detail has been removed and it is precisely this abstract treatment that imparts such an icy
nobility to the head, a nobility and heroic quality far removed from individuality. The hair is carved in a schematic, nonrealistic fashion, arranged according to a definite orderly scheme, with repeated wavy lines to
indicate the general nature of curls but with no suggestion of the actual
softness and silky texture of real hair. This suppression of all allusion to
texture or superficial characteristics conveys at the same time a feeling
of removed impersonality and in the very closed outline of the block of
stone connotes a feeling of massive security and solidity.

Another reflection of the Phidian style may be seen in a copy of the
head of the Lemnian Athena,* the goddess of wisdom and victory and
protectress of Athens (figure 12). The face gives the same awe-inspiring
impression of an untarnished, immaculate beauty as the Olympian Zeus,
a beauty that, as in all Phidian sculpture, keeps the beholder at a distance
by its air of frozen aloofness and impeccable refinement. This refinement
derives from the composition of the head in so many interlocking curved
planes, unencumbered by the least irregularity, that evokes a suggestion
of the remote final beauty in the world of solid geometry. In the present
example the severity of the classical profile has been softened somewhat
by the subtler contours and by the exquisite texture of the marble from
which it is carved. The cylindrical forehead of archaic statues is still
present, as well as the hard edge where the eye sockets meet the brow. The
hair, as in the head of Zeus, is merely a plastic mass with lightly incised
curls to suggest rather than describe the softness of its texture. The mask
is nearly symmetrical in its division, so that each curve comprising the
mask and its features has a balancing counter-curve in eye and brow and
cheek, with a precision of balance never seen in nature. The contours of
the planes comprising the face are smooth and regular with the subsequent elimination of the distracting wrinkles, promontories, and hollows
which interrupt the surface of the face of a living model. The beauty of
the head, in other words, derives from the elimination of the ordinary imperfections of a human countenance and the reduction of the face to an
absolute of imaginable loveliness in purified form. It is precisely this
superiority over the transitory beauty of real men and women that confers

* This statue, formerly on the Acropolis, is described by Pausanias as the finest of
Phidias' works. It was dedicated by Greek colonists of Lemnos between 451 and 448 B.C.

an illusion of divinity on the heads of Zeus and Athena. They embody the shapes and majesty in which Greek poets and philosophers visualized the Olympians. These same qualities are present in the great collection of sculpture carved under Phidias' direction for the decoration of the Parthenon.

Of the many works associated with the name of Phidias, the only surviving original carvings executed by the master or in his workshop are the sculptural decorations of the Parthenon (figure 4). Even in ruin the appearance of the Parthenon is spectacular and moving as it first fills the eye when one emerges from the Propylaea, the shadowed gate of the Acropolis. Its skeleton crowns the summit of the Acropolis, its pillars of white and tawny marble seeming a natural outgrowth of the rocky hill.

The building was a symbolic dedication of the city of Athens to its protectress, Athena. Here was the Athenian universe in stone: the metopes represented the four combats of four ages that marked man's triumph over barbarism; in the pediments were shown the birth and triumph of Athena; and in the frieze the girdling procession of the populus of the Athenian democracy brought tribute to the goddess. All of this iconographical mechanism revolved around that goddess who stood at the very center of the temple, the pole and axis of the Athenian world.

The western pediment originally represented the struggle between Athena and Poseidon for the lordship of Attica, which ended with the goddess' triumph by her creation of the olive tree. The eastern pediment showed the birth of Athena in the midst of a surrounding court of deities framed by the chariots of the sun and moon. The arrangement of the statues of the Parthenon pediments embodies the same type of balance and harmony that governs the architecture of the building. The figures were arranged in such a way that, although there seems to be a symmetrical balance on the axis of the central group, actually there is a flow of movement from figure to figure and group to group across the whole pediment. The figures in the Parthenon pediments served to carry on the feeling of circulation around the central axis of the building suggested by the colonnade and by the moving procession of the frieze. In the metopes, which originally encircled the entablature, were represented those epic struggles in which humanity triumphed over the forces of barbarism and evil. The subjects were the battle of the gods and giants, the triumph of the Greeks over the Amazons and the Trojans, and the victory of the lapiths in the battle with the centaurs. The frieze, which extended around the top of the wall of the sanctuary behind the peristyle, portrayed the panathenaic procession, an annual civic festival when citizens of all ranks united to parade to the Acropolis to present to the statue of Athena a new garment or peplos woven especially for her.

The Parthenon was the work of Iktinos, erected between 447 and 432 B.C., to house the great ivory and gold image of Athena by Phidias. The closed, cubic character of the temple is the expression of the same contained plastic spirit that permeates its sculpture. The organic validity of every part of the architecture and the relation of every part to the whole were just as logical as every part of the plastic decoration, so that the whole is really an expression in architecture of the unity and harmony of the Athenian state. Although architecture is not to be discussed in this book, it is necessary to point out that in such a building the employment of the orders, the unvarying combination of base, column, capital, and entablature imposed an invariable limitation on the structure. It automatically controlled the shape and uniformity of such buildings. One could say that this was the obvious outcome of a completely rational outlook that wished to clothe architecture in the same finite understandable form that governed the Greek view of life. Such a comfortable, comprehensible, and delimited world was exactly what the Greeks wanted. Architecturally this is an illustration of the same self-imposed restraint that governed the ideal forms of Phidias. Technically Greek architects and sculptors of the fifth century could have created fantastic forms of architecture and naturalistic ones in sculpture. That they did not is the inevitable result of their society and their taste for the logical, at once beautiful and self-contained. Just as obviously in the Hellenistic period, when the horizons of science and society itself became enormously widened, when new disturbing questions of life and death and the afterworld upset the security of the old religion, architectural forms became more unstable and dynamic, and sculpture strained for the ultimate in the expression of realism and pathos.

One of the most passionate admirers of the great pediment sculptures of the Parthenon was the English romantic painter, Benjamin Robert Haydon, who first saw the marbles in a shed behind Lord Elgin's house in Park Lane. It was Haydon's enthusiastic defense that was in large part responsible for the acquisition of the collection for the British Museum. His first impression of the great reclining male figure, identified variously as Theseus or Dionysos or a personification of Mount Olympus (figure 13), burns with the fervor of discovery and presents a simple but moving definition of the style as well.

> That combination of nature and idea which I had felt was so much wanting for high art was here displayed to midday conviction. My heart beat! If I had seen nothing else I had beheld sufficient to keep me to nature for the rest of my life. But when I turned to the Theseus and saw that every form was altered by action or repose,—when I saw that the two sides of his back varied, one side stretched from the shoulder-blade being pulled forward, and the other side compressed from the shoulder-blade being pushed close to the spine as he rested on his elbow, with the belly flat because the bowels fell into the pelvis as he sat . . . when I saw, in fact, the most heroic style of art combined with all the essential detail of actual life, the thing was done at once and for ever.[6]

It is really only paraphrasing Haydon to say that the magnificent body and all its muscles are shown in perfect relaxation. There is an easy strength in the pose of the noble frame with no tension or strain in the muscles that enclose it. The whole muscular and bony anatomy is there, but simplified and clarified. The natural curves of the body and its contours are rhythmically exaggerated so that there is a completely unified harmony of shapes and lines and planes building up to a magnificent symbol of humanity. Although we are conscious to a certain extent of the arrangement of the muscles in a pattern, as in the sculpture of Olympia, their disposition presents a far more rhythmic and smooth articulation of the bodily structure. As in all the masterpieces of Greek sculpture of the Great Period the image is at once timeless and self-contained, a reflection of the perfect balance and reason of the mind in the heroic relaxation of the body. The noble quality of man is suggested not only by the large scale but also by the completely self-contained conception of the body, in which no flamboyant posturing or projection of the limbs disturbs the essential mass of the form.

Another superb group from the eastern pediment is that of the Three Fates, a mountainous block of three massively draped women.* We may discern here the same ennobled generalization based on the articulation of real structure that makes for the grandeur of the Theseus-Dionysos (figure 14). The folds of the garments flow over the massive forms in a moving cascade. The lines and masses of this drapery are consciously arranged in a stirring harmony of shapes determined by the ridges and deep

---

* The Three Fates is the traditional identification. The group is also believed to represent Selene, and Aphrodite reclining on the bosom of her mother, Dione.

furrows of the structure that repeat and rhythmically counterbalance one another throughout. At the same time the lines of the drapery follow and emphasize the promontories of the body beneath, suggesting its fullness and swelling warmth. Although the drapery completely reveals the articulation of the body that it sheathes, at the same time the garment exists as a voluminous crust, separate from the body, and with an unmistakable solidity and weight of its own. This is a completely generalized, rather than a particular treatment, and this feeling of breadth with its connotation of the idea of drapery in a universal sense is achieved by carving the contours and furrows with the same sharpness and precision that were employed in modeling heads and bodies in the Phidian style.

The sculpture of the Phidian period is completely free of any artificial exaggeration, as it is free from any affectation of merely decorative ornament and meaningless naturalistic imitation. This nobility, characterized by an incomparable dignity and remoteness, is based on the same heroic aggrandizement of human beings that makes for the grandeur of the characters in the tragedies of Sophocles. It could be said that both Phidias and Sophocles worked with forms inherited from the Archaic period, and in both the wedding of reality and formalism produced an art approximating the real world in a heightened or idealized form. This was an art dedicated to expressing the quality of Arete, which defines the higher merit and nobility of the true nature of man. From its very beginning Greek art had always moved toward a more naturalistic expression, and certainly an artist with the technical capacity of Phidias could, if he chose, have carved infinitely more realistic forms. It must have been his own choice and sense of fitness that led him to impose upon his statues the same abstraction and ideality found in the lofty conceptions of human beings in the plays of Sophocles.

The idea of limitation, self-imposed restraint, and discipline, so vital a part of the classical ideal, is nowhere better expressed in the Parthenon than in the metopes (figures 15 and 16). These were the square sculptured panels projecting from the entablature, where they alternated with the triglyphs beneath the cornice of the building. These compositions were carved in very high relief, some almost in the round. These panels, devoted to the triumphs of the gods over the giants and the Greeks over the forces of barbarism, were limited to two figures. The forms in the surviving metopes devoted to the battle of the centaurs and lapiths are set off against a completely blank background. The compositions are essentially closed, and the greatest movement, even violence, is suggested in extraordinarily quiet, frozen poses. Sometimes the figures seem almost petrified in the most violent action. The real suggestion of movement, of life and death and insensate struggle, is largely implied in the alternation of curves within the contours of the groups.

The sculptural decoration of the Parthenon was completed by the frieze at the top of the enclosing wall of the cella. The subject, as has been noted, is that of the civic procession celebrating the bringing of a new garment to Athena. All classes of the Athenian democracy are represented in this defile of the Periclean world: the mounted knights, the marshals, the water-carriers, the priests and statesmen. The parade terminates at the western end of the building, where its leaders are presented to an assembly of the gods. The tempo of the frieze rises and falls like the sculptural counterpart of a musical score. The procession of mounted knights starts at a walk, gains in momentum to a trot, then a canter, and finally to a gallop by the horsemen in the forefront of the cavalcade (figure 17). In contrast with the wild energy of the stallions is the controlled serenity of the young riders, models of beautiful beings. Their faces and bodies radiate a pride of race, of the strength of young manhood and the easy mastery of their horsemanship. The frieze is restricted to a shallow plane of carving, and the figures are set off against an entirely blank background. Although a certain amount of overlapping of the forms is used to create an abstract illusion of spatial depth, the main impression is of both single figures and groups isolated against the wall of the background. In the Parthenon frieze the aesthetic rapture that stems from the intellectual apprehension of these clear monumental forms is combined with the sensual ecstasy that comes from contemplating a handsome youthful body (figure 18). These carvings of youths are obviously the production of artists who thought of men and boys as beautiful in an erotic, as well as aesthetic sense: their combination of virility and grace, pure form and erotic content, could only have been produced by men devoted to the tradition of homosexuality as it was condoned and practiced in ancient Greece. There is nothing overt in this paean to the beauty of the male body, but, as always in classic sculpture, there is a complete balance between realism and abstraction and the most lucid possible definition of articulation and proportion pleasing to the eye and the senses.

Although the movement constantly changes in the course of this long procession, the cavalcade is presented as though simultaneously seen, arrested at one moment of its progress. This was not the representation of any one particular parade that took place on a given day and year, but a generalized and idealized commemoration of the greatest Athenian holiday. In it the Athenians appear as they wished to be remembered for eternity.

— 6 —

The Fourth Century:
Praxiteles, Lysippus, Scopas

In later times other offerings were dedicated in the Heraion. Amongst these was a Hermes of marble, bearing the infant Dionysos, the work of Praxiteles.

—Pausanias *

WITH the passing of Pericles and his age, the unity and balance of Greek culture and Greek art were forever unsettled. There ensued a period of crisis and national disaster, a period of continuous wars of which the Peloponnesian War was only the most devastating. The fourth century was a time of decentralization and individualism in men as well as in nations. In these troublous times men thought more of their own good than of the state's. There were in this period of social disintegration, great individuals and great philosophers, but their minds and dreams were turned to different dreams, dreams of a more particular and less universal nature. This is the beginning of a cycle of disbelief: the gods descended from Olympus to assume human stature and human passions. Since there was no longer money or need for the dedication of large temples, sculptors turned to the fashioning of small groups or statues dedicated as votive offerings.

An example of this afterglow of the art of Phidias is the statue of Hermes playing with the infant Dionysus by the fourth-century master Praxiteles (figures 19 and 20). It was found at Olympia by the German archaeologists in the nineteenth century and is believed by many to be the only surviving original by the hand of a known Greek master. One is struck at once by the lesser stature of the form: this is a man, beautiful in build, but not a god, carved in a supremely graceful but not noble style. The body is thrown into an S-curve which accentuates the soft beauty

* Pausanias, V. 17. 3

of the sweetly molded limbs. The statue is distinguished by a new realism of technique, perhaps most notable in the carving of the drapery carelessly thrown over the tree stump.

Although Praxiteles seems in some respects to be a follower of Polyclitus in his canon of proportion and block-like composition of the body, there are certain essential differences between the works of the two artists. Whereas Polyclitus' statues are built up in swelling groups of muscles and these blocks of muscles are demarcated by sharp linear boundaries, there are no such blocks or divisions in the work of Praxiteles: He is more concerned with the soft transitions from plane to plane; he aims for an effect of tenderness rather than severity, delicacy rather than strength. A feeling of complete relaxation has replaced the heroic tension of the fifth century.

In statues by Polyclitus and Phidias, the personages seem completely isolated from the spectator, remote in a world of their own, self-sufficient and self-contained. The statue by Praxiteles has a more self-conscious pose which attracts the attention of the beholder. The gods now have the beauty of humans in conformity with the new interest in individual man and his psychology, but they no longer interfere in human affairs, seemingly absorbed, like Praxiteles' Hermes in their own affairs and inner passions. Again, in contrast to the even, generalized texture of fifth-century sculpture, a disturbing change has taken place in the treatment of the surface of the fourth-century masterpiece. There is a new sensuous attraction in the softly graduated modeling, so that one feels in the presence of a physical reality, not an abstraction. By the carving of the body in innumerable transitory planes, the whole statue is bathed and almost dissolved in multiple lights caressing its surface. The fifth-century sculptors made flesh into marble; Praxiteles has turned marble into flesh. As an anonymous writer in *The Greek Anthology* wrote of Praxiteles' statue of Niobe, "The gods turned me into stone from life, but Praxiteles makes me live once more! " [1]

Praxiteles was renowned among ancient critics of art for his ability to infuse a melting gaze into the eyes of his creations. As Diodorus observed, "With consummate skill [he] informed his marble figures with the passions of the soul." [2] This particular quality can be observed in the head of Aphrodite in the Museum of Fine Arts, Boston, the work of either the master himself or a close follower (figure 21). The face has a haunting expression of passionate longing, evocative of the lines of Sappho:

31

> The moon is down;
> The Pleiades have set,
> Times passes, passes,
> And yet I lie alone.[3]

Aphrodite expresses a yearning and passionate tenderness as goddess of love, more courtesan than Olympian. As in the famous Hermes, the beautiful marble has the radiance of living flesh. A web of shadows plays over the face and the dreaming eyes betoken the soft working of the material. Edges and contours are no longer hard, as in the Phidian ideal, so that there is more of an illusion of real flesh and real skin in the recording of the minute transitions from plane to plane. The roughness of the hair, treated in an unfinished, impressionistic fashion, is a device to heighten by contrast the smoothness of the skin surfaces. As the scale is more human, the treatment is more delicate in a technique dedicated to evoking the texture and substance of flesh in stone. The surface of a statue like the Hermes or a head like the Bartlett Aphrodite, this indescribable delicate bloom, might be described as the result of the sculptor's "touch." We speak of *"le touche"* of an artist using brush or pencil or chisel, that indefinable refinement in enlivening the surface of paper, canvas, or marble by just the right kind of pencil mark, brush stroke, or chisel cut that makes his creation alive and vibrant and glowing. Such quality would be totally absent in the deadness of surface characterizing mechanically cut sculpture as in the innumerable copies of Greek art in the Roman period (figure 22).

A sculptor whose name was cherished by all the later writers on the great age of Greek art is that of Lysippus. He was active in the last quarter of the fourth century and is reputed to have been the court sculptor of Alexander the Great. Many copies exist of Lysippus' portrait of the world conqueror. Lysippus was famed for his representations of athletes, in which he evolved a canon of proportion which in this final period of Greek art replaced the earlier system of measurement devised by Polyclitus.

No single original example of the countless works by Lysippus has been preserved, but a statue in the Vatican—the Apoxyomenos, a youth scraping himself with a strigil (figure 23)—is believed to be a replica of a famous bronze original. This statue bears out certain statements by Pliny, as in the more careful treatment of the hair and the illusion of a taller, more slender body enhanced by the appropriately smaller head.

This is a departure from the massive, cubic proportions of Polyclitus, and in the greater muscular tension different from the soft elegance of Praxiteles. In its proportions this statue represents a modification of the Polyclitan canon to a ratio of approximately eight heads to the total height. The greater elegance achieved by this attenuation is in a way prophetic of the perverted grace of the Mannerist style.

The Apoxyomenos is among the few statues that most authorities regard as a reflection of Lysippus' style. The figure seems to shift its weight from one leg to the other, in what is a kind of exaggeration of the Polyclitan system of balance. The device of the arms crossing over the body and the twisting of the torso invite an inspection from more than the one frontal view provided by the masters of the fifth century. The statue has no expression of inner life; its style in the greater animation and the shifting, unstable stance looks forward to the dynamic conventions of Hellenistic sculpture.

It was undoubtedly through the many copies of Lysippus' sculpture that his more restless poses and more elegant proportions were taken up in later periods, especially in the Renaissance and the neoclassic age, by sculptors interested more in the lithe and graceful aspects of the body that are more superficially pleasing than the heavy, static shapes of Polyclitus and Phidias.

Another sculptor of the fourth century whose fame is known through the writings of ancient critics of art is Scopas. His name is associated with the sculpture of the famous tomb of King Mausolus of Caria and the great temple of Diana at Ephesus. A number of his works survive in copies of later periods. One of the most famous is his statue of Atalanta's love, the hunter Meleager. A replica of this image, perhaps carved in Greek times, is in the collection of the Fogg Art Museum of Harvard University (figure 24). In this fragment, which consists of a head and torso, the hero stands with his body slightly bent and his head turned to the left, as though gazing across the hunting field. In more complete versions of the original he holds a spear, and the head of his quarry, the Caledonian boar, rests at his feet. Although the broad handling of the massive muscular planes of the torso is still suggestive of the Phidian ideal, the animated torsion of the frame recalls the innovations of Praxiteles. What is most peculiar to Scopas' style is his animation of the facial mask. Here is a new, dynamic, even passionate expressiveness that is a complete departure from the bland serenity of the fifth century. The lips are parted, as though to suggest the very breathing of the spent athlete. The eyes gaze forth from their sockets with an extraordinary intensity and poignancy, an effect that is achieved by the way in which they are set in literally cavernous sockets and enframed in a swelling muscle at the outer corner of the sockets. The extraordinary suggestion of passionate inner feeling, a kind of daimonic fervor which Scopas achieves by these means, is the prelude to the even greater realism for the expression of pathos in the sculpture of the Hellenistic period.

Another fragment that provides an even more striking illustration of Scopas' expression of passion and divine frenzy is a replica of his statue of a maenad that once stood in Byzantium (figure 25). The companion of Dionysus, her head thrown back, her body bent into an arc, raving in the consummation of the ecstasies of the Dionysian rite—this wildly passionate, abandoned figure seems almost a plastic counterpart of the lines of the poetess Sappho:

> Love has unbound my limbs
> And set me shaking—
> A monster—bittersweet and my unmaking.
> When I look at you
> A fire runs under my skin,
> My tongue cannot speak,
> There is a whirring in my ears,
> Sweat pours down me,
> I am greener than grass,
> And there seems little
> That keeps me from dying.[4]

Not only the wild torsion of the body with its drapery immodestly awry, but also the frenzied passionate expressiveness in the eyes and mouth are completely typical of the trend of sculpture in the direction of not only physical, but psychological, realism. The essentially abstract devices by which this dynamic effect is achieved still imply the persistence of something of the restraint of an earlier age. But at the same time this concern with dynamic movement and the revelation of frenetic passion started Greek sculpture on the road that was to lead to those excesses of realistic description that characterize the work of the Hellenistic period.

— 7 —

The Hellenistic Period
and the Altar of Pergamum

At Pergamum there is a great altar of marble forty feet in height, with colossal sculptures; it contains the battle of the Giants.   —Lucius Ampelius *

O N the night that Alexander of Macedon was born the temple of Diana at Ephesus was burned to the ground, a conflagration symbolical of that fire which was to sweep the world in the person of this great conqueror. With Alexander begins the Hellenistic period, when the culture, once limited to Attica, was spread over all the Eastern world. Alexander's march to the Indus extended Hellenism to the ends of the earth. It brought ruin to the old Oriental monarchies. Ultimately, this expansion led to the conquest of Greek thought, Greek philosophy, and Greek art itself by the mysticism and fatalism of the ancient East. The centuries that followed this Greek adventure in colonialism saw the vast enlargement of experience resulting from this extension of Hellenic power that meant the end of the finite world of the city state. The old Olympian religion became altered by the infiltration of the deities of the conquered Eastern races. At the same time the conception of the gods had been completely altered in the doctrine promulgated by Euhemerus in the late fourth century. This Skeptic mythographer claimed that certain archaic inscriptions had revealed to him that the gods were but rulers and heroes of ancient times who, although they died like ordinary men, had earned deification in the opinion of their adoring subjects. However useful this

* Pergamo ara marmorea magna, alta pedes
  quadraginta cum maximis sculpturis; continet
  autem gigantomachiam.
  —Lucius Ampelius, *Liber memorialis,* VIII. 14

theory may have been for the divinizing of Alexander's successors, the Seleucid emperors of Syria, it inevitably reduced the gods to mortal stature.

The bigger and more modern Greek world of Hellenistic times was one in which material well-being counted for more than civic nobility or spiritual achievement. It was a period of specialization and scientific advance, a period of investigation not only into nature but into the character of the human soul. In this age of insecurity and introspection men thronged the shrines of Aesculapius to heal their bodies and their minds. Just as this age of the great libraries produced philologists rather than poets, so the art that flourished under Alexander's successors was often more the work of imitators than of artists and of men dedicated to exploring new modes of expression of realism and pathos. Hellenistic art often has a breath-taking dynamic force, an expression frequently oversentimental and ornate, in which nothing of the ordered restraint typical of the Periclean age is any longer present. The qualities of restraint and heroic composure were hardly compatible with the ideals of an age that in some respects was more romantic than classic.

In the art and literature of the Hellenistic period men turned to an appreciation and repetition of the past and its treasures. This was in part the result of the Greek colonists' attempt to bring with them and diffuse the art of the remembered homeland to the vast regions under their sway. Actually all that could be said about the old heroic themes had already been expressed. In this age of science and erudition only more complex and pathetic representations of gods and men testified to the investigation of man and his inner emotions. The search for novelty also brings a turn from the divine to the exploitation of the commonplace.

The dominant interests of the age were the evaluation of the past and scientific discovery in the fields of astronomy, physics, and medicine. There was more cataloguing than creation. In the Hellenistic philosophers' search for the one supreme god the old Olympians had little value, except as allegories of divine functions. Temples and altars were erected more to celebrate mortals and mortal triumphs than to reverence the gods. The widening of experience in every realm brought its inevitable broadening of expression in art, which, no longer limited by self-imposed discipline, drew its themes and techniques from the past or improvised tours de force of realism and the expression of extremes of feelings. In many cases these works were as pedantic as the scholarship fostered by the great libraries of Alexandria and Pergamum. Again, the exploration of nature and man by scientists had its parallel in the investigation of realism and psychological expression by artists.

The annals of the Seleucid emperors of Syria reveal a society that has nothing to do with the Greek world of Pericles' fashioning. The accounts of brutal assassinations, the most barbarous atrocities, and merciless conduct of warfare seem to belong to the pages of the history of the ancient Oriental monarchies that Alexander destroyed. Everything associated with Greek restraint and morality is gone, and yet these are the same Greeks on a world-wide stage. The answer to this ambiguity is that even Alexander in the cruelties and absolutism of his last years had ended by becoming a Persian. His successors inevitably were orientalized, too, and their excesses and instability are even further removed from the conduct of the world of Attica. Like colonists everywhere the Greeks in Asia fell easy prey to the temptation of exploiting their realms for material gain and comfort. Commerce flourished as it never flourished again until the American business empire of the twentieth century. The result of this changed society is an inevitable satisfaction in materialism and ornateness in art.

One fragment of the empire of Alexander's successors may be seen in the art of Pergamum in Asia Minor, one of many such Greek cities that grew up in a barbarian environment. This was a colonial city that tried to imitate the homeland, just as in the modern colonial empires Hong Kong and Saigon attempted to copy London and Paris. The rulers of Pergamum did everything in their power to impress Hellenism on the natives. The one claim to fame of the little state was the victories it won over the Gallic invaders in the late third and second centuries B.C., victories that seemed to make the world safe for Hellenism. These triumphs were proclaimed by a giant altar dedicated to Zeus by Eumenes II in the second century B.C.: its principal decoration is a great frieze representing the battle of gods and giants, a raising to an heroic level of the recent conflict that had saved the Hellenistic kingdoms from the barbarians. The Pergamene kings proclaimed themselves the great defenders of civilization and in this monument sought to incorporate the might of their state in architecture.

Instead of the few grandiosely isolated buildings that crowned the Athenian acropolis, this is a new system of town planning, in which each building seems to be laid out in relation to its surroundings and its neighbors, an arrangement symbolical of the expansive universality of Hellenistic civilization in contrast to the limited city state.

The altar at Pergamum is dedicated to Zeus—not, certainly, the old Zeus of the fifth century, but to a new father of heaven and earth, a sort of abstract philosophic concept which shapes all matter and gives it form. Here the mystery cults and philosophic allegories have destroyed the simplicity and equilibrium of the Olympian religion. The subject of the giant frieze—the battle of the gods and giants—is an old one, here applied to the heroizing of a particular event, the victory of the Pergamene mercenaries over the invading Gauls (figure 26).

This extraordinary band of sculpture looks at first like an enormous enlargement of an Ionic frieze, but at Pergamum the colonnade was placed *above* the entablature. Actually this decoration of the base of a monument is just one of many indications of the transformation of Hellenic ideals under Oriental influences; such friezes showing the defile of conquered nations ornamented the base of those palaces that Alexander burned at Persepolis in Iran, an architectural complex also dedicated to expressing the might of a dynasty.

All of the numberless combating gods and giants in the Pergamum frieze were labeled with their correct names and titles; they are the result of book-learning rather than piety, based on an iconography supplied by scholars in the great library up the hill from the altar. The building housed a great collection of books, a vast confused corpus of learning representing a repository, a tomb, rather than any creative dayspring of science. As a testimonial of culture neither this library nor the pretentious altar dedicated to a philosophic conceit could save this exhausted civilization.

In examining the frieze of Pergamum one notices first of all a complete disappearance of all that restraint and balance which characterized the art of the fifth century. A violence of movement and posture seems calculated to express the passion of the struggle, a minute realism of details that is a far cry from the generalization of Pericles' day. The faces of the dying giants are rent by agonized expressions: their mouths open and contorted in pain, their eyes rolling upward under arched overhanging brows combine to give a new and unheard-of pathos to the work (figure 27).

In keeping with the grandiose notions of the Hellenistic rulers, everything is on a colossal scale; everything is exaggerated and contorted to the point of confusion. In contrast to the arrangement of the Parthenon frieze, the figures no longer enjoy an individual isolation against a closed background. They are dramatically swept along in a continuous movement built on strong diagonal accents, a furious rush of turbulent action that flows through the entire crowded composition. All the figures are lost in this whirlwind of tempestuous commotion. Background and planes are there but hardly discernible. The figures exist in a definite immaterial space created by the depth of carving, something quite different from the closed and finite space of the fifth century; space as an immaterial concept was excluded from Phidian art. Here, the forms threaten to move out into the general space which we occupy.

Certain facile comparisons can be made with true Baroque art, as, for example, the emphasis on emotion, pathos, the general disharmony and overladen character of the work, arty and mannered. In comparison with a truly classic relief, although the geometric basis of the composition is different, the arrangement is still in definite planes, and the suggestion of depth rests on a clear stratification of the various planes. There is not the complete and gradual recession into space found in really pictorial Baroque reliefs. The Pergamum frieze, although it may be the most pictorial ancient relief, is still classic, and is in fact more plastic and *less* pictorial than the most plastic Baroque relief.

Comparing the drapery of a typical Pergamum figure (figure 28) with a form from the Parthenon pediment (figure 29), the lines of the garment of the Parthenon goddess follow the rhythm of the deity's movement and at the same time reveal the structure of her form. On the contrary, the drapery lines of the Pergamum figures are not particularly effective in suggestion of underlying forms; they are simply lines suggesting movement, decorative rather than functional, echoing that fury of action that tortures the entire composition. In the same way there is a terrific exaggeration of the muscular anatomy in these enormous exhausted forms, great bulging sinews symbolic of a strength no longer there, no longer present in the art nor in the culture that produced it.

Even if this art seems empty of content and strains every last nerve for melodramatic effect, the total impression of the Pergamum frieze is enormously moving, with its great surge of movement sweeping us along in its Wagnerian power and scale. It was precisely for its new effects of realism, for its rendering of tortured psychic expression, its impressive size, and presentation of thrilling effects of movement and drama, dynamic and awful, that Hellenistic art appealed to Roman taste and to the connoisseurs and artists of Western Europe in the sixteenth century and later. In these times, dedicated to the investigation of new forms of dynamic spiritual expression, Hellenistic sculpture enjoyed an authority and renown that, if anything, exceeded the appeal of what are regarded as the truly classic styles of the fifth and fourth centuries.

— 8 —

A Gallery of Masterpieces

Therefore it may be seen that those who carved these works chose the most beautiful parts from human models and that, aided by their excellent judgment, combined them with great perfection. By this method, to the great wonder of all, the most excellent craftsmen before our day derived the very brilliance and beauty of their manner, as may be brought out by a study of the following statues in Rome: the Laocoön, the Hercules, the Apollo, the Great Torso, the Cleopatra, the Venus, and the Nile, all of which are placed in the Belvedere, in the Papal Palace on the Vatican; and then, among those scattered through Rome, the first is the bronze Marcus Aurelius now placed in the Piazza del Campidoglio, and likewise the giants of Monte Cavallo, and the Pasquino. —Armenini *

Beginning in the later decades of the fifteenth century there began to arise, as though from dragon's teeth in the Italian earth, a whole army of statues. Among these were some of the great masterpieces of later antiquity, like the Laocoön and the Apollo Belvedere, statues that were to exercise an unchallenged authority on Western taste and Western art for hundreds of years. They were installed as veritable norms of perfection, models for the emulation of all. To continue my simile, there was no Cadmus to cut down these giants—none was wanted!—until, in relatively modern times, the real Greek ideal was at last discovered in the works of the Archaic and the Phidian periods. Only then did these *capolavori* of Hellenistic art come to be regarded as mere shadows of an earlier great-

---

* Conciosia cosa che quelli, che scolpirono queste opere, si conosce che essi scelsero il più bello dal natural buono, et che con l'aiuto dell'ottimo giuditto loro, lo congiunsero con molto perfettione insieme, dalla bellezza e bontà delle quali i più eccellenti artefici, che avanti di noi furono, ne trassero con grande stupor d'ognuno il vero lume delle loro maniere, il che si vede uscito dallo studio di Roma, le quali statue son queste: Il Laocoonte, l'Ercole, l'Apollo, il Torso grosso, la Cleopatra, la Venere, et il Nilo, che tutte sono poste in Belvedere, nel Palazzo Papale sul Vaticano: et di quelle che poi sono per Roma sparse; fra le prime vi è il Marco Aurelio di Bronzo, hora posto sullo spatio del Campidoglio, così i giganti di Monte Cavallo et il Pasquino.—G. B. Armenini, *De'veri precetti della pittura* (1586)

ness.* Perhaps the reaction has been too strong against these works which, with their superb dynamic strength and pathos, are only different, not necessarily inferior, productions of the Greek genius. Of these statues enumerated by Armenini in the sixteenth century, I have selected for special consideration the Apollo Belvedere, the Ariadne ("Cleopatra"), and the Laocoön. I substitute the Medici Venus for the Cnidian Aphrodite of the Vatican since this former work was destined to exercise an even greater influence.

THE MEDICI VENUS

> There, too, the Goddess loves in stone, and fills
> The air with Beauty . . .
> The unruffled mirror of the loveliest dream
> That ever left the sky on the deep soul to beam.[1]

One of the most admired statues in this galaxy of Greek masterpieces was the Venus dei Medici (figure 30), which has stood for three centuries in that fancifully beautiful marble octagon, the Tribuna of the Uffizi in Florence. There have been many theories advanced for the exact place of discovery of this image, none of which is supported by conclusive evidence. It was presumably a part of the famous della Valle collection as early as the sixteenth century, but was not brought to Florence until 1677. This is only one of many versions—the Capitoline Venus is another—of the Venus Pudica which are the offspring of Praxiteles' renowned Aphrodite of Cnidos. An inscription on the base proclaims that this was the work of Cleomenes, the son of Apollodorus of Athens.

The statue appears to be a reworking of the Praxitelean formula with an exaggeration of the qualities of prettiness and sensuous allure. This is a slighter, more affected reflection of the fourth-century sculptor's canon in which the self-conscious posture, the demure expression, and slighter stature intensify the goddess' femininity and provide an added erotic attraction. There is almost a suggestion of Mannerism in the proportion of the small head to the body.

Cleomenes, whose name appears in the inscription, was a member of a studio of copyists working in Athens of the first century B.C., a sculptor who evidently sought to reproduce the character of the original, pre-

* Even as late as the eighteenth century, the word "antique," as defined in an edition of the work of the critic Roger de Piles, meant painting, sculpture, and architecture "made in the times of the Greeks and Romans, that is to say, from Alexander the Great to the Emperor Phocas, in whose reign the Goths ravaged all of Italy." (Roger de Piles, *Receuil de divers ouvrages sur la peinture et le coloris,* Paris, 1775, p. 393.)

sumably of the third century B.C., with greatest fidelity. Much of the richness of carving and the subtleties of surface modeling that made for the textural luminosity of the Praxitelean original have been whittled down, so that the body and limbs have a smooth, cylindrical character. The imitation of this already abstracted form, rather dead in execution, seems to have provided a special inspiration for innumerable sculptors of the neoclassic period. It is well to bear in mind that for centuries it was only on the basis of such reflections of Greek originals that the whole apparatus of the appreciation of the classical ideal was built.

THE APOLLO BELVEDERE

O sculptor, among all others the most perfect!
What wondrous art Heaven in you compressed,
And with what superb color your hand tinted
This body, which dazzles every mind?
And with what bonds did Heaven gird your limbs?
So that you are a recipient of its every grace?
So am I moved by your divine style,
To praise it, as if it were a living being? [2]

One of the most famous classical statues in the world is the Apollo del Belvedere (figure 31) found on the estates of Cardinal Giuliano della Rovere near Grottaferrata and placed in the Belvedere when he assumed the Papacy. Its exact authorship remains a mystery, although some regard it as the work of Leochares, a sculptor of the time of Alexander the Great. The statue in the Vatican is in all probability a marble copy made in the first century A.D. after a bronze original.

We can no longer accept Winckelmann's lyric proclamation that "among all the works of antiquity which have escaped destruction, the statue of Apollo is the highest ideal of art." [3] Yet the figure has a superficial sensuous beauty and theatrical excitement about it which have endeared it to millions. The statue has a quality of resilient lightness in this startling apparition of a god revealing himself in a theophany before his shrine. A fleeting moment in an action has been frozen in stone. The face has the soft, unblemished beauty associated with Praxiteles; its radiant smoothness of execution is set off by the intricate convolutions of the crown of hair. An expression of a triumphant confidence darts from the eyes, and an assured supremacy parts the lips in the slightest smile. The portrayal of such an ephemeral expression was a triumph for the Greek sculptor of an age concerned with registering such nuances of inner psychological states in gods and men and the attribution of entirely human reactions and feelings to the masks of divinity. It belongs to a phase of Greek art when the statement of stability and weightiness was no longer the artist's prime concern in his exploration of the momentary and the dynamic. Although Winckelmann was accurate enough in saying that the Apollo seems to tread on air, this feeling of air-borne lightness deprives the statue of the contained balance and ponderation that make for the plastic equilibrium of earlier styles. The smoothness of surface and the absence of veins and muscular structure which led Winckelmann to recognize a form wrought in some divine supraterrestrial substance are the result of the superficial idealization of later Greek art and of the copyist's further simplification of his model.

The influence of this statue has been world-wide. Since the moment of its discovery it has been drawn by every artist visiting Rome. It lives in hundreds of replicas in marble and bronze made from the sixteenth century to the present day, and has served as the model for innumerable figures of gods and men by painters and sculptors of every succeeding age.

THE BELVEDERE TORSO

I have never found that anyone who followed the trail or example of another has been able to equal, what's more, surpass him. Michelangelo provides proof of this, since he was never able to add to the beauty of the Torso of Hercules by Apollonius of Athens, which is now in the Belvedere in Rome, even though he copied it repeatedly.[4]

The so-called Belvedere Torso (figure 32a and b), presumably a representation of Hercules by the Hellenistic sculptor, Apollonius, was known as early as the fifteenth century and a drawing of the early sixteenth century shows the fragment with both legs and the chest still intact. Presumably it suffered still further vandalism with the destruction of papal property during the Sack of Rome in 1527. Its association with the name of Michelangelo made it a venerated model, and it became a standard of muscular perfection to which nearly every later artist paid his respects. There is the unsubstantiated legend that Michelangelo did not wish to attempt its restoration because he felt that the fragment should not or could not be completed. To leave such an important remnant incomplete seems to be entirely against the Renaissance point of view. The cult of the fragment is embodied as a twentieth-century phenomenon that manifests itself in the work of a sculptor like Maillol, who often restricts his work to a torso without head or arms or legs in order to concentrate attention on the pure beauty of form and volume without the distraction of content. The fragment in modern sculpture may invite imaginary completion by the viewer, but the mutilated statue in fifteenth-century Italy seemed to offer an irresistible attraction to complete it by the addition of missing parts. Many distinguished sculptors lent their talents to completing damaged pieces, the core of the antique carving providing an opportunity for an often entirely fanciful restoration. The idea of respecting a torso as such seems to begin in the period of Mannerism, when for the first time we encounter what appears to be the connoisseur's appreciation of the suggestive incomplete. Mannerist artists reveal a tendency to compose from many separate borrowed fragments, and the subjects of their portraits are often shown in association with fragmentary antiquities. Just as the unrestored ruins of Rome became evocative of something mysterious, magic ghostly emblems of a dead and removed past in the piantings of Giulio Romano and Parmigianino, it would seem that pieces of statuary like the Torso for the first time came to be treasured for themselves. Their mutilated beauty, hauntingly suggestive of a lost perfection, revealed a formal beauty even in their incompleteness that satisfied a new connoisseur's delight in form without content.

The lack of interest in the Torso before the sixteenth century was due to its lack of content. In its fragmentary form it had nothing to tell the humanist of the iconography of the pagan gods, nor did it contain a moral or story for the artist. Furthermore, the artists of the fifteenth century in their enthusiasm for the antique preferred complete subjects as models and did not respond to what we would call formal beauty per se. Even though the Torso itself was never restored, many artists, including Michelangelo himself and Raphael, used it as a basis for paintings and sculptures of complete figures. Once that brief period of half-nostalgic, half-formal appreciation in the middle sixteenth century had passed, there arose, especially in Baroque art, an even more concentrated interest in complete images both in the actual restoration of antiques and in their completion in art.

THE ARIADNE

And look at Ariadne, or rather at her sleep; for her bosom is bare to the waist, and her neck is bent back and her delicate throat, and all her right side is visible, but the left hand rests on her mantle that a gust of wind may not expose her. How fair a sight, Dionysus, and how sweet her breath! Whether its fragrance is apples or grapes, you can tell after you have kissed her.[5]

Another greatly admired statue was the Sleeping Ariadne (figure 33), first identified as Cleopatra, which as early as the pontificate of Julius II was placed on a fountain in the Belvedere garden. The theme, often seen in wall-paintings and reliefs, is Ariadne sleeping while Theseus abandons her on Naxos. That the heroine's sleep is an uneasy one, troubled by disturbing dreams, is shown by the restless torsion of the body and the disarray of her drapery. Since it is difficult to imagine the Ariadne as part of a sculptural group, some archaeologists have suggested that this statue is taken from a single figure in a wall-painting of the same subject or of Dionysus' discovery of his future bride. The copy has many defects, especially the lopsided face, but was admired for the fluent ease of the drapery, a restatement of a fourth-century formula, in which the complex folds cling to the form revealing it as through a diaphanous sheath. The expression of emotional disquietude in the figure's twisted pose and confused interweaving of lines of drapery is far different from the static monumentality and fluid rhythms of the group of the Three Fates from the Parthenon pediment. Essentially the description of the drapery is at once more nervous and realistic than the Phidian formula. Such elements as the restless movement and turning of the body and the lineal intricacy of the drapery must have appealed to the sixteenth-century taste for emotional novelty and complexity. Michelangelo himself may have had the Ariadne in mind for his tragic figure of Night for the tomb of Lorenzo dei Medici.

THE LAOCOÖN

The Laocoön, which stands in the palace of the Imperator Titus, (is) a work to be preferred to all that the arts of painting and sculpture have produced. Out of one block of stone the consummate artists, Hagesandros, Polydorus, and Athenodoros of Rhodes, fashioned Laocoön, his sons, and the serpents marvellously entwined about them.[6]

On the morning of January 14, 1506, Michelangelo was called to view the discovery in the Baths of Titus of one of the most renowned sculptural groups of antiquity, a work that was immediately recognized from Pliny's description as the Laocoön by Agesandros, Polydorus, and Athenodorus of Rhodes (figure 34). It was this statue which Pliny described as "a work to be preferred to all that the arts of painting and sculpture have produced." This famous treasure of antiquity at once became the object of the laudatory verses of poets like Sadoleto and a source of inspiration to draftsmen, painters, and sculptors.

The group represents the fate of the Trojan priest Laocoön and his two sons when, suspecting the Greek gift of the wooden horse, he prepared to seek a portent from Poseidon and was immediately attacked and slain by two great serpents raised from the waters by the vengeful gods. The work, as noted by Pliny, is the work of Rhodian masters who were active about 50 B.C., so that it belongs to the very end of the Hellenistic period. It has been the subject of many essays, of which the most famous by Lessing concerns itself with an investigation of the group as an illustration of the description of Laocoön's death by Virgil.

The sculpture is in reality a sort of high relief, so obviously is it meant to be seen from a single frontal point of view. Its theme is the hopeless struggle of Laocoön and his sons to free themselves from the coils of the serpents that sting and crush them. Although there is something repulsive in this description of physical pain, the conception remains a masterpiece of the kind of realism developed in the Hellenistic age. Both the novelty and the violence of the subject are typical of a period dedicated to the exploration of every facet of human feeling and action. All attention is concentrated on the portrayal of inner suffering through the contortion of both bodies and faces. Although this concentration on the representation of the physical and mental torture of a cruel death is essentially hideous, the work is technically marvelous. The superb rendering of the anatomy, the supreme facility and even sensitivity of the carving, the balance of the group and its union in a single plastic mass present a superb tour de force. Laocoön does not cry out, and the beholder is spared the last gruesome details of the mutilation which bodies subjected to the serpents' iron coils would display. The group, although agonizing, is still human and subject to a certain restraint—but not the classic restraint of the fifth century. The one factor that separates the Laocoön from earlier Greek art in addition to the greater realism is the feeling of tension, which in such an extreme form was never portrayed in the art of the Great Period. The fluid movement and alternate straining and relaxation of muscles belong to the final baroque phase of Hellenic art. One reason why the Laocoön group was so extravagantly admired, not only in the sixteenth century but by Winckelmann, Lessing, and Goethe, is that it in a way gave authority to that very portrayal of dynamic movement and straining tension, that suggestion of strident passion still controlled, that formed the ideal of baroque religious art. The agony of a saint suppressing any overt expression of pain under torture was already forecast in the combination of almost superhuman self-mastery and pain in the Laocoön.

Seen from a distance the group is a moving arabesque of forms existing and turning freely in their spatial ambient. It is composed essentially in diagonals dynamically uniting the composition and replacing the closed arrangement in verticals and horizontals of earlier Greek art. The twining snakes, too, provide a sinuous link between the figures in the group. In the treatment of surface and structure we have an even more pictorial type of sculpture than the Pergamum frieze from which it is descended. In a way the broken uneasy rhythms of the forms in their tortured attitudes destroy a sense of continuous, flowing movement in the ensemble. In the same way the intricate carving of the surface, producing a kind of mottled chiaroscuro, creates a dissolution of the earlier solidity of form defined by more precisely demarcated shadows through the definition of simplified planes.

Anatomically the modeling of the individual bodies of Laocoön and his sons is not only a virtuoso performance from the point of view of correct observation, but marvelous in the appropriate suggestion of the strength and weakness in such details as the hands and feet of the separate figures. It was no wonder that not only the group as a whole but the individual bodies and their parts provided models for painters as well as sculptors for more than three centuries.

— 9 —

Painting in the Ancient World

Nicias kept a strict watch on light and shade, and took the greatest pains to make his paintings stand out from the panels. . . . It is this Nicias of whom Praxiteles used to say, when asked which of his own work in marble he placed highest, "The ones to which Nicias has set his hand"—so much value did he assign to his coloring of surfaces.
—Pliny *

The writings of ancient critics, the traveler's guide Pausanias, and the universally observant scientist Pliny, are filled with accounts of the wonders of Greek painting. Not a single fragment of the masterpieces of such artists as Zeuxis, Apelles, and Polygnotus has survived. Although it is sometimes possible to reconstruct the lost compositions of Polygnotus from Greek vase painting, these beautiful ceramic decorations can give only a shadowy idea of painting on walls or panels. As in the case of Greek sculpture the Romans were quick to adopt the subjects, techniques, and styles of conquered Hellas, so that in a measure the great number of wall-paintings discovered in Rome and in the buried cities of Herculaneum and Pompeii can give us some idea of the appearance of the lost works of Hellenic antiquity. The vast repertory of subject matter in these murals includes scenes from mythology, the rites of mystery cults, landscape, still life, and architectural decoration. Although the best of these pictures decorating the villas at Pompeii and Herculaneum may have been done by Greek artists, the vast majority bear the same relation to Greek painting as Roman sculptural copies to Greek originals in stone and bronze. The types of ancient painting available to artists of the fifteenth century and later were occasional examples of what is generally described as the Second Pompeian Style and the form of ornament de-

* Lumen et umbras custodiit atque ut eminerent e tabulis picturae maxime curavit. . . . Hic est Nicias, de quo dicebat Praxiteles interrogatus, quae maxime opera sua probaret in marmoribus: quibus Nicias manum admovisset; tantum circumlitioni eius tribuebat.—Pliny, *Natural History,* XXV. 131, 133

scribed as *grotteschi,* which existed in the Baths of Titus and the famous Golden House of Nero. The so-called Aldobrandini Marriage caused a sensation when it came to light in 1606, and a century earlier Pinturicchio, Raphael, and Michelangelo were enchanted by the painted decorations of the Domus Aurea and the Villa Farnesina. The discovery of the great wall-paintings in the buried cities of Campania produced a veritable revolution in European painting of the eighteenth century.

One of the greatest collections of Greco-Roman painting was discovered in the basilica of Herculaneum. These paintings of mythological subject originally decorated a series of concave niches in the great hall of the building. Since a single one of these compositions will illustrate the character of the style, I have chosen the picture of Theseus Triumphant, representing the hero's return from his victory over the Minotaur (figure 35). This painting was executed in the Flavian period shortly after A.D. 50. It is illustrative of the Second Pompeian Style, in which the epic compositions are dominated by figures of heroic stature. Theseus stands in the middle of the stage surrounded by the figures of the victims he has rescued and children who kiss his hands. The Minotaur lies dead at his feet, and as a personification of the locale the Nymph of Crete with bow and arrows appears above the hero's right shoulder.

The paintings in this mode have been described as sculpture transformed into another medium. The compositions in their complex interrelation of form are like a transposition into painting of the intricate groups of Hellenistic sculpture, such as the Pergamum frieze and its famous descendent, the Laocoön. The figure of Theseus himself is in some ways like a masterpiece of Greek sculpture of the fourth century. Pfuhl, the famous German critic of ancient painting, once described this figure as having the beauty of Praxiteles, the tension of Lysippus, and the passionate fire of Scopas.[1] The body is strongly modeled, so that it stands out like a piece of statuary, and the impressionistic handling of the shining highlights suggests the gleam of bronze. The fresh and sure handling of the brushstrokes that describe the shimmering lights on the torso and the soft locks of the hair imparts a vividness and luminosity that somewhat mitigate the hard academic drawing of the sculpturesque form. The compositional arrangement of this and related paintings from the basilica is relatively simple, with a small number of large impressive figures set off like forms in relief against an unobtrusive background. The grandiose and statuesque qualities of this style are presumably the ultimate reflections of Greek painting of a far earlier period. The suggestion of energy and heroic power is certainly present in the single figure of Theseus. He stands over the dead monster, looking out to triumphs yet unwon, oblivious and aloof from all the jubilant throng. The hero seems almost an embodiment of Theseus in an ancient painting described by Philostratus:

As for Theseus, he is indeed in love, but with the smoke rising from Athens, and he no longer knows Ariadne, and never knew her, and I am sure that he has even forgotten the labyrinth and could not tell on what possible errand he sailed to Crete, so singly is his gaze fixed on what lies ahead of his prow.[2]

There seems to be an attempt in this picture to recapture something of heroic man's detachment and mastery of himself and his fate that ennobled the ideals of a time already long ago.

A painting in a somewhat different mood that may perhaps be traced to an original by a Greek artist of the fourth century is the Pompeian painting of Perseus and Andromeda (figure 36). This composition is believed to be an ultimate reflection of the painter Nikias, who was a contemporary and assistant of Praxiteles. This composition evokes more the romantic than the heroic mood of classical myth. The hero as a kind of classical knight errant elegantly enacts the role of the rescue of a maiden in distress in what seems more a poetic charade than a struggle involving life and death. Nikias was famed for his skill in rendering the volumes of his figures, relieving them against the background, so that it is not surprising that the slender figure of Perseus stands out with sculpturesque clarity of modeling. Far more than the painting of Theseus Triumphant this wall painting is composed in terms of light and space. Not only the sketchy handling, but the soft luminosity of the colors suggests the envelopment of the scene in air and dazzling light.

A type of Roman painting destined to have a tremendous influence on later decoration in the classic manner was the grotteschi, so called in the fifteenth century because they were discovered in "grottoes" or subterranean ruins (figure 37). The present meaning of the word "grotesque" originates in the always playful and sometimes amusingly absurd character of this ornament. The most famous grotteschi were the decorations of the Domus Aurea, Nero's Golden House. This vast complex of buildings and gardens uniting the Palatine and Esquiline hills was constructed by the Emperor Nero after the fire of A.D. 64. Its destruction was begun as a matter of policy by the Flavians, and parts of the complex dis-

51

appeared under the Colosseum. Pliny tells us that the painting of the interiors of the vast palace enclosure was the work of a certain Fabullus, an artist so dedicated to his work that the palace became the "prison of his art." [3]

The ornaments which Fabullus devised for the walls and vaults of the Domus Aurea consisted of a mixture of stucco and painting dividing the surface into a variety of shapes. There were round and square and oblong fields, framed by such motives as the egg-and-dart, astragals, leaves, consoles, and spiraling arabesques. Sometimes the small framed panels were filled with mythological scenes or birds, sphinxes, and griffins. The red and yellow and blue and olive green of the paintings contrasted with the neutral ground to produce a stunning tapestrylike effect. These combinations of floral and geometric ornaments and often spiraling vine patterns were all painted in a light impressionistic style, as befitted such a gay rococo type of architectural ornament. The combination of shapes and colors was endless in variety, and yet completely ordered within the scheme of the total design. Not only the scheme of decoration as a whole, but the fluent painting of the individual scenes, now long since disappeared, invited the pencils of such artists as Pinturicchio, Raphael, and Michelangelo. The absurd elegance and often delicious freshness of invention in the grotteschi were lovingly copied by Francisco de Hollanda. It is in the pages of his sketch book that we find the most accurate records of these lost beauties that in a freer translation found their way into Raphael's superb decoration of the loggie of the Vatican. The grotteschi make their final appearance in the chaste style of interior decoration devised by Robert Adam in the eighteenth century.

It is perhaps well to give some account of landscape painting in the classic period. Elements of this genre find their way into later styles, so that, for example, the backgrounds of many medieval paintings in Byzantine art, in Carolingian manuscripts, and in the proto-Renaissance of the thirteenth century contain reflections of the classical formula for the representation of nature. The term, classic landscape, as used to describe the work of seventeenth-century artists like Claude and Poussin, refers to qualities already present in the painting of the antique period. Used in this context, classic landscape may be said to include everything that is the opposite of the romantic or picturesque.

The sovereignty of man in the Greek view of life and art more than any-

thing else prevented the development of a landscape painting comparable to our modern conception of landscape as a revelation of the poetic
moods of nature or of the romantics' view of nature as an awesome symbol of the divine. So deeply was the concept of anthropomorphic representation rooted in the Greek world view that, the more the Greeks
looked into nature, the more their own likeness was mirrored in it. Nature became animated and personified in daimons of human shape; for
example, in the Pompeian wall-painting of Heracles discovering his son
Telephus in the wilds of Arcadia (figure 38) the magnificent figure of
the Nymph of Arcadia personifies the wilderness—of which no other indication is to be seen.

Pliny informs us that landscape was a flourishing genre in Rome of the
first century A.D. He may have had in mind the idyllic views of coastal
scenery that decorated the walls of villas in Pompeii and Herculaneum or
something like the series known as the Odyssey Landscapes (figure 39)
that once decorated a patrician villa on the Esquiline Hill. This latter
group of paintings serves as an admirable example of ancient landscape
in the Augustan period. The subjects, taken from the Odyssey, include
such famous episodes as Odysseus' adventures in the land of the cannibals, his visit to the island of Circe, and his descent to the underworld.
The paintings which originally ornamented the wall above the dado in the
principal room of the house are framed in bright red pilasters with gold
capitals, so that one has the illusion of looking through this architectural
screen at the barren headlands and the wine-dark sea that are the stage for
Odysseus' wanderings. Enhancing even further the Roman concern with
spatial effects, the architectural members are painted in perspective so as
to convey even more the illusion of gazing out into a natural scene.

In the Odyssey Landscapes there is no interest in the observation of
nature, nor with the artist's representation of a particular locality. They
present no over-all creative vision of nature. These are mythological landscapes in which the activities of Odysseus and his companions dominate
the setting. In a strange way the anthropomorphic element is present even
in the landscapes themselves. The rocks and towering promontories have
a strangely architectural look, as though they were parts of a man-made
stage set representing generalized simplifications of natural forms. The
pictures could be described as idyllic landscapes, in which the lighting
remains static and no meteorological disturbance is allowed to intrude.

Following the usual rule of personification the figures of the wind gods, rather than any darkening of the sky, betoken the oncoming tempest in the first panel of the series. Throughout the series contrasts in mood are provided by contrasts in color or light and dark but entirely by anthropomorphic metaphor, so that in the painting of Odysseus' adventures on the Lastrygonian coast the terrors of the land of the cannibals are symbolized by the figure of a giant killing a Greek, and, by contrast, the peaceful nature of the Aeaean strand across the strait is indicated by a group of nymphs sunning themselves on the headland.

In none of these landscapes is there any uniform or convincing lighting effect. Only in the scene of the underworld, where an unexplained beam of light brightens the grotto entrance, is there any kind of dramatic illumination. From the compositional point of view the setting of each individual panel in the panorama unrolled behind the painted architecture is invariably a shallow stage that projects the actors toward the proscenium and does not in any real sense give the illusion of the existence of space behind the papier-mâché rocks and houses. The representation of conical mountains and bare, rugged promontories in these pictures suggests a stage setting more than reality. Their geological structure is smoothed down to a few salient planes, and the masses are so broadly modeled that they appear as statuesque as the painting of the accompanying figures. Both the simplicity of this formula for mountains and its effectiveness as an unobtrusive and yet dramatic background undoubtedly appealed to artists in the succeeding Byzantine tradition and to medieval artists like Giotto as eminently appropriate for Biblical themes, in which only symbols of nature were necessary to set off the monumentality of the human figures.

A false illusion of depth is provided by the high horizon line that seems to suggest that the spectator is looking down and into the scene. In some of the panels in which distant objects seem to fade one may perhaps infer an intuitive knowledge of the diminution of contrasts in atmospheric perspective, but the effects of light and atmospheric perspective are by no means consistently carried out. Although the occasional streaks of gray and pink on the horizon line might be taken to symbolize dawn or dusk, neither the colors nor the lighting of the landscapes corresponds to any particular time of day. All of these inconsistencies only serve to underline the generalized character of classic landscape and the subordinate role that nature plays in relation to the dominant interest of the human figures and their activities. Only the painting of a kind of all-per-vading luminosity seems to suggest some sensitivity for the beauty of light in nature. But even this is constant and generalized, so that in no particular does classic landscape portray nature as a reflection of the moods and activities of man.

— 10 —

Rome and Roman Art

Listen, queen fairest in all your world, Rome, welcomed among the stars of heaven, listen, mother of men and mother of gods, your temples bring us near to heaven. To you we sing praise and ever shall, so long as fates allow. None shall be wholly forgetful of you. Sooner shall guilty oblivion overwhelm the sun than reverence for you depart from my heart. Your works spread wide as the rays of the sun, where curving ocean surrounds the world . . . A single fatherland you have made for nations far apart. Even the unjust have found it profitable to be taken under your dominion. By offering the vanquished partnership in your own laws you have made a city of what was once a world.   —Rutilius Namatianus *

FOR many centuries the city of Rome was the capital of the world, not only in the days of the Caesars but in the periods of the triumphant church: its contribution in the arts and in literature has exercised a profound influence on the development of later civilization in Europe. This contribution is more than the romanticism and nostalgia provoked by Piranesi's engravings of the skeletons of Roman buildings: in many ways the skeleton of Rome provided the bones of our own culture. Rome was a center of a creative art from about the third century B.C. until A.D. 476, the fateful date of the final collapse of the empire.

> * Exaudi regina tui pulcherrima mundi,
> Inter sidereos Roma recepta polos!
> Exaudi, genetrix hominum, genetrixque Deorum:
> Non procul a coelo per tua templa sumus.
> Te canimus, semperque, sinent dum fata, canemus,
> Sospes nemo potest immemor esse tui.
> Obruerint citius scelerata oblivia solem,
> Quam tuus ex nostro corde recedat honos.
> Nam solis radiis aequalia munere tendis,
> Que circumfusus fluctuat Oceanus, . . .
> Fecisti patriam diversis gentibus unam,
> Profuit iniustis, te dominante, capi.
> Dumque offers victis proprii consortia iuris,
> Urbem fecisti, quod prius orbis erat.
> —Rutilius Namatianus, *Itinerarii,* I. 47–66; translated by Moses Hadas

Both the greatness and decline of the empire of Rome were conditioned by its vast geographical extent, from Hadrian's Wall in Britain to the Euphrates, from Gibraltar to the Danube. Over this great terrain the Romans established an administration, laws, a standard of living that have scarcely been equaled in modern times. The aims and accomplishments of Roman civilization were quite different from the ideals of the Periclean age. The Romans of the empire were dedicated, as no colonial power before or since, to bringing the benefits of their culture to all the world. These benefits were of a more material nature than the ideals of ancient Greece: security through Roman law and security protected by the shields of the legions; freedom of worship, provided it did not interfere with the safety of the state and reverence for the Emperor. For the Romans of the great period there was a sense of a world mission. As Cicero observed, it was part of this mission to regard the whole universe as "one single commonwealth of gods and men" or, as Marcus Aurelius stated, "My city and fatherland is Rome, but as a man, the world." [1] This view of a world with a law and security for all inevitably led to a uniformity in the arts that adorned it, so that there is little difference between Roman temples in Gaul or Africa and Roman shrines in the Eternal City.

In the early centuries of Roman history there was a continuous political struggle between Greek and Latin parties. Such was the revolution which terminated with the accession of Julius Caesar's heir, Caius Octavianus Caesar, the Emperor Augustus. After his victory over the reactionary Romans at Philippi and Actium, Augustus endeavored to reconcile the two elements in morals and religion through his establishment of the principate and the cult of Apollo. For many centuries there was a continuing conflict between Greek and Latin trends in Roman art. In the time of Augustus, and again under Hadrian, the balance swung in favor of Greek forms owing to the personal taste of the Emperor.

Augustan art, although it belongs to the ancient period, also marks the first historical moment when for both political and artistic reasons there is a conscious revival of the forms of Greek art, not only because the authority of this art was recognized but because it provided a peculiarly appropriate enframement for the expression of the ideals of Augustus and the age. In the declining centuries of the empire's power a uniformity of a different kind affected the art of every province. This was the literal conquest of the classical style by the ancient hieratic standards of those very Oriental regions which for so many centuries had been under Rome's political sway.

In contrast to Greece, Rome and her culture were dedicated more to the utilitarian than the aesthetic, as expressed in the great public buildings, in the magnificent plumbing supplied with water from the aqueducts, in the public spectacles and the pomp of triumphs to content the populus and reinforce the legend of Caesar's invincible might. Throughout its history Latin culture was absorbed in celebrating the delights of this world, not the next, except when, in the last centuries of despair, men turned in agonized hope to the mystery religions of the East.

With their strong sense of the practical the Romans translated Greek art into terms suitable for universal use. The forms and techniques of Greek art were appropriated, just as the most famous Hellenic masterpieces were looted to beautify the cities of the Mediterranean world. In the plastic arts the Romans imposed on Greek forms a feeling for realism both physical and psychological and a reminiscence of the sturdy massiveness and dignity of the ancient Etruscan tradition. Roman artists lacked the brilliance, originality, and versatility of the Greeks, so that in the final analysis much of their art is a marvel of adaptation, rather than invention. In art as in other fields the Romans were supreme systematizers, as in the arrangement of education, the formulation of a practical, not a speculative, philosophy, and the wonderful clarity and order of their written words.

The practicality of the Roman genius expressed itself especially in architecture, notably in the enclosing of enormous interior spaces, and in the field of engineering. These achievements, made possible by the employment of the arch, the vault, and the dome, created structures of a magnitude beyond the reach of the simple post and lintel system of Greek architecture. Typically Roman is the remark of Frontinus as he contemplated the fourteen aqueducts totaling 13,000 miles in length that gave Rome a water supply equal to that of any modern city: "Will anyone compare the idle Pyramids, or those other useless though greatly renowned works of the Greeks with these aqueducts?" [2] Size and utility, rather than aesthetic ends, made up the Roman ideal. The ingenuity of Roman builders sometimes achieved, as in the Pont du Gard, an admirable wedding of form and function. Over all Europe, Asia Minor, and North Africa the Romans built splendid cities that were pleasant to live in and a delight to the eye. Their mode of life was at once more comfortable and more hygienic than the common life of Europe today and more gracious than the American. Perhaps it could be said, too, that Roman art was more humanistic than the Greek achievement in catering to common needs.

Like the British today the Romans had a great sense of form and rightness in all things, a reliance on Tradition, and the luck of muddling through. The real source of what may be called Roman character rested on devotion to the family; the Lares and Penates were more important than the dim and distant Olympian gods. In many ways the Romans were a rather strait-laced people, suspicious of individuality and genius, suspicious of art and speculative thought, rather indifferent to science, and incapable of understanding philosophy. The Roman religion was a ritual solemnizing of all phases of public and private life, uniting the family and the nation. The faith that made Rome great was secular, its real religion patriotism. The Romans had few racial or cultural prejudices, and this is what made for an empire in which the aim was unity, not uniformity. The final mistake of the later Christian emperors was the attempt to impose uniformity of worship over all the vast extent of the crumbling realm.

When in the later centuries of the empire the vast Roman machine began to fall apart through corruption and weakness, military and political, the whole classic way of life disintegrated forever, and all Europe collapsed into the night of barbarism, the Dark Ages. In his disillusionment Marcus Aurelius once observed, "What is the end of it all? Smoke and ashes and a legend—or not even a legend?" [3] This might well be an epitaph for Rome's fallen greatness, a civilization which has left far more than legend, a cultural heritage in many fields that has shaped the destinies of all later ages.

— II —

Augustus

This is he, whom thou so oft hearest promised to thee, Augustus Caesar, son of a god, who shall again set up the Golden Age amid the fields where Saturn once reigned, and shall spread his empire past Garamant and Indian, to a land that lies beyond the stars, beyond the paths of the year and the sun.   —Virgil *

The young prince referred to in this passage is Augustus; and it is the great bard of his reign, Virgil, who thus invokes Octavian to rescue the land from seemingly endless war, a miracle performed by Augustus, when, with the final defeat of Antony and Cleopatra at Actium, there came an end to the long and terrible phase of civil war and misery. The gift of peace which Augustus was able to bring after all the waste and tragedy of years of conflict must have far outweighed the unsympathetic aspects of his regime. This is the triumph which Virgil sings in the Aeneid, in which Augustus looms as the real inheritor of the prophecy of his great forerunner, Aeneas. There Virgil creates the myths explaining the history and grandeur of Rome, justifying the dominance of Rome over the Hellenic world and the power of Octavian over the State, and Augustus takes up the mission of his mythical progenitor according to the plan long ago devised by the gods, completing a task begun by Aeneas according to the will of supernatural forces. When he enters the stage of history, Octavian embodies a concept found in all classic cultures, of the hero or savior coming from the East to save mankind. When, as victor over Cleopatra and Antony and pacifier of Asia, Augustus returned to Rome with the spoils of the Orient, he was for all a savior come from the East to

* Hic vir, hic est, tibi quem promitti saepius audis,
   Augustus Caesar, Divi genus, aurea condet saecula qui rursus Latio regnata per arva Saturnus quondam, super et Garamantas et Indos proferet imperium iacet extra sidera tellus, extra anni solisque vias.
                                                        —Virgil, *Aeneid*, VI. 791–796

rescue the Roman State. It was not long before Augustus' unification of the State justified for Virgil the power of this one man, Octavian, over all.

The new order inaugurated by Augustus demanded a new art to express at once its unity and greatness. Just as the Augustan principate was Augustus' special creation, so a new style literally vivified by the Augustan spirit came into being in a merging of Greek and Roman forms. Italy became the center of creation, and a new classicism, the first monumental expression of the Italian spirit, came into being. Just as the ideas of the past and present greatness of Rome were proclaimed in the poetry of Virgil, so in art they find their expression in the Ara Pacis, dedicated in 9 B.C. to celebrate the establishment of the Roman Peace (figure 40). As Augustus proclaimed in the testament he wrote before his death in A.D. 14, "When I returned to Rome from Spain and Gaul, after the operations successfully carried out by me in these provinces, the Senate decreed that on my return the Altar of the Pax Augusta should be consecrated on the Field of Mars and laid down that magistrates, priests, and Vestal Virgins should offer an annual sacrifice at it." [1] It could be said that the Ara Pacis was for Augustan art what the Parthenon had been for the Athens of Pericles. In some respects the altar perpetuates old Roman forms: the rectangular enclosure around the altar proper was an imitation of earlier structures in wood, fences or barriers about a dedicated spot. In other respects, the Ara Pacis is Hellenic in character: the threefold division of subject matter of the reliefs of the sanctuary in a way echoes the themes of the Parthenon sculpture: the procession of Augustus' altar corresponds to the frieze; the panels of myths recall the pediments; and the heroic struggles parallel the subjects of the metopes.

Among the mythical subjects at the east end of the Ara Pacis is the relief of Tellus or Mother Earth, who bestows the riches of the earth upon Rome (figure 40); opposite this composition there is a portrayal of Roma surrounded by trophies of victory. The corresponding panels at the western end of the enclosure are devoted to Aeneas offering at an altar, and Mars with Romulus and Remus. Actually the most dramatic portions of the Ara Pacis are the long friezes on the north and south sides of the building which represent the dedicatory procession (figure 41). Both subject and style of this frieze invite comparison with the Parthenon reliefs. The Parthenon frieze had both a religious and political character. It presented the visible concept of a state of universal Utopia, a kind of symbol of democracy ever renewed in the annual dedication to Athena.

The Parthenon was political and symbolical but not historical, whereas the frieze of the Ara Pacis represents the actual procession that took place on January 30, 9 B.C. All the personages are known by name, and the whole is a monumental history picture completely in the Roman tradition, and, in its embodiment of the Pax Augusta, the highest form of political propaganda.

There is every likelihood that the Ara Pacis is of Greek workmanship, an adaptation of Greek ideals for Roman needs, such as is found in Virgil's adaptation of the Greek epic. The historical relief is truly classical in its originality and power, and it is by no means behind the literary masterpieces in its creative strength. The figures of the Ara Pacis are apart from the Italic tradition in drawing and composition. There is no marked Italic realism. Although some figures are striking portraits, most are conventional types like the types in earlier Greek reliefs, and the style of the monument could be called "neoclassic," since it imitates earlier Greek prototypes. Its designer aimed to place in marble the same motives and concepts which inspired the Aeneid and the Roman odes of Horace. The intentions inspiring the monumental Roman altar put it on a par with the importance and destination of the works of Virgil, Horace, and Livy. The neoclassic style is explained because neither the patron nor the artist could have accepted for such an important monument a style different from that conventionally used as the only one endowed with sufficient *dignitas* for such a project. The copying of classic prototypes in art differed from literature because it did not involve the translation from one language to another. The prestige of classic—that is, Hellenic—art suffocated originality and spontaneity in the plastic arts because, for official purposes, it seems to have engendered a mistrust of the Roman Italic tradition, a mistrust much stronger than Virgil's and Horace's of earlier local literature. One feels that there was more originality in Latin literature, since there was the obligation to express oneself in Latin, making for more sincerity and spontaneity. There was an attempt to equal, rather than imitate, examples. There was an attempt to express concepts and sentiments in Latin within foreign canons and models. The problem to convert Latin into a suitable instrument for such expression is only partially approximated in the sculptural monuments of the Augustan period.

It is in portraiture that a real Latin classicism is achieved, because the only prototypes for the kind of realism demanded were in the Italic and not the Greek tradition. Hellenic influences are universally present in Augustan portraiture, because in this official art there was a need for something more imaginative than externals in portraiture. Indeed, the only technique capable of investing human forms with an adequate dignity was Hellenistic. Although Augustus pretended to Republican simplicity, it is obvious that his dynastic ambitions affected the new desire for the heroic. The portraits of Augustus and his family assume an aloofness that is more than human. There is a loss of the intimacy of the Republican type of portraiture in favor of a new sustained nobility of style. The portraits of the *princeps* became gradually typified and idealized with a diminution of realism, and there is created a figure in which the characteristics remain constant in order to create an official figuration of the personage. There are some realistic elements—like the breadth of cheekbones and the ungracefully attached ears—but most of the features become idealized factors in all the portraits of Augustus. The iconography of his likenesses has an official character which distinguishes it from contemporary portraits in which Roman and Italic traditions survive.

A typical example of the Augustan state portrait is the statue discovered at the Empress Livia's villa at Prima Porta (figure 42). The statue was intended for exhibition in a niche, so that the back is unfinished and the whole effect calculated for a front view. It was very obviously inspired by a Greek prototype. Both proportions and ponderations are borrowed from the Doryphoros of Polyclitus; but in place of the complete relaxation of the Greek athlete the whole conception of the Prima Porta statue breathes lordly will and power. The upper part of the body is erect and tense; the right arm outstretched, the countenance seeming to fix its beholders with a glance. This is no god, no hero, no genius filled with demonic power, but a man as master of reality. Only the motifs of the dolphin and cupid are creatures from the ideal sphere as a symbolic allusion to the descent of the Julian family from Venus. Augustus looms here as the founder of a new antique world. The statue is an organic synthesis of Greek form in the service of the Roman spirit. This is revealed not only in the countenance but in the whole bearing. As in the Ara Pacis there was a deliberate reliance on Greek forms because nothing comparable was available in late Republican art for adequately expressing the combination of majesty and virility demanded by the subject. Perhaps the most purely Roman aspect of the entire statue is found in the historical and political symbolism of the ornaments of the cuirass, where we see the return of the Parthian eagles in 19 B.C. On either side are the figures of sorrowing and discomfited Germania and Dacia. The sun god and dawn goddess above indicate that as far as the sun shines extends the empire of Augustus. The form of Mother Earth below announces the blessing of peace achieved through Roman might.

This type of portraiture is obviously official, the expression of a superhuman perfection which does not admit of emotion. It announces to the empire the calm beneficence of its semi-divine rule; that is, the individual features of Augustus were dignified to express the majesty of the Roman empire, just as the portrait of Pericles (figure 2) showed him as the ideal ruler of men. For the same end, the individual features of Augustus were coerced into a Greek mold (figure 90). The suggestion of individuality in the face, the insistence on concrete reality, is an inheritance from Etruscan art. The reliefs on the armor that celebrate the grandeur of Rome and the submission of the universe itself to Caesar are presented in a typically Roman historical fashion: the surrender of the Parthian standards was a real, not a symbolical, event. The whole statue, together with its symbolical accouterments, is as typical of Augustan Rome as the Aeneid of Virgil: it celebrated past glories and the present greatness of Rome.

The Augustus of Prima Porta is represented in a commanding and eloquent gesture, commanding by the force of his will and intellect. The statue meets the description of Augustus by Suetonius, that he was short of stature, but this was concealed by the fine proportions and symmetry of his figure. There is even a suggestion of what the Roman historian describes as a kind of divine power which Augustus liked to think shone from his eyes. Although in certain respects the statue is suggestive of Greek work, in its insistence on content, the evocation of a real character, a unique person in history, this Roman portrait is totally different both in form and expression from the idealized type of portrait associated with Greek art. It is this insistence on the individual rather than the ideal that distinguishes Latin from Greek art, not only in this classic period but throughout the whole later history of sculpture and painting in the Western world.

Although the features are obviously those of a real individual, like its Polyclitan prototype, the head is a relatively simple cubic mass with simple planes and contours contributing to the feeling of the integrity and solidity of the stone materials. Following Greek precedent, textures are

64

suggested rather than defined. The hair is rendered in a series of little flame-shaped tresses that do not describe the texture of real hair. The eye easily takes in the whole mask, resting on the sharp definition of every plane and contour. The whole is carved with a clarity that must have appealed to the precise mind of Augustus. The commanding air of the figure comes partly from the gesture of the right arm and just the proper tilt to the proud chin. Not only the magnificent accouterments but also the splendid athletic proportions of the body contrive to make the figure enormously impressive in spite of its lack of height. The statue is saved from being completely hieratic and idol-like by the distribution of weight and tension on the right and left sides. Although this may have been a device borrowed from Greek art, it was magnificently appropriate for expressing the vigor and hardiness of the Emperor who followed his armies into the field. It was intended as an artistic evocation of a real man who, through the sheer strength of his will, had risen to be the ruler of the Roman world. And at the same time the statue was a symbol of universal Roman authority and the peace that the power of Augustus conferred upon the world.

— 1 2 —

Hadrian the Hellenophile

O blithe little soul, thou, flitting away.
Guest and comrade of this my play, whither now goest
    thou, to what place
Bare and ghastly and without grace?
Nor, as thy wont was, joke and play.

                                        —Hadrian *

THIS is a memorial to one of the last great emperors and statesmen of the Roman world and one who, perhaps more than any other, could be described as philhellenic. Under him Hellenism became the formative power in the Imperium Romanum. No one knew the empire better: as a lieutenant under Trajan he had witnessed the suicide of the Dacian chiefs in the Carpathian wilds; in Britain he erected the wall against the savage Picts; his travels took him to a diplomatic conference in the silken tents of Osroes, the Parthian king. Then there was the journey up the Nile, a voyage marred by the mysterious drowning of his favorite, Antinoüs. Three times Hadrian visited Athens that was for him the Mecca of philosophy and the arts. He must have been thinking of all these things and places when, on his deathbed, he recited the truly Hellenic lines quoted above.

The monuments which Hadrian left in Athens bespeak his admiration for the ancient center of Hellenic civilization. There is his gate with the inscription on one side, "The city of Theseus," and on the back, "The city of Hadrian." On the plain below the Acropolis there stand, as another memento of his philhellenism, the remains of the great forest of columns of the temple of the Olympian Zeus begun by one of the Pergamene kings and brought to completion by Hadrian.

The one spot in his empire most dearly loved by Hadrian was his villa

* *Historia Augusta, Hadrian;* translated by A. O'Brien-Moore

at Tivoli. There as nowhere else is the reflection of his philhellenic tastes. Most intimately associated with the Emperor was a little pavilion set in a circular pool, an island retreat, where, it is said, Hadrian secluded himself from the world to pursue the arts of poetry, music, and painting. The little building was surrounded by a circular Ionic colonnade, supporting an entablature with a graceful frieze of nereids and tritons. In the vast estate at Tivoli, more a town than a villa, was a reconstruction of the pleasure-groves and lupanars of fabulous Canopus, which the Emperor had visited on his romantic journey up the Nile. An arcade of columns forms a screen around a reflecting pool (figure 43), and under its arches were placed replicas of some of the most famous statues of classical antiquity: the Amazons of Polyclitus and Phidias and the caryatids of the Erectheum which Hadrian must have admired on his pilgrimages to Athens (figure 44). These copies of the Porch of the Maidens are exceedingly interesting for the nature of Hadrianic classicism (figure 45). They are no more than adequate replicas by a copyist who was able to transmit everything except the spirit of the original. Compared with the actual figures in the porch of the Erectheum (figure 46) they have a strangely dry, mechanical appearance, a cold reflection of the warmth and vitality of the masterpieces of the fifth century.

Everywhere the courts and halls of Hadrian's villa were haunted by ghosts of Antinoüs. In Pentellic or Parian marble, in busts and reliefs and full-length statues stood the memorials of the deified Bythnian youth. One of the most famous of these likenesses has found its way to the Museo Nazionale in Naples (figure 47). Its eclectic style presents a kind of anthology of Hadrian's admiration for Greek art, and at the same time, a revelation of the classicism of his day. The proportions and the pose of the figure evoke the familiar Polyclitan athlete. In its very breadth the modeling recalls the Phidian canon. Whereas in the work of a fifth-century sculptor there is a suggestion of warm and pulsing life beneath the marble surface, in this eclectic reconstruction of the Hellenic ideal this feeling of life seems to have been congealed in the smooth, cool, and jewel-like sparkle of the material itself. Although the massive youthful head, framed in its rich curls, may be derived from a Phidian type, this ideal has been transformed into something quite different and strangely moving. The un-Greek, barbarian face of the Bythnian boy has been endowed with an air of mysterious sorrow and introspective languor, largely through the delicacy and carving of the soft planes of the face and the deep shadowing of the eyes. One almost seems to detect here the beginning of that spiritualization of the portrait that more and more comes into prominence in the last centuries of the empire.

Both in its political and artistic aspects the Hellenism of Hadrian's reign marks the last moment in history, when Rome turned to the school of Hellas. In the centuries that followed there is a gradual drifting away from the Greek world that ends in the complete separation of the Eastern empire.

— 13 —

Greek Originals and Roman Copies

Greece, taken captive, captured her savage conqueror, and carried her arts to clownish Latium.
— Horace *

THE question of Roman copies of Greek originals should be examined in considerable detail, not only because even at the present day many lost masterpieces of Greek art are known only through these replicas, but also because until relatively modern times Greek sculpture of the earlier periods was known only through these imitations. In great part the medieval, Renaissance, and even the baroque concept of the classical ideal was based on such Roman facsimiles and the few examples of Hellenistic art that had survived. Copies of famous Greek originals were extensively manufactured in Roman times to ornament the palaces and cities of the entire Mediterranean world. So, for example, a life-size copy of Polyclitus' Diadoumenos was found at Vaison-la-Romaine in Provence. Hadrian's Villa at Tivoli had its replicas of the Erectheum caryatids, the Amazon of Polyclitus, and other masterpieces. These copies can be seen particularly well in the fanciful reconstruction of Canopus at Tivoli. They were made as decorations and mementoes of originals no longer available to collectors. They were the plaster casts of the ancient world. Although reasonably good reproductions were being made by Greek copyists certainly as late as the time of Augustus, the vast majority have a mechanical deadness of execution that inevitably distinguishes them from their prototypes.

Copying probably began even in Hellenistic times, usually with the aim of supplying various sanctuaries with identical likenesses of the same deity. By the first century B.C. the making of replicas had not only become an industry but also a taste developed for eclectic combinations of ele-

* Graecia capta ferum victorem cepit et artes intulit agresti Latio.—Horace, *Epistles,* II. 1. 156

69

ments borrowed from various masterpieces. So, for example, the famous Spinario is a combination of a fifth-century head with the body in the softer style of the fourth century (figure 185).

In Roman times copying was carried out on a literally wholesale basis. The Romans had an insatiable appetite for the luxury of possessing precious objects, which included the work of Old Masters or replicas of their work. The craze for Greek art is retailed not only in Cicero's prosecution of the collector Verres, but also in the cultural pretensions of Trimalchio, satirized in Petronius' *Satyricon*. Not even the wholesale looting of Greece and the provinces could satisfy the demand for statuary and works of art of all sorts for decorations and for patents of *richesse* and culture. The innumerable duplicates of now lost Greek masterpieces reveal how this craving was in part appeased.

Not only the imperial villa at Tivoli but the gardens of the Roman patricians were filled with facsimiles of the works of Phidias, Polyclitus, and Lysippus. Sometimes these replicas are the work of competent craftsmen who did their best to transfer something of the quality of the original into their product. Obviously, in transferring bronze into marble all the qualities of softness and elegance in a molded original tended to become frozen and hard in the attempt to reproduce them in stone. Presumably the replicas were made in Italy from famous works already imported or in Athens from masterpieces still surviving *in situ*. The copyists, compelled to work from originals in a temple sanctuary or public place, obviously could not achieve the most complete accuracy. It may be that they used an occasional cast for guidance and took a minimum number of points in the process of duplicating an original. Although some copies in bronze were made, notably the collection of bronze statues discovered at Herculaneum, the cheaper material of marble was generally preferred.

To illustrate the difference between a Greek original in marble and a later copy of the same style one can compare the Bartlett head of Aphrodite in the Museum of Fine Arts, Boston (figure 21) with a later representation of the goddess of love in the Louvre (figure 22). The Bartlett head is generally regarded as a work of Praxiteles or a close follower. The head of Aphrodite in the Louvre is of the Greco-Roman period, perhaps no later than the first century B.C., a copy of a Praxitelean type, similar to the Bartlett Aphrodite. Superficially the head in Paris is a beautiful object with the sharply cut, crystalline marble suggesting the goddess' lustrous flesh. The regularly carved features still have something of the

70

fragile winsome charm of a Praxitelean original. A closer inspection reveals, however, that in the copy the edges of the contours of the features have become hard and sharp. The surfaces of cheek and brow and chin no longer have the soft gradations of chiseling that impart such a feeling of vibrant, sensuous texture to the original. They are more like mechanically smooth and unbroken planes, like sections of spheroidal forms in the world of solid geometry. There is an uncertainty in carving the hair in rather lumpy masses. Whereas the roughness in the carving of the hair in the original gives an illusion of the mass and texture of the hair, differentiated from the smooth texture of the flesh parts, this quality has completely disappeared in the later imitation. In comparison with the fourth-century original the replica has a harsh and dry quality through the very elimination of the soft transitions in the Praxitelean work. Such a mechanical reproduction can convey only a shadowy impression of the real beauty of Greek craftsmanship.

A comparison of a marble copy of a Praxitelean bronze original and the bronze boy from the Bay of Marathon (figure 48) illustrates what happens in the process of translating metal into stone. The bronze statue, a cast metal replica of a form originally modeled by the sculptor in clay or wax, has all of the Praxitelean character of grace and pliant movement enhanced by the S-curve of the body on its axis, which is apparent in the famous Hermes at Olympia. The fact that the statue was modeled and delicately built up in a malleable material confers a far greater suggestion of fleshly softness than a stone carving of a human form. There is a sensuous warmth in the slight transitions from plane to plane; the muscles seem to move under the skin that is the lustrous surface of the bronze itself. The body gives the impression of lithe, tensile movement and slight feminine grace typical of the Praxitelean school. A differentiation in texture is achieved between the smooth surfaces of the nude body and the crisp definition of the hair in curling locks that seem actually to grow from the head. Although these masses of ringlets are still somewhat formalized in their calculated disarray, they create the illusion of both the mass and fluffiness of the hair. The inlaid eyes add to the lifelike quality of the boy's enigmatic wistful expression.

A comparison with this beautiful Greek original may be found in a Hermes in the Museum of Fine Arts, Boston (figure 49), which is a marble copy of a Praxitelean original. It has the same typical slight and elegant form swaying at the hips, and the face is a translation into stone of

71

the dreamy, yearning expression which we associate with Praxiteles (figures 50 and 51). It is evident at once that the copyist has been unable to capture the nuances of modeling of the metal original, so that the demarcation of the muscular structure is rather sharp and hard. The entire quality of the soft, glowing warmth of skin texture implied in the bronze is lost in the simplification of the stone. The hair no longer gives the impression of a waving crown of light curls, but rather of a caplike encrustation of shells in the marble-cutter's effort to simulate the conventions of the metal prototype. The whole character of the bronze original has been changed in the process of transferring it to carving. There is a simplification of the subtleties of modeling to plain surfaces congenial to the chisel. The body no longer glows with life as it did in the bronze; it has assumed a rather dry and rigid quality.

It was this kind of second-hand abstraction or reduction of the qualities of Greek originals that formed the models for later generations who had no way of knowing the true nature of Hellenic prototypes. It was inevitable that something of the hardness and petrifaction of such mechanical replicas found its way into the repetitions of forms like this in the Renaissance and later. Yet even such shadows of Greek perfection, for all of their shortcomings, had valuable lessons to impart to artists seeking to relearn the mastery of the organic representation of the human form.

A different type of copying in Roman times may be observed in the Horse-tamers of the Quirinal Hill in Rome. These groups of the Dioscuri in a way already represent a classical revival since, although they are derived from the sculpture of the Parthenon pediment, they are not precisely copies of Phidian sculpture but adaptations from it in much the same way that the sculpture of Michelangelo is a dynamic reworking of various Hellenistic prototypes. Both the pose and the proportions of these figures of Castor and Pollux mirror the central statue of the Poseidon of the west pediment of the Parthenon, as it can be seen in the drawing made by Carrey before the destruction of this sculpture in 1689, when the Venetian admiral Morosini made an unsuccessful attempt to remove the pediment statues.[1] Today only fragments of the torso of this statue survive in the British Museum and Athens.

Although the giant figure of the sea god (figure 52) is no more than a torso from shoulders to abdomen, enough remains to reveal the character of the modeling and to indicate the differences between this original and the statues of the Quirinal derived from it. Like the more famous

Theseus on the east pediment, the body of Poseidon is carved in a series of broadly simplified convex planes which not only give an accurate impression of anatomy but suggest the flow and play of the muscles encasing the massive thorax. Although following archaic precedent there is a symmetrical repetition of the shape of the muscles to the right and left of the median axis, there is a soft transition from one swelling muscular element to the next, so that we do not have the sense of hard, linear demarcation of archaic statuary. One has the illusion of a mighty body, alive and pliant.

In the group on the Quirinal Hill the figure labeled "opus Praxiteles" on the ancient base (figure 53) is the closer approximation of the Phidian Poseidon. The companion figure, inscribed "opus Phidiae," is, following a practice often adopted by the copyist for matching statues, a mirror image of its mate. In these adaptations of the Poseidon of the Parthenon, probably made in the second century A.D., the representation of the anatomy is scarcely different from the muscular structure portrayed in the cuirass, which had been introduced to support the statues. Instead of the flowing transitions of the Phidian original we are conscious of a sharp and harsh division between the consecutive groups of muscles. Sometimes these divisions are emphasized even more by deep, separating grooves, so that the entire effect is of the muscles separately appliquéd to the frame like a corselet, rather than a fluid encasing sheath that is organically part of the body. This effect is enhanced by the way in which individual muscles have been exaggerated into swelling promontories. There are also a number of technical deviations from the Phidian ideal, such as the method of indicating the pupils of the eyes by kidney-shaped incisions and the deep pictorial carving of the hair that is more characteristic of Hellenistic art than the manner of Phidias.

Although in many ways the Phidian prototype has been reduced to a rather rigid formula, the very scale and heroic pose derived from the Parthenon sculpture impart a grandeur and even a suggestion of theatrical dynamic movement. In spite of their technical shortcomings at least something of the power and titanic ideal form of the Phidian style was transmitted through these famous Roman landmarks, enough to inspire countless artists, including Michelangelo, to the rediscovery of the ideal and organic representation of the human form in supernatural dimensions.

— 14 —

The Late Antique Period

Attica, the giantess, is fallen
Where the ancient sons of gods now sleep;
In the wreck of marble temples fallen
Deathly silence endless watch doth keep.
Spring-time for the lost ones vainly seeking
Glides downward to Ilissus' holy plain;
But the desert has them in her keeping,
Never shall their forms be seen again.
 —Hölderlin *

FROM the fourth century on, the Mediterranean world presented a far different picture from that of the unified and peaceful empire of Augustus. The period from A.D. 300 to 500 is described by the term Late Antique, a definition for a time when the vigor of the great classic tradition was gradually failing and the life of the old deities was waning. It was an era that could be also called the twilight of the gods. The slow end of the great classical style and the eclipse of the Olympians are the final chapter in the history of the antique world. The span of years from the time of Constantine to the reign of Justinian is sometimes described also as the proto-Byzantine period because it was marked by that coalescence of Hellenistic and Oriental elements making up the style known as Byzantine.

This last phase in the history of the classical world began with the

---

* Attica, die Riesin, ist gefallen,
 Wo die alten Göttersöhne ruh'n,
 Im Ruin gesturtzten Marmor-hallen
 Brutet ew'ge Todesstille nun;
 Lächelnd steigt der süsse Frühling nieder,
 Doch er findet seine Brüder nie
 In Ilissus heil'gem Thale wieder,
 Ewig dekt die bange Wüste sie.
  —Hölderlin, "Griechenland: An Ständlin" (1793)

foundation in 326 of the city of Constantinople. This capital was founded by the Emperor Constantine as a new Rome, and its palaces and sacred ways were modeled on those of the old center of the Roman world. Although its location on the site of an earlier Greek city in the Hellenistic empire made for a continuity of the Greek tradition, Constantine's successors, down to the very last of the Paleologi, thought of themselves as Roman emperors, the heirs of Augustus.

In the period from the fourth to the sixth century the old classical religion gradually sank into oblivion. There was a disappearance of inner conviction, and in many instances the old mythologies become merely themes for stylized exercises in verse and drama. In part the degradation of the ancient faiths was the result of the excesses of the mystery religions. Many of the great shrines dedicated to various forms of the Great Goddess were little more than religious brothels. This was a period when the Olympian cults were further corrupted by the acceptance of a whole host of foreign gods. Anything with an appealing mysterious aspect that in any way coincided with Roman notions of deity was eagerly welcomed.

Even in this period of the degradation of the Olympian religion many believed that the calamities which befell the empire could be ascribed to the baleful influence of Christianity. Many were still sufficiently attached to the old gods to dread that the ruin of paganism would surely cover the earth with darkness and restore the ancient dominion of Chaos and Night.

The period from A.D. 300 to 500 witnessed the emergence of Christianity as the dominant religion of what had been the old classical world. But the death throes of the pagan religion were protracted at least two centuries, after Constantine's Edict of Milan in 313 assured universal tolerance for Christianity. Constantine's own relation to Christianity has never been entirely clear, in spite of the many legends about his miraculous conversion. Indeed, the Emperor had recourse to pagan geomantic practices to secure the fate of his capital by magical means. The representations of pagan deities on his coins show that he maintained at least a nominal allegiance to the old cults, and the syncretic character of his belief is illustrated by the colossal statue of the Emperor as Apollo, which had a rayed crown made from the nails of the True Cross. Although Constantine himself promulgated an edict of toleration for the Olympian religion and his successor, Julian the Apostate, attempted a full-scale revival of the old beliefs, the death warrant of paganism came with the

Emperor Theodosius' interdict and abolition of the Colleges dedicated to the ancient cults. The destruction in the year 401 of the Marneion at Gaza, one of the greatest centers of pagan worship in the Mediterranean world, is sometimes given as a symbolical date for the death of the gods. But, even though the effigies of the Olympian deities were dragged through the streets by Theodosius' chariots and their greatest sanctuaries reduced to smoke and ruin, the worship of the Olympian deities continued in court circles until the reign of Justinian in the sixth century. The forms of classical art were destined to survive even longer.

There were many reasons why the Hellenic tradition should have survived particularly in Constantinople. Constantinople at its founding was a pagan city, and temples to the Dioscuri and the Tyche or city goddess were actually erected by Constantine. In this former Greek center the court continued to sponsor classical learning and literature and the forms of its art. Even after the State acceptance of Christianity as a religion, there seems to have been no conflict between pagan and Christian art productions. Many of the pagan themes were repeated for aesthetic and decorative reasons. Formal elements from ancient art were adapted by Byzantine artists for Christian usage and many classical figure types were amalgamated into Christian subjects for symbolical purposes. For a time at least in Byzantium classical motifs were copied with an attempt to retain the classical composition and style as well.

Under Constantine the new Rome was endowed with some of the most famous works of classical antiquity. Statues by Myron and Phidias, including the Olympian Zeus and the Athena from the Acropolis, decorated the Hippodrome and were only destroyed in the riots at the time of the Venetian crusade. Over four hundred classical statues were set up in front of Hagia Sophia. One can only suppose that the presence of these classical relics made for a persistence of a pagan aesthetic, even though what the form stood for was officially condemned by the Church. Much of the architectural style of Constantine and his successors followed Roman prototypes: the aqueduct of Valens repeats the elevation of the Aqua Claudia even to the range of small arches at the summit of the monument; the triumphal columns erected by Theodosius and Arcadius imitated the helical band of narrative on the pillars of Trajan and Marcus Aurelius. The colossal statues of some of these later monarchs copy a fashion which had been inaugurated with the colossal gold effigy of Nero.

An examination of monuments from this Late Antique period illus-

76

trates the changes which the classical ideal was undergoing in this time of crisis. When pagan themes are employed they are treated in a new romantic idyllic fashion. The subject is no longer a matter of belief, but survives as a theme for aesthetic exploitation almost in the manner of eighteenth-century *chinoiseries*. We notice at the same time, especially in sculpture, an influence of Oriental traditions that transforms the plastic humanistic style into a more linear hieratic formula, and with this abstraction we also discern a new note of gravity and spirituality, a reflection both of Christianity and the political struggles confronting the Empire. The classical themes that appear in mosaics, in ivories, or in the beautiful silver salvers or *paterae* from the fourth to the sixth century are obviously based on Hellenistic originals often very closely imitated but generally revealing a tendency toward a dry, frequently mechanical, reproduction that characterizes the works of these final centuries of the ancient world.

A few lines by Palladas of Alexandria provide a kind of epitome on the fate of the old gods in the Late Antique period:

At the cross-roads I marvelled to see a bronze statue of Jupiter's son tossed from its former place of worship and I declared in my wrath: "O averter of evil and ever undefeatable one low thou art laid today." But at night the god stood smiling beside me and said, "Divine though I am, I have learnt to serve the times." [1]

Although the Olympians were being thrown from their pedestals and their worship decried, this was by no means the final death of the gods. Many of them, like Hercules, simply adopted the disguise of Samson or the Christian virtue of Fortitude, and there is reason to believe that in pagan enclaves throughout the Roman world representations of the old titans continued to be made at once for ritual and decorative purposes until at least A.D. 500. An example of this final hour of pagan art is a representation of Hercules and the Erymanthian boar, now embedded in the façade of San Marco in Venice (figure 54). Most likely this was one of a number of Late Antique fragments stolen by the crusaders from Byzantium in 1204. The relief may be dated in the fourth century and represents the classical hero carrying his giant quarry on his shoulders, while his terrified patron, King Erystheus, endeavors to hide in a cauldron. This work is typical of a moment when the antique style was declining into Oriental patternization. The muscular sheath of Hercules' body is more like a cuirass of separate swelling bosses than an organic structure. The disproportion of this mighty body is also a far cry from the perfected anatomical articulation of a classic figure. The whole has a heraldic appearance that one would never find in works of the ancient period. The combination of linear definition and decorative detail has almost a suggestion of the archaic, but, unlike the formalized vigor of archaic carving, the artistic vitality of the Greek ideal has been transformed into ornament. This formalism is only a part of the reduction of the old gods to symbolic effigies, and it may well be that even in this pagan subject there is an allegory of Christian virtue triumphing over evil.

When seen in the dusky interior of the Archaeological Museum at Istanbul, the relief of Nike which once adorned one of the city gates seems like an evocation from the Hellenic past (figure 55). This is presumably a work of the fourth or fifth century. The winged figure of the Goddess of Victory strides forward, palm in hand with all her drapery flying. In this first glance she seems to have something of the old rhythmic grace of the draped figures of the Parthenon pediment (figure 56). Although superficially the disposition of the garment in long sweeping lines approximates the ideal of the fifth century B.C., in actual execution and arrangement the folds have taken on an essentially more linear and decorative character. There is no longer the implication of the separate existence of garment and body. Here cloth and flesh appear as one undivided substance. It is as though the folds in their depth of carving actually penetrated the substance of the body itself. These deeply channeled lines, like the forms of all Late Antique art, are a dry formalization of organic classical structure. It is only a step from this decorative, rather than structural representation of the body to the completely linear transformation of the classic formula that finds its way into Oriental sculpture.

In some of the ivories of the fifth century there appears a classic quality that is like a resuscitation of the spirit of Hellenistic art. This Hellenistic purity of style in the ivory diptychs has its parallel in the poetry of Claudian, who represents a revival of classical taste in his attempt to infuse life into his writing on the model of the great poets of the Greek and Latin tradition. Although the spirit and beauty of his imagery are somewhat clouded by his dependence on earlier forms, an inscription on a statue dedicated to Claudian in Trajan's forum celebrated him as the synthesis of the spirit of Virgil and the muse of Homer. A particularly beautiful example of Late Antique work in ivory is a plaque in the Victoria and Albert Museum with an inscription of the single word, Symmachorum, above the actual relief panel (figure 57). This fragment is a memento of one of the last great pagan families in Rome before the barbarian darkness shadowed the Western world. Q. Aurelius Symmachus, a man of great wealth and famed as an orator, was one of the final supporters of the Olympian cult. It was undoubtedly his sentimental and patriotic attachment to the old Roman religion that led him to undertake personally the maintenance of the old temples when their state subsidy had been withdrawn through the influence of St. Ambrose in 396. The ivory was perhaps carved as a gift for a friend to commemorate this endowment. The leaf in the Victoria and Albert Museum represents a maiden, either a priestess or a member of Symmachus' family, performing what must have been one of the last sacrifices at the altar of a pagan deity. The serenity of the conception and the precision and delicacy of the execution in its details are extremely suggestive of the finest works of the fourth century B.C. It is almost as though in this their final hour the followers of paganism were striving desperately to rescue not only the ancient cults but the beautiful art that had once embodied them. Although the soft refinement of the features and the crisp carving of the softly fluted drapery may remind us of actual classical reliefs, there is a certain stiffness and formality in the presentation. To repeat the ancient formula is now a studied technical effort, not second nature, for the artist striving to maintain a vanishing taste and style.

The very stiffness of the ivory carving and its maker's meticulous affectation may reflect something of the same pedantry and reliance on the great Latin poets that suffocates the poetry of Claudian. Claudian and Symmachus, like men of every age who see the values of their tradition crumbling, appeared to shut their eyes to the religious revolution that was to destroy their world. In such works as the diptych commissioned by Symmachus one of the last pagan artists clings to the old forms of beauty that for so long had given validity to the cult of the Olympians.

Among the fragments of painting from the Late Antique period is an illustrated manuscript of Virgil in the Vatican Library (figure 58). The scores of paintings devoted to the Aeneid and shorter poems are all of them evidently composed as illustrations, and presumably are not copies of earlier originals. Many of the pages are filled with the most animated details that provide an extraordinary and vivid picture of the pagan world. These paintings mark a final florescence of a style that ultimately goes back to the old Hellenistic tradition. Like the Pompeian wall-paintings, the backgrounds are composed in an atmospheric way. There is generally a rather dashing, even summary, type of brush drawing, and the scenes are laid in a dreamlike ambient of vivid changing colors. There are indications that we are dealing with an art in a period of decline: many of the compositions are decidedly schematic, and the individual figures are apt to be flat and clumsily articulated. The drawing is decorative rather than organic, in much the same way that pagan figure sculpture in the Late Antique period is apt to substitute decorative organization for organic articulation of bodily forms.

All of these tendencies, marking the disintegration of the plastic, organic ideal of the great periods of pagan art, indicate the emergence of a new style more appropriate in its abstraction and symbolical character for the expression of the spiritual ideals of the Christian world. Even in the Late Antique period, these characteristics which were to characterize art for nearly a thousand years were already fully evolved. The appearance of this new style seems to mark the end of the classical ideal in the Western tradition. However, throughout the centuries of Byzantine art and the art of the so-called Dark Ages in the West, it was only the first of many transformations or adaptations of the classical ideal to meet the needs of different societies and times.

— 15 —

Constantine

When I gaze in spirit upon this thrice-blessed soul, united with God, free of all mortal dross, in robes gleaming like lightning, and in ever radiant diadem, speech and reason stand mute.   —Eusebius *

THE conversion of Constantine to Christianity is conventionally symbolized by his vision before the victory over Maxentius at the Ponte Milvio when the legend *In Hoc Signo Victor Eris* appeared in the blaze of the sunset sky. Whether or not Constantine's vision and his adoption of Christianity were only propaganda, a part of a calculated policy, a purely political profession for the unification of the empire, cannot be answered. It remains that under Constantine the Church was built up as a partner of imperial rule and the Emperor's piety is praised by his chronicler Eusebius. There is no question that Constantine was originally devoted to the worship of Sol or Apollo, a monotheistic faith that perhaps made easy the transition to Christianity.

The Emperor's translation from paganism to Christianity is symbolized in the gigantic statue of himself as Sol which was set up in Constantinople and adorned with a rayed crown made, according to legend, from the nails of the True Cross. This gigantic image extolled him as the veritable embodiment of Sol irradiating the Cosmos just as the later colossi of Constantine portray him in enormous size as the transfigured image of the Christ-Emperor, the very scale of which emblematically appears to reveal him as the axial lord of the universe.

The art that flourished under the Emperor Constantine, especially the portraits proclaiming his mastery over the Roman world, introduced a new spirituality or apotheosis in the representation of the living ruler that is related to antique precedent and yet divorced from it in the insistence on the ghostly from the concrete idealism of the ancient period. The rea-

* Eusebius, *Life of Constantine*, 1. 2

son for this change in representation is implicit in the figure of Constantine and in the age he personified.

In the Late Antique period, notably in the portraits of Constantine the Great, a new artistic expression of divinized kingship is encountered. These portraits of the first Christian ruler are the final embodiments of deified majesty in terms both abstract and solemn. Everything is centered on rigid ceremonial grandeur to suggest the superhuman magnitude of the sovereign. There had been earlier attempts to represent the quality of superhuman soaring aspiration in imperial portraits; for example, in the passionate likenesses of Alexander the Great. These Hellenistic heads of the conqueror appear to be moved by a vision of the divine. In the representations of Alexander (figure 59) the suggestion of a kind of tremendous passion and a godlike soulful expression are portrayed in corporeal concrete fashion by the turn of the head, the wild eyes, and the open, breathing mouth. Heads of the Macedonian, like the example in the Museum of Fine Arts, Boston, give a suggestion of ecstatic inner fervor, a connotation of something more than mortal, of a being infused with godly passion, possessed and tortured by the presence of divinity in a mortal frame. In the portraits of Constantine, as in the colossal head from his statue in the Basilica of Maxentius (figure 60), the contact between the Emperor and the heavenly power that deifies him is expressed in a quite different way. The giant dimensions of Constantine's portrait were deliberately intended to suggest the divine stature of the Emperor as the symbolical ruler of the world or cosmokrator. In the head, although the individual elements have not been entirely sacrificed, they have been fixed in a kind of masklike transfiguration of the ruler's personality. The abstract mass of the head is represented without any real organic structure and serves only as a background for the expressive features. The result is a timeless mask filled with a sphinxlike calm, as though the personality was lost in a never-ending vision of a celestial realm, an expression in concrete terms of the higher inspiration that sanctifies Constantine as ruler. His exalted state of spiritual majesty is revealed primarily through the wide-open eyes, staring out with a strange hypnotic power both supernatural and uncanny from under the vaulted shadow of the lids. The impression on the beholder is something quite different from the dynamic turmoil of the Hellenistic portrait. Constantine gazes into a world exalted above terrestrial reality, and it is the personification of supernatural glory that bestows such awesome majesty on the conception. The idea of the supernatural is conferred not only by the enormous eyes but also by the abstraction of the framing concentric curves of the lids and brows. The colossal head looms as an embodiment of divine majesty, rather than of an individual man, a crystallization of the imperial ideology dedicated to expressing the transcendence of the ruler's personality. It was doubtless intentional that the face should have something of the holy look of the portraits of saints, since it was intended as a kind of apotheosis of the sovereign, the Emperor in the earthly likeness of Christ. In this conventionalization or abstract portrayal of ideas and types and the disappearance of individual detail, as well as organic articulation, is the beginning of the symbolic religious art of the Middle Ages. Like the heads of Christ and the saints, the head of Constantine seems to be filled with a spirit straining from the shell of humanity so that it is only a symbol of a fleshly image. The portrait is entirely un-antique in its point of view in the intensity of the ghostly expression so completely appropriate as an absolute effigy of spiritual kingship. Whether the portrait had anything to do with Constantine as he was as a man is unimportant. The very elements of expressive abstraction that determined its form were entirely necessary for a public effigy intended to portray a deified majesty as head of church and state.

In its general shape, its essentially cubic construction, and even in the treatment of the hair the portrait of Constantine is a kind of transformation of the state portraits of Augustus. There the resemblance ends, and in some strange way this head is almost reminiscent of the very beginnings of classical art in archaic times. No physical, biological organism any longer remains, and one sees only a symbolical visual framework of humanity, the constant structure behind the incidentals of phenomenal appearance.

— 16 —

Early Christian Art

God taught the nations everywhere to bow their heads under the same laws. All these did God teach to become Romans. . . . Now the earth is in concord: infuse it, Almighty, with thy presence; now, Christ, a world receives Thee which peace and Rome hold together in a bond.   —Prudentius *

IN the very centuries when the religions of paganism were dying, the early Christian communities both in Rome and the eastern provinces adopted the artistic language of the classical world for the expression of their own iconographical ideas. When pagan idols were being overthrown and famous sanctuaries like the Marneion at Gaza were consigned to the flames, Christian art in its borrowings of forms and techniques was bestowing an immortality on the classical tradition. It was precisely through the strength and continuity of the Christian church that the traditions of paganism were preserved through the Dark Ages, to flourish again in the new classicism of the Renaissance.

Whereas in classical antiquity it had been the aim to create images of the gods in the likeness of men but superior to normal human appearance in their beauty and nobility, this ideal was lost in the Middle Ages under the influence of Christianity. The transcendental aspects of Christianity no longer required the human body as a standard of beauty nor, for that matter, an optical view of this world. The pictorial and plastic language of Christian art required only symbolical representations to be read as a script in readily recognizable unsensual shapes. Antique prototypes continued to be used in a picture language that eliminated or abbreviated what was too complicated in the antique. In painting, for example, from

* Deus undique gentis inclinare caput docuit sub legibus isdem Romanosque omnes fieri . . . en ades, Omnipotens, concordibus influe terris: iam mundus te, Christe, capit, quem pax et Roma tenent.—Prudentius, *Against Symmachus*, II. 603–605, 634–636.

84

Early Christian times onward, there is no further interest in illusionism in space or in light and shade. Heavy outlines replaced fully modeled forms and figures are arranged in planes rather than in space as an optical reality. The reuse of old formulas, transformed for new symbolical needs, replaces any observation of nature. Although the antique artistic forms as well as the classical point of view had vanished, the undying stem of the classical tradition continued to put forth new shoots that produced a transformed classicism in the flowering of Byzantine and Carolingian art. Throughout the Middle Ages the heritage of antiquity was transmitted in literature and in surviving monuments of architecture and the plastic arts. The representation of antique themes from literary descriptions and without pictorial prototypes led to the most varied and bizarre interpretations of classical subjects in every phase of the Middle Ages. Antique monuments themselves were only used as a basis for a new artistic creation when the period borrowing them was right for understanding these prototypes. For centuries the ancient forms were changed into ornament without relation to their original meaning. It is only in the thirteenth and fourteenth centuries that real understanding in the use of the antique is encountered.

Judged by their works, most of the sculptors employed by the Christian church from the third to the fifth centuries were little more than stonecutters, without aesthetic sensibilities or refinements of technique, and yet so dedicated to their task of embodying the object of their worship in a dignified plastic form that the sincere spiritual conception transcends the technical shortcomings of their performance.

A favorite form of Early Christian sculpture was the sarcophagus, the boxlike stone coffin for the interment of the dead. It is on these memorials that have been preserved in great numbers, literally from Arles to Asia Minor, that the earliest representations of Christ and His apostles are encountered. They are usually placed in a pillared arcade, an architectural setting intended to typify the splendors of the heavenly Jerusalem. An early and very fine example, probably dating from about A.D. 400, is the fragment of a sarcophagus from Psamatia, now in the Kaiser Friedrich Museum in Berlin. Christ is represented as standing between two apostles, probably Saints Peter and Paul (figure 61). This figure of the Savior is a perfect illustration of the conversion of pagan iconography and technique to the imagery of the Early Christian church.

The youthful, beardless face of Christ, framed in long ringlets, is obvi-

85

ously taken from the type of the Greek Apollo. There are reasons to believe that not only the supreme physical beauty of the pagan god of light and reason was deemed appropriate for the figuration of the sublime perfection of Christ, but also from the iconographical point of view the radiance and light associated with the old sun god made his luminous mask a suitable emblem for the face of Christ. The texts of early Christianity are filled with references describing Christ's Resurrection as the sun's rising, and His Descent into Hell as the sun's setting; so for this reason the head of Apollo provided a suitable model to symbolize His luciferous character.

In this, as in other Early Christian representations of Him, Christ is dressed in the pallium. This garment had long been associated with the philosophers and teachers of the classical world. This robe was also reserved for both priests and initiates in the mystery cults of the Late Antique world. In the funerary dress of Roman Egypt it is a literal symbol of the reception of the soul of the deceased into the realm of Osiris. There are, therefore, two very good reasons to explain the adoption of the pallium for the earliest portrayals of Christ. The church fathers refer to Him as the Pedagogue, replacing the teachers of the pagan world, so that it must have appeared appropriate to Early Christian sculptors to portray Him in the dress of the teachers of the ancients. A prototype for the figure under consideration is the Hellenistic statue of Sophocles in the Lateran (figure 102), or the Aeschines in Naples. At the same time Christ replaces the priest of the mystery religions as the guide to the other world. On this sarcophagus Christ welcomes the soul to Paradise, so that there was every reason to array Him in the robe of those who in the pagan cults opened the mysteries of the beyond.

From the technical point of view this Early Christian carving is hardly different from the pagan statuary that continued to be made throughout the third and fourth centuries. Although the head of Christ is reminiscent of many Greco-Roman representations of Apollo, the face of the Savior has a much more masklike, dry, and formal quality. This is probably partly the result of a gradual decline in craftsmanship and may also be explained by the fact that, in these final centuries of the Roman Empire, the Hellenic ideal and the old perfection of realistic technique were being replaced by a more abstract Oriental mode of representation. In the same way the folds of Christ's garment are portrayed in a linear formula of sharp ridges and deeply grooved lines, instead of the classic naturalistic treatment of the robe as a weighty, voluminous substance. Although from the technical aspect all of these qualities appear to represent a disintegration of the earlier mastery of craftsmanship of carving, the very formalization of the classical ideal imparts a hieratic and abstract character appropriate to the representation of a new spiritual ideal.

— 17 —

Classicism in Byzantine Art

Arise in glory, Autocrator of the Romans! Arise in glory, Augustae of the Romans! Arise in glory, servants of the Lord! . . . Come, O Emperor, you are called by the Emperor of Emperors, and Lord of Lords!

—Constantine Porphyrogenitos *

I F we could conjure up a vision of Constantinople in the days of its glory, it might resemble a glittering Byzantine miniature with a view of the white-walled city above the blue waters of the Bosporus. Over the marble gates and towers of this circumvallation one could picture the domed churches rising on the hills and, those antecedents of the Moslem minarets, the shining columns of the emperors. In the Hippodrome around Theodosius' Egyptian obelisk and Apollo's tripod from Delphi would be the great bronze masterpieces of Lysippus and Phidias. Add to this the vast palace of the Porphyrogenitos blazing with gold and mosaic and marble amid gardens like Oriental bowers. In the very center of this web, lost in the haze of incense, we could envisage the immobile, idol-like rulers surrounded by the priesthood in glittering vestments, the painted eunuchs and concubines, and men-at-arms from every barbarian race.

In the opinion of some scholars the Roman Empire endured from the accession of Augustus until the death of the last Paleologus on the walls of Constantinople in 1453. According to this view the Holy Roman Empire of Charlemagne was only an interruption without claim to actual descent from the ancient Imperators. Although the emperors of Byzantium, beginning with Constantine, thought of themselves as successors of the Caesars, their civilization as it finally emerged in the sixth century was so totally different from Rome that this heritage from its beginnings was only a symbolical one. Byzantium at its founding was a Greek pagan city in which Greek learning endured throughout the later centuries of

* Constantine Porphyrogenitos, *Book of Ceremonies,* 52. 43, 69. 60

Christian rule. The change of the official language from Latin to Greek under the Emperor Heraclius (A.D. 575–642) finally proclaimed the Hellenic character of the Eastern Roman Empire. Certainly the proximity of Byzantium to the Orient and its contacts in war and peace with the Sassanian empire of Iran had something to do with its rulers' assumption of Asiatic autocracy and the establishment of a naked despotism screened by the pageantry and formalism of sacrosanct and immutable ritual. There is probably some truth in the accusations that Byzantine culture is both artificial and static with no really new creations or ideals to its credit, and that, even though Attic Greek was adopted in the last centuries of the Empire's existence, Greek fire rather than Greek culture preserved Byzantium until the end finally came.

Throughout the millennium of its existence no empire was ever so beset on every side by enemies. There was not only the menace of the waves of barbarians on the European front, but the ever-present danger of the Persians and later the Turks on the eastern borders. It would be surprising indeed if contacts, even although they often appeared to be only on a military level, did not affect the culture of Byzantium itself. Much of the ritual and mystery of court ceremonial were probably borrowings from the Sassanian empire, just as there is reason to believe that the ideas of the Iconoclasts of the ninth century were paralleled in the tenets of Islam. These forces, barbarian and Oriental, converted classical art into the moving decorative formalism described as Byzantine.

The Byzantine sovereigns were given to vices appalling even today. They lacked the ancient Greek virtues of stoical devotion to the State; were often mean and cowardly. Their lives were hedged about by ceremonies calculated to bestow magically an ineffable holiness and power on the person of even the basest ruler. Although their history is filled with injustice, cruelty, and inhumanity that seem to have invited the final debacle, Byzantium, more than the wrecked and ruined shell of Rome in the Middle Ages, preserved the memory of the classical past in literature and in art.

Although no two scholars may agree on the exact moment when Byzantine art can be distinguished from classical or antique art, it is generally conceded that the Byzantine style was formed by the time of the accession of Justinian in the sixth century. Although the Late Antique period saw a prolongation of classical forms, its art is already marked by the emergence of the formalism of Byzantine art. In the same way in the

89

art of the Eastern Empire from 500 to its fall, although generally characterized by the hieratic formula which we think of as distinctly Byzantine,
there are nonetheless persistent, and often very approximate, revivals of
classical forms and techniques. Sometimes this takes the shape of an undisguised borrowing; sometimes a quotation from a classical source.
Throughout the history of Byzantine art the existence of a transmitted
heritage of classical technique manifested itself in the surviving examples of what must have been a far larger corpus of material of pagan
inspiration.

Although Justinian closed the Academy of Athens, in language as in
art the Greek tradition persisted for the thousand years of the Eastern
Empire's history. That it persisted only in a much altered form was the result of the mystical and static character of the Orthodox faith and the
Orthodox empire, that in its ritual beliefs was the very antithesis of the
questing spirit of Hellenic humanism. An admiration for the beauty of
purified reality had no place in the civilization stressing the supernatural
rather than the rational.

Justinian and his reign are the embodiment of the Byzantine Empire
at its moment of greatest power. His ambitions in life were to establish
himself as the new Caesar of a reconstituted Roman Empire and, as
God's vicar on earth, to establish the incontestable power of the Orthodox
church through all the world. His empire ran with the old machinery of
the Roman state, reinforced by dynamic Christian thought. Heir of the
Caesars, like them, he was resolved to be the living law, the fullest incar-
nation of absolute power, and also the impeccable lawgiver, the reformer,
intent upon maintaining good order in the realm. Lastly, in his pride in
his imperial rank he chose to bedeck it with all conceivable pomp and
magnificence. Justinian became, in other words, the sacred Emperor; he
was both Caesar and head of the Church. There was nothing profane or
secular in the Byzantine state. Just as the churches of Byzantium were
embodiments of the sacraments and rituals of the celestial order, so the
life of the Emperor and the court ritual were the figuration on earth of
the divine mysteries.

Justinian's artistic achievement may be seen in the remote Adriatic city
of Ravenna, which became the capital of the Roman Empire in 540 with
the conquest of Italy by his general Belisarius. Among the principal pictorial relics are the mosaic portraits of the Emperor and his consort
Theodora in the Church of San Vitale (figure 62). In these, as in the sa-

cred subjects in the same church, the Byzantine formula is fully evolved: hieratic and monumental forms in porphyry and purple and gold. Justinian is surrounded by his bishops, statesmen, and common soldiers.

Among the classical elements which survive in this mosaic is the display of the figures in a kind of frieze reminiscent of the great official reliefs like the Ara Pacis (figure 41). The individual portrayal of the personages is another survival from Roman tradition. Even the generalized treatment of the robes of the Emperor and his attendants is at first glance suggestive of the ancient world. These are the only lingering reminders of the classical tradition in an art dedicated to formal and ritual ends.

To illustrate the change that has taken place, a comparison is afforded between the imperial mosaics of San Vitale and the Ara Pacis, since both represent dedicatory processions. Just as the Ara Pacis embodied the Augustan principate with the Emperor as ruler and priest sacrificing to the deities ensuring the Pax Augustae, the mosaics of San Vitale symbolize Byzantium with the Basilei offering chalice and paten to their celestial counterpart. This is a contrast between a world of political reality and a world of theocracy. The participants in the Ara Pacis ceremony pass by without looking at the beholder, who is the spectator of an historical event to which the partakers give their undivided attention. The action presumably takes place at a given time and locality. Each figure is a portrait of one of the individuals surrounding the Emperor Augustus.

The arrangement of the Ravenna mosaics is like a procession that has paused momentarily. In the midst of their cortege, the Basileus and his Empress turn to receive the adoration of the spectator. Although most of the heads are probably portraits, there is no indication that Justinian and Theodora and their retinue were even present at the dedication of San Vitale, so that the mosaics are not precise records of an actual event, but rather symbols of the rulers' ghostly presence: the perpetuation of their act of dedication. The hieratic grandeur of Ravenna and the temporal realism of the Ara Pacis are two factors revealing the outlook of two different worlds. The procession of the Ara Pacis terminates in a scene of sacrifice and a relief representing the gods of earth and air and fertile waters, upon which the happiness and security of the city and empire of Rome depended: it is an embodiment of the Pax Romana, the earthly empire of Augustus. The ceremonial defile in San Vitale seems to move toward and to form a part of the apsidal mosaic that shows the Pantocrator in glory receiving the dedication of the earthly church. The mosaics of San Vitale, in other words, present a symbolical picture of the spiritual empire of Byzantium, the Emperor and Empress as worldly embodiments of the Word that rules above. This same mixture of the real and the unreal, Western power and Eastern mystery, the individual and the general, marked the whole fabric of Byzantine civilization.

A comparison of another kind between the mosaics of San Vitale and the Ara Pacis is illuminating to show the break between the classic and the Byzantine world. In the Ara Pacis actual people, real forms are shown as though they could or did exist in the space planes in the stone. They convey a sense of tangible reality enclosed in the space between the front of the relief and the closed background plane. All are definitely solid personages of this world.

In the mosaic the figures no longer seem even to stand on a ground plan; they are suspended motionless and static in the ambient and endless space of the gold background that enfolds them as a light and suggests only an infinity of distance without any closure to the background plane. They have lost all substance. One has almost the feeling that here is a collection of empty ritual garments as emblems, containing no corporeal shape. The whole is at once a surface pattern of marvelous richness, and at the same time it suggests the ghostly existence of these phantoms in an infinite golden space, opening to the golden space of the beyond. Only the heads with glowing hypnotic eyes are reflections of the real, and even these have a feeling of abstraction, a sort of spiritual tension far from the descriptive realism of the Augustan age.

What are the steps, the stylistic and spiritual changes in art, between the classic period and the golden day of Justinian that account for this remarkable transformation? Whereas the realism of Roman art can be explained as the characteristic product of minds overwhelmed by the breadth of human experience and seeking to find significance in real, concrete terms, Byzantine art is the product of minds concerned with the theological mysteries of the divine nature of god and the celestial hierarchy. These minds endeavor to express their awe and their belief in the existence of these immaterial realms in forms which by their very substancelessness and hieratic splendor will express the nature of that other world of the spirit.

The ghostly and disembodied nature of Byzantine art may be illustrated further by a single figure from the mosaics of the choir of San Vitale at Ravenna. This representation of Moses removing his sandals before the burning bush (figure 63) evokes a remembrance of the famous relief of Nike from the balustrade of the Nike temple on the bastion of the Acropolis (figure 64). The pose is sufficiently similar to warrant such a juxtaposition. As usual in Byzantine art the beautiful luminous face recalls the perfection of Hellenic loveliness reduced to an abstract mask of humanity. The drapery is still derived from the generalized garment of antiquity, but there all resemblance ceases. In the Greek figure the drapery, as though drenched with water, clings to the body, revealing its soft, sensuous perfection in a completely organic way. The easy swing of the long, undulating folds has a calculated, logical system of arrangement that is at once a heightening and generalization of the disposition of a real garment. The shadowed saliencies of the carving intervene as a web between the beholder and the body they screen, to produce a fluid design in moving curves which are decorative as well as functional. In the figure in the Byzantine mosaic the drapery has been completely simplified and its form-revealing function has been almost entirely eliminated. The emphasis is entirely on the few lines that explain the mechanism of the dress, and these lines are so strong in relation to the flat areas they enclose that they reduce the figure to a bodiless silhouette. The form of Moses is no more real than the spaceless, textilelike setting in which he is placed. The actual physical articulation of the body is no longer of primary concern. Not even the suggestion of highlights and the flat areas of cool and warm grey, which represent a simplification of the illusionistic shading of Hellenistic painting, can give the figure a feeling of physical existence. The image is a completely spiritualized reordering of the classical formula. This is a style which is part of the Byzantine glorification of the mysterious and supernatural.

In the long history of Byzantine art, from the time of Justinian to the fall of Constantinople, the old forms of the antique world enjoy a kind of autonomous immortality, amidst influences from the East and the barbarian North, influences which had transformed the art of antiquity into the Byzantine formula for the expression of religious sentiments in hieratic terms. The memory of classical art survived as a continuous undercurrent which on occasion became an undertow that drew artists dedicated to religious subjects into the endless ocean of classical form and expression. Classical art survived because of its recognized power of form and expressiveness and because its authoritative language of gesture and pose provided an endless repertory for adaptation to new themes. A theory held by some scholars maintains that the techniques of ancient painting persisted in a now lost secular art to re-emerge in the so-called neo-Hellenistic style of religious art in the tenth and eleventh centuries.

One of these renaissances of the antique took place in the tenth century, and a beautiful example of this revival is the Paris Psalter in the Bibliothèque Nationale in Paris (figure 65). The very sumptuousness of the manuscript as well as its extraordinary Hellenistic character suggests that it was prepared for the court, so that the tendencies it displays must be regarded as part of a rather limited revival of antiquity addressed to a sophisticated audience. This manuscript contains full-page illustrations from the stories of David the psalmist and Isaiah the prophet. One of the finest pages represents the prayer of Isaiah between night and dawn: "Out of the night rises my spirit early to thee, O God." The prophet stands in an attitude of prayer beneath the hand of God, which appears at the upper right-hand corner of the illustration. To the left in a robe of dusky purple stands the personification of Night or Nyx, an inverted torch in her hand and her starry robe billowing over her head. To the right is the child god Orthos, the symbol of dawn, bearing a flaming torch in his left arm. Behind these figures on the low horizon is a row of poppies, the flowers of sleep and night. Two trees partially screen the gold background. In this picture and the others in the same book the episodes are shown as single pictorial entities in the manner of the mythological scenes of Roman and Pompeian wall-paintings. This is no more nor less than a return to the traditional self-contained compositions of the classical period.

The personifications in this picture represent an antique feature and the individual figures of night and Orthos are immediately recognizable as classical reincarnations. Night with her billowing scarf is like the figures of the moon goddess Selene (figure 66), and Orthos is simply an antique *putto* cast in a new role. The attributes of the raised and lowered torches may be seen on Etruscan urns and other ancient sources as emblems of dawn and dusk. An unclassical feature of the composition from the Paris Psalter is evident in the relation of the figures to the landscape, with no suggestion of any continuity or unity of space between the forms and their setting. The gold background appears as a borrowing from the world of mosaic. The illusionistic manner of painting figures and foliate forms with broadly dappled highlights is an inheritance from the antique. The individual forms are extremely classical in appearance; however, they have lost some of the organic construction of true classical form. There is a rather curious inconsistency in the figure of Night, whereby the rather animated, even dynamic, upper part of the body is supported by the static conception of the lower part of the form with its pipelike archaic folds. The figures lack weight; they appear almost as two-dimensional silhouettes with formal gestures and are marked with a curious insubstantial transparency. The artist has attempted the broken play of light and shade, and something of the illusionistic soft modeling of the antique in his draperies, but in actuality the garments dissolve into patterns and stiffly ordered nets of drapery.

The truly classical qualities in this revival of ancient painting can be seen in the suggestion of tactile values and rhythmic linear organization in the figures, a change from the wraithlike forms characteristic of much of Byzantine painting in the preceding centuries. Again, as in Pompeian painting, the figures loom as large and dominant elements in the arrangement. These figures themselves are classical in their details and iconography, but from what is known of the established tradition of Byzantine art it was inevitable that they were drawn with an emphasis on decorative linear design. In many ways this revival appears almost as an attempt to reintroduce the principles of classical art, rather than strict imitation. The color, too, in its radiant luminosity flecked with highlights marks a reappearance of the Hellenistic mode. Although perhaps more decorative in a Byzantine sense in the patternized deployment of lines and accents, one can almost discern a resuscitation of the organic unity of a classical art founded on the monumental beauty of the human form. It is as though the painter of these illuminations recognized the authority and appropriateness of the antique to impart the ultimate in dignity and beauty to his illustration of the Biblical story.

— 18 —

The Barbarian Period

Where is the Senate? Where the people? The bones of Rome have been reduced to dust, her flesh consumed, the splendor of her ancient grandeur has vanished. The host of her people is no more, and we few who still survive every day see swords pointed at our hearts. Every day calamities without end overwhelm us. And indeed if the Senate is no more, if the people have perished, if every day increases the sorrow and lament of those few who still remain alive, this signifies that Rome has become a desert already consumed in flames.   —Gregory the Great *

THE final collapse of antique civilization and the beginning of the "Dark Ages" came with the death of Justinian in 565, which left all Europe open to barbarian rule. Even in the days of Justinian the destruction of ancient Rome had begun. The Goths had cut the aqueducts and General Belisarius defended the walls by hurling down on the ranks of the foe the giant marble statues that girded the summit of Hadrian's tomb. The Byzantine empire plunged into an abyss through sheer economic exhaustion brought about by Justinian's costly expeditions and relentless taxation. In the East, from Alexandria to Byzantium, the terrible raids of the Persians and later the Arabs depopulated the lovely Eastern provinces and reduced these regions to a state of barbarism from which they have never recovered. Something like a dark pall settled over Europe, with wars raging from one end of the continent to the other. The barbarian conquerors' policy of massacre and enslavement so reduced the populations that the economic mode of life dropped to an appalling level. Civilization was pushed back to conditions of 1000 B.C. As the great cities of the empire gradually fell into ruin, commerce and the arts

* Ubi enim Senatus? Ubi iam populus? Contabuerunt ossa, consumptae sunt carnes, omnis in ea saecularium dignitatum fastus extinctus est. Excocta est universa compositio eius. Et tamen ipsos nos paucos qui remansimus, adhuc quotidie gladii, adhuc quotidie innumerae tribulationes premunt. Quia enim Senatus deest, populus interiit, & tamen in paucis qui sunt, dolores & gemitus quotidie multiplicantur, iam vacua ardet Roma.—Gregorius Magnus, *Opera Omnia,* Book II, 1595

of peace came to an end. Every branch of the great Roman system was shattered. Nothing any longer worked. The great roads that once spread like arteries from the heart of the empire gradually became clogged and impassable. For hundreds of years the population of Europe was despoiled by successive waves of barbarian armies—Goths, Huns, Franks, and Saracens. In this succession of debacles literacy itself threatened to disappear, and the techniques of all the monumental arts vanished in the holocaust. Only in the monasteries, isolated citadels of Latin culture, was a semblance of education kept alive during centuries so dark that it seemed no dawn would ever come.

In Europe one-third of the population had died during two dreadful visitations of the plague during the sixth century. Added to these woes were the invasions of the Lombards. The complete disruption of Italian society that ensued with the onrush of these savages had its inevitable counterpart in the total collapse of the arts. Both the character of the Lombards and the art they brought with them were calculated to exterminate any vestiges of the ancient tradition. The unbelievable ferocity of these invaders, their indifference to any refinements of civilization, and their entire political incompetence brought about the barbarization of the country. Italy was fragmented into a series of duchies extending from Pavia to Beneventum, in which the native populations were the slaves of the barbaric chiefs.

Whereas an earlier barbarian, Theodoric the Ostrogoth, had confided the care of the Theater of Marcellus to the great family of Symmachus and enjoined the preservation of classical statues, the new invaders had little concern for the preservation of Roman culture. As a writer of the sixth century says, "Many illustrious Romans were slain out of greed and the remainder shorn of a third of their possessions by the Lombards. The churches have been reduced to rubble and the priests murdered; the cities have become deserts and the people destroyed. Where once were the homes of the people, today is the domain of wild beasts." [1]

Although it is customary to envisage the Middle Ages as a dark interregnum between the luminous ideality of the lost classical world and the bright effulgence of the Renaissance, the tenebroso shading of this picture has perhaps been somewhat overdone. Undoubtedly for long periods from the sixth to the fourteenth century the peoples of Europe existed in such conditions of misery and brutality that there were neither hearts nor hands to tend the arts, but at the same time this dark period was responsible for transmitting the ancient learning to the true Renaissance. The preservation of classical texts through the diligence of scholarly monks is a cliché of every history book. At the same time the old gods and their powers, however altered in shape, were preserved in learned works that converted pagan lore to Christian symbolism.

Neither edicts, nor exorcism, nor the demolition of their temples and images could extirpate the old gods. Even though officially banished, their worship persisted in remote country districts at the end of the sixth century in the papacy of Gregory the Great. They were not regarded as myths or poetic inventions. Jupiter, Venus, and Mercury were still very present to Christians as spirits moving in the air, in the dark groves and abandoned sanctuaries, ever ready as demons to pervert any man foolish enough to pay them homage. To the church, paganism was still a danger, just as imminent and powerful as communism today. No wonder that Gregory the Great sought to discourage the study of classical literature since the beauty and seduction of its content might prove only another snare of demons.

As early as Pope Gregory's day, the plundered buildings of Rome were falling into decay, and, although the Pope himself has perhaps been unjustly accused of destroying the ancient statues of the capital, a countless number of the thousands of sculptures that once decorated the temples and the forums had already fallen victims to barbarian sack, to iconoclasm, and the lime pit. At the same time, ancient works of art were frequently reused, so that, for example, ancient sarcophagi were employed not only for Christian interment but often as the frontals of altars. If a baleful magic was attributed to all survivals of pagan times throughout the Middle Ages and even later, many classical objects in metal and precious stones were eagerly adapted for church furniture. One has only to recall the delight of the Abbot Suger at the refashioning of an ancient vase into a Christian chalice for his great church at St. Denis. Magical properties were attributed to ancient carved gems and cameos that could bestow upon the owner the boons of invisibility, treasures, or success in love. Many of these ancient intaglios found their way into the decoration of Christian crucifixes and reliquaries.

Throughout the Middle Ages the memory and the reverence of the classical past never disappeared either in literature or the arts. Many of the revivals or renascences of ancient forms in the Byzantine, Carolingian, and Romanesque periods are regarded more as survivals of a tradition never entirely broken than as sudden and deliberate renewals of the vanished heritage of the ancient world. An aesthetic sensibility and appreciation for fragments of antiquity, although certainly long dormant for reasons of superstition, comes into the open in the later centuries of this so-called dark period.

It is not possible to find illustrations of anything remotely resembling antique forms and techniques in this dark period, but examples of such a survival do occur in a few isolated monuments. The complete degradation of the antique tradition may be illustrated by a single example, a fragment of a sarcophagus built into the wall of the cathedral of Calvi, near Capua (figure 67). This is a type of carving that may be seen in many examples of barbarian workmanship such as the Altar of Ratchis at Cividale. Although there is a total deterioration of craftsmanship, it is interesting to observe the attempt to preserve an ancient model. The composition of tritons with nereids on their backs bestriding the waves to uphold a medallion with a portrait of the deceased is a motif frequently found in Roman sarcophagi (figure 68). The classical figures at Calvi have disintegrated into flat ornamental forms, as flat as the strip of Lombard interlace that decorates the lateral rim of the panel. The arms of the sea gods are scarcely more than flattened ribbon shapes. The faces of the marine deities, like the head of the personage in the medallion, are the crudest of simplified masks. With such a complete disappearance of sculptural capacity as this stone reveals, the nadir of the Western plastic tradition was reached; looking at this total collapse of technique it is almost impossible to believe that the lost art was ever to be resuscitated. The very attempt to emulate the antique, however pathetic in its failure, is noteworthy if only because it reveals the persistent authority and stimulus of ancient art even in these darkest days, a stimulus that centuries later was to make possible the resurgence of Western art in the later Middle Ages and the Renaissance.

— 19 —

The Carolingian Renaissance

After this on the natal day of Our Lord Jesus Christ one and all congregated again in the said Basilica of the Blessed Peter the Apostle, and then the venerable and glorious pontiff with his own hands crowned him with a most precious crown. Then all the faithful Romans . . . with one loud voice cried out by the Will of God and of the Blessed Peter Keeper of the Keys of the Kingdom of Heaven, *To Charles most pious, Augustus, crowned by God, great peace-bringing Emperor, life and victory!*   —Muratorius *

THE restoration of Europe to a unified rule, the deliverance of Italy from the centuries of misery under Lombard rule, and, in a measure, the resuscitation of the grandeur of Rome and her past came with the rise to power of Charlemagne, King of the Franks, and his coronation as Holy Roman Emperor in St. Peter's on Christmas Day, A.D. 800. Against the background of the Dark Ages the Emperor Charlemagne's reign shines with a greater luster, and, only with his restoration of an ordered administration, was there possible a revival of economy and the arts of peace.

The term Carolingian renaissance describes the efforts of the Emperor to renew the Roman past. This period extends from 771, when Charlemagne became King of the Franks, to the death of Charles the Bald in 877. Charlemagne, after he was crowned as the heir of Augustus by the Pope, was guided by the idea of a renewal or renovation of the Roman Empire. This imperial effort began as a revival of classical literacy and liturgy in an attempt to provide a good Latin style for the secular and ecclesiastical administrators of Charlemagne's realm and ended as a full-

---

* Post haec adveniente die natali dominis nostri Gesu Christi, in iam dicta Basilica Beati Petri Apostoli omnes iterum congregati sunt, et tunc venerabilis almificus Pontifex manibus suis propriis pretiosissima corona coronavit eum. Tunc universi fideles Romani . . . unanimiter altisona voce Dei nutu atque Beati Petri Clavigieri regni Coelorum exclamaverunt, *Carolo Piissimo Augusto a Deo coronato, magno, pacifico Imperatori, vita et victoria.*—Ludovicus Antoninius Muratorius, *Rerum Italicarum Scriptores* (1723)

scale attempt to renew classical antiquity in support of the political idea of reviving the Roman Imperium.

For the first time since Hadrian and Marcus Aurelius there was a ruler who took an interest in art and literature and the carrying out of a cultural program of his own. Charlemagne, who considered himself as the heir to the ancient emperors, conceived the idea of return to pre-Byzantine Rome. He was to be a renovator, not precisely of pagan Rome, but the Rome of Constantine, in which, according to the spurious donation of Constantine, the imperial power had been conferred on the papacy. With this ardent desire to revive the hallowed past came an attachment to the city of Rome and its buildings as a kind of symbol of that moment when Rome and Christianity merged under Constantine. The real basis of the Carolingian renaissance was in the monuments of the Christian Roman emperors, with the Emperor Charlemagne as the pivotal point in this philosophy of renewal. Charlemagne thought himself a new Constantine to the extent that his palace at Aachen was built as an imitation of the Lateran Palace of Constantine. He even imported a supposed equestrian statue of Theodoric from Ravenna as an emblematic parallel for the famous bronze of Marcus Aurelius, which throughout the Middle Ages stood in the court of the Lateran and was piously regarded as a likeness of Constantine.

Charlemagne's reconstruction of the classical world began with his efforts to train a staff to administrate his domains in schools teaching Roman literature to provide a Latin style for an official language. This was a program that led to the rediscovery of the Roman tradition in every branch of the arts. For the first time classical antiquity became a cultural experience, the discovery of something which had been lost; and classical culture became the distinguishing mark of Western man.

In the writings of Bishop Theodulf of Orléans, the author of the *Libri Carolini,* one finds passages so sophisticated in their admiration for antiquity as to amount almost to a doctrine of art for art's sake. This is one of the first appearances of a humanistic aesthetic regard for classical art encountered throughout the Middle Ages in works ostensibly dedicated to political and religious themes. On one occasion, in his *Ad Iudices,* Theodulf gives a loving and meticulous description of a great silver vase embellished with the labors of Hercules, and he describes too the map of the world painted in his refectory with a beautiful figure of Mother Earth as nurse of mankind, her head diademed with a mural crown and sur-

101

rounded by the Twelve Winds.[1] This description cannot fail to evoke memories of the beautiful figure of Terra Mater of the Ara Pacis and the personifications of the earth mother that appear with other classical emblems in the ivories of the Carolingian period. Excerpts like these are enough to show that on occasion the Carolingian *renovatio* was something more than a grandiose political expedient that partook of the nature of a true renaissance with a truly humanistic interest in both the iconography and forms of the ancient gods.

The classical art of the Carolingian renaissance was at best secondhand; it derived from Roman art of the fourth and fifth centuries as refracted through Byzantine and Christian ideas. The majority of Carolingian art was on a small scale. Insofar as is known there was no interest in monumental sculpture, and the few attempts at monumental architecture were rather strange travesties of classical prototypes. The so-called classical renewal under Charlemagne was in general directed to the Late Antique, rather than the Greco-Roman period, because it was found appropriate to typify Charlemagne's *renovatio* in the artistic framework of his Christian predecessor, Constantine.

As far as the preservation of the art of the classical world is concerned, the Carolingian period was at best a holding action, inaugurated by the interest of the court and restricted entirely to the Emperor's circle and to the products of monastic artists under imperial patronage. Unlike the art of the Renaissance of the fifteenth century this was not a public revival of classical taste. It could have influenced only a limited group. The only exceptions to this rule might be occasional works of architecture, like the Palatine Chapel at Aachen or the basilican gate at Lorsch, which represent the same superimposition of vaguely classical or Late Antique forms on a medieval framework that is seen in the surviving examples of painting and sculpture.

Not unexpectedly it was in the realm of portraits of sovereigns that Carolingian art officially proclaimed its admiration for antique precedents. These prototypes were no more antique in the classical sense than Charlemagne's architecture but, like it, evocations of the Constantinian or Late Antique period. The portrait of Lothair in his famous Gospels (figure 69) is a restatement of the imperial portraiture seen in the Missorium of Theodosius (figure 70). The general pose of the ruler seated on a cushioned throne, his right hand leaning on a scepter, the refinements in the representation of the bodily form, its *contrapposto* and weightiness, indicate a similar prototype as does the trough of folds in the figure's lap. Lothair's men at arms are borrowings from Late Antique consular diptychs, such as the helmeted figures of Rome and Constantinople. More Carolingian than Late Antique is the interest in stirring bodily movement and the suggestion of a kind of intense psychic activity in the penetrating glance, the tension of the guards and also the essentially linear portrayal. The head of Lothair, although a tiny drawing, has something of the concern and pathos of a late Roman portrait.

The works that most clearly demonstrate the zeal of the classical *renovatio* in Charlemagne's empire are the illuminated manuscripts, particularly the group of books produced in the scriptorium of Reims in the early ninth century. Among these sumptuous books are the Coronation Gospels (figure 71), now in the Schatzkammer at Vienna, a book which the Emperor Otto III found on the knees of Charlemagne when he opened his tomb at Aachen. The figures of the Evangelists in these beautiful pages are massive forms dressed in broad classical garments rendered in full modeling in light and shade. They are placed in spacious landscapes, illusionistically painted. These figures unmistakably show the artist's discovery of some classical source. Like the Gothic sculptors of the Cathedral of Reims, who four centuries later turned to classical fragments for inspiration, the painter of this book was obviously acquainted with some original, either classical or Byzantine, in which the illusionistic technique of the Hellenistic mode of Pompeii was still in evidence.

The great scholar of Carolingian manuscripts, Wilhelm Koehler, discovered the inscription of Demetrius Presbyter in the Schatzkammer Gospels. Although it has been impossible to determine whether this is the signature of the scribe or the artist of the manuscript, the importance of this evidence is that Demetrius was a stranger brought to the Carolingian court from the region where the Hellenistic tradition was still alive. This is a strong confirmation of what must be true of the entire Carolingian *renovatio;* namely, that this revival must have been fostered by the importation of artists from Byzantium or Italy, and it becomes apparent that the vital Hellenistic spirit of works like the Gospel book of Charlemagne cannot be explained by the mere presence of ancient models as an inspiration for the craftsmen attached to the Emperor's court.

The individual figures of the Evangelists in these pages are placed in a landscape setting, which in classical fashion is animated by the dashing

103

technique of brushstrokes with a feeling of atmospheric luminosity. The Evangelists in this manuscript and those in the Gospels of Ebbo (figure 72) have a weighty, senatorial dignity. A first superficial impression is of a classical draped statue with its costume composed of many closely pleated folds, the same type that was followed in the Visitation group at Reims in the thirteenth century. It soon becomes apparent, especially in the Ebbo Gospels, that, while using a classical model with full shading to bestow a properly statuesque quality on the forms, the painter has completely transformed this precedent into a dynamic explosion of brush organization. The vibrant swirling movement of the folds of the garment seems almost calculated to suggest the apostle's ecstatic response to divine inspiration. The psychic tension imparted to these forms by the demonic movement of the linear rhythm transforms them into symbols of ghostly inspiration. The painting of the figures is organized in an explosive swirl of brushstrokes, sweeping in wavelike ripples across the forms. These many calligraphic flourishes only superficially described the nature of the classical garment, but they impart an extraordinary suggestion of supernatural energy to the forms. The individual figures of Evangelists loom like phosphorescent clouds against the background. They appear to be composed of a moving, fiery substance that is almost like a symbolical condensation of the saints' inspiration in this dynamically moving skein of lines. This is a transformation of the solidity and serenity of classical forms by the Northern tradition of expression through wildly nervous draftsmanship that is the essence of the Teutonic Celtic style.

For the most part the classical forms which appear in Carolingian painting are presented in a Christian context and not as free agents. They are like quotations from classical writings by someone who has no intention of composing in classical meters. There is as yet no thought of using classical images for the creation of new pictorial poetry. The salvaging of classical form and content may seem rather limited and transitory, but this renewal served to transmit these ancient forms to later periods where they enjoyed what was in every way a rebirth.

This same quality is present in the Utrecht Psalter (figure 73) in which the drawing is charged with nervous energy, and the beholder is again vaguely conscious of Late Antique or Constantinian models in the poetic fantasy in the rendering of nature. All of these paintings are the work of artists who were able to recapture the real syntax of Christian antiquity to a far greater degree than their contemporaries in the field of architecture. Like the Gospels of Reims, the style of the Utrecht Psalter is a translation into linear terms of the impressionism of the Roman tradition. The backgrounds in this manuscript are suggestive of the Odyssey Landscapes or the decorative topographical landscapes of Pompeii and Herculaneum. Just as in the Odyssey Landscapes, scores of little figures move in backgrounds of infinite space. The nervous zigzag pen drawing is a kind of calligraphic imitation of Roman impressionism by an artist who was evidently familiar with the Celtic linear style. Interesting, too, in this manuscript are the classical personifications of seasons and elements of nature.

As Panofsky has pointed out, one of the greatest contributions of the Carolingian renaissance was the reinstatement of the old gods, each authentically antique in pagan content and artistic form.[2] A beautiful example of this temporary rescue of the Olympians is the manuscript of Aratus at Utrecht (figure 74). The individual divinities of the constellation, probably copied from a Late Antique original, are comparable to figures in Pompeian murals. They are modeled in a truly statuesque fashion, and their rich colors flecked with milky highlights recall the mode of the Augustan age. Although the painter's forms are rather stiff-jointed manikins than actual human bodies, the original model for them must have been such an ancient painting as the Theseus from Herculanaeum (figure 35). Nature is seen only through the prototype the artist had before him. He was interested not in creating natural forms but only in trying to present shapes appropriately classical for the ancient text he was called upon to illustrate. The use of the Byzantine gold background shows that he was affected by contemporary conventions as well: the isolation of the figures in this manuscript against gold backgrounds only intensifies their sculptural "antique" quality. Although the union of classical form and content seen here was abandoned in the late Middle Ages, it was through the preservation of classical types in the Carolingian renaissance that they came to enjoy their ultimate revival in the Renaissance of the fifteenth century.

— 2 0 —

The Late Middle Ages
and Classical Antiquity

Rome, thy grand ruins; still beyond compare,
Thy former greatness mournfully declare,
Though time thy stately palaces around
Hath strewed, and cast thy temples to the ground.
—Hildebert of Lavardin *

R EADING Gibbon on the barbarian enslavement of Europe in the Dark
Ages one might suppose that the white sepulchral splendor of the Roman
world melted like snow from the face of the West in these centuries of fire
and pillage. The fact is that this material shell of the classical past—its
buildings, sculpture, and treasure, cracked and crumbling to fragments
from the destruction of both Christians and barbarians and from centuries
of neglect and vandalism—still survived in considerable quantity as a reminder of pagan days. The medieval annals are filled with descriptions of
the excavation of Roman temples and villas and graveyards in France and
Italy. It is not surprising that Roman tombs were sometimes identified as
the graves of Christian martyrs. More often than not these enterprises were
mere treasure hunts, although as early as the seventh century Gregory
of Tours devoted himself to the serious study of Roman remains. Sometimes the magic relics of paganism were piously destroyed, and, especially in the Gothic period, the old ruins were used as quarries for new
buildings. Sarcophagi and relief fragments were frequently rescued by the

* Par tibi, Roma, nihil,
  Cum sis prope tota ruina;
  Quam magni fueris integra fracta doces.
  Longa tuos fastus aetas destruxit, et arces
  Caesaris et superum templa palude jacent.
        —Hildebert of Lavardin, *De Roma* (twelfth century)

clergy to be used as altar tables; even pagan statues were included in the decor of medieval churches. Sometimes these fragments were regarded with positive awe as revelations of what must have seemed an almost magical perfection of craftsmanship surpassing the capacities of Carolingian and Romanesque stonecutters. Ancient gems, including cameos of Augustus and intaglios that had been magic talismans for invoking astral powers, found their way into the setting of Christian reliquaries and processional crosses.

We marvel today at the nearly perfect preservation of the handful of monuments of Roman Provence, but these temples and amphitheaters at Arles and Nîmes are only a tiny legacy of the great number of such surviving remnants of the classical past that stood throughout the Middle Ages in Italy and France. Many, like the amphitheater of Orange, were only destroyed in the eighteenth century. However incapable of profiting from them the masons and carvers of the Dark Ages were, the very presence of these works preserved the memory of the monumentality of ancient art, until eventually in the twelfth century they kindled a revival of Roman methods in the architecture and sculpture of Provence.

From the iconographical point of view, the pagan gods, although no longer venerated, enjoyed a survival in medieval encyclopedias as parallels for the strength and virtues of Biblical personages or as inventors of those arts that made possible the transition from barbarism to civilization. Sometimes the Olympians were explained as magicians, superior beings practicing a good and useful magic, so that Apollo is transformed into a god of medicine, a kind of patron and pioneer in the healing arts. It was the aim of the Christian fathers not so much to destroy the old gods as to Christianize them or, as was often the case, to use them as useful parallels for Christian virtues. Part of this campaign is the importance attached to the Sybils as prophets of the age of Christ. Familiar examples of this process are the relation between St. Sebastian, the plague saint, and Apollo, the slayer of the pestilential hydra, or Hercules' identification with Samson or the personification of the Christian virtue of Fortitude.

There are many indications before the true Renaissance of the fifteenth century that a sense of pride in the classical heritage persisted throughout the darkest periods after the fall of Rome. The fragments of ancient statuary and metalwork that were so often lovingly installed in churches for safekeeping are the outward evidence of such sentiments just as the legends of the foundation of civilization in France by refugees from the Trojan War illustrate this reverence for the prestige of the ancients in the Chansons de Geste.

The term "renaissance" is sometimes applied to a return to the classical past that took place in the twelfth century. This revival or proto-humanism began as a kind of erudite antiquarianism with a new emphasis on Roman classics and good Latin. It comprised the rise of vernacular poetry in France and Italy, and witnessed the development of some of the great universities like Salerno, Oxford, and Paris out of the old cathedral schools. The century also saw the appearance of collectors of classical art, like Bishop Henry of Winchester, who to the amazement of his contemporaries ran himself ragged acquiring fragments of statuary from the ruins of Rome. This Renaissance witnessed not only a revival of interest in the Latin authors but also the production of Latin prose and verse, notably the poems of Hildebert of Lavardin on the ruins of Rome that might almost have been written by some Late Antique author like Rutilius Namatianus. This whole awakening takes place in the shadow of Rome. For the first time since the fall of the Empire, the ruined center of Western civilization is referred to as *Roma Caput Mundi.* As early as the twelfth century there appeared a guidebook for the benefit of visitors, the *Mirabilia Urbis Romae (The Marvels of Rome)*, full of references to the magical and legendary origin of the monuments and clichés on the passing of the grandeur of the material world.[1]

Before Petrarch, the twelfth-century poet Hildebert writes of the pathetic reminders of the distant past, the ruins of Rome, with a fervor that suggests the Renaissance humanist's quest for nostalgic antiquity. In the Renaissance, however, the fall of great cities is associated with the glamour of individual destiny, so that it takes on the flavor of historical romanticism. Hildebert declaims on the feebleness of his own time before these remains of Roman grandeur. Their vision, even in its fragmentary state which he laments, aroused a suggestion of the original grandeur of form. Only a Renaissance man could admire the intrinsic beauty of these vast, melancholy ruins. For Hildebert there is always a moral in these remnants, because a heavenly realm is attainable only by the fall of earthly splendor. The Roman monuments in their dilapidation symbolized the decline of the worldly realm, and their aspect could in no sense provoke a desire for a *renovatio.* They are reminders of divine chastisement, and their greatness impresses the beholder with his own weakness.

Two episodes in the twelfth century may stand as symbols of the point of view toward antiquity in this period which, since it was illumined by the dawn of classical studies, is sometimes referred to as the Proto-Renaissance. One is the dedication of a house or tower by a certain Nicholas Crescentius; the other the strange tale of a friar's admiration for classic statuary. The so-called House of Crescentius is a memorial to the brief revival of Roman glory in the late Middle Ages (figure 75). This stump of a ruined tower stands on the Via del Teatro di Marcello near the Foro Boario. The structure is built of medieval brickwork with inset fragments of Roman friezes and entablatures. It once commanded the bridge over the Tiber and was erected by one of the most powerful of Roman families. It bears the following inscription:

> Nicholas, to whom this house belongs, well knew that the glory of the world was vanity. He was induced to build this dwelling, less by vanity than by the desire to restore the splendor of ancient Rome. Within a beautiful house be mindful of the grave and remember that thou hast not long to live in thy dwelling. Death travels hither on wings. No man's life is eternal . . . Here stands the name of Nicholas' father, Crescentius, and of his mother, Theodora.

Nothing could be more typical of this moment than the spirit of this inscription with its reminder of the brevity and vanity of this life and worldly glory. At the same time it shows a man of the twelfth century who considered himself heir to the Roman Empire, making this small effort to restore the splendor of ancient Rome, and as he says elsewhere in the inscription, the glory of his fathers. One seems to discern here that same wistfulness for the vanished greatness of Rome that is recorded in *The Marvels of Rome,* referring to "the temples and palaces of emperors, consuls, senators, and prefects that were in the time of the heathen within this Roman city. How great was their beauty in gold and silver and brass, ivory, and precious stones we have endeavored in writing as well as we could to bring back to the remembrance of mankind." [2] This insignificant house, sometimes wrongly referred to as the House of Rienzi, is a kind of symbol of Cola di Rienzi's attempt to reunite Italy under the leadership of Rome that for a brief moment saw the Senate reinstalled on the Capitoline. This architectural episode is a kind of prophecy of the real Renaissance that was to come.

A second incident illustrates the sensuous magic which the antique exerted even on pious minds. It is a story related by one Master Gregory, an English visitor, who in the twelfth century encountered Venus in the ruins of Rome:

109

This statue was dedicated by the Romans to Venus in that guise in which, as it is said in the story, she showed herself naked to Paris with Juno and Pallas in the rash competition . . . This figure is executed of Parian marble with such marvellous inexplicable art that it seems more a living creature than a statue, for there are traces of rosy color on the face, as though she were blushing in her nudity, and those who look close seem to see the blood warming the snowy face. Because of its marvellous aspect I was drawn, I know not by what magic attraction, to revisit the statue three times, although it was two stadia a distance from my lodging.[3]

This episode is recounted in Master Gregory's version of *The Marvels of Rome,* and some have thought that perhaps the Capitoline Venus (figure 76) may have been the object of his admiration. (One wonders if he could have known the old legend of the youth who inadvertently placed his wedding ring on the finger of a statue of Venus and found himself thereafter in her demon thrall.) Certainly astonishing and significant in his account is the completely aesthetic evaluation of the image, regardless of the unChristian pagan allure of the goddess' nudity. It has been said that Master Gregory's description might well have been the eulogy of a connoisseur of the Renaissance. At the same time this quasi-magical regard of ancient statues as superior living beings has its counterpart in the lines of Hildebert of Lavardin:

> Here might the gods be amazed by their own images,
> Desiring only to equal their sculptured grace:
> For nature despaired of giving her gods that grandeur
> Which man infused into his mighty statues,
> Breathing a power which prostrates all beholders,
> Man's art eclipsing the fabled might of the gods.[4]

Here also is the old idea of art's improving nature which was to be repeated ad infinitum in the Renaissance and later. It is an early instance of a dawning recognition of ancient masterpieces as marvels of human craft. The two episodes, Crescentius' dedication and Master Gregory's Venus, both laid in Rome, are symbolical of the spell that the monuments of the ancient city were once more casting on Western man, an enchantment that was to lead him not only to classical beauty but to the discovery of himself.

The first to express a truly modern point of view toward classical antiquity in the thirteenth century was the poet Petrarch. In his writings for the first time the concept of antiquity appears as something removed, separated from the writer's time by the intervening Middle Ages or *Medio*

Evo. The mighty ruins of Rome appear to him as venerable and untouchable relics of the past, and he inveighs against the curtain of the Dark Ages that separates him from this distant golden vision. This was a point of view that made possible the study of the past as detached from the modern epoch and as an integral unity. This perspective was necessary for the development of modern archaeology as a science dedicated to the study of remote cultures in their own context. Petrarch's view was entirely different from the conventional medieval historical insistence on a development from pagan darkness to Christian light.

Professor Panofsky has pointed out that the medieval mind was totally incapable of realizing the unity of classical subject matter and classical form. Classical subject matter lost its original form, and classical form, its subject matter. Only in the Renaissance of the fifteenth century were they reintegrated. Actually, a union of classical subject matter and classical style would have been meaningless to the average artist and patron, so that classical motifs, when they were used, appear disguised in contemporary terms. Invariably, the classical prototype lost either its original form or its meaning. A connoisseur like Master Gregory could appreciate the beauty of Venus *in propria persona* and not as a star-goddess arrayed in a medieval gown.

For the medieval mind the ancient period was something far away like the world of legends or the fantastic wonders of the distant East. At the same time it was real and dangerous in the presence of the old gods changed into demons. The fact that pagan monuments are often referred to throughout the Middle Ages as the works of "sarrazins" demonstrates the confusion of classical antiquities with relics from the Orient. The classic past was remote and distant and yet linked to the present in much the same way as the Old Testament was regarded as the ancient foundation of the New. The idea of continuity with the classical past rather than a separation from the ancient world persisted in the myth of the German emperors' inheritance of the mantle of the Caesars. In a similar way, the Roman Empire of the Middle Ages was hopefully regarded by many as the last of many monarchies in which the world had known universal peace, just as Augustus brought peace to the Roman world in a time when Christ simultaneously bestowed the boon of spiritual peace. With the development of Petrarch's ideas in the Renaissance of the fifteenth century men came to regard antiquity as a cultural entity removed from the present, an ideal to be longed for rather than a foreboding, if useful, reality. With this perspective, classical art became the object of everlasting nostalgia, and there developed a yearning for hallowed antiquity as a lost paradise to be regained by reconstruction and emulation. The century of Hildebert of Lavardin was not ready for such a fervent turning to the past: Hildebert sorrowfully concluded that no *renovatio* could restore Rome to her former glory; and Rome herself is made to say, "I prize my ruin above my greatest triumphs . . . once ruler of cities, I now rule heaven." [5]

— 2 I —

Classical Forms in
the Romanesque Period

One sang of Cadmus, who, exiled and far from home, founded the city of Thebes; another of Jason and the sleepless snake; another told of mighty Alcides, another of how Demophoön had his sweet will of Phyllis. One told how Narcissus, drowned in the well in which he worshipped his own face, another how Pluto ravished Orpheus' fair wife from his side.   —Anonymous *

THE term Romanesque is used to describe the art of Western Europe from about 1000 to the early thirteenth century, a period when a new monumental art finally emerged to mark the end of the ages of barbarism and degradation that ensued with the fall of the Western Empire. Romanesque art is a resumption and culmination of what had only been begun briefly under the Carolingian empire. The very term Romanesque implies the same derivation from Roman forms as the designation Romance languages indicates the basis of these tongues in the Latin tradition. Certain factors contributed mightily to the character and extent of this revival of architecture and the plastic arts. In Italy the emergence of the free communes made possible at once the patronage of the artist and his emergence as an independent craftsman. At the same time the character of Roman-

---

* L'un dis de Cadmus quan fugi
Et de Tebas con las basti,
L'autre cantava de Jason
E del dragon que non hac son;
L'us conte d'Alcide sa forsa,
L'autre con tornet e sa forsa
Phillis par amor Demophon.
L'un dis com Neguet en la fon
Lo belz Narcis quan s'i miret;
L'us dis de Pluto com emblet
Sa belle mollier ad Orpheu.
               —Anonymous, *Flamenca* (thirteenth century)

esque art was unified by the spread of the influence of the Cluniac order over the Western world. An exchange of ideas and techniques that at times seems to bestow upon Romanesque art a kind of international character was brought about by the transmission of iconography and technique along the great pilgrimage roads that unrolled over France toward the great shrine of Santiago at Compostela. The term proto-Renaissance is sometimes applied to certain aspects of Romanesque art that reveal a peculiarly intensive adaptation of antique prototypes. This Romanesque revival of antiquity is a strictly Mediterranean phenomenon that had its beginnings in southern France with a sudden awakening on the part of architects and sculptors to the models in the form of Roman buildings and carvings that lay all about them in the ruined cities of Provence. This turn to reproducing monumental imitations of ancient art is in itself different from the timid small-scale borrowings of the Carolingian period.

The word Romanesque in its literal sense may be applied more aptly to the style of Provence than any other. It was inevitable within a district that still preserved so many superb monuments of ancient architecture—like the Pont du Gard, the great amphitheaters at Arles and Nîmes, and the triumphal arch at Orange—that builders should be influenced by these examples before their eyes. Perhaps this emulation of the Latin heritage was partly occasioned by the recognition that these relics, too, were fragments of old Rome, the ancient center of the world and of the church, that now once more began to cast her shadow over Western Christendom.

This turn to Roman forms is nowhere better illustrated than in the sculpture of the Church of St. Trophîme at Arles. The façade itself is suggestive of an ancient triumphal arch; its columns are a reasonable approximation of the Corinthian order, and its entablature is a modification of a Roman prototype. The sculptural decoration of the portal marks a return to monumental stone carving. Some of the individual figures, like the massive forms of the Apostles with their garments carved in closely pleated folds (figure 77), are suggestive of Roman workmanship of the period of Constantine (figure 83). The heads of the apostles have something of the gravity and pathos of Late Antique portraits. Above them the continuous frieze of densely packed figures appears to be an imitation of the carving of Early Christian sarcophagi. It is evident at once that the craftsmen who were active at St. Trophîme did not exercise any particular discrimination in their choice of models to follow. A work of Roman or Early Christian antiquity would serve them equally well in their efforts literally to invent a style of monumental figure carving appropriate to a monumental architectural enframement. In comparison to actual Roman forms the figures of the apostles at St. Trophîme are lacking in any sense of beauty of proportion; their squat, rigid bodies are scarcely articulated beneath the mesh of lines that symbolizes, rather than describes, the structure of plausible folds. At the same time, the ability of the sculptor, however limited, to create such massive, even three-dimensional, form shows the lesson timidly learned from the plastic grammar of the ancient world. In a way different from the aim of a classical sculptor, the impression these figures were intended to create was not strictly plastic, since in their application to the wall as columnar verticals the carver obviously intended them to fulfill the function of architectural accents.

It is no wonder that the old gods should have briefly reappeared from their long sleep in Provence during the literary and artistic renaissance of the twelfth and thirteenth centuries. The heroes of the Golden Fleece, Alexander, and Julius Caesar were the familiars of the troubadours. In the twelfth-century epic *Eraclius* they sang of the miraculous exploits of the Byzantine emperor Heraclius and the mighty demigod, his prototype. A feast described in the thirteenth-century novel *Flamenca* was enlivened by the jongleurs' recital of legends heroic, touching, and tragic from the worlds of mythology and the Old Testament. One of the favorites from the troubadours' repertory, Hercules, puts in an appearance in a Christianized role at Saint Trophîme (figure 79a). The great god, whom we have not seen since his last appearances in Late Antique art, may be recognized in a strange figure on the north side of the west façade in a long narrow panel just above the base of the elevation. The god is represented prone, as though swimming or floating on an endless current. Since the hero holds a lion's paw in his right hand and a club in his left, there is an evident allusion to his adventure with the Nemean lion. The hide with hoof and horns draped around his shoulders is a trophy of the Labor of the Cretan bull. In later medieval art the subject of Hercules and the Lion is virtually interchangeable with the triumph of Samson over a similar antagonist as an allegory of the victory of good over evil. At Saint Trophîmes, however, the mythological hero is brought even more intimately into the service of Christian theology. In the panel immediately above his recumbent effigy Hercules appears again, upholding two dwarf-like forms (figure 79b). As in ancient portrayals of his capture of the Cecrops, Hercules is represented as gazing up at St. Michael weighing souls. It seems

115

immediately apparent that Hercules' role here is that of a celestial gen-
darme engaged in carrying wicked spirits to hell. That the inverted figures
he carries are not the poisonous dwarfs of ancient legend, but damned
souls is made plain by their stopping their ears to the Gospel. Hercules, in
other words, appears as a prefiguration of the archangel and his assistant
or psychogogue.

The nudity of Hercules and accuracy of his attributes indicate at least
that the carver was familiar with a classical model, and the composition of
the hero staring at the psychopomp of St. Michael must owe something to
a portrayal of the Cecrops story as it often appears in Attic vases or in
the archaic metope at Selinunte.[1] The "swimming" Hercules most likely
represents a coercion of a standard figure on a sarcophagus into this unusual pose that was so obviously contrived to fit a definite architectural
space. Although this figure has been very much mutilated, it is apparent
even in its present state that the carver had at least some feeling for the
modeling of the nude; he was evidently striving for certain effects of realism, as in the emphasis on the god's sagging paunch. Although there is very
little beyond the *élan* of the figure that is aesthetically moving, it is none
the less apparent that the sculptor had learned at least something about
the articulation of the human figure from the observation of antiquity.
From what remains of the head one can observe a revival of the Antonine
drill technique. It is of course only necessary to compare these carvings
with the barbaric relief at Calvi to illustrate the reëmergence of sculpture
as a monumental medium.[2] The resemblance of the conception of Hercules as bearer of souls to the old arrangement of the Cecrops myth is interesting not only because of the resemblance of this subject to ancient reliefs, but because the style of the representation at Saint Trophîme may
be described as "archaic" just as much as the Selinunte panel: the vigor
of the direct conceptual statement is as typical of this period of the rebirth of the plastic tradition in twelfth-century France as it was of Greek
art of the seventh century B.C.

The qualities observed in the sculpture at Arles are even more marked
in the façade of the Church of St. Gilles, which was begun in 1116. The
façade of this building itself gives the impression of a temple with its order of Corinthian columns surmounted by a heavy entablature, and at
the same time the tripartite division with the three deeply recessed portals
recalls the arrangement of a triumphal arch. The whole conception appears as a kind of Romanesque attempt to recreate the impression of big-

ness and lavish decoration that the master builder had observed in some Roman ruin like the theater and triumphal arch of Orange. The carving of the friezes with their many densely crowded figures are an obvious derivation from the arrangement of Late Antique or Early Christian sarcophagi. Even the heavily drilled folds with the body showing through this network of lines, as though encased in a web, are a medieval adaptation of the style of the fourth or fifth century. Because of this mannerism, these figures have a kind of rhythmic animation imparted largely through the decorative organization of the lines that gives them a feeling of dynamic movement which is quite different from the inert and lifeless forms of the Early Christian grave reliefs.

Certain individual figures at St. Gilles were unquestionably inspired by earlier and, more properly speaking, classical forms. An illustration of this is the image of St. James the Great that is carved in very high relief on the middle portal (figure 78). The immediate model for the apostle appears to have been a maenad (figure 183). The sculptor, without understanding the meaning of this bacchic figure, has taken over the slight bend of the body to impart a feeling of animation to his shape, and from the same source he seems to have learned something about the organic conception of the anatomy. He has borrowed rather literally some of the passages of the drapery, and he apparently was most interested in the way in which the repeated curving and moving lines of the ancient figure gave it a suggestion of animation. In the Christian figure the borders of the garments move and twist with a stirring serpentine rhythm almost suggestive of the wild convolutions of medieval penmanship.

In imparting a spiritual life to his forms through abstract linear rhythms the sculptor is entirely in the Romanesque tradition. The convoluted animation of the drapery folds on the surface of the figure seems almost a wilful denial of its solid structure, dissolving the form into a weightless phantom. But the body itself, as though to maintain its columnar function in the architectural ensemble, remains strangely still. This faint awakening to the classical tradition in southern France came to a complete end with the devastation of the Albigensian crusade in the thirteenth century, but its influence spread throughout France and Italy to establish the firm reinstitution of monumental art in the West. It remains that the borrowing from ancient sources in southern France is completely within the framework of the Romanesque style. Although it may, according to some, have exercised some influence on developments in Italy, it never approached the far closer understanding and adaptations of the Roman tradition in the work of the pioneer Italian sculptors in the twelfth century.

The development of the Romanesque style of sculpture in Italy furnishes telling examples of the persistence of the Latin tradition. This factor may be considered with particular profit in the work of the two key figures in the development of the plastic tradition in Lombardy in the twelfth century: Guglielmo of Modena and Benedetto Antelami. The style of Italian Romanesque art, especially in its most vigorous phase in the northern provinces, is a development out of a variety of earlier indigenous traditions. The barbarian style of the Dark Ages, as well as Byzantine, Carolingian, and, finally, antique styles and iconography, all contributed to the formation of a mode of plastic expression that is just as national and just as original as the Romanesque styles of France in the twelfth century. Although many attempts have been made to demonstrate the influence of Languedoc or Provence on the workshops of Guglielmo and Antelami, it appears evident for a number of reasons that the work of these sculptors represents a parallel development that at the same time deviates very strongly from the dynamic calligraphic character of French Romanesque in its firm adherence to the antique tradition. Many of the details of the sculpture of Provence give the impression of imitations of Early Christian sarcophagi or Byzantine ivories enlarged to fill a vaguely classical architectural framework, whereas the carving of Romanesque Italy impresses one to a far greater degree as a direct return to Roman models. What is more important for later developments, these adaptations of antique motifs and techniques are handled with an understanding of ancient form and plastic structure.

The real founder of the Romanesque style in Italy, Guglielmo of Modena, in his return to Greco-Roman models steered Italian sculpture in a different direction from the course of Romanesque art in France. One may detect Guglielmo's classical qualities most notably in certain decorative idioms and in his renovation of classical forms. On the cathedral of Modena the device of the frieze interrupting the bare wall of the façade appears as a reminiscence of ancient architectural sculpture and is very different from the usual scheme of concentrating ornament in the tympana and door jambs of Romanesque churches. Guglielmo also employed ancient fragments, such as the Roman lions of the portico. These crouching beasts are ill-adapted to supporting the columns and are far removed in style and spirit from those fearsome apparitions which are the true Romanesque lions of later Lombard cathedrals. On the south façade of the cathedral is another classical motif of Guglielmo's: panels showing reliefs of funerary genii with reversed torches (figure 80), a motif borrowed from Roman sarcophagi.

It is apparent at once that there has been a change in the sense of this motif in its transference from pagan to Christian usage. When it appeared on Roman sarcophagi, the Cupid extinguishing a torch (figure 81) was intended to suggest the passing of life into a drowsy limbo of eternal sleep. Professor Panofsky has suggested that the presence in one relief of the ibis, a bird with an unsavory reputation in the bestiary, indicates that the cupid with this emblem and the companion figure were two aspects of carnal love.[3] With its adoption here by Guglielmo as a Christian symbol the motif of the sleeping Cupid promised awakening to immortality rather than death. Whatever the meaning, like no other Romanesque sculptor before him Guglielmo was seduced by the decorative beauty of the ancient motif. He has made an evident attempt to capture something of the calm repose and quiet nobility of the Roman model. At the same time Guglielmo has achieved a softer modeling and composed his form in more massive rhythms. In his archaic way he has produced rather solid and robust plastic forms that are quite different from the dryness of late Roman carving. Guglielmo of Modena is certainly the real progenitor of all later Italian sculpture in his feeling for the antique and the monumental quality of his figures. In these panels of funerary genii the carver had not only a sense of anatomy probably derived from his observation of antiquities but also a positive feeling for the nude as living flesh. For all the awkwardness and heaviness of his forms Guglielmo represents the first real awakening to the beauty of the human form since the fall of the classical world.

Guglielmo's most distinguished follower in the great twelfth-century revival of sculpture in Lombardy was Benedetto Antelami, chiefly remembered for his magnificent sculptural decoration of the baptistery of Parma. The plastic iconography of this building includes a vast repertory of subjects that, following the plan of the sculptural decoration of the great French cathedrals, presents the theme of man's salvation foretold by the prophets and realized with the coming of Christ and the ultimate triumph of the redeemed in the Last Judgment. Included in this scheme of plastic decoration which fills the portals and interrupts the exterior walls of the octagonal building are a number of figures of archangels set in niches. They are to be regarded most likely, not only as the benevolent watchmen and guardians of humanity, but as heralds of the Last Day. It is especially in these forms that Antelami displays the typical Italian reliance an antiquity inaugurated by Guglielmo. The angel chosen for illustration (figure 82) represents a typical example of Antelami's peasant-like robustness of form and his conception of the body and head as massive cubic shapes. At the same time the archangel reveals a particular ancient prototype. The style of the drapery as well as its scheme of arrangement indicates that the sculptor had a Late Antique model in mind. It is not necessary to suppose that Antelami ever undertook a journey to Rome, but his archangel is so close to the Victories at the base of the arch of Constantine (figure 83) that he must have had access to a somewhat similar piece of sculpture. The robe of the angel at Parma resembles the dress of the fourth-century Nikes in its composition of a veritable mesh of densely pleated folds. In following the complicated drapery system of the Constantinian model the sculptor was not always entirely sure of the exact structural relation of the lines in the Late Antique carving, so he presents a somewhat superficial and confused impression of the classical fold scheme. He has also copied the Constantinian formula of incising the lines of the folds so deeply that they seem literally to penetrate the substance of the body which they clothe. Antelami must have been fascinated by the surface richness of his Late Antique model and has used the rhythmic repetition of the multiple undulating lines of the robe both to accentuate the voluminous fullness of his figure and, by the very movement, this stirring web of lines to offset the feeling of weighty immobility. Just as Guglielmo was moved by the decorative fluidity of the ancient cupids at Modena, Antelami here has discovered other elements of a different antique style to develop his own conception of sculpture. In this figure of the archangel and another example of his manner to be investigated Antelami had already achieved a complete definition of the Italian conception of sculpture, in which the figure is conceived as a massive, even ponderous volume, definitely existing in space and at the same time relieved and lightened by decorative manipulation of its superficial form.

Although the sculptor was undoubtedly aware of some ancient model, his treatment of the form is an interpretation rather than a copy. The vigorous carving of the body as a solid plastic mass and the uniform stylization are more Romanesque than classic. At the same time this sure, powerful handling of high relief displays again the lesson the sculptor could have learned only from the observation of the antique. The form of the Archangel may seem clumsy and ponderous. It is readily apparent that bodies in Romanesque sculpture do not reveal the easy, organic articulation nor the concern with the rhythmic flow of the drapery associated with classical statues. Romanesque sculptors like Antelami were concerned only with the most general shorthand description of the body as a solid impenetrable volume, simplified to tell as an architectural accent and so dense and robust in its abstract cubic structure as to impart a great feeling of both structural integrity and physical power.

— 22 —

The Gothic Period

Can Christ, like Jupiter, favor idols,
Or does our Mary, like Vesta, desire them to be graven?
—Abelard *

WITH the Gothic period in the early thirteenth century a new intellectual life in Christian Europe made for an inevitable change in the artistic expression. The selective spirit in the study of the classics that had flourished in the renaissance of the twelfth century now came to be regarded as useless and even pernicious. Theology comes largely to replace literary studies. One would have to take note also of St. Bernard's indictment of figural decoration, especially of the rather frivolous representation of demons and monster forms that had particularly enchanted the carvers of the preceding century. Gothic sculpture as an art form takes on a specifically autonomous expression; that is, it tends to develop without relying for models on manuscripts, textiles, and classical precedents. A realism based on the observation of natural bodies replaces the earlier imitation of classical figures, just as natural leafage replaces the stiff classical acanthus in capitals. There is a new spirituality in the combining of real and ideal elements in the faces of the saints.

Even for Thomas Aquinas who may have seen the work of Frederick II's Campanian classic school, realism and beauty in art were a new means for the revelation of truth. Even though idolatry may have arisen in primitive times through man's deception by the beauty of graven images, according to St. Thomas, the men of his day, as Christians, had no reason to fear this snare. This is the beginning of an acceptance of beauty and realism for the sake of veracity, the faithful representation of the

---

* Numquid amare potest ut Jupiter idola Christus
Aut sculpi ut Vesta nostra Maria volet?
—Petrus Abelardus, "Versus ad Astralabium Filium"

122

reality which the senses perceive. In such a view, realism in Gothic art becomes the measure of the supernatural.

There are, however, what might be described as little islands of resistance in this Gothic world, in which there are even more pronounced indications of a real classical renaissance than was apparent in twelfth-century Provence. There is, for example, a sculptor, or perhaps better to say a sculptor's workshop, at Reims, which seems to have taken the keenest interest in classical prototypes. Here we have something more than just an imitation of the superficial aspects of classical models. We have for the first time some suggestion that, following real classical fragments, the figures are conceived with a realization of the natural organic correspondence between the body and its garments. There is a combination of freedom and stable balance of posture, especially in the use of *contrapposto,* that gives the impression that the figure is entirely self-centered and controlled from the axis within itself.

Admiration for the antique went hand in hand with the rediscovery of nature. The examination of antique fragments was interesting to artists of the thirteenth century, not from an archaeological point of view, but because it showed them how the artists of the Roman past saw nature or, better, how they made things look real in the way that the advanced painters and sculptors of the Dugento wished to have them look. This is simply another factor leading to the artist's free observation of reality without the impediment of the medieval intellectual point of view. When we discern a seeming dependence on antique models, it is in reality a translation of the antique prototypes into contemporary terms. When, for example, the thirteenth-century French artist Villard de Honnecourt looked at classical statues and sketched them, he was entirely insensible to their volume and was interested only in their external profile and linear features. The lines of the muscles of an antique statue drawn by Villard de Honnecourt reveal little understanding of anatomical articulation, but are translated into linear rhythms, stemming from the centuries-old manuscript illumination (figure 84).

The Gothic experiment in reconciling reality with universals is a stage in the journey toward the rationalization of visual phenomena in the Renaissance. The basic difference between the Gothic and the Renaissance approaches to reality is that in the Renaissance what had been intuitively achieved in the thirteenth and fourteenth centuries was scientifically integrated with the new concepts of space and perspective to produce an illusion of three-dimensionality in both painting and sculpture. Gothic art represented a much more abrupt change from Romanesque art than did the transition from the Gothic to the Renaissance point of view. Gothic art was new because its vision was centered on a humanized realism based on experience rather than reliance on absolutes or recipes. Many facile comparisons could be made with the thought of nominalist philosophers and scientists to illustrate the common turn to expressing both the universal order of the divine and the individuality and ever-changing nature of the real world in a union of the conceptual and the concrete. Part of this revelation of nature was the use of classic forms, not with any intent to be classical, but to aid in the achievement of presenting human forms in a convincingly real way from the lesson of antique models. The notebooks of Villard de Honnecourt, filled with his drawings of things he himself had observed, including classical images, are typical of the Gothic vision. At the same time this master builder's sketches are concerned with systems of proportion and measurement enlarging the real to the universal. Like so much of Gothic art, Villard's approach is a combination of the conceptual and the recording of actuality.

The famous group of the Visitation at Reims (figure 86) has appeared to some scholars as a kind of re-evocation of the Phidian style, so much so that they have even romantically supposed the presence of Greek artists in France or concluded that the carver of these figures must himself have undertaken a journey to Athens in the days of the Crusades. These beautiful images seem to belong to an intense but short-lived imitation of antiquity at Reims, probably shortly after the first quarter of the thirteenth century. These are to be sure not the only examples of a turn to classic models in Gothic France. There are many echoes of Greek and Roman art of many periods in the sculpture of the cathedrals of Chartres and Corbeil. The figures at Reims are unique in their suggestion of the great style of the fifth century B.C.

These statues are not exactly copies of ancient prototypes, but on the contrary reveal a rather broad understanding of the real form of the antique. They have sometimes been compared to the drawings in the notebook by Villard de Honnecourt, a craftsman who must have been intimately associated with the work at Reims. Villard's drawings (figure 85) generally give a sure general impression of an antique prototype, upon which the draftsman unmistakably impresses his own artistic personality. Both the naturalism of Villard's images and their animation through line are Gothic and not antique. The rhythm and movement of the calligraphic sweeps of his pen confer a spirituality on his interpretations that is quite different from the static linear organization of his models. Somewhat the same analysis can be made of the statues on the façade of Reims. Another important factor that the drawings and sculpture have in common is that they reveal unmistakable evidence for the copying of antique statues, rather than the relief fragments which earlier had provided models for the Romanesque carvers of Provence. One of the most classic qualities of Gothic sculpture is the isolation of plastic figures and groups, together with a new study of bodily structure and movement on the basis of the antique. However, even in this most classic phase in the late medieval world, an art concerned primarily with recapturing a visual naturalistic representation of the human body and a revelation of its spiritual state could not concern itself except incidentally with the return to the antique in a properly speaking archaeological or archaistic way. These figures are important, perhaps most of all, as a step from the Romanesque to the Renaissance concept in the representation of corporeal form. The Gothic artist was interested in presenting a credible and realistic, not a symbolical, organization of the body and its mass, and in vitalizing it so that it seems to be animated by a hidden inner force.

In this revelation of the bodily function the really antique drapery of the Visitation group plays its part: both the Madonna and St. Elizabeth are dressed in the Roman *palla,* and the heavy folds of these garments, perhaps more than anything else, give the suggestion of majestic breadth to the figures. The drapery of the Reims statue in its interesting complexity has a kind of life of its own and does not entirely reveal and clarify the structure of the body beneath. The forms are centered around their axes so that they have a suggestion of the statuesque autonomy of antique sculpture. It is apparent, of course, that these extraordinary Gothic statues were based on actual surviving classical prototypes, probably Gallo-Roman copies of the Phidian style. There are indications that Reims in the thirteenth century was still a veritable quarry of classical statuary. Surviving fragments of Gallo-Roman sculptures show at least the kind of prototype that the Reims master must have had before his eyes. There is a bronze in Lyons that is a late copy of the Phidian type, and a marble torso (figure 87) in the Musée Calvet at Avignon is another classical fragment remarkably close to the figures in the Visitation group.

Perhaps the closest prototype of all for the figure of the Madonna is a draped statue of a Vestal (figure 88). In view of the revival or the persistence of ancient forms in Rome of the first century of our era it is not at all surprising that this Augustan portrait reveals the same type of Phidian classicism in the drapery that was ultimately adopted at Reims. Mary's face in the Visitation group has something of the same elegiac mood and reflective dreamy expression of the classical prototype, but the Madonna's mask has been converted to a typically Gothic and more spiritual type by the subtle elongation of the face and by the precision of linear definition, notably in the treatment of the hair and the sharp contour of the high, arching brows. The massive fullness of Phidian statuary was recaptured in many statues besides the prototype mentioned; it appears most likely that the Greek quality to be vaguely discerned in the famous Visitation group may be explained by the fact that the sculptor invented the images of Mary and Elizabeth from Augustan statues of Vestals which were available to him in the thirteenth-century ruins of Reims.

Although superficially the garments of Mary and Elizabeth seem extraordinarily close to the antique formula for drapery, the resemblance remains a superficial one. In the same way, although the head of St. Elizabeth suggests a Roman portrait and the head of the Madonna has even been compared with that of the Venus dei Medici (figure 30), both of these Gothic masks differ from the classic ideal in the sculptor's suggestion of a spirituality, an ecstasy of expression, that is quite different from the purely physical ideality of the antique prototype. The actual differences between the Gothic and the antique extend to the conception of the figure as a whole. Although there are indications that there was at least some interest in classical proportions at Reims, as may be seen in some of Villard de Honnecourt's diagrams, these experiments with the ancient canon were not applied to the sculpture of the cathedral. In the figures of the Madonna and St. Elizabeth the heads are actually too large for the bodies and the bodies themselves too squat to bear comparison with any Grecian canon of proportion.

In a classical statue we have the feeling that the whole body, warm and organically alive, is present and moving under the drapery. The rhythmic organization of the folds of the garment invariably enhances this feeling of form and movement. Although revealing the body the classic drapery still has a life of its own as a design and a substance apart from the body that supports it. In the Gothic statues at Reims the nature of this classical relation is suggested in a superficial way only. The draperies seem like shells or wrappings that contain no substantial corporeal form. The stiffened hulls stand by themselves, with no real conviction that a material body exists beneath. There is perhaps some suggestion of the balanced distribution of weight in classical sculpture by the contours of the forms, but the classical garment is presented more in accordance with a system of moving linear rhythm in the drapery folds that is almost calligraphic in its nervous convolutions. At least the implication is present that the figures are articulated around an axis, so that their existence in space as figures in the round is suggested.

Here as everywhere in Gothic sculpture the sculptor was striving for reality. He found the Gallo-Roman prototypes from the ruins of ancient Reims a short cut to the solution of his problem, and at the same time he translated these models into the linear framework of his tradition. How these same Roman fragments served as inspiration for Carolingian painters has been seen in the great paintings of the Evangelists in the Ebbo Gospels (figure 72). In their naturalism and linear animation these Gothic images at Reims present a kind of spiritualized reality that is the thirteenth-century transformation of the antique. If the images of the Visitation suggest a weightless ethereal quality, it is because the basic concept of the classic statue as a form balanced between immobility and action has been transmuted by the Gothic artist using essentially linear terms into movement without any real concern for ponderation, so that the figures have another kind of spiritual expression, which is no more than a ghost of the Phidian style.

— 23 —

The Augustan Revival
of Frederick II

And here he caused his image to be carved in eternal and immortal memory.
—Andrei Ungari *

IN the inscription over the gateway at his favorite city of Capua the Emperor Frederick II styled himself Imperator Fredericus Secundus Romanorum Caesar Semper Augustus. This title is in every way appropriate to a ruler whose lifelong ambition it was to restore the absolute monarchy of the Roman emperors. In Frederick's attempt to revive Roman life and forms the real beginning of the phenomenon known as the Renaissance may be discerned. Frederick's dream of the renewal or renovation of the ancient and universal power of Rome as capital of the world had both a political and metaphysical basis. The Emperor's efforts to establish Rome as the capital of a united Italy with himself as its Caesar was part of his plan to unseat the popes as the successors of the emperors by the donation of Constantine. Frederick's revival of the antique had a further mystical explanation in that it was an expression of Frederick's conviction that the age of Christ and the age of Augustus had come again with him. Apparently Frederick saw himself as cosmokrator, a world ruler endowed by God as Adam was the ruler of the world before the Fall. In his law and justice the Emperor saw an abstract power that might lead men back to the better nature possessed by the first man.

"We recall the ancient Caesars to men's minds by the example of our own person." This statement of the Emperor Frederick's is the complete expression of his conception of himself as the new Augustus. This mystical enactment of the role of the ancient Caesars found its formal expres-

* Ibique suam ymaginem in eternam et immortalem memoriam sculpi fecit.—Andrei Ungari, *Descriptio Victoriae Karolo Provinciae Comite Reportatae.*

sion in Frederick's patronage of an art sacred to himself as emperor, just as the art of Augustus was dedicated to the glory of the Imperator and the Pax Romana. It was an art calculated to invite faith in the new Caesar Augustus. The Greek and Roman forms that Frederick caused to be imitated in the architecture of his gateway at Capua and the palaces of his Apulian and Sicilian domains was a natural part of his program to revive Roman tradition as a unifying symbol of the latinity of Italy. From a political point of view this revival of Roman art completely secular and dedicated to the immortalizing of the Empire and its ruler was specifically intended to be something different and quite apart from the accepted church art of the thirteenth century. It was an attempt to express in classic form Frederick's emulation of the age of Augustus and to present the Emperor himself as a new Augustus come to institute a new Christian world empire. Not since the fall of Rome had there been such a conscious resumption of classical forms. Although there had been many sporadic returns to antiquity throughout the Dark Ages, the craftsmen engaged in Frederick's program of reviving the Augustan age produced the first reunion of ancient concepts and styles. This was, in anticipation of the Renaissance of the fifteenth century, the first instance of the substitution of the authority of antique art for the prescriptions of the tradition of Christian art. The wonder and pomp of Roman art with its realistic aims replaced the coloristic linear symbolizing of the spiritual world in Christian art.

Nowhere are the idea and the form of Frederick's renewal of the Roman Imperium more evident than in the colossal head of Frederick, now in the German Archaeological Institute in Rome (figure 89). This extraordinary portrait of Frederick was found some years ago at Lanuvium on the Via Appia to the south of Rome. The head, now cut off at the neck, was originally part of a bust or draped statue. It is carved of fine-grained Italian marble and was perhaps originally adorned with a metal diadem. It represents a man of forty to forty-five years of age with deeply shadowed eyes, an energetic, rather youthful mouth, and a powerful chin. The somewhat long face is perhaps to be taken as a Hohenstaufen characteristic, since this is always a notable feature in other likenesses of Frederick and his race. The head is characterized by an extraordinary naturalism in the rendering of individual features. This naturalism in itself is suggestive of Gothic art. Another rather un-antique feature is to be seen in the manner in which the head is composed of so many separate interlocking planes, like the facets of a jewel, in distinction to the inner unity of form to be discerned in classic sculpture. Another aspect of this stylistic characteristic may be noted in the isolation and sharpness in the carving of the individual features and the way in which those features appear as elements separately joined to the mass of the head and not organically part of its form. The hardness of the carving and the isolation of the parts give the head a rather strong, sharp, plastic character that is most effective when the head is seen in the full illumination of outdoor light.

Although the stylistic qualities described in the preceding paragraph are all definitely un-antique, at the same time the thirteenth-century sculptor must have had a special antique prototype in mind, which he translated into his own medieval idiom. In a strange way the head is a combination of the cool serene character of the portraits of Augustus (figure 90) and the absolute transcendental embodiment of the majesty found in the portraits of Constantine (figure 60) and his successors. Actually, the head of Lanuvium is something more. Almost like the heroic and titanic portraits of the Hellenistic period, it is a personification of a tyrannical will and a ruthless power remorselessly dedicated to the breaking of all opposition. Its suggestion of activity and force are in a sense more suggestive of the *terribilità* of the Renaissance portrait.

Further, whereas the heads of Constantine seem lost in the contemplation of infinity, the narrowing eyes and knitted brows of Frederick in his portrait from Lanuvium are concentrated on an earthly rather than a heavenly goal.

It becomes immediately apparent that the treatment of this head as a component of so many different isolated forms separates it from the antique, and at the same time the carving of these isolated features differs from the technique of the ancient period. The hair, for example, is made up of a collection of separate locks treated as plastic masses, with the individual hairs indicated schematically by incised lines. This completely unnatural rendering of the coiffure is exactly like the schematic portrayal of lions' manes, as may be seen in many Romanesque examples both in Italy and northern Europe.

The very first gimpse of this colossal head reminds the beholder in some indefinable way of the portraits of the Emperor Augustus, but it is also immediately apparent that the true Augustan quality has been lost in the process of medieval stylization. One has the impression that, perhaps under the orders of the Emperor himself, the artist strove to reproduce a typical Augustan physiognomy with something of the spirit and style of the Imperial portraits of the fourth century. One has the added impression that on this stylistic combination individual traits of Frederick's actual appearance have been superimposed. The precise relation of the head from Lanuvium to actual portraits of Augustus is difficult to put into words. The ancient prototype shines through the Lanuvium portrait, but it has become confused with the frontality and hieratic bearing of Constantinian portraiture. The problem is further complicated by the fact that portraits of Constantine are sometimes described as neo-Augustan in character. The chief resemblance of this portrait of Frederick to the heads of Augustus resides in the essentially cubic, closed form of the head and in the treatment of the hair. Although the seemingly free disposition of the hair in sickle-shaped curls over the forehead recalls the familiar hair style of Augustus, the separate treatment of the individual locks and their arrangement in rigid axial symmetry are a complete formalization of the technique of the Roman prototype.

Within the antique framework the elements of a naturalistic representation of a distinct personality can be discerned. One has only to look at the carving of the mouth and nose, the long Swabian face with its characteristic strong, small, and short chin, and the unelegant thick neck supporting the head. Actually the Lanuvium portrait in its combination of the generality of the antique with a typically Gothic naturalism corresponds very closely to the portraits of Frederick on his famous gold coins or *augustales* (figure 91). The Emperor's likeness on these medals is based on the same combination of prototypes already described in the account of the Lanuvium portrait. The actual head again is generally reminiscent of an Augustan type, but the use of the bust on coinage as we see it here only made its appearance in the second half of the third century. Here again something of Frederick's actual likeness has been coerced into an ideal antique model, so that the portraits on these gold coins closely resemble the sculpture both in physiognomy and style. Just like the heads on the coins the marble portrait from Lanuvium differs from the alive and smooth forms of Augustan portraiture by the way in which it is carved in a hard technique almost suggestive of wood carving concentrated on the representation of individual plastic forms attached to a cubic core.

The Lanuvium portrait showed Frederick as he wished to be seen, not

131

as a true naturalistic portrayal of Frederick himself as he really was, but rather as a "picture of Caesar," a monumental embodiment of the power of the Imperator as the mighty and inflexible cosmokrator and judge of mankind. What we have is a portrait of the new Augustus, a symbol of might embodied in the personal genius of Caesar. Politically it was only natural that Frederick as the opponent of the papacy should wish to have himself shown in this portrait as a kind of heir and legitimate descendant of Augustus, a Caesar come to renew the Imperium Romanum as world judge and universal ruler opposed to the worldly might of the Pope. One may therefore think of this portrait, like the portraits on the *augustales,* as artistic propaganda to legitimize Frederick's claim to imperial might. The Lanuvium head was an embodiment of Frederick's idea of the *renovatio,* an effigy calculated to impress the beholder with the idea of godly majesty, and, as such, a purposeful echo of the official art dedicated to absolute power in the state portraits of Augustus and Constantine. The head in its combination of Augustan and Constantinian portraits, its unsparing naturalism and Gothic structure, shows the way in which the sculptor took antique forms and reworked them in the new and expressive medieval idiom.

— 24 —

Nicola Pisano

Nicola (Pisano) . . . saw amongst much booty won by the Pisan fleet certain ancient sarcophagi which are now in the Campo Santo of that city. One of them was of particularly fine workmanship and depicted Meleager hunting the Caledonian boar . . . Nicola was so impressed and delighted by the merits of this work that he set himself to imitate its style and that of other fine sculptures on these antique sarcophagi, with such effect that he soon came to be considered the best sculptor of the time. —Vasari *

NICOLA PISANO is mentioned in every textbook on art history as the designer and carver of the magnificent pulpits in the Baptistery of Pisa and the Cathedral of Siena. He is usually singled out, too, as the one Italian sculptor of the late Middle Ages who produced a new and meaningful style of religious art by his assiduous study of classical precedent. Some writers have concluded that he must have gained his mastery of the classical idiom by an apprenticeship in the archaizing workshops dedicated to producing a new Augustan art for the Emperor Frederick II. Nicola's style, however, is different from the archaistic manner of Apulia both in spirit and form, and at the same time it has much in common with the local schools of Tuscany and the north. His adoption of classical prototypes, furthermore, seems entirely explained by Vasari's story of his studying the Campo Santo fragments. Nicola's particular adaptation of antique formulas for contemporary needs must form the basis of any study of his work.

* Ed essendo fra molte spoglie di marmi stati condotti dall'armata de' Pisani, alcuni più antichi, che sono oggi nel Campo Santo di quella città; uno ve n'aveva fra gli altri bellissimo, nel quale era scolpita la caccia di Meleagro e del porco Calidonio con bellissima maniera. . . . Niccola, considerando la bontà di quest'opera e piacendogli fortemente, mise tanto studio e diligenza per imitare quella maniera, ed alcune altre buone sculture che erano in quegli altri pili antichi, che fu giuricato, non passò molto, il migliore scultore de' tempi suoi.—Giorgio Vasari, *Le vite,* I, 293–295; *Lives,* trans. Foster, I, 61

The monument in which this classical influence is most clearly revealed is the pulpit which he executed for the Baptistery of Pisa in 1260. It could be said first of all that Nicola recognized the technical superiority of ancient sculpture and adapted it to the religious sentiment of his time. This is a point of view that has little to do with the archaizing and pagan imitation of the antique sponsored by Frederick II. That revival was an entirely secular archaistic phenomenon without any real organic foundation, a school that sprang up at the Emperor's command and died with him. Nicola Pisano's different and truly creative use of the antique is magnificently illustrated by certain figures and panels on his Pisan pulpit. We may take as an example of his style a single figure, the representation of the Virtue of Fortitude (figure 92).

This statue, isolated from its setting, might almost be identified as an antique representation of Hercules. The complete nudity of the form and the pagan god's attributes of the club and lion are all part of the classical iconography. This is only one of many instances in the art of the Middle Ages, in which this great deity, the invincible preserver of the Roman emperors, assumes a Christian guise. There are many commentaries that point to Hercules as a pagan parallel for Samson, because of his strength and because both he and the biblical hero died for the love of woman. Dante in *The Divine Comedy* seems to point to Hercules' subjection of Cerberus as a prefiguration of Christ's Descent into Limbo.[1] In similar fashion the invicible strength of the ancient god came to be adopted as an appropriate personification of a Christian virtue. Nicola Pisano's model for his figure of Fortitude may have been the nude of Hippolytus in the Phaedra sarcophagus of the Campo Santo (figure 93). An even closer precedent exists in a sarcophagus with episodes from the Hercules myth in the Museo Nazionale at Rome (figure 94). Both the position of the legs and the arms and the tilt of the head in Nicola's figure are related to this antique prototype. Although seemingly so close to a classical model, Nicola's figure is in no sense a literal copy of this or any other precedent. He was interested in achieving a degree of naturalistic representation that would make more alive and meaningful the Christian symbols in scenes that he was called upon to depict; so that his figure is in no sense a merely retrospective use of antiquity, but the realization of a new visual reality achieved through the lessons provided by classical fragments. Part of Nicola's formula for creating a sense of the vital existence of his figures was to imbue them with a feeling for mass and bigness that was in a sense a simplification of the anatomy of his Roman models. In this respect his figure already has something of the power and monumentality of all later Tuscan art. The figure has a certain dryness of execution, a certain stiffness of pose that belies his not completely successful combination of the antique with nature. Like all of Nicola Pisano's images this one differs from its ancient prototype in the animation and expressiveness of the facial mask that seems to reveal the presence of inner thought, as though this personification of Christian strength were brooding intensely on the deployment of its physical strength. How successful this first nude of the Italian proto-Renaissance is in the sculptor's powerful suggestion of the organically integrated anatomy—an anatomy that once again evokes the combination of realism and abstraction of truly classical works. One need only compare it with the conventionalized, dry, and segmented representations of the nude in the Late Antique period to discern how completely successful Nicola Pisano has been in creating a new classicism.

Nicola's study of the Roman remains in the Campo Santo is evident in all of the panels illustrating episodes from the life of Christ on the pulpit of the Pisan Baptistery. In the scene of the Adoration of the Kings (figure 95), the figure of the Madonna has clearly been inspired by the enthroned Phaedra on the famous sarcophagus in the Campo Santo (figure 96). Here again the antique has only been a point of departure, not the final aim of the sculptor's art. Although the pose of the two figures is generally similar, Nicola Pisano has suppressed the intricate linear rhythms of the drapery in the Roman fragment in favor of a much broader and simplified handling of the folds, a technique that he apparently found useful for impressing a peculiarly heroic monumentality on his forms.

— 25 —

Classical Forms in
Fourteenth-Century Italy

[Giotto] of illustrious fame, not only equal of the ancient painters but superior in art and genius, restored the art of painting to its ancient dignity and renown.

—Villani *

THE fourteenth century—or the Trecento in Italy—is one of the great moments in the development of Western art. Its achievement could be regarded as the beginning of the modern world. The greatness and originality of this period of expression depend mainly on two factors which happened to converge in this moment of time. One was the discovery of the antique world; the other, the development of an Italian language, that is, an Italian language in literature and an Italian language in art.

In their puny mastery of architectural techniques and capacity in the plastic arts, the men of the thirteenth and early fourteenth centuries were like pygmies living in a giant's carcass, the skeleton of the classical past. Yet, all through the darkest period of the medieval night Italians remained conscious of the greatness of the Roman world. In the ninth century Alcuin observed, "Rome once headed the world; the world's pride, the city of gold stands now a pitiful ruin, the wreck of its glory of old." [1] By the fourteenth century little jingles invited the visitor to admire the monuments of Rome: "Come hither, and thou shalt see how fine my castles were, my towers, my mighty palaces and triumphal arches." [2] The famous medieval guidebook, the *Mirabilia Urbis Romae* (The Marvels of Rome), advertised for the pilgrim such famous sights as the Tombs of Romulus and Remus, the so-called statue of "Constantine" outside the

* [Giotto] non solum illustris fame decore antiquis pictoribus comparandus, sed arte et ingenio preferendus, in pristinam dignitatem nomenque maximum picturam restituit.
—Filippo Villani, *Cronica universale* (1348)

136

Lateran, the wreckage of the Colosseum, and the famed groups of horses on the Quirinal Hill. Some of these landmarks began to be included in paintings as symbolical indications of a Roman setting, and it was not long before the more progressive artists, in search of means to produce a moving realism for their dramatic presentation of Christian legend, discovered the models for their conceptions in the fragments of antiquity.

Many parallels could be drawn between the attitudes toward the ancient world exhibited in the creations of the great artists and writers. In this morning of the Renaissance which is the fourteenth century, Dante Alighieri shines like a bright star in the lightening firmament. The great artists who are his companion luminaries illustrate his method and thought in the conception of the classical world of this period. It is evident that his great work, *La Divina Commedia,* was an attempt to reforge a link with the classical world, in a way comparable to Frederick II's earlier attempt to reconstitute the empire of Augustus in the spheres of politics and art. For Dante, the value of the classical past was as a background for the Christian tradition just as much as the Old Testament was regarded as a forecast of the New. In the mind of the poet Christianity had superseded as well as absorbed the pagan tradition, and he did not regard it, as Petrarch did, as an entity separated in time from the world of the late Middle Ages.

The classical elements in the *La Divina Commedia* are not difficult to find. Dante's synthesis in his use of both Latin and Italian has its parallel in the living synthesis of ancient and medieval art forms in the work of Nicola d'Apulia and Ambrogio Lorenzetti. The key to an analysis of Dante's classicism in his relation to Virgil. "Tu se' lo mio maestro e'l mio autore," he writes in the *Inferno.*[3] Virgil is the model for Dante's style and he is chosen as the poet's guide through the regions of the next world, a journey that had its precedents in the visits of Odysseus and Aeneas to the realm of the shades. Virgil in his prophecy in the fourth Eclogue of the birth of a miraculous child provided a link between paganism and Christianity, and no less important from Dante's point of view was his heralding of the greatness of Rome and its empire, that same empire which Dante believed had endured to the Holy Roman Empire of his own day. Dante's admiration of his Augustan predecessor was also based on Virgil's loving descriptions of Italy in which Dante recognized the greatness of his country and the latinity of his own past. This sense of the Latin tradition so pronounced in Dante explains how artists turned to this same tradition in this period of rebuilding on the classic Italian heritage of Rome. Dante took his style from Virgil just as the artists of the Trecento awakened to the form and style of antiquity. In the same way, Dante's simplification of Virgil's poetic style parallels the simplification of Graeco-Roman fragments by painters and sculptors of the Trecento who adapted these models to their own Italian manner. Dante's transformation of the imagination and heroic concepts of the *Aeneid* into modern terms may be compared to Giotto's creation of a timeless visual language, both antique and Italian. Turning to the details of Dante's reliance on Virgil, his introduction of the creatures of antique fable—the centaurs, the harpies, the gorgons, Cerberus, Minos, and Charon—has its counterpart in the reappearance of this mythological repertoire in art.

Another aspect of Dante's relation to the pagan past is his knowledge of classical writers. It is not the number of ancient poets and philosophers known to him that is important, but the fact that he was able to discriminate on the worth of the ancient writings available to him. This literary discrimination of Dante's has no parallel in contemporary art: it is not until the sixteenth century that a similar selectivity in the appraisal of ancient works of art is noticeable; only in the writings of post-Renaissance men like Dolce and Armenini can one find a studied list of ancient masterpieces to be regarded as superior to all other surviving fragments. In Dante's time, and throughout the fifteenth century, the use of ancient models for their own inspiration by artists was completely undiscriminating with regard to both period and style.

Petrarch in a sonnet dedicated to a portrait of his dead love, Laura, painted by Simone Martini, wrote:

> And now to an image alone I cling—
> Made not by Zeuxis, nor Praxiteles, nor Phidias,
> But by a greater master of far higher genius.[4]

Here, and in another sonnet comparing Simone to Polyclitus, the facile recitation of the names of famous men of antiquity is mere rhetoric. The inclusion of these phantoms which Petrarch knew from literary sources indicates no knowledge of their artistic personalities but only a reverence for the vanished greatness of the world of Greek art which now appears to be imagined as a standard of final beauty which modern artists must emulate or surpass. It is the beginning of that nostalgia for the classic world that characterizes the true Renaissance of the fifteenth century.

There is a kind of lull in the pursuit of classical forms and techniques in the early fourteenth century before the veritable wave of antiquarianism that engulfed all the arts at the close of the Trecento. Among the artists of this period there are only sporadic borrowings to testify to the persistence of the classical heritage as a living tradition. Sometimes these borrowings are so completely disguised as to be almost unrecognizable. When Giotto uses the Temple of Minerva at Assisi as a background for one of his frescoes of the Life of St. Francis, he converts the Roman temple into a kind of Gothic pavilion decorated in the fashionable style of inlaid marble. There are other instances of this sporadic borrowing, as may be illustrated by Ghiberti's famous story of Ambrogio Lorenzetti and the Venus of Lysippus. Typical of this period, when antiquity was regarded as a kind of curiosity and even with a certain nostalgia, is the curious episode recounted by Gibbon, when in 1332 many Roman nobles died gallantly under the horns of wild bulls in the ruins of the Colosseum in the re-enactment of a gladiatorial show. In this period of seeming neglect of the classical past the Italian phase of Gothic art was devoted wholeheartedly to the achievement of a new realism illustrated at once in the convincing monumentality of the human figure and the expressiveness of gestures that at times seems an attempt to capture in pictorial terms the dramatic effectiveness of liturgical plays. If some observed classical remnant could aid in this development of an heroic language of painting, well and good; the antique, as much as nature, might be used to this end. But at the same time there was not the least interest on the part of artists in the aesthetic qualities of bygone art. In some ways the art of the Trecento in Italy is not unlike the development of thirteenth-century sculpture in France, in which, as at Reims, only an occasional exploration of classical form interrupted a general trend in the solution of problems of realism.

The examination of a few examples of recognizable borrowings from the antique by the Italian masters of the fourteenth century reveals the tenor of the age. One of the most beautiful panels in the famous *Maestà* by the Sienese painter, Duccio di Buoninsegna, is the Three Marys at the Tomb (figure 97). This panel is one of a long series devoted to a detailed pictorial history of Christ's life and Passion in the altarpiece completed in 1311 for the Cathedral at Siena. The composition is a familiar one, with many antecedents in earlier Byzantine and Romanesque art. At the left are the three Marys, and at the right, seated on the tilted lid of the open sarcophagus, is the luminous apparition of the angel who announces that Christ has risen. It is the figure of this celestial visitor that is of special interest. The angel is dressed in a radiant white robe, an adaptation of the classical himation worn over an inner vest or chiton. The drawing of this beautiful figure is spectacular in its evocation of the linear poetry of a draped classical statue. The dazzling snowy whiteness of the angel's robe is intensified by the bluish-green tinge of the modeling. This dress is represented with an intricate system of bunched folds that have the same suggestion of the arrangement of a classical garment as the famous Visitation group at Reims (figure 86). In a somewhat parallel way Duccio's drawing of this figure suggests the same kind of translation of a classic image into linear terms that is seen in the Reims group and even more in the drawings of draped figures by Villard de Honnecourt. One cannot be sure if Duccio's beautiful drawing of the angel (figure 97) is actually derived from a classical fragment or whether, as in so much of this artist's work, this is another indication of contact with the Gothic north, in this case with the master of the classical figures at Reims. This is the only detail in all of Duccio's work of what seems to be a real apprehension of classical form. Although this is an evocation of an angelic being, it displays a real feeling for the solid articulation of the body beneath the waves of its shining drapery. Again, as in all of Duccio's work, the drawing shows his sensitivity for an exquisitely composed silhouette and a softly fluid rhythm of lines here deployed in the complex transformation of classical form into animated linear pattern.

A remarkably interesting document of classical taste in the Trecento is the miniature painted by the great Gothic artist Simone Martini for a codex of Virgil belonging to his friend Petrarch (figure 98). The poet had lost this precious manuscript, and this frontispiece presumably was added when the book finally came to light. This little illumination is a work of Simone's last years, when he and Petrarch were resident in Avignon, the sea of the exiled papacy. Petrarch dedicated a number of sonnets to his painter friend and added some words of praise to this picture which Simone painted for him.

> Like Mantua which Virgil hymned in song
> So Siena rejoices in Simone who painted her thus.[5]

This illustration seeks to personify the works of Virgil. At the top Servius, the annotator of the codex, draws a curtain to reveal Virgil to

Aeneas. Below, a peasant with a pruned grapevine stands for the Georgics, and a shepherd milking an ewe for the Eclogues. Simone's painting has little to do with Petrarch's nostalgic yearning for antiquity. It is more a medieval fantasy of the pagan past than a borrowing from antique sources. It represents that familiar tendency in medieval art to reduce the classical to contemporary terms. Aeneas is a dapper figure dressed in a modification of Byzantine armor usually reserved for the representation of warrior saints. Virgil himself, reclining, book in hand and looking to heaven for inspiration, is like a representation of St. John on Patmos. His beautiful white robe with its long flowing lines is typical of Simone's sinuous Gothic draftsmanship. Typical also is the rather weightless, wraithlike character of Virgil and his visitors. In striking contrast are the figures personifying Virgil's bucolic poetry: the vivid action and homely realism of these tattered *contadini* are obviously something recalled from everyday observation that has nothing to do with any ancient source.

Another name in the story of painting in Siena that has always been linked with an awareness of antiquity is that of Ambrogio Lorenzetti. This association is based largely on a story related by Lorenzo Ghiberti in his commentaries. The Florentine chronicler, after describing several classical statues dug up in various parts of Italy, goes on to say:

> Still another one was found in the city of Siena for reason of which they made great holiday and by the intelligentsia it was deemed a most marvellous work, and on the base was written the name of the master, who was a most excellent master: his name was Lysippus. . . . I saw this statue only as drawn by a very great painter of the city of Siena who was called Ambrogio Lorenzetti. . . . Everyone praised the statue greatly, and also the great painters who then were in Siena—to every one it seemed absolutely perfect.[6]

The honors bestowed upon it, with its setting up in the Piazza del Campo, were blamed for the subsequent reverses in Siena's endless conflict with Florence, and so the statue was smashed to fragments and buried in Florentine territory. It is not certain whether this image was a representation of Aphrodite or Poseidon, and no single figure in Lorenzetti's work suggests such an antique original. There is, however, one detail in the artist's fresco of Good Government in the Palazzo Pubblico in Siena that has often evoked comparisons with classical prototypes. This is the figure of the personified Pax or Peace (figure 99), which occupies a prominent position in the group of virtues typifying the benefits of just rule in the

Commune. The figure is part of the painter's complex allegory of the common good, the *bonum commune,* uppermost in the minds of the citizenry of medieval Siena. Although Peace and Concord are associated with the common welfare in the political philosophy of St. Thomas Aquinas, these virtues were also the twin ideals of Roman political thought as expressed by writers like Cicero and Sallust. It is perhaps for this reason that the resemblance in the figure of Peace to classical art is not pure coincidence. Peace is represented as a woman reclining on a couch, dressed in a loose garment like a shift, and decked with a laurel wreath. She is reminiscent of reclining figures on Roman coins or of certain figures of the goddess Phaedra on Roman sarcophagi (figure 100). The almost diaphanous garment worn by the figure is painted in a web of flowing parallel lines which creates the impression of the thin stuff clinging to the body and revealing the soft form of breasts and abdomen with extraordinary success. Whereas the painting of the upper part of the body reveals an approximation of a classical prototype, the folds of the garment draping the legs are painted in the conventional Gothic formula that reduces the drapery to a succession of V-shaped forms and pipelike vertical masses. One has the feeling that Ambrogio Lorenzetti was like a man with a limited vocabulary in a foreign language, falling back into his own tongue when unable to find the proper phrase. In addition to the figure of Peace there are other indications of Ambrogio's awareness of classical forms, such as the busts of the seasons that are part of his decoration in the Palazzo Pubblico. Collectively these borrowings reveal an artistic personality sensible to the appropriateness of the antique both for the quasi-classical erudition of his allegories and for the realization of convincingly solid forms.

Many critics of the painting of the Trecento have pointed out the classical qualities in the mosaics and frescoes of the great Roman painter, Pietro Cavallini. Although certainly the breadth of his handling in the painting of the monumental forms in his wall-painting of the Last Judgment in Santa Cecilia in Trastevere may suggest the massive plasticity of Early Christian or Roman painting, Cavallini has a typically Gothic tendency to muffle his figures in heavy garments so stiff and full that they completely conceal the articulation of the bodies beneath. Like the dress of the figures at Reims (figure 86) they might be thick outer shells that do not appear to contain a real corporeal form. Much more classical in his technique and in his adherence to antique precedents is an unknown Roman artist, perhaps a pupil of Cavallini, who painted a series of frescoes devoted to the story of Isaac in the upper church of San Francesco at Assisi. This artist is usually referred to as the Isaac Master.

Following a Greco-Roman precedent already re-established in tenth-century manuscripts like the Paris Psalter, each episode in the Old Testament story is related in a separate panel, just as was the case in the Pompeian wall-paintings of events in classical mythology. Many of the draped figures in the Isaac Master's frescoes show an unmistakable classical feeling; so, for example, the robe of Abraham in the scene of the Sacrifice of Isaac (figure 101) is like a pictorial version of the drapery of the famous Sophocles of the Lateran (figure 102). In the Hellenistic statue the folds of the pallium pulled tightly across the body stand out as sharp, weltlike ridges. In the thirteenth-century painting a similar garment is worn by the prophet, and similar folds are indicated by painting a salient highlight reinforced by a streak of dark shadow, so that as in the statue these ridges stand out prominently in relief over the flat areas of the drapery. Many of the heads in these frescoes with their dark rose complexions shine with lustrous gleaming highlights, so that the effect is almost like polished bronze. This effect may be seen particularly well in the beautiful head of Isaac in the scene of Jacob's Offering (figure 103). The painting of Isaac's beard as a shimmering web of highlights gives an impression of the metallic crispness of the hair in an ancient metal image. The presentation of the drama in poignant Biblical stories has a peculiarly moving psychological tension established by the moving glances and gestures uniting the participants in the individual panels. This poignancy of dramatic expression is in itself more Gothic than antique and is a quality which, together with his statuesquely composed forms, seems to relate the Isaac Master to the greatest of the Florentine painters of the fourteenth century, Giotto di Bondone.

Particular classical elements in Giotto's work are rather difficult to pin down to exact precedents, perhaps because this master's classicism has a truly universal character, a monumental form language of his own creation. In all the great works of his mature period, notably the great series of frescoes illustrating the lives of Christ and the Madonna in the Arena chapel at Padua, Giotto developed a peculiarly classical generalized type. By classical in the present instance is meant that the features are indicated in a few generalized smooth planes with sharp breaks in the transition from one surface to another to produce types suggestive of the idealized masks of classical sculpture. The modeling of the bodies as well as the faces is simplified to an arbitrary reinforcement of the contours to make the shapes stand out in relief. This formula confers a kind of super-human nobility to Giotto's heads and figures. Their massive rock-cut proportions connote their more than mortal strength and stature. The very bigness of bodies and features is intended to give them a majestic and properly speaking statuesque monumentality. As in the work of Nicola Pisano the humanity and tangibility of the sacred personages is heightened by Giotto's painting them in such solid, unmistakably real form.

The accepted tradition of clothing Biblical figures in timeless classical garments was an aid to the artist in the painting of figures of monumental breadth. In this final consolidation of his style everything that Giotto paints has the hardness and solidity of stone. There is a tremendous emphasis on the realizing of the solidity of the forms, which appear to be literally hewn from one universal substance. This is the final realization of Giotto's monumental style. But even this tremendous solemnity is relieved by such piquant touches as the dog fawning on Joachim, which makes the whole conception dramatically alive.

One of Giotto's noblest compositions is his portrayal of the Mourning over the Body of Christ, a scene of overwhelming tragedy and grief cast in an heroic mold (figure 104). Even in this scene of violence and un-restraint there is a composure and dignity that save it from degenerating into bathos. The figure of Christ appears as the core in the plastic organization of the composition, which in its general arrangement may have been borrowed from a classical relief representing the Death of Meleager (figure 105). There is a completely logical articulation of the story and a very large design which completely embody the pathos and grandeur of the Scripture with an elimination of all triviality and, one might say as in classic art, giving the most intrinsic significance of the event in concrete form. It has the unity of a great pediment composition. All the gestures and glances of the figures converge in the cat's-cradle of hands about the head of the dead Christ. The individual faces show expressions of grief, but these expressions are really the abstractions of tragic masks. The grief is more strongly expressed by the pose and gesture

144

of the great weighty forms, like blocks of marble sunk in sorrow. Even the landscape bends to the universal grief, and the human tragedy has its shrill antiphonal in the lamentations of the angels who, like birds of woe, fill the whole sky with their distress.

Giotto was one of the few men of his time to have the universal vision which Dante revealed in *The Divine Comedy*. In both cases this was un-questionably a universality that was rooted both in the observation of nature and on the foundation of a classical past. Giotto was one of the great pictorial geniuses who created a world that was both timeless and in its poignant naturalism an intensification of the life of his own time. Giotto, in addition to his absorption of the lessons of monumental classi-cal art, was like Dante in his study of nature and in his observation and realization of characteristic human actions with real vivacity and in-tensity. One could point also to the artist's creation of dramatic and pathetic scenes, and he is like Dante in his creation of an expressive art based on his own human experience. It could be said that Giotto's crea-tion was a greater achievement, since in his renewal of painting he did not have behind him a great unbroken tradition such as Dante found in medieval and classical poetry. Like all the artists of his period Giotto's knowledge of the Greco-Roman tradition was based only on those few scattered fragments of indifferent quality that had survived the ages of barbarism. In a truly classical way both Giotto and Dante bestow a monu-mentality on their creatures by the way in which they simplify nature to colossal universals, so that nature is raised to a transfigured and absolute level. Their personages are like colossal actors on an earthly stage. Giotto's personages, although recalling the titanic aloofness of classical statues, are so based on nature in gesture and detail that they assume a moving dramatic expressiveness through this foundation in reality.

— 26 —

The Renaissance in Italy

The history of the Renaissance is not the history of arts, or of sciences, or of literature, or even of nations. It is the history of the attainment of self-conscious freedom by the human spirit manifested in the European races. It is no mere political mutation, no new fashion of art, no restoration of classical standards of taste. The arts and the inventions, the knowledge and the books, which suddenly became vital at the time of the Renaissance, had long lain neglected on the shores of the Dead Sea which we call the Middle Ages. It was not their discovery which caused the Renaissance. But it was the intellectual energy, the spontaneous outburst of intelligence, which enabled mankind at that moment to make use of them. The force then generated still continues, vital and expansive, in the spirit of the modern world.

—Symonds *

THE Renaissance or, to give it its Italian name, the *Rinascimento,* is a period in history associated with the revival or rebirth of the learning of the ancients. It was dominated by the twin interests of humanism, which could be defined as the intelligent comprehension of antiquity, and individualism or the realization of personal psychology. The Renaissance was the period of the first great explorers: Amerigo Vespucci, who gave his name to a small continent, Cabot, and Columbus. All discoverers, all voyagers know in advance what they are to find, and so when they reached the palmy shores of Hispaniola they knew they had reached the mysterious Indies. So other seekers in art, humanities, and science, searching for man, were bound to find him, and artists and humanists in their exploration of antiquity felt sure they had discovered the secrets of Phidias and Apelles.

Actually in Italy the Renaissance represents an acceleration of tendencies that had always been there: the enthusiastic study and imitation of classical literature and classical art, which had survived the Middle Ages through the Italians' sense of their Latin past. The fifteenth century

* John Addington Symonds, *Renaissance in Italy*

brought what was only a more scientific study of this classical tradition and its adaptation to the present. The very presence of antique fragments had always stimulated a kind of unscientific imitation of these models. In a literary way these fragments had inspired Hildebert and Petrarch with dreams of the golden age of Roman greatness.

Perhaps the first real Renaissance personality was Petrarch in the fourteenth century with his learned approach to antiquity and his interest in ancient Rome as something remote that yet had a significance for the present. His mind was filled with a dream-image of the classical period based on his admiration for Virgil and Ovid, so that he was concerned with sites rather than monuments, in what was a literary approach. For Petrarch the ancient monuments were not so much aesthetic treasures of a past age as emblems of Roman virtue that promised future greatness in the poet's vision of the revival of Rome as *caput mundi:* they were symbols, tangible reminders of the pagan and Christian past, testaments of Roman virtue; for the collector, the possession of such antiquities was to incite the owner to follow the ways of the ancients which these tokens personified. The monuments, both inscriptions and figures, were only images of antiquity in a moral, political, and literary sense, mementos of great men and their virtue and testimonies to ancient heroes. This was a nonvisual approach, not unlike the literary outlook of the modern historian, philologist, and sightseer—an interest in the associations evoked by famous monuments rather than their artistic properties.[1]

In the Renaissance men recognized in the antique a concrete ideal of spiritual independence, a guide to the constitution of a truly humanist world. Ancient literature in its emphasis on morality, valor, and virtue offered a confirmation of the importance of man in his earthly role to dominate the universe by the force of his individuality and spiritual fiber. In a similar way the beauty of ancient art could be adapted to endow the representation of man with a dignity and heroic pride appropriate to his new place at the center of the cosmos. The humanist poets recognized an absolute norm in the writings of the ancients, not only as a stylistic authority but as a way of life, thought, and usage. The beauties of antiquity, plastic and literary, hidden in the earth or in the pages of ancient folios, emerged to sweep through the learned and artistic world like a revolutionary fire. For artistic invention as well as the creation of the mystical concepts of Neoplatonism the love of ancient things was the agent for the birth of a new spiritual world. Just as Alberti, echoing a fundamental

147

Neoplatonic concept, sought a reconciliation of Christian and pagan ideas, so in art the adoption of the ancient forms converted Paradise to Olympus.

It was nothing new in Italy for artists as well as critics to reinforce their practice and arguments by reference to ancient literature. The late Gothic master, Cennino Cennini, was aware of Quintilian, and Petrarch proposed to base his accounts of the arts on Pliny. In the Renaissance these old sources were restudied so that their wisdom could be used by artists to create anew like the ancients. By the middle fifteenth century the whole corpus of classic literature and the arts had been systematized into a body of knowledge indispensable to every artist.

It should not be supposed that the empirical codifying of ancient systems of ancient proportion, color, and drawing led to an archaistic resuscitation of the antique. The Renaissance was more a transfiguration than a resurrection of the classical ideal. The many individual artists from 1400 to 1550 were primarily concerned with the imaginative expression of reality rendered grand and harmonious by the principles of science. The study of the antique was only a part of that science. Whether art, as for Leonardo, was a divine instrument for the universal clarification of all phenomena, or, as for Michelangelo, the means for externalizing his titanic vision of the human journey to God, the antique was only one contributing factor for the realization of a true classicism, a great formal harmony joined with the expression of thought and sentiment. The reminiscences of ancient things are present in the work of Renaissance artists because these men recognized their authority as much as they acknowledged the value of scientific laws of vision, just as earlier artists had relied implicitly on the styles of their masters and on the rules of the craft.

The fifteenth century brings the first direct study of Hellenic culture lost for one thousand years. It is a period marked, too, by the devotion of the greatest minds of the age to the study of antique sources. There appeared new translations of classic texts and a frantic search for surviving manuscripts of classical writers, a treasure-hunt which unearthed, among other things, the famous writings on architecture by Vitruvius. Accompanying this enthusiasm for the tangible remains of the pagan past was the foundation of academies modeled on their ancient predecessors, in which the members not only took antique names but adopted a pagan mode of living as well.

In conjuring up a picture of a glorious age, devoted to the higher beauties and philosophy of the classic period, one should not forget that the society of the humanist, the artist, and their patrons was as remote from the people as the metaphysical concepts of scholasticism were beyond and apart from the common folk of the Middle Ages. The antique virtues and wisdom celebrated by the humanists had no actuality in a life even more brutal and sordid than the age that preceded it. The ruthlessness of medieval tyrannies was only intensified and systematized in the Renaissance. "It was an age of treachery and devotion, brutality and civility, vice and grace, all fired by love of gold, of beauty, of pleasure, of fame, and sometimes of God." [2]

Of this mundane devotion to material joys and pedantic erudition the classical art of the Renaissance was an integral part, but in the case of many artists, even the great Botticelli, classical motifs were only an overlay on a medieval structure. The work of a sculptor such as Ghiberti is filled with medieval survivals. His pictorial conceptions in bronze with their tall flamelike figures often seem like metal counterparts of the still Gothic composition of a painter like Lorenzo Monaco. The fragile beauty of Botticelli's Venus is almost more evocative of a tapered Gothic Madonna in ivory than of a classic statue. For all the artists' enthusiasm and erudition for the renewal of the ancient past, their actual styles were not matched by an advance in the unified application of the new discoveries in the sciences of perspective and optics until well on in the Quattrocento. This is the achievement of the High Renaissance, the age of consummation in the sixteenth century, which saw painters and sculptors creating a new classic language in art with a unified vocabulary of expression far different from the halting phrases ventured by the pioneers of the fifteenth century.

Whereas in medieval art the aim of artists under the direction of priestly authority was to emphasize unreal and spiritual forms through the splendor of material evoking the luster of paradise and to present symbols of moral and religious import in accordance with traditional recipes, in the fifteenth century science and art were dedicated to rendering the outside world intelligible in a rational way and in accordance with newly discovered scientific laws governing appearance. The science of perspective and reliance on the models of antiquity were more important than Cennino Cennini's emphasis on the chemistry of colors. In such a world the old symbolical art which relied on the beauty of unreal, even abstract, shapes had no place. In the Quattrocento, the study of nature, the investigation of laws of perspective, and especially the formal lessons of the antique provided a new and different discipline. A reliance on vision replaced the formulas of the recipe books in the quest for the presentation of a rational view of reality. Intellectually, as Alberti maintained, it was preferable to imitate gold in colors than to employ the gold leaf of earlier tradition.

The enthusiasm for the aesthetic beauty of classical art in the early Renaissance might be compared to the discovery of the primitive by Gauguin and Picasso. Just as these painters made a fragmentary use of South Sea island fetishes and African masks, both as a protest against academic tradition and for the intrinsic formal expressiveness they discerned in these idols, so fifteenth-century artists like Ghiberti, Brunelleschi, and Donatello introduced borrowings from classical sources because they found these prototypes aesthetically exciting, and because they were useful models to achieve a realism more moving than the rigid conventions of the Trecento. The use of primitive art in modern times never approached the scientific ordering of classical sources that followed in the later decades of the Quattrocento, but the initial employment of these native arts parallels the Renaissance infatuation with antiquity.

The circumstances that made this revival of antiquity possible were the stability and independence that had gradually grown with the establishment of the Italian communes and the desire of these citizens of the Latin world to develop in the pride of their heritage a culture that would match the vanished splendor of antiquity. It was part of the opportunity that, with security and a measure of liberty, enabled men to examine themselves and the world of which they were a part. The pursuit of antiquity was only another aspect of the rational scientific exploration of that world in its totality that is associated with Leonardo's experiments.

To stress the change that took place in the Renaissance art of the fifteenth century a distinction could be drawn between the attitude of the Romanesque, Gothic, and Renaissance periods toward the achievement of realism. Whereas in the Romanesque period the dominant aim was to create the realism of the supernatural world in appropriately symbolical terms with no reference to the world of nature, the Gothic artist, conceiving nature as a reflection of the beauty of God, took nature as a point of departure for a preconceived and still abstract idea of beauty combined with the unscientific recording of many observed details. In the Renaissance, which was not a religious period, the beauty of man and

150

nature prevails over all and they are the object of scientific study for their own sake in order to create in art the objective reality of a world of which man was the center and measure.

Romanesque art included in its symbolical representations a great many inheritances of misunderstood classic forms and techniques. There is a naïve visual approach to antiquity, as in the twelfth-century sculpture of Provence, an attitude that continues in the Gothic period with an only more direct imitation of actual models. At Reims and with Nicola d'Apulia, antiquity becomes a second language for the realization of a divine beauty to be revealed in apprehensible terms. There is nothing scientific or antiquarian about the Gothic approach. It is only in the Renaissance that such a scientific imitation of antiquity begins as part of a program dedicated to realizing in the fullest possible way the beauty man discerned in himself. Now for the first time the recognition of the beauty of the human image in fragments of ancient statuary could be utilized to surpass and not imitate nature. The antique becomes part of man's efforts to create a truly objective image of the homocentric world. The beauty of ancient forms and the poetry of mythology become a new and never-ending source of creative imagination.

For Early Renaissance artists like Ghiberti, Brunelleschi, and Donatello, it was as though the shell of an observatory had been opened to reveal to their eager eyes a new universe, the classical realm, inviting unlimited imaginative exploration. Ghiberti's passionate delight in the discovery of ancient statuary reveals how in the fifteenth century these relics were appreciated for their aesthetic attraction rather than for what they represented as symbols of past glories and religious, as well as historical, associations. Just as classic literature came to be valued for reasons of its style rather than its moral content, classical art, which had survived the Middle Ages, assumed a new aesthetic importance. The writings of Cicero and Virgil attracted the humanists by the beauty of their style rather than by what they had to say. Now the sculptors and painters suddenly found a whole new world for secrets of representation that would enable them to create forms not only real but beautiful. The burning excitement that drove Brunelleschi and Donatello to ransack the ruins of Rome for the discovery of lost principles of beauty was different from Nicola d'Apulia's mechanical repetition of the lessons of the Pisan sarcophagi. Antiquity had been rediscovered as a fascinating novelty, but the real novelty lay not in these ancient remains but in the way of looking at them.

Classical subject matter had been used for illustration by painters and sculptors in medieval times either as an illustration of the appearance of the ancient deities, as decoration, or in moral allegories. There was no savoring of the myths for their own intoxicating and dangerous pagan allure. Part of the Renaissance attitude was the awakening to the beauties of ancient literature for its own sake and for its revelation of the nature of the gods. Once again, the gods take on their ancient shapes in the attempt to recapture the forms and wisdom of the ancients, their poetic imagination, and their knowledge of the world.

The Olympians, when they appeared in medieval art, were accoutered in the dress of the time, and only in the fifteenth century did artists desire to reveal their true nature, partly for Neoplatonic reasons, partly for the creation of aesthetic delight. In this respect the study of the antique representations of the vanished titans was indispensable to artists who only followed Politian's lead in evoking the beauty and fire of the gods in the verses of *La Giostra.*

Salutati's work of 1396 on the Labors of Hercules, recounting the adventures of the god for their own sake and not for any Christian symbolical reasons, has its parallel in the portrayal of the classical hero as a pagan figure by an anonymous Florentine sculptor on the Porta della Mandorla of the Florentine Duomo. It is perhaps not surprising that, given the survival of works of ancient sculptors and the absence of ancient painting in the fourteenth century, sculptors should have availed themselves of examples for improving their medium before painters turned to the very same source of inspiration. Botticelli's Venus follows the description of Aphrodite Anadyomene, as provided by Politian in his poem, so closely is it like an attempt to reconstruct a lost masterpiece of Apelles. For a visual aid it was natural that Botticelli should turn to one of the many versions of the Venus Pudica such as the famous example in the Medici collection.

The old themes, set in a dreamlike world, became a source for hidden allegories relating to the hopes and loves of mortal princes, a complex language of symbolism inspired and dictated by the humanists' passionate exploration of the mysteries of Neoplatonism. The gods became emblems of gallantry and cosmological magic, and it is not at all surprising to find, in an early edition of *La Giostra,* a woodcut representing Giuliano dei Medici invoking Pallas Athena to bestow upon him fame and valor, inevitable components of the Renaissance man's ruthless pursuit of *virtù,* the ultimate ideal of personal achievement and grandeur.

The dawn of the fifteenth century inaugurated the evocation of the antique world for learned humanists in a new and complete visual interpretation based on actual study of antique fragments. The antique came to impress artists as a means for creating "better than nature" precisely by following these ancient norms. From such a study grew a more relaxed treatment of the human form, the realization of tactile value and the organic articulation of the body.

At first the humanist scholars were interested only in the subject matter of antiquity; the artists, in its aesthetic quality. In the later decades of the Quattrocento there was a gradual integration of these points of view. This rapprochement comes about with the humanists' collecting of antique fragments and the artists' approach to classical remains in their artistic and scholarly aspects. In the resulting exchange of ideas art becomes an accepted part of the humanists' endeavor and program.

On the whole the Quattrocento artist was indebted to antiquity for motives rather than for any code of formal aesthetics. Later these motives became so transformed as to defy identification. Antiquarianism and artistic stimulation from the antique take many forms. For one thing the artists of the fifteenth century display a stylistic diversity in the variety of ancient styles from which they choose their models. For them there was an equal worth to all fragments of the illustrious past. There is apparently no selective evaluation of ancient masterpieces in this opening period of the Renaissance, no attempts at establishing a canon of taste. The Quattrocento approach to the antique shows how every artist sees what he is prepared to see in each ancient work of art. He is apt to select isolated quotations from ancient sources, details of costume and furnishing to give historical accuracy to his scenes, or items like triumphal arches selected for purely symbolical reasons. Often quotations from a number of ancient figures are absorbed and recombined in a single new creation. This is part of the Renaissance artist's dependence on the antique translation of nature for his conquest of reality, most of all for his mastery of perfected anatomy. Again the early Renaissance owes the sculpturesque quality of its pictorial style to the vision of antiquity. It is important to note that the style of the ancient models is never literally copied; in the process of assimilation and digestion of antique motifs the artist comes to create in the antique style rather than producing strict imitations of classical prototypes.

The difference in point of view that separates the Renaissance of the fifteenth century from the Middle Ages is that, whereas in the Gothic world antiquities were occasionally used in a rather practical way as models to make forms more convincingly real, in the Quattrocento there was a gradual awakening to the intrinsic beauty of these ancient shapes to create a new beauty worthy of the pride and confidence artists now felt in themselves and in their time. Ancient objects of all kinds from sculpture to gems, although used by some scholars mainly as illustrations of the appearance of the gods described in literary sources, also began to awaken a new aesthetic response. Vasari's account of how Donatello was regarded as the first modern sculptor to vie with the ancients is an indication of the recognition of the perfection of Greek and Roman antiquity. Alberti's treatises on architecture, sculpture, and painting were only the scholarly systematization of what, in the late fifteenth century, was an established taste and an established authority. What in the opening decades of the Quattrocento had been a haphazard enthusiasm, a deliriously exciting discovery of a new source for a whole world of visual images and techniques, came more and more to be ordered into such systematic compendia. This trend to classify and codify becomes increasingly evident in the High Renaissance. The catalogues of classical images to be admired in Rome and Michelangelo's measuring of the Horse-tamers of Montecavallo are only two instances of the evolution from random enthusiasm to scientific method in the appreciation and use of the antique as an ultimate authority of perfection.

Whereas in the Middle Ages the works of ancient writers like Cicero and Ovid and Virgil were a source for moralizing parallels with Christian concepts or prophecies of Christ's coming, in the Renaissance these classic works came to be regarded more for their style than their content: the beauty of the prose and verse in which they expressed themselves mattered more than what they had to say. Similarly, the aesthetic appearance of the surviving works of antique art was now more important than what they represented. Artists became fired with the ambition of themselves achieving or indeed surpassing the intrinsic beauty recognized in the ancient marbles and bronzes.

The collecting activities of humanists like Poggio Bracciolino and Niccolò Niccoli were only another aspect of the new fervor of discovery

154

that, according to Vasari's legend, sent Brunelleschi and Donatello to explore the wreckage of ancient Rome. Although earlier men, such as Master Gregory and his Venus,[3] may have looked with something approaching aesthetic curiosity at works of ancient art, such instances were sporadic in the Middle Ages. The novelty in the fifteenth century was not the material, which had always been available, but in the way of looking at it. The excitement of discovery and admiration shines through Ghiberti's accounts of the antique masterpieces he had seen in all parts of Italy.

Before 1450 it was the scholars rather than the merchant princes who collected antiquities. The humanist Niccolò Niccoli collected all kinds of things—coins, statues, portraits, bronzes, and gems. These things were prized for their evocation of history. Niccoli lived among his antiquities as a stimulating surrounding to relive and revive the past; he also liked his objects to be beautiful. Another famous collector and hunter of manuscripts was Poggio Bracciolino, who, although he had something of the usual literary interpretation of ancient monuments, actually made a list of the ruins in Rome; that is, as monuments and not as sites of events in history. This approach marks a complete change from the entirely literary interest of Petrarch in the previous century. Poggio relates: "I have had my bedroom furnished with marble heads; one is elegant and intact, the others have had their noses broken off, but still they will delight a good artist . . . My disease is that I admire too much perhaps and more than a learned man should, those marbles carved by great artists." He speaks of how the ancient sculptors "represent even emotions of the soul so that a thing which can feel neither pain nor joy looks to you as if it laughed or mourned." [4]

The last act in the interaction of humanist and artistic pursuits reveals the spectacle of the humanists' guiding artists to ancient art so that the painters and sculptors would be able to create the new world of revived antiquity which the humanists longed for.

— 27 —

Lorenzo Ghiberti

Also, I have seen in a diffused light the most perfect sculptures which were executed with the greatest skill and care. Among these I saw in Rome in Olympiad 440 [1447 A.D.] the statue of a hermaphrodite . . . which had been made with admirable skill . . . Also I saw in Padua a statue . . . a marvel among the other sculptures. Among the other admirable things I saw is a wonderful chalcedony intaglio which was owned by one of our citizens, Niccolò Niccoli. He was a most diligent man and in our time was an investigator and collector of many excellent antique things.   —Ghiberti *

THE first great sculptor of the Italian Renaissance who based his style on classical antiquity was the Florentine Lorenzo Ghiberti. The legends of antique sculptors reported by Ghiberti in his commentaries, together with his descriptions of statues he had himself seen, testified to this sculptor's studied devotion to ancient art. Like every Renaissance artist it was his aim to extract an idealized image of reality from nature, and to this program the study of antique sculpture was intimately linked. Classical sculpture for Ghiberti was not nature itself, but it could reveal the principles and rules governing nature. There he could find ready for use an already edited and improved presentation of nature.

Ghiberti's earliest important work is the bronze panel representing the Sacrifice of Isaac (figure 106), which he submitted in 1402 as his entry in a competition for the commission to execute the bronze doors of the

* Ancora ò uedeto in una temperata luce cose scolpite molto perfette et fatte con grandissima arte et diligentia, fra'lle quali uidi in Roma nella olimpia quattro-cento quaranta una statua d'uno Ermafrodito . . . la quale statua era stata fatta con mirabile ingegno . . . Ancora uidi in Padoua una statua . . . questa statua è merauigliosa fra l'altre scultur[e]. Fra l'altre egregie cose io uidi mai è uno calcidonio intaglato in cauo mirabilmente el quale era nelle mani d'uno nostro cittadino, era il suo nome Nicholaio Nicholi: fu huomo diligentissimo et ne' nostri tempi fu investigatore et cercatore di moltissime et egregie cose antiche.—Lorenzo Ghiberti, *I Commentarii,* ed. Schlosser, III, 4

Baptistery at Florence. At the upper right of the panel the figure of God leans from the sky to arrest the hand of Abraham at the very moment when he is about to sacrifice his son Isaac, who kneels nude upon an altar. The left-hand side of the panel is occupied by the figures of two servants and a donkey before a stylized rocky landscape. All of the figures are gilded and stand out in magnificent relief against the dull brown patina of the background. The quatrefoil enframement of the composition is an inheritance from Gothic times and had been used in 1330 by Andrea Pisano for the south doors of the Florentine Baptistery. Ghiberti's arrangement of the figures in groups is not integrated in accordance with a unified compositional harmony, so that these different parts of the episode, as in many medieval reliefs, appear haphazardly combined. The depth of the relief is reminiscent of the illusionistic spatial treatment of Roman carving of the Flavian period, a mode that must have been especially congenial to Ghiberti, who more and more with the development of his sculptural career created his reliefs almost as pictures in bronze. This competition panel of Ghiberti's also provides an example of the artful assimilation of antique motifs that the sculptor increasingly pursued throughout his life. The beautiful figure of the kneeling Isaac is an amazing revelation of how, for the first time since the end of antiquity, a sculptor could create a pulsing and lyrically articulate nude body. The flow of muscles under the shining sheath of skin is wonderfully rendered. The qualities of warmth and taut aliveness in the youthful frame are partly the result of a study of an actual body, partly the result of ordering the inequalities of a particular anatomy according to the simplified scheme of an already idealized nude of classical times. Although it is not entirely possible to point to the particular source of Ghiberti's inspiration, the rendering and pose of his figure of Isaac recall one of the kneeling boys from the Niobe group (figure 107) or a torso now in the Uffizi that is reputed to have been in Ghiberti's possession (figure 108). It is apparent that this sensuous perception of the beauty of the naked body and its convulsive animation are quite different from any antique prototype. By comparison the Fortitude by Nicola d'Apulia, in itself a remarkable achievement for the thirteenth century, appears like a stiff mannequin laboriously achieved.

Other details in the composition reveal Ghiberti's passionate search in the dustbins of classical statuary that had lain so long neglected. The head of Abraham is a classical Zeus and, as Professor Krautheimer has pointed out, the attendant servants are borrowings from a sarcophagus with the Pelops story, which exists in a number of versions.

Ghiberti won the contest for the Baptistery doors from his nearest rival, the architect Filippo Brunelleschi, probably because Ghiberti's composition was so completely suited to the rising classical taste of the day. Ghiberti had had a predecessor in the resuscitation of classical form and content in the anonymous sculptor who carved the decoration of the Porta della Mandorla on the Cathedral of Florence between the years 1391 and 1396. The contrast between the classical subjects of this carving and the entirely Gothic character of their enframement is very striking, as is the representation of Hercules (figure 109), which unmistakably implies a classical prototype in the feeling for plastic values, the entirely fluid movement of the body, and the sculptor's subtle treatment of the small interlocking planes of the anatomy. This is not only one of the earliest illustrations of a modern sculptor's selecting an antique model for the solution of his problem in the representation of reality, but also one of the first examples since ancient times of the use of the antique motif without change in iconography. Hercules appears as himself. It seems possible that there may be a connection between this figure and the writings of the humanist, Salutati, on the Labors of Hercules, which appeared in the last years of the fourteenth century. It is perhaps not too much to suppose that these antique motifs on the Porta della Mandorla were proposed to the sculptor by the commission in charge of the work. It is from his first step in the dedication of classical form and classical technique to ecclesiastic decoration that the art of Lorenzo Ghiberti emerges.

Although Ghiberti continues to quote from antique sources in the panels of the north doors of the Baptistery, for which he had won the award, it is not until the work on his masterpiece, the so-called Gates of Paradise or east doors of the Baptistery, that he uses ancient forms in a completely integrated authoritative fashion. In these marvelous reliefs begun in the late twenties of the Quattrocento Ghiberti plays with antique themes, developing one, two, or even three variants, each reminiscent of classical originals in one or two features, but never alike. Sometimes he uses a mixture of classical elements and there is the most complete originality and freedom in the treatment of the stance, gestures, and drapery of the figures.

158

A typical example of Ghiberti's method is the beautiful panel of the Genesis story (figure 111). Like so many artists of the Renaissance, Ghiberti retains a number of medieval idioms in his vocabulary. The telling of the story according to the traditional method of continuous narration, in which a number of episodes from the same story are presented within the confines of a single composition, is familiar enough in medieval art. The arrangement of this panel and even the conventions for trees and clouds, together with the Gothic elongation of the forms, is reminiscent of the work of some belated medieval artist like Lorenzo Monaco, or even Ghiberti's younger contemporary, Fra Angelico. Ghiberti appears to have been interested in creating a kind of painting in three dimensions in these finest works of his career, and the illusion of depth was certainly based on his study of the deeply carved relief of Roman sarcophagi. The panel of the Genesis legend illustrates how Ghiberti made a selective use of many Roman models that were parts of his homogeneous image of antiquity. Ghiberti's mind and his sketchbooks must have been crammed with dozens of ancient motifs upon which he drew freely for his own creative expression in the artistic language of the antique. An examination of only a few of the figures in this crowded composition shows how Ghiberti proceeded. The kneeling figure of Adam in the scene of the first man's creation at the extreme left of the composition is derived from such a precedent as the fallen hero in the sarcophagus of the Adonis legend (figure 110). Unlike the crumpled figure of the dying Adonis, Ghiberti's Adam is filled with a positive suggestion of his awakening, struggling into life in a manner almost prophetic of Michelangelo's great conception of the Creation of Man. In the center of Ghiberti's relief the beautiful figure of Eve rises from the rib of the sleeping Adam at God's command. Both the pose and the proportions of this figure recall some of the svelte representations of nereids in Roman marine sarcophagi. Ghiberti's Eve in her elegant attenuation is perhaps more Gothic than antique, and the suggestion of her floating upward as a pristine symbol of feminine beauty is an invention of Ghiberti's own. The technique of imparting to the bodies a soft, sensual warmth is one that Ghiberti had already displayed in his panel of the Sacrifice of Isaac. These details from the Genesis panel show Ghiberti working in an antique manner, rather than copying. These borrowings are his inventions in a classical mode, easy variations rather than direct or literal imitations. A final detail from the Genesis relief, the

159

Expulsion from Eden, reveals that Ghiberti was one of the first Renaissance artists to adapt the pose of some famous classical statue of the goddess of love, such as the Venus dei Medici or the Capitoline Venus (figure 30), for his conception of Eve. Although the pose is roughly similar, Ghiberti has gone far beyond the placid sensuous serenity of the original to suggest the pathos of the shame and sorrow which Eve feels in this moment of tragedy. This is a direct illustration of how Ghiberti could use the poses of ancient models for the revelation of human emotions that have nothing to do with the classical prototypes. All of these comparisons from his Genesis panel confirm that for Ghiberti the attraction of ancient art resided in the stylistic interpretation he could put on these classical forms. What he looked for in antiquity were such things as elegance, slim figures, moving forms, and the expression of exuberant action. The result is that the style of these reliefs which Ghiberti intended to be antique is really his own. Ghiberti recreated antique models according to his own taste, which was founded in the Gothic tradition; he succeeded in producing a new concept of beauty which is in every way typical of the artist and his period.

— 28 —

Venus Reborn

I also saw in a private house in Florence a statue of Venus wonderfully wrought in marble in that guise in which formerly Venus was portrayed. For she was a woman completely naked, holding her left hand over her privy parts, her right hand over her breasts; and this was said to be a work by Polyclitus which I do not believe.   —Benvenuto de Rambaldis da Imola *

J UST as Hercules weathered the Middle Ages in the disguise of Fortitude or Samson, so on occasion Venus descended from her planet to impersonate Prudence or Mother Eve. These theophanies of the goddess of love began with her appearance on the façade of the cathedral of Traù in the twelfth century and continue in the work of more famous masters like Giovanni Pisano in the thirteenth century and the great pioneer of fifteenth-century painting in Italy, Masaccio. All of these manifestations presuppose the artists' acquaintance with some famous ancient prototype like the Venus dei Medici (figure 30) or the Capitoline Venus, both descended from the famous Cnidian statue by Praxiteles. In every case, whether or not the sculptor or painter recognized Venus for what she is, he found her pose and gesture eminently suited to represent the apprehensive modesty of Prudence or the shame of Eve.

In the ancient examples of the *Venus Pudica* the gesture with which the goddess somewhat ineffectually covers her nakedness was never a realistic portrayal of modesty, alarm, or shame, such as might be assumed by a real woman: it was a marvelously effective symbol of modesty, like an unmistakable gesture in a ballet that at the same time bestowed a certain coquettish provocative charm on the goddess through this feigned chastity and demureness. Its meaning was immediately clear; it provided

* Ego autem vidi Florentiae in domo privata Statuam Veneris de marmore mirabilem in eo habitu in quo olim pingebatur Venus. Erat enim mulier speciosissima nuda, tenens manum sinistram ad pudenda, dexteram vero ad mammillias et dicebatur esse opus Polycleti quod non credo.—Benvenuto de Rambaldis da Imola, *Comentum super Dantis Aldigherii Comoediam* (1375)

161

a ready model for artists seeking to portray a similar situation in the realm of Biblical story or allegory.

An instance of such an adaptation is the figure of Prudence, one of the Virtues carved by Giovanni Pisano for the pulpit executed for the cathedral of Pisa in 1302 (figure 112). Again, there is the famous figure of Eve in the Expulsion scene, painted by Masaccio in Sta. Maria del Carmine somewhat more than one hundred years later. These examples not only offer comparisons with the antique prototypes but are interesting for the contrast between the Gothic and Renaissance approach to classic models. Giovanni Pisano, the son of Nicola d'Apulia, belongs to a period, the early fourteenth century, when the impact of the spirit and style of French Gothic began to be felt in Italian art. It is not surprising, therefore, that in his figure of Prudence Pisano abandons the sturdy Roman forms and serenity of his father's style in favor of a more pictorial and nervous realism. Although the Prudence is obviously copied with some accuracy from a statue the sculptor must have known, Giovanni Pisano has adapted the classic pose to the realistically rendered form of a human model. The elegant, coquettish grace and allure of the Greek original have vanished, leaving a figure of rather squat proportions carved with an evident interest in a realistic portrayal of the flabby folds of flesh. The intensity of the facial expression, a strange study in apprehension, is reinforced by what has become a rather militant gesture of self-defense. This is an attempt to animate the bland passivity of the classic with a new fervor of spiritual expression appropriate to the personification of a virtue, and at the same time this treatment illustrates the Late Gothic quest for reality that for a time overshadowed the interest in the ideality of the antique.

Masaccio's employment of the Venus Pudica, which will serve as an interesting comparison with Giovanni Pisano's statue, corresponds to that absorption of ancient forms into an individual artist's style such as that exemplified by Ghiberti. Masaccio completes a great trinity with those pioneers in the evolution of modern art, Brunelleschi the architect and Donatello the sculptor. "Giotto, born again, starting where death had cut short his advance, instantly making his own all that had been gained during his absence, and profiting by the new conditions and the new demands —imagine such an avatar, and you will understand Masaccio." [1] These words by Bernard Berenson epitomize the new monumentality that this painter brought to Western art.

The precise origins of Masaccio's art are obscure, but it is apparent immediately that he originated a style of heroic naturalism which immediately impressed itself upon his contemporaries as a perfect and appropriate embodiment of a new view of man in his environment. His Expulsion of Adam and Eve from Eden (figure 113) is an illustration of Masaccio's ability to construct statuesque figures in a grand style and to describe their psychological state through expressive gestures. Masaccio's relation to the antique is just as difficult to define precisely as Giotto's borrowings from classical sources. In the Expulsion the figure of Eve provides an illustration of how Masaccio adapted the Venus Pudica. The antique type had been altered to emphasize the overwhelming shame and despair of Eve, just as hopeless remorse is portrayed in the slumped form of Adam. The figure of Eve has none of the superficial sensuous delicacy of the classical original. It lacks the particularized realism of Giovanni Pisano's statue. All of Masaccio's forms are heavy, powerful creations that in their robust strength and massiveness are evocative of the solidity and grandeur of Etruscan art. Although Masaccio's figures are ennobled, they have the simplicity and sturdiness of the Tuscan peasant. He achieved this new dignity in the painting of human beings by the great breadth of his fresco technique, in which all details are eliminated and the articulation of the forms indicated in strong contrasts of light and shade that bestow a truly statuesque monumentality on his creations. Masaccio's powerful modeling, like the chiaroscuro of ancient paintings, makes the forms stand out almost as sculpture in the round, with a suggestion of the grandeur of monuments of antique art. Although the figure of Eve appears as a definite borrowing from antiquity and the heads of other figures by Masaccio suggest the severity and gravity of Etruscan art, it is evident that the painter, like Giotto, had so completely absorbed the lessons of antiquity that its influence is almost hidden in his original creation of an art dedicated to visual objective reality and the revelation of the psychology of individuals.

Masaccio copied an ancient Venus just as literally as did Giovanni Pisano, particularly in the position of the hands, but his expression is no less different from the antique. The animation of the figure through the striding posture and the dramatic contortion of Eve's weeping face are elements totally absent in the classical. The convulsive movement of the arms is an indication of conscious nakedness, rather than a poised symbol of modesty. As in Giotto, perhaps the most classical feature of Masaccio's art is his realization of human forms as fully rounded and architectural. Their massiveness is like the solidity of statues, weighty and firmly planted on the ground, with a completely tactile value recalling the ancient Roman sculptural tradition. Masaccio continued Giotto's new dramatic conception of Biblical events as possible happenings in the everyday world and not as symbolical and hieratic abstractions. What differentiates his work from Giovanni Pisano's and makes it so typical of the Renaissance is the presentation of the poetic beauty of the organically articulated human form as an instrument for dramatic emotional expression in monumental form.

Vasari wrote of Masaccio, "He imparted a life and force to his figures with a certain roundness in relief, which render truly characteristic and natural . . . The works produced before his time should be called paintings, but his performance, when compared with those works, might be designated life, truth, and nature." [2]

— 29 —

Piero Della Francesca

I have taken the trouble to describe the principal measurements of man, not the peculiarities of this or that man, but rather I have wished insofar as possible to determine that exact beauty, the gift of Nature, bestowed in certain fixed proportions on many bodies, and this too I have wished to commit to writing . . . I have selected many bodies governed by those that are most healthy and beautiful, and from all of these I have obtained measurements and proportions.   —Alberti *

PIERO DELLA FRANCESCA is the true descendent of Masaccio. He continued the tradition of the great Florentine's massive Etruscan forms to create an art of his own, no less filled with monumentality and dignity and ordered by Piero's feeling for the ineffable purity of geometric shapes. The mathematical construction of his figures was affected unquestionably by his acquaintance with the mathematical researches of Alberti.

Alberti was searching for an abstract ideal in the figural arts in his attempts to reconstruct the canon of Polyclitus. He actually made up a table of dimensions on the basis of measuring beautiful forms. For Alberti the most beautiful figures were apparently to be the most general and typical, an ideal to be arrived at almost literally by an arithmetical average of proportions. This trend toward an idealized figure style was far ahead of the rather particular realism of the fifteenth century and looked forward to the idealized figure style of the High Renaissance. This search for an ideal anatomy was part of the Renaissance man's search for human perfection, and the appearance of the idea that man can be improved. One way that he could be improved was through his environment, and for Alberti the alteration of any environment for the better was the real

* Ho presa questa fatica, di descrivere cioè le misure principali che sono nel uomo, e non le particolari solo di questo o di quell'altro uomo; ma per quanto mi e stato possibile, voglio porre quella esatta bellezza concessa in dono dalla natura, e quasi con certe determinate porzioni donata a molti corpi, e voglio metterla ancora in scritto . . . Ho io scelti molti corpi, tenuti da colori che piu sanno, bellissimi, e da tutti ho cavato le loro misure e proporzioni.—Leone Battista Alberti, *De Statua* (1464)

justification of architecture, providing an appropriate setting for the dig-nity of man. For him beauty was the principal aim in architecture, and that beauty he saw reflected particularly in the laws, the ceremonies, and even in the military tactics of the ancient period. In a building beauty, rather than the satisfaction of necessity, came uppermost, with the idea of function somewhere in the back of his mind. For the creation of a style based on blocklike definition of volume and clarity of formal definition, the abstraction and refinement of the human body suggested by Alberti's theories and already achieved in classical statuary provided ready models for Piero's embodiment of the dignity of man in statuesque form. In the elimination of all concern with the irregularities of surface texture and the reduction of the surfaces themselves to the simplest rounded planes he created an art that anticipates the lucid plastic volume of Seurat.

A single figure by Piero della Francesca will serve to illustrate his par-ticular use of the antique: this is the standing figure of Hercules (fig-ure 114), a wall-painting that once decorated the Villa Graziano in Borgo San Sepolcro, a house perhaps occupied by Piero himself. It is most likely a fragment of a larger scheme of decoration with other paintings of heroes of antiquity.

The figure suggests a mirror image of the famous Farnese statue (fig-ure 176), but is actually even more closely related to certain Hercules statues in the tradition of Lysippus (figure 115). Piero's Hercules has the elongation and slight *contrapposto* of Lysippic statues such as the Hermes of the Belvedere, and the actual modeling of the muscular anatomy ap-pears to be the artist's adaptation of such a fourth-century original. The rose-buff color of the flesh seems to be a facsimile of the tint and surface quality of a Roman copy.

Over and beyond the original inspiration from the antique Piero's Hercules is completely indicative of his method in what amounts to a creative transformation of an ancient marble. Here, as in so many of his heroic forms, the artist has evidently been inspired by the simplicity and planular composition of the anatomy offered by the classical model. He has used this framework to build a form that in its simplification contains a prophecy of cubism in the way in which it is composed of smooth, un-interrupted convex surfaces approaching the perfection of geometric forms. He has imposed on this frame a purely Renaissance head, which in the bold assurance of its expression is the very embodiment of the idea of *virtù,* a spiritual strength transcending the expression of muscular power in the body. The modeling of the face is executed with the same blocklike simplification that bestows a sculptural aspect on the torso.

The body has the largeness and nobility of classical art: that perfect balance between a plastic and decorative conception of the human frame associated with the sculpture of the Great Age. The Hercules reveals Piero's passion for geometric solidity to the extent that the figure has the appearance of having been carved from solid stone. The form at the same time has something of the simplicity and massiveness, the intellectual purity, found in Alberti's architecture. These qualities bestow a peculiarly objective and crystalline sublimity even on an isolated form like the Hercules. The modeling of the torso displays the artist's love of smooth rounded forms, surface meeting and marrying with curved unbroken surface like the interlocking concave and convex planes in a shape in the world of solid geometry. This simplification and total elimination of textural detail not only convey a feeling of statuesque roundness but impart that feeling of refined purity of form associated with Greek marbles. It has been said that Piero approached the noble abstraction of classical antiquity through Euclid rather than Homer. One has the feeling that there is a geometric basis for all the shapes in Piero's forms—spheres, cylinders, and cones—and yet these are never lifeless geometrical shapes, because, although the artist may draw a shoulder in a perfect arc or enclose a limb in a perfect cylinder, he varies this outline to impart a tense aliveness to the defining line. In his selective inspiration from the formal values of classical sculpture, Piero attained a severity and monumentality, a rational absolute beauty, that represents the classical Mediterranean style at its best.

— 30 —

Botticelli and the
Neoplatonic Ideal

In the tempestuous Aegean in Thetis' lap
One saw . . .
Born in the sea, free and joyous in her acts,
A damsel with divine visage
Driven ashore by the ardent zephyrs
Balancing on a shell; and it seemed the heavens
rejoiced thereat.   —Politian *

SANDRO BOTTICELLI belongs to that world of poetry and Neoplatonic
philosophy that flourished at the court of Lorenzo dei Medici, himself a
notable poet and patron of the arts in Florence in a period when the
Medici family had developed from the business executives of Masaccio's
generation into a family of princely, aristocratic rulers.

Botticelli's art is based partly on the science of the early Quattrocento,
partly on medieval tradition, and partly on his own interpretation of the
antique. Above all, he is a poetic creator of a dreamlike reality and in his
style perhaps the most individual of all Renaissance painters.

The mystical and poetic qualities that pervade Botticelli's art may be
explained by his absorption not only in mystical Christianity, which profoundly affected his last works, but also in the doctrines of Neoplatonism.
Neoplatonism can be described as a philosophy or way of life based on
Plato and systematized by the humanists in the circle of Lorenzo the Mag-

* Nel tempestoso Egeo in grembo a Teti
  si vede . . . nata in atti vaghi e lieti
  una donzella non con uman volto,
  da zefiri lascivi spinta a proda,
  gir sovra un nicchio, a par che 'l cel ne goda.
                                        —Poliziano, *La Giostra*, I, 99–101

nificent. It was the aim of scholars like Marsilio Ficino not only to make Platonic ideas available in Latin translations, but also to order the great mass of material contained in the works of Plato and his followers like Plotinus into a system that would give new life to every branch of classical studies. This was not in any sense simply a pagan revival, but an attempt to integrate Platonism with Christianity; so that it is not surprising that one of Ficino's most famous works bears the title *Teologica Platonica.* Neoplatonism struggles with the task of determining the relation of god and man to the universe, in which the whole cosmos is thought of as a series of spheres irradiated by the divine influence from God descending to the material world itself. All things on earth are influenced by celestial bodies which determine their nature. Man is possessed of reason and mind, the former attached to experience and the senses, the latter communicating with the essence of the cosmic mind which contains the angelic prototypes of all things existing in the lower spheres of being. Man is always torn by the struggles of his mind and reason imprisoned in a body from which the soul longs eternally to escape to reunion with the divine. Art became not only a means of illustrating the abstruse concepts of the Neoplatonic universe, but the contemplation of beauty a means of ascending to the celestial realm. In Neoplatonism the gods become the familiar spirits of the humanist circle—visitors from the spheres of Neoplatonism disguised in the vestments of Christian allegory. In Poliziano's *La Giostra,* Giuliano dei Medici invokes Pallas Athena and Aphrodite to bestow valor and virtue upon him and to open the gates of fame.

The new and fervent interest in ancient art and poetry in fifteenth-century Florence is revealed in Botticelli's famous picture of Spring, the Primavera, a panel that seeks to recapture the pagan verses of Lucretius and Horace, who described the blossom-strewing Flora, Spring blown in by the West Wind, and the Graces dancing their solemn and erotic measure before Mercury (figure 116). Typical of Botticelli is the stirring, nervous outline of his forms, the light and floating grace of all the forms that is the artist's signature. The scene is laid in a darkling grove; a strange melancholy heightened by the cool submarine colors pervades this painting, in its somberness so far from the real warmth and joy of returning Spring. There is a definite classical inspiration in the group of the Three Graces, a free adaptation of the famous antique group redrawn in Botticelli's linear idiom (figure 117). Botticelli displays a wonderful feeling for the growth and vital articulation of living forms expressed in

169

terms of line: the flowerlike twining hands of the goddesses in their supple, abstract structure suggest the drawing of hands in Oriental art. The flowers that carpet the ground of this twilight bower are no longer the merely patternized blossoms of earlier days; in them we have the same feeling of actual growth, the proper appearance and structure and pliancy of real flowers that Botticelli has adapted to his mystic language of draftsmanship, so that they are endowed with a wonderful vibrancy and life.

The picture is conceived as a kind of frieze, in which the figures with their demonically animated drapery, inspired by the flowing lines of neo-Attic reliefs (figure 118), move with a nervous frenzied energy that is the peculiar instrument of Botticelli's art. Botticelli's types have an extraordinary realism and individuality, filled with a strange poignancy of expression, both yearning and wistful. The forms in their linear construction have a moving fragility that is beyond this physical world. Botticelli's poetic neo-paganism is even more expressively present in another great panel painted after a visit to Rome, the famous Birth of Venus (figure 119).

This painting was done for the Medici villa at Castello in 1478 and was directly inspired by Poliziano's poem *La Giostra,* describing the birth of Aphrodite in a lost painting by the Greek artist, Apelles. Venus stands upon a shell, wafted to the shore by the blowing winds, the *zefiri lascivi* twined in erotic embrace. She glides to the strand where the Hour of Spring spreads a flowered mantle to receive her, while roses fall from the breaths of the zephyrs to perfume and, like the seed of the divine Cronos, to fertilize the foaming sea.

The panel is a marvelous illustration of the sensuous allegorical interpretation of mythology that was offered by the humanist poets who descried in Venus a queen risen from the shades of the classic past to be the inspiration of their Prince's thought and genius. To penetrate the complex allegory behind Botticelli's Venus we must understand that Venus was at once a figure from the bowers of courtly love and an embodiment of divinity in the Christian sense. The ancient goddess of love and beauty was invited by the poets to the Medici court to make Florence her abode, to preside as an ideal of refinement and culture, and in the Neoplatonic sense as a guide to the highest spheres. In Neoplatonism, beauty is a gateway to the divine. Venus is the embodiment of Ficino's idea of the nobility of sight and the sublimity of visual beauty for the apprehension and translation of the divine. Venus as a symbol of that planet of the humanists' devising, Humanitas, is a heavenly body that engenders in man all manner of virtues and is herself a guide to the higher realms that impinge on divinity. She was thought of as arousing feelings akin to religious fervor kindled by beauty. Love itself incarnated in a goddess is a symbol of divinity. In the Neoplatonic sense her domain is more Paradise than Olympus, and Botticelli's painting as much a religious allegory as a classical fable.

Renaissance artists like Botticelli in their search for the true image of the ancient gods turn not only to fragments of classical art but to ancient literary sources. Like so many Renaissance pictures Botticelli's Venus is a theme from the literary accounts of ancient painting translated into visual imagery and a kind of tribute to the vanished glory of antiquity. In many respects Botticelli's panel is more medieval than Renaissance in its stylistic aspects. This quality is particularly notable in the disregard of perspective and the decorative use of gold on the tree-trunks and on the locks of the goddess. Even the arrangement suggests a religious composition like the Baptism of Christ by Masolino (figure 120). These memories of medieval procedure are perhaps in part the result of Botticelli's training and personal predilection. He seems intuitively to have applied a familiar arrangement from religious art to the unexplored antique theme. Perhaps this medievalism was deliberate, too, this strangely religious atmosphere in a pagan myth. Botticelli may have wished by this subtle concealment in a framework suggestive of religious painting to imply the Christian symbolism hidden in the Neoplatonic subject.

The central figure of Venus is obviously inspired by the classic type of Praxitelean derivation known to us in the Capitoline Venus and the famous Aphrodite that only later entered the Medici collection (figure 30). Strangely, Botticelli's goddess appears more Gothic than classical; her body has the curve of a Gothic ivory. And, unlike the ponderation of classical statues, she appears completely weightless. She seems to float through the air, the suggestion of lightness enhanced by the stream of linear movement that both animates and etherealizes her form. It is apparent that Botticelli's goddess was created in competition with, not in imitation of, the classic past. It is the strange fragility and ethereal purity of the form that make this figure the very embodiment of that divine love which the Neoplatonists saw revealed in the beauty of mortal shapes.

The entire painting is typical of the artist himself. His types, notably the Venus in this painting, have an extraordinary realism and individuality filled with a strange poignancy of expression both yearning and wistful. From what has already been said of the nature of this allegory it is not surprising that the face of the goddess of love resembles Botticelli's paintings of the Madonna. Botticelli's particular instrument of expression is line. His emphasis on silhouette and movement transforms his figures into weightless phantoms and at the same time endows them with a wonderful vibrancy and life of their own. It is these qualities that make Botticelli's painting a poetic, rather than archaeological evocation of antiquity, the artist's creation of his own humanist poetry based on the vanished beauty of the classical past.

Although Botticelli's ideological treatment of the poetry of classical mythology may evoke the spirit of pagan antiquity, his handling of the forms, even when derived from classical sources, is strangely anticlassical. Botticelli as an artist relies on draftsmanship in much the same way as an Oriental painter. It is the wiry linear outline that tellingly defines the volume of the body in space almost more than the use of modeling. The artist's line conveys a sensation of eccentric decorative pattern to his pictures, one of many lingering suggestions of the Gothic mode. The movement of the lines themselves imbues the shapes with a strange nervous animation. In a painting by Botticelli it is the skeleton of drawing and its tremulous vitality that attract the eye more than solid forms, so that for this very reason Botticelli's calligraphic mode of expression negates the very corporeality of the sculptural prototype on which the Venus in this panel is based. At the same time the nacreous pallor of the flesh tints adds to the wraithlike incorporeality of his gods. Botticelli's painting, based so largely on his fascination for the rhythm of now angular, now sinuous, lines, was in its way eminently suited for the creation of such allegories as this. In the Birth of Venus the reduction of his forms to insubstantial weightless phantoms consumed like flames in their own movement was wonderfully appropriate for expressing these spirits from the astral realms of the Neoplatonists.

— 3 1 —

Donatello

His productions displayed so much grace and excellence with such correctness of design that they were considered to resemble the admirable works of the ancient Greeks and Romans more closely than those of any other master had ever done . . . insomuch that he has not only remained unsurpassed in that style but has never been equalled by any other artist, even down to our own days.   —Vasari *

THE greatest sixteenth-century biographer of Italian artists, Vasari is an authority who commands our respect for his information on the great men of the fourteenth and fifteenth centuries. In writing of the Florentine sculptor Donatello, Vasari also describes a journey that Donatello undertook with the architect Brunelleschi to Rome for the express purpose of studying the remnants of antiquity. He relates how the two young men stood in amazement before the marbles of the ancient city and how they earned the soubriquet of treasure-seekers for their zeal in excavating fragments of Roman buildings and statues. Whether the story of the Roman trip is true is beside the point, since the legend is at least a symbol of Donatello's study of antiquity that made it possible for the sculptor to produce a kind of original classical art of his own. It is everywhere apparent that Donatello was an original artist and not merely an antiquary.

One of Donatello's most famous statues is the bronze David which at one time ornamented a fountain in the Medici Palace (figure 121). This statue has first of all the unique distinction of being the first freestanding male nude to have been wrought by any sculptor since the fall of the Roman Empire. It would seem as though it should be relatively easy to es-

* Ed ebbono l'opere sue tanta grazia, disegno e bontà, ch'esse furono tenute più simili all'eccellenti opere degli antichi Greci e Romani, che quelle di qualunche altro fusse giammai . . , e gli fece con bellezza più che ordinaria; perciocchè, non che alcuno artefice in questa parte lo vincesse, ma nell'età nostra ancora non è chi l'abbia paragonato. —Giorgio Vasari, Le Vite, II, 396; Lives, I, 469

tablish a correspondence between this statue and some classical proto-type. The pose of the body in a kind of S-curve might be compared with some Praxitelean type (figure 122), but there is no precise comparison in any one ancient work. Perhaps the explanation for this lies in what Vasari said: "The animation, truth to nature, and softness manifest in this figure make it almost impossible for artists to believe that it has not been molded on the living form." [1] And it is precisely the suggestion of a kind of breathing life in the warm youthful body that separates it from the static perfection of the antique. The face has a strangely sensuous, in-ward, and brooding expression that is again far different from anything to be found in antiquity and is another illustration of Donatello's interest in imbuing his statues with the suggestion of inner psychic life. The figure has little or no suggestion of the Biblical hero and may be properly de-scribed as classical only in the sculptor's feeling for the moving organic beauty of the nude body. Although the antique basis is there in some Praxitelean type, this is an illustration of the Renaissance sculptor's cre-ative reworking of the classical ideal in the interests of his own realistic and psychological expression. What is so strikingly original about Donatel-lo's David is that he could see the Biblical hero as an antique god, with a sense of form and material in bronze that he might have learned from the study of some famous antique precedent such as the Spinario. De-spite many deviations from the classical standard, Donatello has made the rediscovery of antiquity. He has found the secret of physical beauty and has presented it with various nuances of modeling and pose to make the youthful body sensuously appealing.

The loveliness and aesthetic attraction of the statue do not rest so much on our recognition of the heroic subject as on the entirely frank portrayal of the fluid organic mechanism of the nude body. The intrinsic beauty of the bodily form is displayed for our aesthetic admiration as it had not been since ancient times. There is no denying the fact that, show-ing through the veil of Biblical association, the figure has an almost pro-vocative erotic appeal, a quality which in this naked hero, just as much as in the young men of the Parthenon frieze, is an indication of the taste of the time and of the sculptor. Whether or not the love of beautiful youths was condoned in fifteenth-century Florence is unimportant beside this revelation of the admission of the nude as an intrinsically beautiful theme, as it had been in antiquity. It is this more than anything else that stamps Donatello's work as a humanist creation. This presentation of a

174

pagan form in Biblical disguise was only a means for gaining acceptance for what was in every other respect a classical point of view.

Most notable among Donatello's many achievements was his equestrian statue of the professional soldier, Gattamelata, ordered by the city of Padua to commemorate his victories (figure 123). Here again there are certain suggestions from the antique, which are subordinated as usual to Donatello's contributions in the psychological and realistic interpretation of the individual. Although there had been a few attempts at equestrian statues in the Middle Ages, this is the first really monumental treatment of such a subject since classical antiquity. The general inspiration for the figure probably comes from some such source as the famous Marcus Aurelius statue in Rome (figure 124). The pacing horse itself owes something to the famous horses of St. Mark's in Venice (figure 125), and the type and muscular construction of the proud head suggest certain fragments of classical equestrian sculpture that had come to light during the Renaissance such as the classical bronze head of a horse in the Museo Nazionale, Naples. Gattamelata's armor is Roman; his cuirass and the saddle are covered with a wealth of archaeological detail. Certain elements of the base are not unlike the decoration of Roman tombs. But all of these borrowings from the antique have been creatively used by Donatello to forge a tremendous portrait of an individual. He is a veritable personification of military genius, the appropriate embodiment of craftiness and heroic composure. As is usual in Donatello, the whole suggestion of Gattamelata's strength and intelligence is concentrated in the face which presents a complete idea of his inward character. The countenance radiates a kind of intellectual force; Donatello's evocation of both the physical and ghostly attributes of a personality is what makes his work typical of the Renaissance.

— 32 —

The Labors of Hercules

Such is the spiritual allegory: Hercules is interpreted as the contemplative life or as a man following the contemplative life . . . many monsters did he slay because he overcame many temptations of the flesh by which he was sore tempted in many ways. He conquered rivers, monsters, wild beasts, kings, and dominions, that is he overcame troubles, vices, desires of the flesh and the wealth of the worlds.

—Ghisalberti *

LIKE every other phase of Renaissance art, the later development of relief sculpture is characterized by a closer approximation of its style to the general appearance and technique of antique reliefs. This approach replaces the earlier borrowing of selected details already noted in Ghiberti. The change is most notable in the treatment of actual mythological subjects and may be studied in a number of examples of the representation of the Labors of Hercules by Central and North Italian sculptors. The examination of these panels will, at the same time, afford an opportunity to note the differences in the understanding of the classical styles in the art of these regions of Italy.

Antonio Federighi was a Sienese sculptor known principally as the carver of a number of fonts in the cathedral of his native city. Although little known outside Siena, Federighi's work is interesting as a reflection of the style of his famous master, Jacopo della Quercia, who already had manifested some of the antique traits that take the ascendant in Federighi in the late Quattrocento. One of Federighi's most interesting works is an octagonal font in the Capella di San Giovanni of the cathedral, in

---

* Allegoria spiritualis talis est: Hercules interpretatur vita contemplativa vel vir vitam contemplativam dicens, et dicitur ab her quod est lis et cleos quod est gloria quasi gloriosus in lite vel labore vite . . . , multa monstra interfecit quia multas temptaciones carnis superavit secundum quod multis modis caro temptatur. Flumina, monstra, feras, reges, terras superavit, idest inundationes, vicia, motum carnis, copia terrenorum superavit.—F. Ghisalberti, *Integumenta Ovidii* (1933), p. 63

which a series of reliefs from the Genesis story are combined with episodes from the Labors of Hercules.

Such parallels are frequent even in medieval art. Hercules in his role of defender of mankind against a variety of monstrous enemies had in the moralized editions of Ovid come to be an emblem of Christ in triumphs over evil. The victory of Hercules over the Nemean lion (figure 126) symbolizes the defeat of pagan pride by Christian virtue, just as the Expulsion humbled the presumption of Adam and Eve. The companion panel of the slaying of Nessus, like the hero's other adventures with the hydra, the boar, and the stag with brazen hoofs, is a symbol of how Christ himself, "conquers all sin and every vice, all error and all malice." [1]

Although this is a piece of church furniture, an effort has been made to make it look like a classical artifact, just as Alberti's design for Sant'Andrea at Mantua made that church resemble the structure and decor of a Roman bath. In Federighi's font, the panels are set in what is a reconstruction of a Corinthian order terminating in a projecting cornice; the ornament is purposefully antique throughout; and the figures in the sculptured stories are carved, as in ancient panels, in such high relief that they give the illusion of existing in the round.

The total effect of Federighi's reliefs is that of the separate panels of mythological subjects on an antique sarcophagus, like that devoted to the Hercules story in the Villa Borghese (figure 127), wrapped around the octagonal form of the font and, as in the ancient prototype, separated by Corinthian pilasters. The effect of the individual panels with the forms of Hercules and his victims or Adam and Eve silhouetted against empty backgrounds follows the Roman precedent as well. The panels of Hercules' Labors at Siena, the encounters with Nessus and the Nemean lion, do not exactly follow the arrangement of these scenes on the Borghese sarcophagus, but the imitation of antique models is apparent throughout.

Although the careful attention to the musculature of the hero's torso imitates an antique prototype, there are certain aspects of Federighi's style which are inherited from his master, Jacopo della Quercia. This latter artist had evolved a canon of proportion which in its stockiness and implication of physical power was in some way suggestive not only of a Polyclitan canon but also of the rugged strength of Etruscan art. Like no other Italian sculptor Jacopo suggested the presence of sheer animal force and vigor in the mighty peasant forms of Adam and Eve in his reliefs at San Petronio, Bologna. These characteristics are if anything exaggerated

177

in the work of Federighi who, as is to be expected, shows at the same time a more intimate and direct acquaintance with the antique. This is apparent not only in the accuracy and delicacy of the architectural members of the enframement, but also in the panels of erotes and dolphins in the basement of the font, motifs obviously derived from nereid sarcophagi. This greater classicism reveals itself also in the thoroughly Polyclitan form of Adam in the Temptation scene and in the individual figures of Hercules. In the relief of his struggle with the Nemean lion Hercules is struggling with a beast that might have risen from its place outside the portal of a Romanesque cathedral: the tail curled under the hind leg and the flamelike conventions for the mane are more medieval than antique.

Federighi's style is typical of the late fifteenth century in the complete mastery of anatomical structure and peculiarly Tuscan in the uncouth vigor of the physique and the expression of the animal-like vitality of the human body. In this period, for the first time since antiquity, the human nude appears as accepted as animals in a state of nature.

Turning back for a comparison with Late Antique reliefs of the Labors of Hercules, it becomes apparent that once more in the Renaissance, the human body was represented as a beautiful organic entity and not as a reduction of its essential appearance to an emblematic schema with no regard for the articulation of a real animate form.

A series of panels devoted to the Labors of Hercules on the façade of the Colleoni Chapel in Bergamo serves as a comparison between the treatment of antique forms and techniques in Tuscany and North Italy. As in the font at Siena episodes from Genesis are combined with the Hercules cycle. It is apparent once again that in these compositions the sculptor was aware of ancient representations of the Labors of Hercules. The author of these carvings was Giovanni Antonio Amadeo, the late fifteenth-century sculptor, whose style, like that of so many artists in Lombardy and the Veneto, was a mixture of elements of medieval, northern European, and antique forms. Amadeo is remembered chiefly for his decoration of the richly encrusted façade of the Colleoni Chapel, more like an enlarged Gothic relic casket, set with a variety of carvings and colored stones, than a structural building in the sense of Florentine Renaissance design.

In the reliefs devoted to the Hercules myth, the treatment is totally different from the approximation of the antique in Central Italy. The reliefs are filled with picturesque details, and the depth of cutting is another

Lombard device attempting to make reliefs approximate painting. This tendency is carried to the extreme of deeply undercutting the contours of the figures, evidently with the idea of having the resulting band of surrounding shadow make them stand out from the background. Actually, this technical device only serves to make the figures appear as appliqués attached to the background.

The figure of Hercules himself in these panels (figure 128), although perhaps generally inspired by an antique prototype, is at the same time obviously drawn from a rather plump human model. The sculptor's attempts at a daring *contrapposto* are not entirely successful: the demigod's left leg is dislocated into an anatomically impossible position. The whole relief is typically Lombard in the accumulation of multiple picturesque details, and the particularized naturalism of Hercules' anatomy strongly suggests the German taste that had been prevalent in northern Italy since Gothic times. The relief is typical of a region in which there never was as in Central Italy and Rome an intellectual understanding of antique art nor any attempt to recapture its clarity and idealism.

— 33 —

Mantegna

Squarcione . . . to the end that Andrea [Mantegna] might know more than he did himself, caused him to work diligently from casts moulded on antique statues, and after pictures on canvas, which he had brought from various places.

—Vasari *

O<small>F</small> all Renaissance artists Andrea Mantegna was the most anti-quarian in the true sense of the word, because of his genuine attempt to preserve the intrinsic aspect of the ancient fragments which he copied so lovingly. Mantegna's style grew out of his admiration for antiquity, the perspective of Paolo Uccello, something of the statuesque grandeur of Piero della Francesca, and to a more limited degree the color of the Bellinis of Venice, his relations by marriage. Mantegna's distinguished career as a painter was concentrated largely on his work for three genera-tions of the Gonzaga family at Mantua and, finally, for that great con-noisseur, Gianfrancesco Gonzaga's chatelaine, Isabella d'Este. His com-pletely intellectual approach to both antiquity and reality relates him to such great contemporaries as Piero della Francesca, as does the quiet mysticism that pervades his religious paintings.

Mantegna's training in the workshop of the Paduan painter, Squar-cione, seems first to have acquainted him with the study of the antique. This was the beginning of Mantegna's lifelong admiration of the classic past. There is the possibility he made a trip to Rome, perhaps coming in contact with Donatello there in 1432, and certainly many of Mantegna's paintings are filled with mementos of the Eternal City. Many famous monuments, such as the Septizonium, the Pyramid of Cestius, the column of Trajan, and the Colosseum, appear in the backgrounds of his paint-

* Squarcione . . . acciocchè Andrea imparasse più oltre non sapeva egli, lo esercitò assai in cose di gesso formate da statue antiche, ed in quadri di pitture, che in tela si fece venire di diversi luoghi.—Giorgio Vasari, *Le Vite*, III, 385–386; *Lives, II*, 263

180

ings. According to Vasari, it was at the time of Mantegna's marriage to the daughter of the Venetian painter Jacopo Bellini that Squarcione, piqued at his pupil's alliance with this rival school, wrote a withering critique of Mantegna's frescoes in the Eremitani Chapel in Padua. These works, Squarcione said,

had nothing good in them because Andrea had therein copied antique marbles, from which no man can perfectly acquire the art of painting, seeing that stone must ever retain somewhat of the rigidity of its nature, and never displays that tender softness proper to flesh and natural forms, which are pliant and exhibit various movements. He added that Andrea would have done much better with those figures if he had given them the tint of marble and not all the colors: they would then have been nearer to perfection, since they had no resemblance to life, but were rather imitations of ancient statues in marble.[1]

Vasari goes on to say that Mantegna was of the opinion that antique statues were more perfect than nature

which rarely assembles and unites every beauty in one single form, wherefrom it becomes necessary to take one part from one and another part from another. He thought, moreover, that the muscles, veins, nerves, and other minute particulars were more distinctly marked and more sharply defined in statues than nature, wherein the tenderness and softness of the flesh, concealing and covering a certain sharpness of outline thus causes them to be less apparent.[2]

In certain respects this criticism seems justified, but there can be no doubt that, as Vasari also states, Mantegna did modify his studies of antique models with reference to humanity.

A perfect example of Mantegna's work is his St. Sebastian in the Louvre (figure 129). The saint is bound before an elaborate fragment of an arch with an engaged Composite column. In the distance amid fantastic stalagmite promontories supporting miniature towns one can recognize the arch of Septimius Severus. The saint stands on a fragment of broken entablature and, just as in the Forum today, an acanthus plant grows beside the support of Sebastian's martyrdom. A most interesting and telling detail appears at the lower left in the shape of a fragment of a sculptured foot of a draped statue. It is extraordinary how the precise glyptic definition of this little piece of statuary, perhaps in Mantegna's own collection, hardly differs except in its tonality from the painting of the foot of St. Sebastian himself. Both of these feet give the illusion of stone rather than living flesh. Turning our attention to the complete figure of the martyred saint, it is immediately evident that the beautiful torso has been taken from an antique model, presumably of the Polyclitan type figure 130). The necessity of joining this fragment to the legs has been obviated by the intervention of the massive loincloth, but it is apparent that these members exist only as a support for this superbly sculptural trunk. The artist has painted the magnificent torso with its intricate case of rippling muscles as though glistening with the silken sheen of a piece of marble carving. The head of St. Sebastian with the eyes turned to heaven has something of the pathos of the mask of an ancient barbarian, here turned to the expression of the saint's mystic and serene acceptance of his martyrdom. The strangely mystic element of this painting appears to derive from the serenity and detachment of its construction. The sky is filled with enormous cumulous clouds drifting over a sunlit landscape, fantastic and even romantic in its forms. The empty quiet beauty of this setting seems indifferent, apart from the cruel martyrdom it enfolds. Even Sebastian's executioners, engaged in quiet colloquy in the lower right-hand corner of the painting, are completely apart from the recent target of their arrows. The figure of the saint himself has at once the solidity and serenity of a classic victor, and in this serenity and calm and detachment from all that moves around him Mantegna seems to imply that the saint is alone with God. If Mantegna delighted in painting flesh in imitation of the lustrous beauty of the ancient marbles he loved so well, he perhaps sensed at the same time that the very petrifaction of his forms bestowed upon them an air of timelessness and mystery, as though the saint's body in its purity had been miraculously transmuted into immortal stone.

— 34 —

The High Renaissance

Imitating Nature in part, one should therefore select the most perfect form. This is what Apelles did, he who painted the famous Venus rising from the Sea . . . from Phryne the most renowned courtesan of her day; and likewise Praxiteles carved the beautiful statue of the Cnidian Venus from the same young woman. And in part one should imitate the beautiful statues in marble and bronze of the ancient Masters. Those who fully savour and possess the admirable perfection of these will surely be able to correct many defects of Nature, and make their Paintings attractive and pleasing to everyone; because antiquities contain all the perfection of art, and may be exemplars of all that is beautiful.

—Ludovico Dolce *

Wιτη the High Renaissance of the early Cinquecento there is a consummation of various tendencies already inaugurated in the fifteenth century: the works of the great artists in their separate ways move toward the creation of a new classicism, a canon of form that is at once conservative and timeless. This new classicism was an appropriate and inevitable production of Rome, the city that once again takes its place as the center of Western civilization. This brief moment in the first quarter of the sixteenth century marks the culmination of the Pope's revival of the Roman empire, a period when the pontiffs lived as emperors with their families and cardinals established as a lesser nobility. In a society in which every emphasis was on solemnity, majesty, and glory it was inevitable that the artists employed to embody its ideals were almost bound to create in a

---

* Devesi adunque elegger la forma più perfetta, imitando parte la Natura. Il che faceva Apelle, il quale ritrasse la sua tanto celebrata Venere, che usvica dal Mare . . . da Frine famosissima cortigiana della sua età; et ancora Prassitele cavò la bella statua della sua Venere Gnidia dalla medesima giovane. E parte si debbono imitar le belle figure di marmo, o di bronzo de' Mestieri antichi. La mirabil perfettion delle quali chi gusterà e possederà a pieno, potrà sicuramente corregger molti difetti di essa Natura, e far le sue Pitture riguardevoli e grate a ciascuno; perciocchè le cose antiche contengono tutta la perfettion dell'arte, e possono essere esemplari di tutto il bello.—Ludovico Dolce, *Dialogo della pittura intitolato l'Aretino* (1557)

183

sublime and grand manner. This was an art dedicated to the immortalization of the papacy rather than the glorification of God. The grand manner could only grow in the service of a society completely confident in its power and wealth and dedicated to the ostentatious perpetuation of its own magnificence on the grandest possible scale. Such an art had little or no contact with the people, and even if people could have seen Michelangelo's Sybils or Raphael's School of Athens it is doubtful that these sublime intellectual conceptions would have had the slightest meaning. This was a classical art, but more limited in its appeal than Greek classical art. There are other similarities to the art of the Great Period. The painting and sculpture of the sixteenth century represent an intensification of the naturalistic and scientific achievements of the previous period. Just as the sculpture of the Parthenon is more anatomically correct according to normal experience than the carving at Olympia, so the forms in Michelangelo and Raphael are treated more freely, naturally, and as a matter of course than by the painters of the fifteenth century. The figures are now completely organic in their composition, and they stand firmly on their feet, a stability not always achieved in the work of the previous period. Everything is completely balanced and controlled. Something of the ideal stylization that marks the work of the High Renaissance masters has its beginnings in the fifteenth century. The attempt to achieve ideal types and proportions in imitation of classical practice had already been formulated by Alberti.

Raphael's wall-paintings, and even his tapestry compositions, have sometimes been called the Parthenon sculptures of modern art, because, like classical sculpture, their heroic forms do achieve a kind of balance between realism and abstraction. It must be admitted, however, that, compared with Greek art, the modern counterpart is lacking in warmth and immediacy, since it is always in certain respects a derived and retrospective manner. From the social point of view the classical art of the sixteenth century is a perfect reflection of a society filled with reminiscences of Roman heroism and medieval chivalry, a society trying to appear to be something it is not, by following an artificial social moral code which stylizes the whole pattern of life, as may be seen in the prescribed codes of etiquette and morality devised by Castiglione in his famous work on the perfect courtier. The classical art of Raphael describes this society as it sees itself and wants to be seen. Raphael presents an appropriately aristocratic art, both conservative and ideal, and, like the classical art of

184

old, suggesting permanence and continuity in its very stability and serenity. Raphael's art is a kind of symbol of the moderation, the calm and security of the ruling class. Again, as a parallel to the classical art of the fifth century, what we see in Raphael is an enhanced, ennobled reality, free from everything transitory and banal. He creates an heroic race in the full bloom of ripe, sensuous beauty, expressing a sublimity appropriate to an aristocratic society.

In the fifteenth century artists were indebted to the antique for selected motives; later these motives became so transformed as to defy identification. The artists of the Quattrocento depended on the antique translation of nature for their own conquest of reality and the mastery of anatomy, just as they took ideas from ancient drapery patterns to impart movement and life to their own creations. Whereas the work of the Early Renaissance was marked by a great variety of styles and motives, there was a new synthesis in the High Renaissance. Antiquity comes to be integrated into a unified artistic language and the artists really create or invent their own *arte antica*. In the sixteenth century we have a complete synthesis of antique form and content in a unified expression based on ancient models. The old Greco-Roman types are reactivated in the artist's invention of his own classical art. The classic normative quality of the sixteenth century and its society resulted in an attraction to the most classical examples of antiquity, the ideality of the fifth century, as well as the more rarefied grace of the Apollo Belvedere. It could be said that the High Renaissance approach to the body approximated classical art in the concern for ideal physical beauty and organic rhythm, that quest for the typical and general already inaugurated in Alberti's famous essay on sculpture. This fascination for the serenity and nobility of truly classical art is interrupted only by the great Michelangelo, who in his search for the heroic and dynamic turned for inspiration to the unclassical phases of ancient art: the Hellenistic period and the Antonine baroque.

The sixteenth-century ideal is based on the effort to surpass rather than to imitate nature, an ideal that becomes more and more prominent in the learned discussions of the functions of painting and poetry. There did exist perforce a conflict between the concept of ideal imitation or exact imitation, as the latter is described in Pliny's accounts of antique painters deceiving animals and even men by the realism of their portrayals. Critics and artists, too, in this learned age were aware not only of the ancient literary descriptions of this kind of verism but also of Horace's advice that it was better to follow the perfect models of Greece in art and poetry than to strive for new invention. This controversy assumed a pedantic character in the disputes which arose over whether the painter should follow Zeuxis in composing his ideal from many perfect models or, as reported of Praxiteles, derive his form from one perfect human form.

What emerges from an examination of all of this philosophical writing and learned art is that, as never before, artists, under pressure to produce a perfect art, an art properly superhuman like that of Phidias, turned more closely to an intensive study of what ancient models could teach them. An artist like Raphael, setting out to draw a beautiful female form from the imagination would have his mental image conditioned not only by his knowledge of anatomical structure but by his memories of how a perfect body was represented in a statue he had seen in the Vatican. The High Renaissance artist's intelligent acquaintance with the principles and proportions of classical sculpture was such that it became second nature for him to draw in the antique manner. In this way it was inevitable that a gifted artist, learned and sensitive to the inner beauties of the antique, could truly create his own classical art "per superar la natura."

The perfect embodiment of the ideal nature of Cinquecento art, already described, may be seen best of all in the work of Raphael Sanzio, whose dates are 1483 to 1519. His artistic education began at the humanist court of Urbino, where antique principles of architecture and war were being studied for their utility to contemporary needs. Raphael took the antique to reanimate a mode that had been dead for centuries. He used classical art as a formula for his own sublime mood. The sources of Raphael's art are the sentimental religious paintings of his master, Perugino, the scientifically marvelous drawing of Leonardo, and finally, particularly after his removal to Rome, the example of classical art itself. Like almost every artist of his day, Raphael was affected by the grandeur of Michelangelo.

One of Raphael's earliest works, which already reflect his acquaintance with humanist ideas, is the little panel sometimes identified as The Three Graces in the Musée Condé at Chantilly (figure 131). The group, like the earlier one in Botticelli's Primavera (figure 116) is almost certainly derived from the antique group at Siena (figure 117) or even a classical painting of the theme (figure 132). An odd feature of the little painting is that each of the figures holds a golden apple, so that they are probably to be interpreted as the Hesperides. This picture was originally part of the panel entitled The Knight's Dream in the National Gallery, London. The sleeping knight is Scipio Africanus who, according to legend, had a vision offering him the life of arms or of letters or of pleasure. The guardians of the golden apples are there as emblems of action, and the knight's questing typified by the adventure of Hercules. The whole thing was therefore a kind of elaborate allegorical present for the young Scipio Borghese on the occasion of his Confirmation.

The figures of the three maidens, although certainly derived from the ancient group, are animated by a charming feeling of warmth and breathing aliveness. As in all of Raphael's figures, the painting of the flesh has a kind of glow and radiance, and here the vital and luminous figures are in complete harmony with the poetic Umbrian landscape that enfolds them. Compared to Botticelli's wraithlike maidens, Raphael's Graces are closer to the antique precedent, not only in the pose of the three figures but also in the studied interest in the beauty of the nude, still somewhat hard and relief-like in quality, but already revealing the broad, generalized treatment of anatomy that monumentalizes Raphael's mature style.

Whereas the women drawn by Picasso in his classical vein are filled with real erotic attraction, a sensual warmth in the fullness of forms often provocatively distorted and conveyed by the artist's succinct and loving abbreviation of desirable bodies in the simple cursive line of the Greek vase painter, Raphael's goddesses are, like the heroic Phidian sculptures, remote from everything except a very generalized suggestion of sensual beauty and attraction. Their heroic scale and frozen intellectual perfection of form place them on an inviolable superior plane in which transitory sexual attraction has no place.

Raphael's Galatea

I have hither bidden by the wave and breeze,
The Graces of the Sea, the Dorides,
Olympus bears not, nor your lucent arch,
Such lovely forms, in such a lightsome march:
They fling themselves, in wild and wanton dalliance,
From the sea-dragon upon Neptune's stallions,
Blent with the elements so freely, brightly,
That even the foam appears to lift them lightly.
In Venus' chariot-shell, with hues of morn,
Comes Galatea, now the fairest, borne;
Who, since that Cypris turned from us her face,
In Paphos reigns as goddess in her place.
Thus she, our loveliest, long since come to own,
As heiress, templed town and chariot-throne.

—Goethe *

T HE vision of the sea gods' sporting beneath the towering moon on the Aegean is Goethe's poetic recollection of one of Raphael's greatest paintings, the Galatea of the Villa Farnesina (figure 133).[1] Like Goethe's lines from *Faust,* the Umbrian painter's conception of the loveliest of nymphs was inspired by Philostratus' *Imagines.* For the great scholar of

* Die Töchter hab'ich alle herbeschieden
  Die Grazien des Meeres, die Doriden.
  Nicht der Olymp, nicht euer Boden trägt
  Ein schön Gebild das sich so zierlich regt.
  Sie werfen sich, anmuthigster Gebärde,
  Vom Wasserdrachen auf Neptuns Pferde,
  Dem Element auf's zarteste vereint,
  Das selbst der Schaum sie noch zu heben scheint.
  Im Farbenspiel von Venus Muschelwagen
  Kommt Galatea, die schönste, nun getragen,
  Die, seit sich Kypris von uns abgekehrt,
  Zu Paphos wird als Göttin selbst verehrt.
  Und so besitzt die Holde, lange schon,
  Als erbin, Tempelstadt und Wagenthron.

—Johann Wolfgang von Goethe, *Faust, Sämtliche Werke,* ll. 8136–8147; translated by Bayard Taylor (Boston, 1871) the Renaissance, Burckhardt, this wall-painting represented "an awakening of love in its full majesty, pure and lovely," [2] a marvelous evocation of the ancient poetry of nature. The thread that links Raphael's composition to antiquity loses itself in the famous Thiasos of Scopas, which, according to tradition, was brought to Rome, and reflections of which undoubtedly survive in the reliefs of a number of sarcophagi. Raphael's conception reveals a vitalization and reuse of one of these decadent prototypes, just as some of the individual figures show the artist's selective borrowing from other antique models. The motif of the figure striding forward with one foot advanced like the Galatea may be found in a number of ancient precedents, such as the Venus of Capua in Naples (figure 134), whose attitude and drapery provide a possible model for Raphael's sea nymph; [3] the sea horse at the left is taken from one of the famous groups on the Quirinal (figure 53).

The fresco as a whole, however, eludes any such attachment to specific models and is rather a wonderful recreation of the classical spirit without reference to a particular prototype. Here is a reactivation of a number of old types in the artist's invention of his own classical art, an art that is now marked by a complete absorption of antiquity with a synthesis of form and content and an inspiration from ancient art embracing form as well as motifs. The old antique shapes really become Raphael's personal possessions, and he uses them to raise his forms above the earthly, so that what we see are ancient figures animated by a new life and worked into a completely harmonious style.

The artist is so much the master of the syntax of classical art that his figures are like a revivification of the ideals of antiquity. In the largeness of the forms placed in a shallow stage, even in color, they are in a way comparable to the wall-paintings of Pompeii and Herculaneum. The painting of Galatea marks the culmination of classical rhythmic organization and pictorial composition suggesting ancient frescoes already apparent in the early panel of The Three Graces.

As Raphael painted the subject, the Galatea is an original interpretation of antique myth based on Theocritus and Ovid or their modern translators, Politian and Bembo, more moving in its recapturing of the Greek sense of life and pathos than that of the most learned humanist.[4] The very spirit of the sea and its creatures is evoked in the painting, with nature portrayed in metaphorical and mythical forms as in the great wall-paintings of Campania. Just as in the famous mural of Hercules and

Telephus (figure 38) the Arcadian grove is figured by the heroic form of the nymph of the glade, so Galatea and her company represent the sea. In the sky above the nymph's triumph are erotes shooting arrows to indicate the amorous nature of her dynamic cortège, with Nereus' daughter as another Aphrodite wafted over the sea filled with gods lost in tender dalliance.

Raphael's antique style does not reveal itself as in the evanescent and melancholy interpretation of Botticelli, but with the same full forms of the artists of imperial Rome: solid, corporeal forms, disposed with a splendid balance of masses. The shallow composition in overlapping planes in itself suggests the arrangement of a Roman relief or Pompeiian wall-painting.

These resemblances of Raphael's work to classical paintings perhaps require a little further explanation. The figures in the great painting cycles of Pompeii and Herculaneum have the pliant rhythm and statuesque volume of Hellenistic sculpture, noble and compelling forms executed in a completely humanistic manner. In their attitudes and solidity many appear to be derived from statues. They are balanced and massive, and, as in statuary, the drama and action are related in composed, contained poses and gestures. The bright tones, not always related in any definite unified color harmony, are lightly, even impressionistically, brushed in, and the lighting is usually a diffused, generalized luminosity with no logical light source for the shadowing of the separate parts of the composition. The forms suggest space by their own volumes and are placed in a shallow stagelike setting. All of these qualities of Pompeiian painting are suggested in Raphael's Galatea. Whether he had some acquaintance with similar antique murals already uncovered in Rome, as in the Domus Aurea, or whether, working in a manner so saturated with classical learning and procedure, he independently arrived at a somewhat similar effect is a question that cannot be answered categorically. The parallel only serves to strengthen our impression of the degree to which Raphael was able to associate himself with the classical mode, so that he ended by producing a kind of sixteenth-century counterpart.

In truly classic fashion Raphael in this apotheosis of Galatea symbolizes a triumph of life, a life flowing in the throbbing vortex of the senses, suggested at once by Galatea's rapt expression and the wild embraces of her companions. The universal poetic quality of the picture is the result of the graceful and wonderful invention of Raphael, an inven-

190

tion based on his mastery of the generalized antique idiom and his power of creative ideation from a completely formed and ordered mental image.

An important clue for an understanding of Raphael's procedure in his great imaginative classical subjects is found in a letter discussing the Galatea which he wrote to Baldassare Castiglione:

In order to paint a beautiful woman, it would be necessary for me to see many beautiful women, but since there is a scarcity of them, I make use of a certain Idea which comes to my mind.[5]

This is the first appearance of the word Idea which occupied the attention of all of the leading critics of the sixteenth and seventeenth centuries and has been the subject of scholarly examination by modern art historians as well. Ultimately this concept goes back to the Aristotelian definition that the excellence of an artist's production resides in his knowledge of universals derived from particular experience, whereby many scattered beauties are joined in one composite exemplar of them all. Raphael's Idea, explaining it as simply as possible, is really an expression of the artist's creative ideation of an ideal form, that perfected image shaped in his mind on the basis of remembered visions of nature or antiquity. "The 'Idea' of the painter and sculptor," to quote the critic Bellori, "is that perfect exemplar in the mind, with an imagined form, which by imitation, the things that appear to human sight resemble." [6] The creature of Raphael's imagining is based on an inward mental image and selective imitation; that is, a selective imitation of nature modified and ennobled by an intelligent adaptation of the antique. This does not mean an imitation of external nature as it exists, but a generalization, whereby in an Aristotelian sense nature is represented not as she is, but raised above all that is local or accidental so as to be in the highest sense representative. In arriving at his particular universal and statuesque forms, Raphael's kinship with classical thought as well as classical art is apparent. The expression of the idea that the masterpieces of antiquity provided a beauty surpassing nature is mentioned over and over again by Italian critics of the sixteenth century. Bellori insists that "it is necessary to study the most perfect of the antique sculptures, since the antique sculptors used the wonderful *Idea* and therefore can guide us to the true beauties of nature." [7] Or, as Dolce put it, "It is necessary to imitate the beautiful figures in marble and bronze by antique masters . . . because ancient statues contain the whole perfection of art and may be exemplars of everything beautiful." [8]

— 36 —

Francesco Penni and
the Statuary Style

Wherefore these artists acquired the true and antique manner from the marbles
and the bronzes of Rome, and ever imitating these on their walls, they thus achieved
a great and miraculous success, and so did they exceedingly in every kind of thing,
and such fine inventors were they, and so universal, that their pictures by reason
of the divers riches that they held, were so much esteemed by painters, and so
necessary to them that all hastened to copy them.   —Armenini *

T HE lengths to which Raphael's pupils went into the literal transcription of ancient prototypes is apparent in the decorations by followers like
Francesco Penni, who completed the decoration of the Villa Farnesina
after the master's death. Whereas Raphael's gods in the Galatea fresco
were informed with a throbbing pulse of life, moving in a subtly contrived
composition, an imaginative recreation of ancient poetry and ancient
painting, the panels in the vaults of the Sala di Psiche show a far different
approach.

Such a composition as Giovanni Francesco Penni's Council of the
Gods (figure 135) gives the impression not of a gathering of human
shapes, but of a gallery of statues disposed in serried rows like the arrangement of a deeply carved Roman relief. It need only be noted that
the figure of Hercules in the foreground, like the Vulcan above him, is an
almost literal copy of the Belvedere Torso (figure 32a, b). The sphinx
comes from the group of the river god Nile in the Vatican, and a Praxitelean statue, perhaps one of several in the Medici Collection, inspired

* Conciosia cosa che essi presero la vera, & anticha maniera da' marmi, & da' bronzi
di Roma, & quelli tuttavia immitando nelle facciate loro, riuscirono così grandi, & mira-
bili, & si fecero così copiosi in ogni genere di cose, & così belli inventori, e tanto universali
che le loro pitture per le diverse ricchezze che vi sono, sono da' Pittori talmente desiderate,
& così ad essi necessarie, che ogniuno vi corre à torsi le copie.—G. B. Armenini, *De' veri
precetti della pittura* (1586)

the figure of Mercury to the left (figure 122). This by no means exhausts the repertory of familiar types, whose antecedents may be recognized in classical sculpture.

This composition is an example of an unresourceful artist's taking quite literally the injunctions of sixteenth-century critics on the value of studying the antique. In the writings, of course, the aim was not this kind of direct copying, but the use of ancient masterpieces as a point of departure for creation, the imaginative evocation and classical life transformed by the artist's own Inward Design (*disegno interno*) into a transfigured reality.[1]

Just as Giulio Romano, Raphael's most distinguished pupil, seems to have been concerned with creating another Roman art in his architecture and painting, so to an even greater extent Penni appears to have been so hypnotized by the ideality of ancient statues that he substituted them literally for representations of credible human beings. The result is a frozen, stony counterpart of humanity, characterized by a hardness of modeling that betrays its origin in marble. Penni, in painting like this, deserves the designation of "skillful statuary," inadvertently applied by Shakespeare to Giulio Romano as a condemnation of this uninventive reliance on the antique. It was no wonder that some of the more imaginative artists like Pontormo should have turned to experiments that led away from this final *reductio ad absurdam* of the classical style to inaugurate the novelties and ambiguities of Mannerism and a totally different interpretation of the classical tradition. Nor is it surprising that the general impression of Penni's fresco of Olympus anticipates the hollow sham of the neoclassic pastiche of Anton Raphael Mengs.

Michelangelo

When my rude hammer to the stubborn stone
    Gives human shape, now that, now this, at will,
    Following his hand who wields and guides it still,
    It moves upon another's feet alone:
But that which dwells in heaven, the world doth fill
    With beauty by pure motions of its own;
    And since tools fashion tools which else were none,
    Its life makes all that lives with living skill.
Now, for that every stroke excels the more
    The higher at the forge it doth ascend,
    Her soul that fashioned mine hath sought the skies;
Wherefore unfinished I must meet my end,
    If God, the great Artificer, denies
    That aid which was unique on earth before.

                          —Michelangelo *

M ICHELANGELO, like Picasso today, was a figure who completely dominated the artistic stage. His conceptions were so tremendous and so superior to the talents of his contemporaries that in the end they could produce not pupils but only imitators. There were none capable of continuing the grandeur of his ideation, because there were none of his intel-

    * Se 'l mie rozzo martello i duri sassi
       Forma d'uman aspecto or questo or quello,
       Dal ministro, che 'l guida iscorgie e tiello,
       Prendendo il moto, va con gli altrui passi,
       Ma quel divin che in ciel alberga e stassi
       Altri e se più col proprio andar fa bello;
       E se nessun martel senza martello
       Si puo far, da quel vivo ogni altro fassi.
       E perchè 'l colpo è di valor più pieno
       Quant'alza più se stesso alla fucina,
       Sopra 'l mio questo al ciel n'è gito a volo.
       Onde a me non finito verra meno,
       S'or non gli da la fabbrica divina
       Aiuto a farlo, c'al mondo era solo.
                —Michelangelo, Sonnet 61; translated by Symonds

lectual and technical stature. His art became a canon for artists and was ranked with the accepted norm of classical art. The piecemeal imitation of his work combined with the fragmentary copying of isolated ancient motifs produced the precious formula of the Mannerists. Although there is perhaps some truth in the contention that Michelangelo's work is so much the unified organic body of a single genius that it is improper to dissect it into fragments for separate analysis, the fact remains that these fragments, as much as the whole, can often reveal the totality of his thought and art, and in their isolation demonstrate his absorption in the antique.

Many art historians have been baffled by the phenomenon of Michelangelo for the reason that his own life seems so incompatible with the artistic expression of his thought in painting, sculpture, and poetry. There exists a marked dualism between Michelangelo the man, or social being, and Michelangelo the spiritual and artistic personality, so much so that there appears to be an incredible dichotomy between the bourgeois circumstances of his birth in 1475 and the simplicity of his whole physical life, and the dreams of heroic grandeur that he realized in marble and fresco. He never raised his daily existence to the level of his ideal, nor did he seek to incorporate the experience of his own life in his works—perhaps for the reason that Michelangelo's Platonic education in the courts of the Medici kept the two apart. In his art, Michelangelo strove to express a world of absolute truth which, in the Platonic sense, was apart from, and greater than, the deceptive world of appearances.

Michelangelo lived in the last generation of the Western Christian world, when it was still literally possible to regard paganism and Christianity as different manifestations of the same universal truth. Through his intimate association with Lorenzo the Magnificent and the great Neoplatonist Marsilio Ficino, Michelangelo absorbed the pagan philosophical doctrines that, for a great part of his life, seemed to contend with his devotion to Christianity. Michelangelo inevitably resorted to Neoplatonism in his search for ideal visual symbols of human life and destiny: this very abstraction of thought combined with his assiduous study of the antique as a very embodiment of the spiritual ideal he sought made for the heroic grandeur of his forms. In the same way, many of Michelangelo's painted and sculptured figures seem to express in their physical struggles the Platonic idea of the soul of man striving for union with God through the magnetic power of divine love.

Neoplatonism colored Michelangelo's thought and art: even the edition of Dante that he used had a Neoplatonic commentary. In love also Michelangelo was Platonic in his relations with both sexes. The resulting frustration, this inactivation of normal impulses, the conflict of spirit and desire, are often cited as being psychologically and pictorially expressed in the internal struggle that seems to rack Michelangelo's figures and in their imprisonment in the matrix of the stone. This torment and movement without locomotion in Michelangelo's figures are at once his spiritual adaptation of the violence of Hellenistic sculpture and an inevitable psychological expression of the dualism of pagan and Christian thought, of desire and chastity, embodied in Michelangelo's own life.

Everything in Michelangelo's artistic education contributed to the titanic structure of his later creative achievement. The most significant factor in the formal foundation of that structure was his study of antiquities preserved in the Medici gardens. Closely related to the knowledge of the beauty of organic form in sculpture which he learned from this source under the direction of his master Bertoldo was his assiduous copying of the figures in the great cycle of frescoes by Masaccio in the Brancacci Chapel of Santa Maria del Carmine. From these heroic, dignified forms presented with a massive plastic form, simplified and yet organically superior to Giotto, he learned to depict humanity in proportions more than life-sized with a suggestion of superhuman nobility and sculptural mass. It was the plastic nobility of the Masaccio paintings that appealed to an artist who always considered himself primarily a sculptor. His study of the antique provided him not only with poetic themes but also with models for that beauty of organic articulation of the human body that ultimately enabled Michelangelo to literally invent his own anatomy for the expression of his soaring ideas. The antique is always a controlling governor and norm imparting an expression both ideal and dynamic on his work. The structure of Michelangelo's formal education was crowned by his introduction to the doctrines of Neoplatonism that formed the way of life and the philosophy of the Academy of Lorenzo the Magnificent. Later, in conflict with this pagan thought, Michelangelo came under the spell of Savonarola. The mysticism of the great Florentine preacher and his teaching of the soul's redemption through suffering on the journey to union with the godhead find their inevitable tortured expression in the art of Michelangelo's later years. Every artist of every age perforce is the legatee of traditions and techniques of his predecessors. To the factors that made up Michelangelo's artistic personality must be added the intangible influence of his time with its political, social, and religious pressures affecting his psychology and the even more indefinable quality of originality that wrought these many heritages into something peculiarly his own. In Michelangelo this catalyst was partly his own individual genius and his supreme mastery of the techniques within which his spirit and hand expressed themselves. The character of Michelangelo's genius and the dynamic explosion in art of his personal psychology will become apparent in the analysis of his individual works.

Not the facile recognition of his models but rather the discovery of how the antique was the ever-renewed wellspring of his inspiration is the reason for studying Michelangelo's relations to ancient sculpture. Throughout his life, Michelangelo wrestled with the classical as an antagonist that could, in this lifelong competition, enable him to solve his own problems in the expression of states of being unknown to the ancient sculptors. Over and over again, in painting as well as in sculpture, he confronts the Laocoön or the Belvedere Torso to score his own triumphs in the representation of psychic as well as physical energy in the spiritual delirium of the Ignudi or the torpid dream state of the statues of the Medici Tombs.

One of Michelangelo's earliest works, which he must have executed while still a youth, is a stone relief of the Battle of Centaurs and Lapiths, still preserved in the Casa Buonarroti in Florence (figure 136). The crowded mass of figures and the deep incision into the plane suggest the technique of the battle sarcophagi of the Antonine Period (figure 137), and this is the first instance of Michelangelo's turning to one of the most baroque phases of classical art: the rounded, generalized forms of the individual heroic forms have almost a suggestion of the grandeur of the Phidian ideal. Most striking of all, perhaps, is the artist's use of antique prototype to create a composition of passionate dynamic struggle and emotion. One notices for the first time the contortion of the individual bodies in the interests of passionate expressiveness in this first appearance of his personal ideal of beauty.

Michelangelo's first really monumental commission was that for his heroic statue of David, certainly one of the most famous statues in the history of Western art (figure 138). It was carved from a gigantic block of Carrara marble, which had been offered to a number of famous artists, including Leonardo, before Michelangelo finally accepted its challenge.

This colossal nude statue of an adolescent youth shows the biblical hero with his sling, just before his struggle with the giant Goliath. The immediate classical prototype for this work of Michelangelo's was one of the horse-tamers, or Castor and Pollux, colossal statues nearly twenty feet high, which ever since the fall of the Western Empire and all through the Middle Ages had stood among the Roman ruins on the Quirinal Hill (figures 53 and 164). Few such colossal statues had survived from ancient times, and the dimensions of the horse-tamer and the David are nearly identical. The pose is the same, and Michelangelo has also borrowed the *contrapposto* and the deep-set eyes from this source (figure 139). One has the impression that the David was not carved from one actual model, but from Michelangelo's marvelously accurate memory of the articulation of the human frame in its separate parts reënforced by his study of the statues of Montecavallo. The image is one of tremendous force and power brought about by the twisting of the body on its axis, and the balance and alternate relaxation and tension of different parts of the body. Within the essentially classic and generalized form there appears a wonderfully accurate picture of the awkwardness and disproportion of the adolescent body, which seems in some magic way to be tremulous with pent-up force before the expected struggle. The torso of the David has something of that wonderful harmony of reality and abstraction associated with the Phidian ideal, but this Apollonian serenity is disturbed and made into something new and dynamic by the twist and strain of the head and the vibrant arm. The statue looms as a huge and dynamic embodiment of heroism that in its scale and force is far removed from the slight, inscrutable, sensuous prettiness of the youth by Donatello, Michelangelo's David (figure 140) has certain points of comparison with the famous statue of Hadrian's favorite, Antinoüs (figure 141), which in the early sixteenth century was in the Farnese Collection in Rome. The head is a kind of free adaptation of this revived classical ideal.

Michelangelo's David continues the fifteenth-century conception of this Old Testament figure as a hero rather than a kingly psalmist. His strength is implied in a physical and spiritual sense rather than by any active combat. The resemblance to a youthful Hercules (figure 94) in this statue is not entirely accidental. The idea of character, strength, and courage had always been associated with the ancient god, and in the Middle Ages Hercules together with David appears as a symbolic personification of Fortitude. Both were the spiritual victors over evil. There is evidence that for a time Michelangelo contemplated a companion figure of Hercules to stand with the David as defender and just governor of the city of Florence. In this way, the David was as much a political as a religious symbol, a secular duty emphasized by the installation of the statue in front of the Signoria.

The sixteenth-century critic Lomazzo implies that Michelangelo adopted the disproportionately large heads of the Montecavallo giants to provide, by a similar optical illusion, a sense of correct proportion in the David,[1] although this relation of head to body may be taken as an example of Michelangelo's knowledge of the adolescent frame in which parts like head and hands may appear disproportionately large for the ungrown body. There can be no doubt that Michelangelo did take over other technical features of the horse-tamers such as the fluid treatment of the hair, the thin nostrils, and the handling of the eyeballs with kidney-shaped holes for the pupils to intensify the flashing glance.

Although its complete nudity and giant scale recall ancient sculpture, the David is completely typical of Michelangelo's individual expressiveness in the sculptor's realistic representation of ungainly youthful anatomy and in its suggestion almost of an animated being in marble. Its gigantic nakedness was a symbol of indomitable fortitude, a wonderfully imaginative conception of a Herculean defender of justice. At the same time Michelangelo with his enchanted love for the mechanical beauty of the human form was able to endow his heroic stripling with a body that seems almost to breathe, the suggestion of possible movement in the tension of muscles and sinews, taut over the giant frame, ready for the emergency that the youth sees with his marble eyes. Such a conception has no single existing prototype in classical art, and so it is only in occasional aids to his dynamic embodiment of youthful strength that the great sculptor called upon his memory of antiquity.

Michelangelo's connections with the monuments of the classical past may be illustrated by an analysis of a number of the great monuments of his long career: the ceiling of the Sistine Chapel, the slaves which he executed for the tomb of Julius II, the Medici Tombs, and finally the painting of the Last Judgment in the Sistine Chapel.

The tremendous scheme of decorating the vault of the Sistine Chapel was undertaken in 1508. The fundamental conception of this tremendous scheme is the setting forth of the prophecies and prototypes in the Old Testament forecasting the coming of Christ and the redemption of man.

The most notable evidences of Michelangelo's classical preoccupations are in the figures of nude youths which appear above the titanic figures of the Prophets and around the biblical scenes in the center of the vault. These strangely moving forms, which in their contortions seem expressions of every form of feeling and passion—almost like illustrations of different tempos in a symphonic composition—were for Michelangelo expressions of the platonic idea of the divine love that raises men to God. They may perhaps be identified as the souls of the seers and sybils seated below them. They exemplify the soul—the *anima razionale*—in the Neo-platonic scheme of the cosmic order. The poses of many of these figures are taken deliberately from ancient statues, perhaps because Michelangelo believed that the idea of beauty was thereby manifested in the purest form.[2] Some suggest poses taken from the Laocoön group, and still others are unmistakably derived from the Belvedere Torso (figure 32). None of these derivations is a slavish copy; all seem like vitalized statues pulsating with life, in which the attitudes of the models have been transformed into a new dynamic life, with a musical quality in the rhythm of the contours. This wonderful inner life and movement stem in large part from Michelangelo's violent dislocation of the forms in *contrapposto*.

A comparison of one of these Ignudi (figure 142) that appears to be a free adaptation of the Belvedere Torso with Michelangelo's employment of this same fragment for a statue of Giuliano deí Medici illustrates the wealth of creative ideation that the artist was able to extract from his antique model. In the Genius of the Sistine ceiling the giant body, racked by the exertion of its spiritual struggle, seems to collapse into a posture of tormented exhaustion. The pathos of this ghostly symbol of the soul's striving is enhanced by the colossal proportions of the form, whose Herculean strength appears paralyzed by the effort of straining toward the divine. In the statue of Giuliano, Michelangelo again employed the Belvedere Torso to create a haunting image of a ruler sunk, like Michelangelo himself, in shadowy meditation on the woes of Italy. There appears once again the theme of spiritual frustration in a figure strangely powerless despite the implications of giant strength in the mighty frame. Even though there is something ungainly, almost repellent, about the exaggerated anatomy of Michelangelo's giant youths, we can accept this proportion as aesthetically valid if we realize that the artist did not intend them as normal human bodies, but as symbolic portrayals of transfigured angelic spirits to whom such a supernatural anatomy is completely appropriate. Since they are creatures not of human flesh, he has given them these heroic proportions in every way superhuman to indicate their celestial race. In the process of arriving at such a transfigured conception of humanity, the antique, with its already perfected canon, especially in the turbulence and pathos of the Laocoön, served Michelangelo in this invention of a new giant race to typify spirit rather than flesh. Michelangelo's figures, like the famous Adam (figure 143), are poised on a tremulous bridge between life and death, between the world of matter and the world of spirit. The extraordinary beauty of features veiled in dreams and filled with a haunting melancholy and pathos complements the spiritual stature implied by their colossal bodies. They reveal the same tragic poetry found in Michelangelo's sonnets.

The masterpieces of classical art, which were always present as shadows waiting in the corridors of the artist's mind, had achieved a supreme realization of perfected physical humanity that in its ideality connoted the perfection of divinity. Neither Phidias nor even the dynamic masters of the Hellenistic period were concerned, however, as Michelangelo was, with the expression of moments in the transitory journey of the soul enclosed in its mortal shell—its birth or ecstasy or dissolution as revealed through the action, the pantomime, of its earthly body.

The giantism of Michelangelo's forms is already forecast in an only less dynamic way in the sculpture of the Parthenon pediment (figure 13), where Phidias by a similar exaggeration of the normal stature of man implied the divine perfection of his subject. Whereas Phidias' Theseus is entirely finite. Michelangelo's figure of Adam in its straining unease is an embodiment of dynamic becoming rather than being. Michelangelo symbolically shows the human race in its beginning, straining into life at the divine touch, as in the completion of the cycle of salvation it struggles to return to the godhead that first enlivened its clay.

Although the figure of Adam extended on the barren crust of the primordial world may suggest the titanic figure of Theseus from the Parthenon, Michelangelo's man has none of that suggestion of superior physical and spiritual well-being implied in the complete inertness, relaxation, and lack of tension. Even if the Adam in its giant bulk may suggest such an ancient pediment sculpture, the pose with the muscles collapsed in inaction gives the impression of a great being, the inanimate clay of God's forming, waiting as a yet uninhabited fleshly shell, for the quickening touch of the divine. The great form seems to stir ever so slowly, already miraculously enlivened by the approaching vision of his maker who calls him to life.

A suggestion of inner life and psychic agony is communicated through the violence of bodily poses in the series of figures of captives which were originally destined to decorate the unfinished Tomb of Pope Julius II (figure 144). The exact symbolism of these moving figures has never been entirely clear. They may represent the arts and virtues chained in Julius' death, or more likely, embodiments of the Neoplatonic concept of souls struggling to be free of the trammels of material existence. This symbolism seems the more pointed in the unfinished forms of giants, in which the bodies are literally imprisoned in the core of the stone. All of these figures in varying degrees display the influence on Michelangelo of the famous Laocoön group that had first come to his attention in 1506. This Hellenistic tour de force itself embodied an expression of agonized passion and flow of life, which Michelangelo has raised to a kind of higher spiritual level through his very intensification of the movement of the bodies. Once again one has the feeling that Michelangelo began where the antique left off; in some magical way stretching his hand across the centuries to raise the forms of Hellenistic art to a new spiritual expression. All of these figures are filled with an extraordinary pathos. In every case one feels that the titanic forms are animated by something more than a merely physical struggle. They are images of heroic emotional effect that far transcends the violence of the Laocoön, no matter how much that group may have anticipated the needs of Michelangelo for a model of physical violence.

The most finished of the slaves, now in the Louvre, seems to show an indebtedness not only to the figure of Laocoön's younger son (figure 34) but even more pointedly in the pose to the Dead Niobid.[3] Michelangelo has adapted this inert, lifeless figure to an erect position and in a marvelous way given the suggestion of a body spent in a titanic struggle from which life seems to ebb with the crumpling of the exhausted youthful form. Neither this nor the other slaves is a copy of any one antiquity: Michelangelo transmuted remembered forms and poses into his own supremely plastic expressions of spiritual agony in stone.

One of Michelangelo's greatest commissions was for the Medici Tombs in the sacristy of San Lorenzo in Florence (1521–1534). These were memorials of Lorenzo Duke of Urbino and Giuliano of Nemours. The elaborate architecture presents the tomb as a kind of palace of the dead, and the fundamental conception of the group is that of the universe lamenting the decease of the Medici princes symbolized in the figures of Day and Night, Dawn and Twilight, as symbols of the destructive power of time, placed beneath the statues of the two dukes. The Medici Chapel is conceived as a kind of holy crypt, another world, Michelangelo has sought to symbolize in the combination of his architecture and sculpture that this is indeed a realm of departed souls. The effect on the beholder is created partly by the supernatural dimensions of the figures so large and overwhelming that they make the beholder himself feel that he belongs to this world of shadows. The statue of Giuliano (figure 145) is another illustration of Michelangelo's adaptation of the Belvedere torso (figure 32a, b) in such individual aspects of the torso as the folds of the abdomen, the muscles over the ribs, and the wavelike play of the muscles. But this colossal physique is dominated by the shadowed tragedy of the face, an embodiment of Michelangelo's own political and religious depression. The most remarkable figures are those on the lids of the sarcophagi, representing the times of day. These statues sit sunk in a strange paralysis that is neither sleeping nor waking. Such reclining types go back to classical antiquity. Michelangelo found at least a part of his inspiration in the Ariadne of the Vatican. Night (figure 146) is derived partly from the Ariadne (figure 33), partly from an ancient Aphrodite (figure 187). The strange form appears as though petrified in a dream, possessed by a sleep that is but unfulfilled desire. She is surrounded by creatures of night that disturb the soul: the owl, the satyr-mask, emblem of sensuality, and the bunch of withered poppies.

These giant figures, in addition to their symbolism of time, are metaphors of the transient states of the soul: of sleep, death, and waking. The figures of the two dukes are the images of departed souls lost in contemplation. The inertia and grief of the huge figures seem to express an endless mourning for the dead. These giant forms are symbols of the pain of souls for all ages. Michelangelo once wrote a quatrain on the giant uneasy figure of Night:

> Dear is my sleep, but to be mere stone,
> So long as ruin and dishonour reign:
> To hear nought, to feel nought is my great gain;
> Then wake me not; speak in an undertone.[4]

All of the figures are illustrations of Michelangelo's ability to create giants in a mighty formula of his own. Michelangelo's contortion of the gigantic forms has rendered the body far more dynamic and organic than the classic prototype; so that, for all its great bulk, it seems to rest weightless on the tomb. Whereas the classic precedents for these images were always intellectual and impersonal, Michelangelo's statues are completely individual and emotional. Their deadly weariness is a concrete expression of the artist's own disillusionment and frustration.

Michelangelo's titanic painting of the Last Judgment (figure 147) might be described as the artist's final pictorial expression of his lifelong search for the kingdom of God. In simple explanation of this vastly complicated iconographical tragedy one could say that the underlying concept of the Last Judgment is that unity of mercy and vengeance, of punishment and salvation, expressed in the sermons of Savonarola—the idea that punishment itself is an act of mercy since the soul, by suffering in Purgatory, may find at last the way to Paradise. In looking at this picture we find ourselves gazing into a vast space, a void beyond the laws of time and perspective, the limitless expanse of the universe itself. At the summit Christ stands at the center of a vast solar system (figure 148). He is the real sun of the Apocalypse, beside whose splendor the physical sun turns to ashes. He is a kind of Christ-Apollo, Christ-Helios, the Sol Justitiae, who has replaced the Sol Invictus of paganism. Again, as in the ancient astral myths, the skies are peopled with innumerable souls, freed from their bodies and drawn ever magnetically to their guardian stars. This is no more nor less than the Pythagorean concept of the aspiration of the souls of the elect to the sun, an idea well known to Dante, which Michelangelo has pictorially embodied in his conception of the wingless forms that rise magically to the Apollo-Christ. Michelangelo's work is a prodigious cosmic vision that presents an echo of his old Neoplatonic beliefs: man, the son of earth, formed from its clay, is after his death returned to the highest sphere; he is subject to new powers and a new age begins for him.

The Christ of Michelangelo's Last Judgment, although suggestive of the Apollo Belvedere (figure 181), is in no sense a copy of that statue. It belongs to a period when Michelangelo no longer drew from nature or the antique, so that all of his late designs are inventions, in which he was not so much concerned with even plausible anatomical construction as with the creation of forms as emblems of eschatological magnitude. Never confined to the quality of matter, these forms are dredged up out of the depths of Michelangelo's memory so that, like the remembered dreams of a lifetime, they contain reminiscences of his youthful attachment to the antique transformed into a completely personal vision. In order to explain why the vision of Apollo swam into Michelangelo's mind when he was drawing the colossal Judge, one can only say that there probably still lurked in his mind the Neoplatonic appropriateness of the sun god to represent the luminous Christ. The features and krobylos echo the Belvedere statue, but the form is petrified in the very action of loosing thunderbolts against the damned. Although Michelangelo could scarely have known the role of Apollo in Greek tragedy, the Judge of the World has taken on the features of Apollo. Michelangelo must have had a presentiment of the Olympian godliness in the Apollo Belvedere which led him to attribute Apollonian qualities to the face of Christ the Judge, a face which not only resembles the Apollo in pose and detail but has something of the victory-breathing sublimity of its features. There are other Apollonian elements in the Last Judgment, such as the giant figure of Niobe punished of old by the sun god, just as there are many allusions in Michelangelo's sonnets to Apollo and the sun or Christ and Apollo that make one wonder if here, as so often in his life, Michelangelo was thinking of a fusion of Christianity and paganism.

— 38 —

Titian

In the other, one sees Jupiter
Changed by love into a superb white bull
Bearing off his treasure rich and sweet.
Her face turns to the fading shore
In terror, while her golden hair
Stirred by the heading wind, plays over her bosom;
Her gown billows and blows back in the wind;
With one hand she clasps the bull's back
And with the other clutches his horn.

—Politian *

OUR mental picture of Venice in the sixteenth century is of an opulent and splendid marble city floating like a golden mirage above the lagoon, filled with the riches her argosies brought from the treasure-houses of the Levant. Venice had never enjoyed the intellectual renaissance of Florence in either a philosophical or artistic sense. It was a society more dedicated to the experience of sensuous pleasure than the pursuit of science or the cold mysteries of the Platonists. In art the Venetian renaissance expressed itself in a dazzling and sensuous display of color, almost as a tangible reflection in art of the light that engulfed her palaces and waterways. It was as though the frozen fire of the jewels and gold of her ancient Byzantine mosaics had liquefied into the sensuous glowing warmth of oil color. The Venetian artist painted to record things in their outward visual

---

* Nell' altra in un formoso e bianco tauro
si vede Giove per amor converso
pontarne il dolce suo ricco tesauro,
e lei volgere il viso al lito perso
in atto paventosa; e i bei crin d'auro
scherzon nel petto per lo vento avverso;
la vesta ondaggia, e indrieto fa ritorno,
l'una man tiene al dorso, e l'altra al corno.
—Poliziano, *La Giostra,* I, 105–106

aspect as veiled in light and vibrant air to the negation of the tangible definition of sculptural form.

It was inevitable that the sensuous mythology of Ovid's poetry should have exercised an appeal to artists concerned like the poet Aretino with the evocation of the erotic and sensuous pleasures of the golden ancient world. One of the greatest interpreters of the pagan legend was Venice's famous painter Titian. This sixteenth-century master owed his command of color and the creation of poetic allegories to Giovanni Bellini and Giorgione. In his long lifetime he visited Rome, where he came under the spell of Michelangelo and the antique. His paintings were commissioned by the greatest courts of Europe. In the last decades of his life after 1560 he evolved a style which with its vibration of light and the atmospheric envelopment of nebulously defined form anticipates the vision of Rembrandt and the modern Impressionists. It is to this period that his greatest paintings of pagan mythologies belong. Titian's evocations of classical myth are, like Botticelli's poetic inventions, based on literary descriptions of paintings in Catullus and Philostratus and on the legends related by Ovid. They are to an even greater extent reinforced by references to actual classical fragments, and always Titian's mythological subjects are pagan in intent as in form with no suggestions of Neoplatonic symbolism.

The sixteenth-century critic Albani, writing of Titian and Correggio, observed that "it was better for them that they did not meddle with statues. Statues, no matter how beautiful, are a dangerous model for a painter." [1] Albani was wrong in asserting that Titian did not base himself on antiquity. There is no Renaissance artist in whose work the classical element emerges so insistently as a constantly present and active factor. From his visit to Rome and his study of the marbles in the Grimani Collection in Venice, Titian had gained an intuitive understanding of ancient monuments and the possibilities for new creations concealed in an ancient motif. He had little concern for archaeological accuracy nor was he interested in ancient art for its naturalism. Titian's was an entirely personal interpretation. His borrowings from ancient art became ever more free and individual in the work of his later years. Ancient art was useful to him, as it was to Michelangelo, for the achievement of an heroic style, especially in the painting of the human figure. Titian's selection of ancient prototypes was based on the effectiveness which he described in a gesture or movement appropriate to the expressiveness of his own work. Invariably he transformed his models into his own pictorial style, and he shows complete liberty in using classical forms in a context totally different from their original meaning. In his last style these shapes themselves dissolve in a flood of color and light, a style which the poet William Blake contemptuously referred to as "disorganized blobs." [2] Titian's use of color almost as a film or a series of veils concealing the forms is totally opposed to the sharp sculptural mode of the Florentine masters of the Renaissance. In the works of his last years there is an almost total disregard of the original destination of his ancient models in the way in which the artist completely reorders them into new compositions. It is everywhere apparent that Titian was never interested in renewing the intrinsic forms of ancient art, like a Mantegna, but he was always sensitive to their beauty and utility, for the emotional expressionism that became ever more the principal aim of his art.

One of the most beautiful of paintings from the point of view of sensuousness of color is Titian's Bacchus and Ariadne in the National Gallery in London (figure 149). This poetic interpretation of classical legend is a wonderfully constructed arrangement, almost like a musical composition, in the building up, interlocking, and repetition of the shapes that comprise it. As on a stage we see Bacchus and his noisy train burst from a wooded glen onto an open strand. As though swayed by a divine ecstasy, Bacchus whirls to leap from his chariot, deserting his cortege of revelers to pursue the love of Ariadne. The heroine seems to flee into the infinite vista that opens into this sunlit landscape. Above her a starry crown beckons from the skies. The frenzied figure of the wine god is very obviously based on the raging Orestes from a Roman sarcophagus (figure 150). Ariadne and some of the figures in the Bacchic rout are drawn from similar sources. It is apparent at once that the resplendent colors bear no relation to ancient marbles, and the way in which the figures are literally dissolved in a vibrant envelopment of color provides a sensuous, rather than intellectual interpretation of a mythological incident.

Another wonderful example of Titian's transmutation of classical forms into a world of paint and color is The Rape of Europa in the Isabella Stewart Gardner Museum in Boston (figure 152). The Europa is an example of Titian's building his composition almost like an exercise in music, with countless repeated phrases and echoes. These harmonies were developed in preliminary sketches as the painter moved into his creation. The canvas is dominated by the figure of Europa, swooning in fright across the back of the bull that floats effortlessly over the azure sea. At the lower left a putto on a dolphin provides a comic echo of the major motif. On the distant strand Europa's companions wave and call in helpless anxiety, and in back a succession of blue headlands recedes into a fiery sky. Hovering overhead two cupids with arrows speed the erotic abduction. The poses of these erotes are only slight variants of the pose of Europa herself, and other motifs like Europa's flying scarf repeat the movement of the heroine's arms. The reclining posture of Europa, as Dr. Brendel has pointed out, is taken from the statue of a falling Gaul among the marbles in the Grimani Collection (figure 151), a borrowing that illustrates Titian's adaptation of antique shapes for purposes totally different from their original destination. The cupids are slightly altered transformations of a Phidian Eros. The sculpturesque character of these classic prototypes has been completely dissolved in Titian's creation of a painting in gauzy areas of color.

In the passage already referred to, in which Albani stated that Titian avoided the use of statues as models, he goes on to explain that the drapery in statuary appears so well-defined in its shadowed grooves and ridges that the painter copying sculptured drapery may fall into the trap of emulating this very hardness. "That is why Titian," he says, "in painting the darks, used to leave in the grooves of the draperies an impasto blended in accordance with nature." This analysis could apply very well to the scanty drapery of the Europa, which, although from a distance may remind us of the chiton of a classical Amazon, becomes on close inspection only a loosely defined texture of contrasting lights and darks and pigment alternately thick and thin. The darks of the drapery grooves are painted, as Albani implies, in variegated values of burnt umber and neutralized sienna. This method is indeed the method of the whole painting, a mode in which the statuesque prototype has been transformed into pure pigment, which is neither flesh nor stone, so that every element in the painting exists only as a color shape in a dematerialized memory of solid form in the gauzy glowing world of pure color.[3]

— 39 —

Mannerism

Wherefore, the continued making and drawing of well-made objects is the means of making these yours by infallible rule: this is certainly true, because imitation is nothing else but a diligent and judicious means that one uses to become like unto other excellent artists by such observations. But in order that you may realize fully the basis by which you may mirror these excellent masters, whereby you can surely determine what is finest, chiefly with regard to capital examples, we place before you certain of the most notable ancient sculptures which are the most intact that have survived to our times and which, moreover, come nearest to the very perfection of the art.
—Armenini *

Between the art of the High Renaissance and the true Baroque art of the seventeenth century there is an interregnum, a type of art that does not belong entirely to one or the other of these greater trends. This is the painting and sculpture of the Mannerists, so called because their critics accused them of working in the "manner" of Michelangelo or Raphael or Correggio and distorting that manner to their own purposes. In this new art there are no further discoveries in the representation of phenomena in the outside world.

The artists retreat to a kind of inner world of their own making, in which new methods and new tricks of drawing and painting replace the earlier recordings of the realm of visual experience. There is a return to medieval conceptions of pictorial construction and deliberate elongation of forms, replacing that convincing rendering of normal space and pro-

* Conciosiacosa che il continuo fare & il continuo ritrarre le cose be fatte è cagione che si facciano le sue per certa regola benissimo, & è certo cosi, poiche l'imitatione non è altro, che una diligente, & giuditiosa consideratione, che si usa, per poter divenne col mezo delle osservationi simile à gli altri eccellenti. Ma accioche da voi si conosca à pieno il fondamento da potervi specchiar in esso, & per dove possiate capire con sicurezza il buono, & massimamente delle figure per essempi principali vi si porranno innanzi alquante scolture antiche delle più note, & che sono piu intiere à i tempi nostri, & che più ancora si accostano alla perfettion vera dell'arte.—G. B. Armenini, *De' veri precetti della pittura*

portions that had concerned the scientists of the fifteenth century. The colors are no longer realistic, but emotional, in that their unreal and yet jewellike brilliance is designed to affect the mind directly. This new art is characterized by the quality of grace, a kind of sweetness and elegance which seems to parallel the refinement in manners described by such writers on courtly etiquette as Castiglione, who said, "The courtier ought to accompany all his doings, gestures, demeanors, finally all his motions, with a grace." [1] In addition to deliberate posturing designed to suggest the aristocracy and refinement of the figures, it became a convention to endow the forms with small heads and long limbs to insure the required elegance. Such distortions echo the ideas of practitioners like Vasari, who opined that, in order to achieve final perfection, art must improve on nature and not be concerned merely with what he describes as the dry imitation of natural objects found in the work of his predecessors. [2]

In contrast to Renaissance pictures, whose figures have normal, harmonious proportion, the forms by Mannerist artists are strangely contorted into new serpentine rhythms; violent zigzags and diagonal lines replace the closed rectangles and horizontals of the Renaissance compositional formula; there is an instability and lack of balance; an arbitrary metallic lighting replaces the natural light of the fifteenth century; besides, there is a morbid, subjective quality in both the mood of the paintings and in the whole hypersensitive exotic organization of their composition. What is the explanation of this turn in art? Is it the result of the same malaise that disturbed Michelangelo? Is it the result of the moves of the Council of Trent? Is it a reaction against the academic classicism of the Renaissance? All of these explanations are partly true. This mundane quality present even in religious art, this facile grace and preciosity is partly an exploration of new forms; it is also intended to tickle the tastes of an affected, decadent society. As early as the sixteenth century the work of artists like Pontormo, Parmigianino, and Bronzino was explained as an imitation or exaggeration of the *maniera* of the giants of the High Renaissance. More recently the style has been characterized as anticlassical in its deviation from the norms of the Renaissance. One thing is certain, that Mannerism is just as autonomous a style as that of any other period. It also appears certain that, although admittedly anticlassical in their performance, the Mannerist artists, both painters and sculptors, were still committed to the antique, if only in a different and fragmentary way, for the achievement of *la bella maniera*.

211

In Mannerist art the antique became a subject for detached academic study. Artists discovered novel aspects of antiquity to satisfy new creative needs; there was a romantic nostalgia for pagan antiquity as an image of a remote and unapproachable realm. Whereas Roman buildings had been objects for admiration and scientific study in the Renaissance, for the late sixteenth-century artists the vestiges of ancient Rome assumed all kinds of magical and emotional overtones, as mysterious and evocative fragments of a vanished order. The ruins became enchanted relics, without any real archaeological value.

The Mannerist period witnessed a return to specific models, as in the fifteenth century, but without need to conform to any concept of the balance, harmony, or logical unity of the ancient forms. Mannerism is an art of symbolical fantasy and poetic idealism. The Mannerist artists of mythological subjects required special models as a confirmation for their own artistic invention that could be quoted or transcribed from any phase of any ancient style. In this strange period the classical becomes an embodiment of physical beauty, carnal desire, and heroic pathos. The interpretation of classical subject matter in painting and poetry becomes for the real world of tensions and suppressed emotions, a visionary enclave of untroubled beauty and vitality.

In the Mannerist period there unfolds a new secret world of antique influences; the artists express themselves mostly in a veiled absorption of the antique style difficult to distinguish. They are no longer interested in monuments with an ideal norm, as the High Renaissance, but those which express all kinds of eccentric invention and a subjective mannered deviation from rational naturalism, so that obviously there is a new interest in Hellenistic sculpture presenting the most complicated poses. In the same way there seems to be a new interest in Roman relief sculpture of the second and third centuries A.D. for their expression of spiritual agitation: the melancholic emotionalism of Mannerist art is intensified by a new and different study of the complex style of the later Roman sarcophagi. Mannerist artists are interested in those aspects of antiquity that confirmed their own emotional excitement or heightened the ferocity and phantasy of conception and the expression of force, by the disquiet of every form.

In the sixteenth century critics like Vasari and Armenini presented a selection of classic masterpieces, a roster including the Laocoön, the Apollo, the statues of Montecavallo, the Ariadne, and the Nile of the Vatican. The fame of these selected masterpieces promptly spread far and wide, through copies, prints, and casts. But what induced Primaticcio to make bronze replicas of these famous statues and to buy ancient marbles for Francis I was no longer the same impulse that caused Brunelleschi to go on foot from Florence to Cortona to draw a modest Roman sarcophagus that Donatello had told him about. For the original religious fervor for antiquity is substituted the zeal of the collector and the archaeological method. Ancient works were looked at with different intentions; they were interpreted with new canons and rules, an interpretation more nearly approaching archaeology. This more systematic ordering of antiquity in a way relegates it to a cold and distant past. Sometimes in Mannerist works classical fragments under a veil of affected mysticism assume once more the medieval concept of antiquity as an unknown forbidden wisdom, a magical secret.

In this period there was a search for beauty per se, a new intellectualized, abstract, and unique beauty. This beauty could be achieved in part, it was thought, by what is described as the *serpentinata,* the trick of twisting the figure in a kind of gyratory fashion on its axis, which presumably had its origin in the more violent aspects of Hellenistic art, although the definition of its principle is credited to Michelangelo, who is supposed to have told one of his pupils "that he should always make a figure pyramidal, serpentlike, and multiplied by one, two, or three, in which precept the whole mystery of the art consisteth." [3]

That perfect harmony of classical form which was achieved in the brief moment of the High Renaissance was upset in the period of conflict and crisis in the sixteenth century. This was part of the same struggle that brought the philosophy of Bruno and the science of Galileo into conflict with Christian dogma. The artists suffered in the struggle between their Christian beliefs and their admiration for pagan antiquity in this period when classicism and the nude were repudiated to the extent that Michelangelo's Last Judgment had to be outfitted with clothes. The earlier admiration for classical beauty was transformed into a self-conscious feeling composed of reluctant admiration, disquieting scruples, and a cool archaeological interest. The fig-leaf, invented in the sixteenth century, is a symptom of this new self-consciousness and uneasiness. The artistic situation was further complicated by the emergence of medieval tendencies in conflict with classical principles. The objection was to classical forms, especially nude forms, in Christian art, so that what was incompatible with Christian culture became an all the more perfect harmony in itself.

There was never any conflict in the antique. Physical beauty, carnal desire, and heroic pathos had never been in conflict with moral or theological precepts. Attempts to classicize Christian subjects were frowned upon, but genuine classical subject matter was quite acceptable. For the poetic soul classical antiquity becomes a beckoning, nostalgic realm, an abode of beauty, sensual love and *dolce-farniente*. This marks the beginning of the conception of the classical past as an enchanting Utopia, surrounded by a halo of sweet and melancholy resignation, antiquity as an idea of bliss and happiness. The classical past now looms as a visionary refuge, offering an ideal fulfillment of all unappeased desires, a paradise lamented.

Although Mannerism is an outgrowth of the High Renaissance and its attachment to the classical, it is at the same time an art that seeks for the exotic and the new in its general performance as well as in its use of the antique. Like any original style it was produced by the artists themselves, partly as a result of a dissatisfaction with the static perfection of the High Renaissance style, partly as a result of inner and outer pressures, but most of all as the result of a desire for the exploration of new effects of pictorial expression, necessitated by the artist's inner imaginative stimulus to depart from the classic forms of the High Renaissance to produce new visual and psychic influences on the beholder by the purposeful manipulation and distortion of reality. If the antique was used only for isolated figures and poses, this was completely in line with the new cult of the esoteric and ambivalent from both the pictorial and iconographic points of view. The classic models were disguised, just as the meaning of the learned allegories, replacing the older free transcription of classical subjects, concealed and titillated by only half-suggested implications.

Parmigianino

Were I a Parmesan, I would feign call
That Little Parmesan, "Child of the Graces,"
Swift and more graceful than a dancer,
Light (one might say) as the wind itself.
—Boschini *

Even in his own lifetime Parmigianino was designated as Raphael re-born. Although, as his contemporaries recognized, he had inherited something of the gentleness and statuesque composure, he transformed the Umbrian's style into an idiom that in many ways appears the antithesis of classicism. Parmigianino's art was formed from his association with the great Renaissance colorist Correggio, and inevitably from his acquaintance with the work of Michelangelo and some of the Mannerist pioneers in Rome of the first quarter of the sixteenth century. To a far greater degree than his Parmesan forebear, Correggio, Parmigianino utilized antiquity, and, like all Mannerist art, his paintings have an abstract beauty unknown to the High Renaissance. His paintings are filled with *venusta,* which in contemporary criticism meant a kind of indescribable inner loveliness, and with the quality of *grazia,* a word that implied not only grace but that air of exquisite refinement of manner and movement prescribed for the perfect courtier by Castiglione. The effect of the psychologically disturbing distortions of reality is at once precious and lewd.

Parmigianino is a typical Mannerist in the way in which he disguises the antique and interweaves it with religious as well as pagan subjects.

* Se fusse Parmesan, voria chiamar
Fio de le Gracie quel Parmesanin,
Suelto, e legiadro più d'un Balarin,
Agile (se puol dir) del vento alpar.
—Mario Boschini, *Arte del navagar pittoresco* (1660)

That he was abundantly aware of the antique is evident in drawings after ancient monuments, notably two studies of the head of the older son in the Laocoön group. The ancient head is made even more expressive by the intensification of the gaze and the strangely wiry quality of the drawing.

Many of Parmigianino's paintings of the Madonna are filled with undisguised recollections of the ancient world in the shape of triumphal arches and columns as an allusion to the pagan order overthrown by Christianity and as a concession to the awakening archaeological taste in hallowed antiquity. No painting of Parmigianino is a more notable example of the Mannerist transformation of the classical than the Madonna of the Rose in the Dresden Gallery, painted about 1530 (figure 153). From the point of view of its sensuous charm and strangely affected grace it would be hard to imagine a less religious painting of the subject. Although ostensibly a religious picture it is completely profane.

It would almost seem that the legend current in the sixteenth century that the picture was begun as a Venus and Cupid may have been manufactured from the obvious resemblance to an antique type. Whether or not the painting was originally designed as a pagan allegory for the poet Aretino and then altered when the picture was acquired by Pope Clement VII, the fact remains that the pose of the Madonna was quite literally borrowed from the Cnidian Venus or the Venus dei Medici (figure 30). This classical source is superficially disguised, since the Madonna is draped in a diaphanous robe, but the very employment of this fragment of antiquity and its concealment as in a pictorial rebus is typical of Mannerism, a parallel for the conceits of Mannerist literature. This drapery hides the pagan form, just as allegory provides a thin shield for other more daring ventures into the forbidden pagan themes by Mannerist artists like Parmigianino and Bronzino. Although the exquisite pose of the hands had an obvious function in the classical statue, it is quite meaningless here. Not only was Parmigianino enchanted by the gesture of the Venus concealing her charms, but its adoption for the Madonna only adds to the haunting ambiguity and mystery of the conception. Above all, this posture, however meaningless, served to confer a hyper-refinement and sensitive grace to the figure. The movement of the pliant arms is repeated in the tortuous involutions of the draperies that move around the figure of the Madonna in undulating rhythms. Not only the pose but the statuesque modeling reveals Parmigianino's fascination for the hard, stony precision of sculpture, and the sharp, cold definition of the Madonna's regular features specifically suggests a model in statuary.

Save for the rose as a symbol of Christ's sacrifice and the globe emblematic of His dominion, it would be difficult to recognize this panel as a religious painting at all. The painting has a quality of sensual attractiveness that projects itself forcefully to the beholder both in the physical charm of the model and the delicious luxuriance of the technical handling. The artist's flesh tints have a marblelike luster, the sensuous enjoyment of which is excited by the painting in blended pearly tones of variegated touches of cool and warm hues. As in so many Mannerist paintings the microscopic delicacy of finish in the picture seduces the beholder into a lingering sensuous examination of its every part.

In a painting like this the effects are just as strange and contrived as in Parmigianino's famous self-portrait in a convex mirror. It is as though the fascination of the strange distortions of reality seen in the glass had led this imaginative painter to experiment in yet other deviations from the normal forms and normal space of the High Renaissance to the exploration of a strange exciting world in which the effects of balance and clarity were purposefully disturbed. Part of the excitement and novelty of the Mannerist un-classical composition lies in the uncertainty of the position of objects in space. In a strangely medieval way the elements in the picture seem to be pressed in the slide-glass of the foreground plane, but at the same time their strange serpentine rhythms seem struggling to free them from this arbitrary imprisonment. This movement in surface arabesques is completely in harmony with the Gothic elongation of the figures in the over-all rhythm of the design. All of these qualities, like Parmigianino's disguised use of the classical, are parts of a style formed not so much in nature as in the artist's own mind.

Another example of Parmigianino's hidden devious transformation of an antique motif through his Inward Design (*disegno interno*) is his painting of Amor or Cupid (figure 154). The source is ostensibly a literary one. Not only the painting of Cupid's golden locks but also his activity of fashioning the bow are from descriptions in *The Golden Ass* of Apuleius. Vasari explains the child erotes at the bottom of the composition when he tells us that one of these children is trying to force his companion to touch Cupid and that this crying, obviously female, Amor resists, because she fears to be burned by the fire of love.

From the formal point of view the figure of Cupid appears to be a combination made in Parmigianino's own interior vision of several figures by his master, Correggio, and the memory of such an antiquity as the Cupid by Lysippus existing in various copies (figure 155). With only slight variations the pose of the classical statue of Cupid unbending Hercules' bow has been altered to the needs of the present conception. Here to an even greater degree than the Madonna of the Rose the sensuous qualities of Parmigianino's painting both entrance and repel. There can be little doubt that the figure of the god of love is intended to be provocative from a sexual point of view. The beauties of the androgynous adolescent body are rendered more piquant by the slyly malicious, knowing glance of the Cupid, whose feigned labor in the shaping of the bow is only a pretext for the overt pose. The solid statuesque modeling appears as another of Parmigianino's translations of stone into a soft lustrous substance that is neither flesh nor marble but a substance rendered sensuously attractive by the artist's gradations of tone and hue within the nacreous areas of the naked form. The disguise of the classical source and the obscurity of the subject are once more typical of the Mannerist game of pictorial enigmas. This representation of Love punished by the labor of fashioning the bow, taken together with the unhealthy overt connotations of the nude boy, seems to contain further hidden meanings, the dangers or punishments of the type of love the image suggests.

Bronzino's Allegory of Luxury

I omit infinite other lascivious actions which I might heere rehearse, or at the least point at, (although perchaunce they would bee necessarie for the instruction of the painter, whom they may oftentimes stande in steede, either to satisfie the humors of the Great Princes and noble men, or else his owne private affection) thinking it better to passe them over in silence, because it is impossible to set them downe in civill and chaste tearmes.   —Lomazzo *

THE sixteenth-century critic Ludovico Dolce, advising artists on the attainment of perfection in art, makes a specific recommendation for the employment of antique precedents:

And in part one should imitate the beautiful marble or bronze figures of the antique masters. Those who fully savor and possess the admirable perfection of these will surely be able to correct many defects of Nature, and make their paintings attractive and pleasing to everyone, for the works of antiquity contain all the perfection of art, and may be models of everything beautiful.[1]

Again in his *Dialogo della Pittura* he noted "that painters often take their inventions from poets, and poets from painters." [2]

These observations of a writer who lived in a period when the Mannerist style possessed the imagination of all Italian artists find their illustration in one of the great masterpieces of sixteenth-century Florence: the *Allegory of Luxury* by Agnolo Bronzino (figure 156).[3] This beautiful and enigmatic work is typical at once of the intellectuality and obscurity of the painter's invention. Its complex iconography shows the snares of sensual love unveiled by outraged Time and Truth. Beneath these figures at

---

* Altri atti infiniti di lascivia che si potrebbono quivi raccontare, o almeno accennare, con tutto che forsi sarebbe necessario per istruttione, & avvertimento del pittore, à cui sovente occorre, o per compiacere à Principi, & signori, ò anche per suo proprio capriccio di dovergli esprimere, ho giudicato che sia megliò tralasciare, non potendo essere che in così fatto ragionamento non venga à dirsi alcuna cosa obscena & possa contaminare i buon costumi.—G. P. Lomazzo, *Trattato dell'arte*, 1584; translated by Haycocke

the top of the stage an adolescent Cupid embraces the kneeling Venus; their coral lips brush lightly in a kiss. At the right, above a pair of masks that symbolize Fraud, is a dancing putto whom Vasari identified as the figure of Jest; and behind him, in the strange mineral depths of the picture, is the figure of a girl with a serpent's tail, who symbolizes Deceit.

In looking at this beautiful picture in the National Gallery the beholder's first impression is that of the strangely provocative nudes, seemingly wrought of some alabastrine substance, set off against the mineral blue of the grotto formed by the curtains in the background. Indeed everything in the picture seems to be made of some precious substance that has no correspondence with the matter of the objects represented. The masks, as well as the human figures, have a common marblelike quality. The picture resembles a piece of sculpture in which all the elements are represented in the likeness of stone. This effect is marvelously enhanced by Bronzino's painting of the bodies of Venus and Cupid in a *grisaille* palette of white and pearly gray with faint touches of rose. In the exquisite precision of the rendering of every detail the picture has almost the appearance of a colossal *nature morte*. There is something magical about the evocation of the separate parts of this composition that in its exaggeration almost approximates surrealism. This is in no sense a complete realism, but rather a fragmentary one. Part of the novelty and invention of the Mannerist painter consisted in this almost veristic, plastic definition of details additively combined within the composition. There is a combination of many details drawn from reality or from the antique, rather than a complete painting from the life. One notes an emphasis on the details of the composition, each presented in its separate essential form regardless of its relation to a complete pictorial whole. The picture gives the general impression of a screen of figures and limbs with glimpses of isolated hands, heads, and other details in the background, and even within the shallow stage it is difficult to decipher the planes that comprise it. In some respects the painting almost gives the impression of a relief rendered in painting, with only the figures of Venus and Cupid looming in the round.

The painting illustrates the new attitude toward the unclothed body—naked, rather than nude, provocative in the self-conscious posturing and filled with hidden lascivious allusions. Bronzino's picture has its counterpart in the erotic suggestion of Donne's verses in which lubricity is veiled beneath the Neoplatonic allusion to the soul's release from the body.

License my roaving hands, and let them go
Before, behind, between, above, below . . .
Full nakedness! All joyes are due to thee,
As souls unbodied, bodies uncloth'd must be,
To taste whole joyes.[4]

Many of the Mannerist qualities of the painting and its character as a whole can be explained by Bronzino's special use of antique precedents. The figures and their separate parts represent a kind of compendium of Bronzino's peculiar antiquarianism. These antique borrowings are so many fragments taken from a variety of sources. The head of Venus herself is Bronzino's own exquisite refashioning of the Cnidian Aphrodite (figure 157), which on other occasions served him for the head of the Madonna in the Holy Family of the Uffizi. The upraised right arm of the goddess of love has been borrowed from the so-called Hestia Giustiniani. One could go on enumerating the scattered inspirations from the antique that went into the making of Bronzino's picture. The important thing is that his joining of these many isolated details is completely typical of the artist and Mannerist invention in general. From the formal point of view the picture represents a kind of culmination of the artist's admiration for antiquity that had revealed itself in a number of his earlier works. Some of his most distinguished portraits, for example, show the sitter in association with some carefully delineated antique statuette or fragment. And in some of these the subjects of the portraits themselves have a statuesque self-contained quality that points the way to the artist's greater and greater use of statues for the allegorical subjects from the end of his career. Of these, the London painting is the most splendid example.

The Mannerist ideal as represented by Bronzino is at once an outgrowth and distortion of that search for an ideal beauty to express the divinity of man in the work of Michelangelo. In a Mannerist painter like Bronzino there is more of a search for elegance and the expression of beauty at once intellectual and abstract. The strange uneasy rhythms of the Mannerists spring from their formalized use of a serpentine line that is itself an exaggeration of a formula inaugurated by Michelangelo. Michelangelo's sculpture and painting possess an intricate rhythm which this great artist developed out of his admiration for the examples of the baroque art of the ancient period. A Mannerist artist like Bronzino formed his own personal style not so much on nature as on the precedent of forms already existing in art, in his case the art of Michelangelo and

221

the antique. In the invention of the Mannerists these formal conventions are presented with a new intellectuality and obscurity.

Another and remarkable instance of Bronzino's always inventive and always hidden use of the antique may be discovered in his monumental fresco of the Martyrdom of St. Lawrence commissioned by the Grand Duke Cosimo for the church of San Lorenzo and unveiled in 1569. This vast composition is filled with a dense throng of nude and semi-nude forms which revolve in a varied counterpoint of movement around the central figure of St. Lawrence. Many of these giant figures, far more Michelangelesque than the graceful slender shapes in the Allegory of Luxury, have vague suggestions of remembered classic statues. The figure of the saint himself, serenely recumbent on his gridiron, evokes memories of ancient river gods and ultimately of the heroic personification of Cephissus from the Parthenon. Another single figure is even more worthy of analysis to illustrate Bronzino's Mannerist transformation of the antique (figure 158). This is the huge huddled form in the lower right-hand corner of the composition. After looking at it for some time it becomes apparent that this is Bronzino's personal disguised translation of the famous Belvedere Torso (figure 32b); the titanic back with its waves of muscles is unmistakable, and so, too, is the arched curvature of the spine. This is the one personage in the entire composition who, withdrawn from the scene of torment, seems convulsed with sorrow and despair at St. Lawrence's agony. As though to indicate in physical terms the paroxysm of sorrow that convulses the giant frame, Bronzino has twisted the arms and legs added to the memory of the Belvedere Torso in a violent serpentine *contrapposto* expressive of the strange tension that seems both to move and paralyze the Herculean body. One could have no better illustration than this single figure of how a Mannerist painter like Bronzino uses a fragmentary quotation from the antique—his borrowing from the Belvedere statue—to invent a new anatomy that is both moving and strange in its psychological and formal connotation.

— 42 —

Benvenuto Cellini's Narcissus

His Excellency sent to Rome post-haste for a block of Greek marble, in order that I might restore his antique Ganymede, which was the cause of that dispute with Bandinello. When it arrived, I thought it a sin to cut it up for the head and arms and other bits wanting in the Ganymede; so I provided myself with another piece of stone, and reserved the Greek marble for a Narcissus which I modelled on a small scale in wax.   —Cellini *

THIS passage from the *Autobiography of Benvenuto Cellini* has served to identify one of his most beautiful statues, now in the Museo Nazionale in Florence.[1] There was perhaps something appropriate in Cellini with his learned antiquarianism and enormous self-esteem choosing the subject of Narcissus (figure 159a, b). This beautiful statue, although not so well-known as the sculptor's great bronze of Perseus, is a magnificent example of the Mannerist style that Benvenuto's art embodied. It is the sculptural counterpart of Cellini's great contemporary, the Florentine Bronzino.

Mannerism, whether exemplified in sculpture or in painting, is primarily an intellectual art that in strange complexity seems to spring from the spiritual suffering of the artist. The works of Mannerist painters and sculptors are like tropic plants with roots both deep and dark. The work of these men of the middle sixteenth century may be described as a virtuoso style, the combination of a precise scholarly approach and a reliance on obscure literary sources, an equally complex theoretical basis. This was a many-sided cultivated generation of artists, many of whom read

---

* Con molto prestezza mi fecie venire 'l Duca un pezzo di marmo greco, di Roma, acciò che io restaurasi il suo Ganimede antico . . . Venuto che fu 'l marmo greco, io considerai che gli era peccato a farne pezzi per farne la testa e le braccio e l'altre cose per il Ganimede; et mi providdi d'altro marmo, et a quel pezzo di marmo greco feci un piccol modellino di cera al (quale) posi nome Narciso.—*Vita di Benvenuto Cellini,* ed. Orazio Bacci (Florence, 1901); translated by Symonds

both Greek and Latin. For Cellini and his contemporaries no concept was too complicated and no program too profound. This was no longer the unified one-sided organic art of the Renaissance, but a many-faceted compound of beautiful details. As one instance of the change that was taking place it might be noted that, whereas Michelangelo's statues forced the beholder to concentrate on one view which strikes him as complete and final, in the work of Cellini and his contemporaries we are confronted with the revolving view, the *figura serpentinata,* which in its twisting on its own axis, compels the beholder to circle around it to enjoy not one, but many different views. There is something strangely insecure, unstable about this type of sculpture that may well be regarded as a reflection of the cultural malaise of the times.

All of the artists of this period, Cellini included, studied the work of Michelangelo, as an actor learns his role, in order to immerse himself in the dramatist's work, and, as is to be expected, they studied the antique in order to achieve a *bella maniera.* The antique, as in the days of the High Renaissance, was still the accepted norm to be followed to achieve an ideal of beauty in the Mannerist virtuoso manner. In Bronzino's painting it appears to have been the Mannerist's aim to captivate and interest, to intimate all kinds of dark, hidden meanings in his work. This is an art so steeped in literature that it almost requires another literature to explain it.

By the middle sixteenth century, which saw the florescence of Mannerist artists like Cellini and Bronzino, the well-known classic myths like the stories of Hercules, Venus, and Bacchus had been presented so often that there was nothing more to say. Following the learned research by humanists into the most abstruse classical iconography, the artists of this generation turned to new and more obscure legends like the history of Perseus, inventing an iconography and symbolism that, although understood in current learned circles, would have baffled the ancients.

The Mannerists were artists who in modern terminology wanted to "show off," to display not only the greatest technical virtuosity and delicacy of execution, but also to reveal their easy mastery of bodies in fascinating and disturbed postures and their fluent knowledge of the vocabulary of expression in the antique manner.

As might be expected, Benvenuto Cellini's dashing account of his life is not without its mentions of his interest in antiquity. On one occasion he mentions his study of the ancient remains in the Campo Santo, and

224

again of the passionate enthusiasm he experienced on seeing some drawings by Filippino Lippi of the antiquities of Rome. Later he tells us that
when he first reached the Eternal City he spent as much time as possible
in the study of the antiquities themselves. Cellini was an artist so learned
in antiquity that it was in a way second nature for him to quote from
classical sources on every possible occasion.

His Narcissus is an admirable example of this sort of borrowing which,
without being in the least antiquarian, contains distinct reminiscences of
classical prototypes. The pose is vaguely suggestive of the bronze Faun
in the Naples Museum (figure 160) or some similar precedent. Cellini's
acquaintance with the antique was at firsthand in more than one way. As
the quotation which opens this chapter explains, the very piece of marble
that Cellini used for the Narcissus had been intended for the repair of
Grand Duke Cosimo's Ganymede (figure 161). Benvenuto built up the
fragmentary torso into a completely new composition of his own. In the
process the classical myth has, in true Mannerist fashion, been darkly and
symbolically transformed. The young eagle which the boy holds in his
hand presents an allegorical riddle having nothing to do with the classical
story. The restored Ganymede has something of the graceful elegance and
beauty of detail found in the Narcissus. Cellini had made a terra-cotta
model for his Narcissus that already shows the motif of the arm circling
the head, a pose borrowed from Michelangelo and here used to intensify
a suggestion of the subject's vain self-satisfaction. Cellini himself tells that
the attitude of his figure was conditioned by two holes in the block of
marble that forced him to elect this pose. In a first glimpse of this statue
the eye inevitably moves in a twisting curve from the right foot through
the leg and the long, undulating torso to the right arm that embraces the
head. This tortuous movement which, when the statue is seen in the
round, exists in depth is an illustration of Cellini's *figura serpentinata*.
The spiral composition was perhaps suggested by the violent dislocation
of Hellenistic statues like the Laocoön. The Narcissus has something of
the extraordinary attenuation preferred by Mannerist artists: the elon-
gated torso imparts a suggestion of svelteness and implied grace, and at
the same time its exoticism tells us that we are looking at an essentially
affected art which, by such devices, was trying to express something new,
and in its departure from the normal canon perversely stimulating. This
violent, uneasy movement and distorted proportion were not only an exaggerated reworking of Hellenistic precedent, but it was also a means to

the artist's mastery of the most complex interplay of the body and its muscles. Here, as in other marble works by Cellini, the artist seems to be trying to simulate his own technique in bronze in the sharpness of modeling and the precise finish of every detail. As in Benvenuto's metalwork the muscles seem to shine through the skin that is stretched over them, and the slender body is both taut and pliant. A haunting placid beauty radiates from the face; the weary adolescent loveliness of this mask seems almost an echo of Praxiteles. For all dependence of the Narcissus on remembered classical ideals such features as the disturbing mobility and the sharp, particularized anatomy are typical of this Mannerist performance.

— 43 —

Replicas in Bronze

I have seen replicas of the Laocoön in wax, no more than two palms in height, which could be said to be that very one in Rome in little.   —Armenini *

THE spectacular casting of large bronze figures in the work of famous sculptors like Donatello and Benvenuto Cellini is so familiar that the statuettes in bronze made in the fifteenth and sixteenth centuries are apt to be overlooked. These are often the works of master craftsmen in this rediscovered art which began to make its appearance as early as the fifteenth century in Florence. A hundred years later whole workshops were devoted to their manufacture. Many of these small masterpieces are original creations, while others are miniature replicas of antique works of art made to satisfy the desire of connoisseurs for mementos of famous classical originals no longer obtainable. Patrons like Isabella d'Este specifically commissioned sculptors to make small copies of the most famous pieces of ancient sculpture in Rome and Florence. Many of the statuettes, in addition to their intrinsic aesthetic appeal, are important documents for the spread of the antique taste and its uses. These little cabinet pieces were not made to deceive as forgeries of antiquities. They were made as objects of *virtù* and as bona fide miniatures of famous and admired originals. Although generally faithful to the prototype, the replicas are all different in some respects and from one another, so that they may be regarded as works in which the artist shows his own personality and originality with the antique as a point of departure.

As early as the Quattrocento there were numbers of reproductions of the Spinario; these were joined in the next century by copies of such

* Io ho veduto il Laocoönte ritratto di cera da quello di Roma, il quale non passava due palmi di grandezza, che si può dire che era il proprio in quella forma.—G. B. Armenini, *De' veri precetti della pittura*

works as the Apollo Belvedere, the Medici Venus, the Laocoön, and the Belvedere Torso. There are several copies—or better, variants—inspired by the Belvedere Torso (figure 32a, b), which are interesting both for the history of the influence of this famous fragment and as reflections of the changing taste of the Cinquecento. A particularly beautiful reflection of the Belvedere Torso is to be found in a sixteenth-century bronze in the Victoria and Albert Museum (figure 162). The statuette represents the Torso in its present mutilated form, with the addition of a head of a stolid cubic Hercules type.[1] By leaving his reduction unrestored, the sculptor wished to call attention to the formal beauties of the muscular structure—that complex rippling, wavelike rhythm of interlocking planes singled out by Winckelmann in his famous description of the original.[2] The beauty of this small bronze is further enhanced by the silken sheen of the green patina. The manufacturers of such bronzes as this often took care to bestow an antique quality by such a beautiful artificial surface. Patinas of different colors, from basalt black to malachite green, could be obtained by dipping the bronze in blackened oil, in acid or vinegar, and then imparting a final luster by the application of wax. The bronze under discussion is a rather exact copy of the Torso. Although the torsion of the body is just as marked as in the original, the treatment of the muscles has been somewhat simplified by the exigencies of the tiny scale, and the bronze medium has conferred a softer, more fluid form to the hero's mighty frame. The head appears derived from an earlier, more severe style of ancient art. The retention of the fragmentary form of the original reveals the new appreciation for formal beauty and the evocative appeal of the incomplete.

This intellectual taste for the fragmentary and the riddle such incompleteness presents are completely typical of the Mannerist point of view. Reflections of this taste may be seen in Bronzino's portraits, in which the sitter is often shown with a small fragmentary statue,[3] and in a family group by Bernardino Licinio, in which a youthful sculptor holds a statuette of the Belvedere Torso. Once this brief period of half-nostalgic, half-formal appreciation of the fragment had passed, one finds, especially in Baroque art, an even more concentrated interest in complete images, both in the actual restoration of antiques and in their completion in art.

In the middle eighteenth century the trade in antiquities was still brisk, especially as conducted by men like Gavin Hamilton and Thomas Jen-

228

kins. They purveyed marbles, more often than not heavily restored, to the English gentry. Originals in good condition were becoming exceedingly rare, and many foreign visitors who wished to acquire elegant decorations for their stately homes resorted to having marble copies made to order after the famous and admired masterpieces. Many with less simple purses were pleased by a new commodity: the miniature replica of antique marbles in bronze, porcelain, or terra cotta. Although a small number of reductions of renowned statues had been offered by Massimiliano Soldani as early as the 1690's, the business of manufacturing small copies of ancient statuary really came into its own about 1760 under the direction of the silversmith Giacomo Zoffoli. After his death in 1785, the work was continued by his brother, Giovanni Zoffoli. Visitors to Rome in these years could find listed in the Zoffoli catalogue "a series of figures, made or to be made in height one and a half palms standard Roman (measurement)." [4] The list included many of the famous masterpieces of Hellenistic and Roman times admired in the eighteenth century.

The architect Charles Heathcote Tatham who was in Rome in 1795 wrote to his patron, Henry Holland, that "all their execution is superlatively good, having artists employed who study the antique with Attention and model with great ingenuity and taste." The Zoffoli studio was apparently a cooperative enterprise. Clay reductions of the statues to be made were furnished by one Vincenzo Pacetti, perhaps with the collaboration of "other artists who studied the antique with Attention." The Zoffolis themselves prepared the wax models for casting and presumably with their silversmith's training added the final chasing and patination. The result was a faithful reduced replica of a famous antique with the addition of something of the softness inherent in the bronze technique.

The replica (figure 163) of the Capitoline Antinoüs (figure 47) is a typical product of the Zoffoli workshop. Like all the pieces described in the catalogue it is "un palmo e mezzo," or approximately 13 inches in height. Since it was made in an age when fidelity to the original was a primary criterion there is superficially little to differentiate this statue from its prototype except scale and material. Obviously the artistic worth of such an object cannot be measured entirely by the fidelity of the reproduction. As a reflection of the lingering rococo taste the proportions of the Antinoüs have remained somewhat more svelte and the expression more piquant, the modeling reduced to smooth, uninterrupted planes has something of the quality that was to distinguish Canova's neoclassic style. It is easy to understand how graceful pieces like this were sought after for the decoration of Adam interiors. A collection was acquired by the first Earl of Morley for Saltram Park in 1793. Such miniatures were not only influential in the diffusion of classic taste, but with their shining patinas and elegant craftsmanship were beautiful objects of *virtù*.

— 44 —

Montecavallo

These figures combine the irresistible energy with the sublime and perfect loveliness supposed to have belonged to their divine nature . . . the sublime and living majesty of their limbs and mien, the nervousness and fiery animation of the horses they restrain, seen in the blue sky of Italy, and overlooking the city of Rome, surrounded by the light and music of that crystalline fountain no cast can communicate.
—Shelley *

THESE spirited, evocative lines of Shelley's written during the poet's happy and turbulent years in Italy are among the last tributes to one of the most famous antiquities of Rome, the Horse Tamers, Castor and Pollux, which today as in the ancient period crown the Quirinal Hill before the presidential palace (figure 164). The colossi of Montecavallo, as the hill was also called, are among the few works of ancient art that were never engulfed in the earth with the destruction and decay of the old imperial city, so that they stood as impressive landmarks and mementos of the Roman past throughout the Middle Ages. They are an example of the kind of interpretation placed on pagan relics in the medieval period as well as an illustration of the influence exerted by such famous surviving works of ancient art.

Descriptions of them are first encountered in the guidebooks of the Eternal City that began to appear for the convenience of pilgrims and tourists as early as the twelfth century. The author of the *Mirabilia Urbis Romae* identified Phidias and Praxiteles, whose names appeared on the ancient bases, as two philosophers or fortunetellers who were commemorated with these memorials by the Emperor Tiberius. Since nudity was neither accepted nor understood, the writer explains the nakedness of the figures as a symbol of the naked truth of their revelations, their twin steeds emblematic of the agility of their wits. Although miniature repre-

* Percy Bysshe Shelley, Letter to Thomas Love Peacock, 23 March 1819

sentations of these landmarks appear in some of the earliest maps of Rome, it was not until the fifteenth century that they came to the attention of artists.

One of the first artists attracted to the Horse Tamers was the Veronese Pisanello. As a painter Pisanello is known through his decorative and still largely Gothic religious paintings and by the magnificent medals celebrating famous personages of his time. In addition he was one of the most distinguished and original draftsmen in the Western tradition. Pisanello's training was received, it is thought, in the workshop of a belated Gothic master of fourteenth-century Venice. His art provides a transition from the particularized realism and formal splendor of the courtly style of the late Middle Ages to the more generalized ideation of forms typical of the Renaissance of the fifteenth century.

Pisanello, above everything else, reveals that passionate return to the observation of nature that characterizes the early Quattrocento. His approach is in many ways still intuitive, but especially in the magnificent drawings of birds and beasts there is an exactness in the rendering of the traits of the species and its vital articulation that anticipates the entirely scientific recording of Leonardo. If many of his drawings of living creatures appear as painstakingly additive presentations of the parts and surface texture, this is still an inheritance from the medieval visual approach to reality. Much the same method typifies Pisanello's studies from the antique.

Pisanello in his copies of the antique is a kind of Pygmalion who transforms the ancient statues into human beings. His drawings are not only copies of ancient statuary, but among the first to attempt to use the movement and poses of these models for a realistic portrayal of the human figure in action and form. His sketches from classical statuary retain everything which is essential with regard to the pose and general appearance of the original, but the nude bodies that he draws are not marble. Their proportions invariably become slighter, almost Gothic, in the spare, sinewy anatomy. They are described in terms of line with a slight reinforcing modeling, and they move with a nervous pliancy that is not part of the antique model. His recordings of ancient statues and reliefs are charged with a wiry, electric energy that suggests portrayals of human, rather than statuesque, models. Like his drawings of birds and beasts, Pisanello's style in his drawings after the antique is particularized. The bodies appear more as additive combinations of the separately observed and recorded parts than that generalized ideal conception of an organic form that typifies his antique prototypes.

A remarkably interesting drawing of Pisanello's is his sketch of Montecavallo, which shows the Horse Tamer attributed on the ancient base to Phidias (figure 165). The figure is shown without the horse and holding a staff in the right hand. It is recognizable as a reasonably accurate transcription of the original, but certain changes are immediately apparent. Although the artist in studying the antique has been careful to describe very accurately the complicated muscular structure of the torso, the proportions of the figure have been attenuated so that the form has far more tense and wiry energy than the prototype. It is as though the ancient statue was recorded in a general way, but that at the same time the artist thought in terms of a particular human model. The drapery over the left arm is drawn in the fine Gothic linear scheme that characterizes Pisanello's style. What is most remarkable about Pisanello's drawings after the antique is that they reveal an artist combining the study of ancient models with the objective recording of nature to produce a new, realistic, and organic description of human forms. This is the beginning of the Renaissance artist's natural assimilation of the lessons of antiquity that has been observed in the only more scientific classical studies of Florentine artists like Ghiberti and Donatello.

A small drawing which, together with a larger version in Dresden, is probably a copy of a lost sketch of the late Quattrocento, shows the group as it appeared before it was rearranged in the sixteenth and eighteenth centuries (figure 166). In this representation the statues are immured in the dilapidated brick masonry of a small house that was built between the bases of the groups. The horses, already badly damaged at this time, are supported by columns of brick. To the right is one of the four colossal statues of Constantine, two of which later were installed on the balustrade of the Capitoline, and a third found its way to the narthex of St. John Lateran. The style of the drawing immediately suggests a topographical recording, a note made by an itinerant artist of one of the sights of the city. The drawing of the marble giants is rather cursive and flimsy and not particularly accurate with regard to the actual appearance and proportions of the originals. One has the feeling that it may once have been part of a collection of such records as were made by known visitors to Rome like Martin van Heemskerck or Francisco de Hollanda in the sixteenth century, a cursive note with no particular sensitivity for the beauty of the classic forms. On the bases appear the ancient inscriptions, *Opus Fidiae* and *Opus Prxb,* a curious corruption of Praxiteles which adds nothing to our estimate of the artist's concern for accuracy.

The point of view toward the antique is far differently expressed in the beautiful prints devoted to this subject by the sixteenth-century artist Antonio Lafreri as parts of his vast compilation of illustrations of the monuments of ancient Rome, the *Speculum Romanae magnificentiae.*[1] Lafreri's plate (figure 167) shows the great sculptural groups magnificently outlined against a cloudy sky. Their bases are still imbedded in medieval masonry and the broken carcasses of the horses still rest on piles of brick. The print may be taken as an illustration of the new archaeological interest in the most noteworthy masterpieces of classical antiquity that appears in the Mannerist period. The Lafreri drawing is an accurate portrayal of these groups with regard to their scale and a faithful recording of the heroic and severe style. In these Roman copies it is difficult to discern any special differences in the style of the sculpture assigned to Phidias and Praxiteles: both appear to be echoes of the grandeur of conception and simplified powerful anatomical structure associated with the Parthenon pediments. The artist has faithfully transcribed these characteristics, just as in other prints he gives an accurate record of the more realistic, dynamic style of the Laocoön and the Pasquino.

Even today the visitor to Rome may be shocked to find people living in squalor in the crannies and embrasures of the Aurelian Wall: this is only a survival of a time when all the old monuments were used as shelters by the poor, so that the horsemen of the Quirinal, as may be seen in the drawing and Lafreri's print, were literally imbedded in the masonry of hovels built from the ruins of the Baths of Constantine that once stood on the Quirinal Hill. In the Middle Ages ruined Rome might be imagined as a giant's carcass inhabited by the verminous survivors of barbarian destruction.

The Castor and Pollux of Montecavallo were the inspiration of many artists throughout the Renaissance and Baroque periods. Michelangelo's interest in these giants and their relation to his David have already been noted. Raphael introduced the head of the horse from the "Phidias" group into his famous Galatea. Later, in the seventeenth century, the Horse Tamers in a violently dynamic adaptation reappear in the famous horses of Marly by Coustou in the Place de la Concorde.

As objects of intrinsic classic beauty their interest continues in the

work of more archaeologically minded sculptors. A miniature bronze replica (figure 168) in the Wallace Collection in London is probably the
work of a sculptor of the eighteenth century, when the groups had been
rearranged and restored in the Quirinal Piazza. In this replica something
of the hardness of the marble is transferred to the representation in
bronze, and the accuracy of the copy points to the more scientific study
of antiquity in the neoclassic period.

* Bronze copies of the famous Montecavallo groups were made as early as the
sixteenth century by Guglielmo Fiammingo (Museo Nazionale, Florence). The replicas
in the Wallace Collection, although described as Italian, may be the work of a French
family of bronze makers, "Les Keller," active in the early eighteenth century.

— 45 —

The Renaissance in France

La grande Diane ancienne
Grande Déesse éphésienne
Fut renommée et reclamée
Et de maint poète clamée:
Mais la Diane Francienne,
De la grand' France tant aymée,
La surpasse ore en renommée
—Fontaine *

I<small>T</small> was not until the reign of Francis I (1515–1547) that the Renaissance and classicism were introduced and there begins the classical chapter in the history of French art. Francis' interest in culture, as exemplified in Italian and classical art, was partly an outgrowth of the rivalry with Charles V and his desire to raise France to a position of preëminence in every sphere. With Francis I there really begins a French style, marked by an absorption, refinement, and clarification of the intellectual discoveries of the Renaissance and the merging of these borrowings into a single art, a combination of logic and good taste and a classical elegance that were to characterize French art in later centuries. For a few years Francis I had enjoyed the council of the aged Leonardo, and shortly after his death the King imported the Florentine, Il Rosso, the North Italian, Primaticcio, and the famous Florentine sculptor and philanderer, Benvenuto Cellini. In addition to his collection of antique medals and cameos Francis also imported a few fragments of antique sculpture. But the most important of all for the diffusion of classical taste in France was the collection of bronze casts of all the famous classical masterpieces venerated in sixteenth-century Rome.   These included reproductions of the Laocoön, the Apollo Belvedere, the famous Ariadne, the Venus of Cnidos, and

* Charles Fontaine, *Odes* (1557)

the colossal statue of the river god Nile in the Vatican. The decorations that the Italian painters Il Rosso and Primaticcio created for Francis in Fontainebleau belong to the Mannerist tradition exemplified in the work of Bronzino and Parmigianino. Il Rosso's decoration for the gallery of Francis I at Fontainebleau is an adaptation of that style of decoration, partly in stucco, partly in painting, that had been discovered in the Golden House of Nero and the Baths of Titus. Primaticcio is if anything even more classical, especially in the works executed after 1540 in which his forms suggest the delicacy and softness of late Hellenistic statuary combined with something of the elegance associated with Mannerism. The classical elements are present, of course, in the humanist subject matter both mythological and allegorical and in the universal predominance of the nude. Invariable attributes of this transformed classical canon are the long tapering limbs, thin necks, and exaggerated classical profiles.

The gods of the ancient world in appropriate classical form took their place in the charade of Olympus enacted at the court of Fontainebleau. The divinizing of the king and his courtiers in poetry and art was only the most playful aspect of imperialism in Renaissance France. In the writings of Ronsard and Joachim du Bellay the sovereign is described as Jupiter, his constable as Mars. In the Galerie François Ier at Fontainebleau, Francis I enacts the role of a long line of heroes in a cycle of paintings by Il Rosso. This series "under the cloak of fables shows forth the enterprises, the warlike exploits, the defeats, the victories, the misfortunes, the successes, the magnanimity, the good counsel, the patience, the benevolence, the liberality, and all the other virtues of the king, demonstrated in war and peace, in life as well as death." [1]

One of the principal objects of divinization popular at the French court was Diane de Poitiers, mistress of Henry II. She is encountered repeatedly in the guise of her Olympian prototype in the paintings of the Fontainebleau school and in the famous statue attributed to Jean Goujon that once graced the park at Anet. A fascinating example of this type of portrait allegory is the painting of Diana the Huntress in the Louvre, a work attributed to a follower of the Italian founders of the Fontainebleau school (figure 169). The panel shows the goddess nude with a quiver and bow striding to the left, accompanied by a greyhound before a dense screen of trees that almost completely obscures the sky. Whether this is an actual portrait of Diane de Poitiers has sometimes been questioned.

There is at least a generic resemblance to other portraits of this famous courtesan, such as the drawing by Jean Clouet at Chantilly, and it would be highly likely that this is one more complimentary allegorical reference to her identity as the moon goddess. The pose and attributes of the figure are reminiscent of the famous Diana of Versailles (figure 170), which in the time of Francis I belonged to his mistress, the Duchesse d'Étampes. But the antique prototype has been endowed with a kind of coquettish elegance, a sort of hyper-refinement of aristocracy, composed in part by the Mannerist canon of form. But the sensuous attraction which may be analyzed as a kind of combination of innocence and sophistication marks the emergence of a purely French taste in which the classical prototype has been completely transformed. The picture reveals a superimposition on a classical ideal of a taste for the piquant and the elegant that even in Gothic times had been a part of the French tradition.

In this painting the familiar Mannerist canon of a towering short-waisted figure with long, tapered legs has been exaggerated to produce a form of peculiarly affected grace. There is a further trick of distortion of the body that is typical of Mannerism. Whereas the back is seen in three-quarters view, in order to display the provocative contour of the virginal breast, the front of the body is drawn in profile in a manner organically impossible, but effective for the total sensuous appeal of the presentation. Although the beautiful body still has something of the calligraphic emphasis on contour typical of Mannerism, its naturalism in the presentation of a warm and desirable body is typically French.

The emergence of what may be described as a French classicism in sculpture is likewise notable in the century of Francis I, particularly in the works of Jean Goujon, a sculptor of notable attainments. His date of birth and artistic origins are somewhat obscure, but many have thought that his acquaintance with the classical idiom both in architecture and sculpture presupposes a period of study in Rome. He first appears as a designer of columns for the organ loft of the Church of St. Maclou at Rouen, a design that already shows a complete familiarity with classical prototypes.

The real masterpiece of Goujon's career is the Fountain of the Innocents in Paris, in which the decoration consists of tall reliefs of draped nymphs and panels of nereids and sea-monsters (figure 171). The panels of tritons and mermaids must have been rather literally copied from prototypes of this subject matter in Roman sarcophagi. The tall attenuated figures of nymphs reveal a reappearance of the mannered, agitated style of neo-Attic reliefs. The Mannerist canon of proportion and the decorative, rather than functional, connection of the draperies with the bodies perhaps reveal an influence of the famous Nymph of Fontaine-bleau by Benvenuto Cellini. The drapery of these figures with its multiple closely pleated folds is decidedly classical in appearance, in a way ulti-mately evocative of the famous draped figures from the balustrade of the Nike Temple on the Acropolis (figure 64). But, whereas Goujon's figures strike a kind of classical balance between voluptuousness and re-straint, the undulation and *contrapposto* are no less suggestive of the ele-gant attitudes of Primaticcio's Mannerism. The note of elegance and piquant sensuousness are the most French elements of this French classi-cism—as is the nicety of execution and the exquisite sense of surface pat-tern and texture.

— 46 —

Albrecht Dürer

The pagan people attributed the utmost beauty to their heathen god "Abblo" (Apollo); thus we shall use it for Christ the Lord, who is the most beautiful man, and just as they represented Venus as the most beautiful woman, we shall chastely display the same features in the image of the Holy Virgin, Mother of God.

—Dürer *

THE classical tradition finds its way to Germany with Albrecht Dürer, a northern counterpart of the many-sided Italian genius of the Renaissance. His point of view toward antiquity was in certain respects still medieval and Christian. Like his contemporaries, Dürer found many things in antique art to support his own investigations, notably the expressive power and beauty of the human body, the scenes of passionate drama in antique reliefs, and the self-contained serenity of ancient statues. It is not entirely certain whether Dürer's acquaintance with the antique was directly through his knowledge of ancient statues or through the intermediary of Italian artists of the Renaissance.

Dürer was the first northerner to display a nostalgia for the beauty for antique art that was so foreign to northern tradition. To paraphrase Professor Panofsky, Dürer believed that the beauty of classical art could be rewon by understanding and achieving the principles of its creation.[1] Even before the evolution of his theory of human proportions his experiments were directed to capturing and ordering systematically those qualities of the antique portrayal of the body which could be used to instruct himself and his German fellow-artists in an approximation of classical form and movement.

Beautiful examples of Dürer's quest for the antique ideal are a series

* Dan zw gleicher weis wÿ sÿ dy schonsten gestalt eines menschen haben zw gemessen iren abgot abblo also wolln wir dy selb mos prawchen zw crÿsto dem herrn der schönste aller welt ist und wy sy prawcht haben fenus als das schönste weib also woll wir dÿ selb zirlich gestalt krewschlich darlegen der aller reinesten jungfrawen maria, der mutter gottes.—Martin Conway, *The Writings of Albrecht Dürer* (New York, 1958), pp. 178, 203–204.

of drawings and prints of a similar figure used sometimes for Apollo (figure 172) and sometimes for Adam, which appear to be related to the Apollo Belvedere or some similar antiquity available to Dürer in Germany. It might be added parenthetically that Dürer endowed Christ with the form and features of Apollo, perhaps, like Michelangelo's great figure, as a reference to the Renaissance concept of Christ as the sun of righteousness, the descendent of the pagan Sol Invictus.

Although Dürer may have looked upon the antique as an improved and ennobled nature, the achievement of the ideality he sought eluded him for the very good reason that classical art in its serenity and ideality was fundamentally different from the ever-dominant concern of German art with the pictorial and the particular. In Dürer's print of Apollo, the figure has such a marked resemblance to the famous statue in the Vatican that some scholars have presumed that Dürer must have known a similar classical statue in Germany or a replica of the original. The differences between the print and the classical statue are such as to rule out any firsthand acquaintance, and at the same time these variations describe the gulf that separated the German and Italian conceptions of classical art. In Dürer's Apollo the definition of the sinewy anatomy of the body and the insistent accurate recording of the muscular mechanism belong to that same German concern for the particular, which five centuries later made Böcklin paint his mermen not so much as creatures of fable, but as credible specimens in a zoological collection. Dürer's emphasis on the wiry body and its muscular sheath almost approaches an *écorché,* so that it is infinitely more realistic in this respect than the Apollo Belvedere, in which the muscles are reduced to smooth, unobtrusive planes. One has the feeling that the drawing was intended to serve a didactic purpose as a model of perfectly legible anatomical structure at the same time that it reproduced the characteristic pose of a venerated image of antiquity. Neither Dürer nor any other German artist had what could be called a real aesthetic interest in *sacrosancta vetustas* (hallowed antiquity). The German artist's investigation was scientific and literary in contrast to the Italians' concern with beauty rather than subject and history. In Dürer's drawing the pose of the god has been adapted to display as effectively as possible the scientifically recorded anatomy of a human model. At the same time Dürer's Apollo reveals a taut, nervous energy that is not in the least like the balanced serenity and poised weightless elegance of his classical prototype.

It seems likely that Dürer's acquaintance with the antique must have been through the intermediary of Italian graphic art of the Quattrocento, such as the prints of Mantegna and the drawings of antiquities by artists like the Master of the Codex Escurialensis. He worked, one could say, from such contemporary Italian translations of the language of antique art. If Dürer's Apollo has a certain flatness and seems to be composed primarily as a silhouette, this may be taken as a further indication that we should assume the intermediary of a drawing or print between Dürer's composition and the antique original.

— 47 —

El Greco

What shall begin and what shall end my lay?
The hapless father and his children twain?
The snakes of aspect dire in winding coils?
The serpents' ire, their knotted tails, their bites?
The anguish, real, though but marble, dies?
The mind recoils and pity's self-appalled,
Gazing on voiceless statues beats her breast.

— Sadoletus *

EL GRECO, DOMENICO THEOTOCOPOULOS, was born in Candia in Crete and, it is generally believed, received his earliest training as a painter in the surviving tradition of Byzantine icon-painting. As a youth he went to Venice to undergo the coloristic influence of Titian and Tintoretto and finally to Rome, where he fell under the spell of the great Michelangelo and of the classical ambient of the Eternal City. His style is a combination of all of these varied elements and has besides a special baroque quality in his concern for endless space and luminosity. El Greco's space and light are like no other painter's. When he finally settled in Spain his style developed into a mystic expressiveness that in its distortion anticipates the modern world.

In his religious paintings El Greco's figures become substanceless phantoms, fashioned of light and color in a conflagration of flamelike shapes. There is no longer any real organic articulation, nor is there any

* Quid primum, summumve loquar? miserumne parentem
  Et prolem geminam? an sinuatos flexibus angues,
  Terribili aspectu caudasque irasque draconum,
  Vulneraque veros, saxo moriente, dolores?
  Horret ad haec animus, mutaque ab imagine pulsat
  Pectore, non parvo pietas commixta tremori.
  —Jacobus Sadoletus, "De Laocoöntis Statua Quae Romae in Vaticano Spectatur"
  1538

243

texture except the texture of pure color and pure light inherent in the pigment applied to the canvas. The miraculous becomes credible in terms of light and movement and space. The movement is tempestuous, the forms bodiless wraiths, not earthly men but ineffable forms of the celestial sphere. El Greco often seems to paint in that released frenzy of religious fervor of the dreams of St. John of the Cross and St. Theresa of Avila. All of these qualities are completely anticlassical but, even within El Greco's frame of mystic expression, there are suggestions of an indebtedness to the old tradition.

No more striking illustration of El Greco's reworking of the classical tradition could be studied than this dramatic canvas of the myth of Laocoön (figure 173) in the National Gallery in Washington.* The death agonies of the Trojan priest and his sons take place, like so many of El Greco's religious scenes, before the walls of Toledo. In El Greco's composition Laocoön lies on the ground in mortal agony; one of his sons is already dead; the second struggles with a serpent. At the right stand Apollo and Artemis, the gods whose anger at Laocoön's sacrilege raised the dragons from the deep.

El Greco probably saw the famous Hellenistic marble of Laocoön (figure 34) during his stay in Rome from 1570 to 1572. If the theme suggested the picture, certainly no greater change could be imagined in the presentation of this minor tragedy at the Fall of Troy. The differences are not only the dissimilarities between El Greco and the ancient world, but between El Greco and the artists of the High Renaissance who extravagantly admired this statue. In the classical group the interest is concentrated on the representation of the death agonies of physical men through the Herculean straining of the muscles and the distortion of the pain-racked faces. In El Greco's painting one senses that a spiritual struggle is going on. The one surviving victim seems powerless to fend off the attack of the serpent which, bent like a tensile spring, appears to twist and bend the youth struggling to avoid its sting. Little of the great classical composition appears to survive except perhaps in the facial type of Laocoön and in the hieratic enlargement of his form. The position of the recumbent priest was probably suggested by the same Hellenistic statue

---

* The Inventories of El Greco's works list a number of small and large canvases of Laocoön. His acquaintance with the statue is further demonstrated by his including the head of Laocoön in a canvas of Christ Healing the Blind. Cf. Harold E. Wethey, *El Greco and his School* (Princeton, N.J., 1962), I, 24; II, 83–84.

244

of a falling Gaul (figure 151) which influenced Titian's Europa. The atmosphere, as in El Greco's religious paintings, is that of a mystical vision. The luminous and incandescent bodies flicker like flames against the darkness of the storm which shrouds the background.

Although no definitive explanation is possible, it appears as though some symbolical Christian drama, rather than the pagan tragedy, were being enacted. Toledo, the city of miracles and Christian mystics, here stands for the fabulous Ilium. El Greco had used the town before as a background for the drama of the Crucifixion; perhaps here, in this ghostly combat between the flame-tall men and the serpents, is an allegory of the struggle of the soul and the material body. The painting is like El Greco's religious subjects, in which the spiritualized forms seem to flow upwards in windswept fiery movement to union with the divine.

A comparison between the struggling youth in El Greco's painting and Michelangelo's Bound Slave (figure 144) suggests itself both from the point of view of style and that of expression. Michelangelo has shown the giant form, a transformation of an ancient Niobid, spent in the exertion of a hopeless struggle. Its pathos and tragedy are enhanced by the implied futility of the youth's battle against a power that is the greater because it is not seen but felt. The already attenuated and tortured form may have inspired El Greco's figure, which in its frozen impotence suggests one of those strange nightmares in which the dreamer is incapable of movement in the face of danger. The classic and the Michelangelesque seem present only as memories in this conception which El Greco has raised to a strident and frenetic pitch in the towering shape that sways in the wind.

El Greco was undoubtedly haunted by the ancient myth of Laocoön's martyrdom, perhaps as a symbol of the divine injustice of the pagan gods transformed into Christian allegory. Even in his wildest phosphorescent explosions of pure color—as here in the Laocoön—El Greco, like the great Titian in his final paintings where color is dissolved into light, seems to have conjured up the remembered stability of classical form as a scaffold for his dreams.

— 48 —

The Baroque

Our business is to imitate the Beauties of Nature, as the Ancients have done before us, and as the Object, and Nature of the thing require from us. And for this reason we must be careful in the Search of *Ancient Medals, Statues, Gems, Vases, Paintings, and Basso Relievo's:* And of all other things which discover to us the Thoughts and Inventions of the *Graecians;* because they furnish us with great Ideas, and make our Productions wholly beautiful. And in truth, after having well examin'd them, we shall therein find so many Charms, that we shall pity the Destiny of our present Age, without hope of ever arriving at so high a point of Perfection.

—Du Fresnoy *

THE great artists of the seventeenth century, the so-called Baroque period, lived in an environment far different from that of their predecessors in the Renaissance. This was a time of great expansion in every field of human endeavor, a time marked by the rise of the modern sciences of astronomy, physics, and medicine. It was the period of the philosophers who subordinated the world to human reason. It was inevitable that in this worldly period of expansion and vitality there should be reflections of worldliness, expansion, and a new scientific unity in works of art as well. The complexity and variety of the world showed itself in the spaciousness, the dynamic movement, and naturalism of Baroque artists. As the Baroque scientist extended his vision to the conception of infinity, the

* Sed juxta antiquos naturam imitabere pulchram,
Qualem forma rei propria, objectumque requirit.
Non te igitur lateant antiqua numismata, gemmae,
Vasa, typi, statuae, caelataque marmora signis,
Quodque refert specie veterum post saecula mentum:
Splendidior quippe ex illis affurgit imago,
Magnaque se rerum facies aperit meditanti;
Tunc nostri tenuam saecli miserebere fortem,
Cum spes nulla fiat rediturae aqualis in aevum.

—C. A. du Fresnoy, *De arte graphica* (1668); translated by John Dryden (1716)

Baroque painter sought a more comprehensive and broader concept of nature with a new integration of all factors affecting visual reality—space, light, and atmosphere, the dynamic animation and integration of all things in the natural world, expressed in realistic and pictorial terms.

The Baroque period, like our own, was shaken by voyages into space, and, with the acceptance of the theories of Copernicus and Galileo, a world that was once the center of the universe became a part of limitless infinity. The sixteenth century had seen the beginnings of the adventures of the explorers who mastered terrestrial space with their girdling of the world. This discovery of space celestial and terrestrial coincided with voyages in the field of art in a search for the definition of unlimited space filled with realistic forms which, as never before, were presented as tangible images in terms of paint that described form, texture, and light itself. In a similar way, the language of the sculptor was accommodated to an expression of reality that at times approached the pictorial.

This was an age of absolutism in ecclesiastical and secular spheres. It was the period of the great absolute monarchies of the Hapsburgs, the Bourbons, and the Stuarts, and of the supreme spiritual authority of the church of Rome. All of these powers demanded a new grandeur and a new realism to command adherence to the faith and to the divine power of the sovereign in pictorial and plastic terms. For religious art the aim was above everything else concentrated on an overwhelming persuasion to belief. The church, imperiled by the rising Protestant tide, found in the arts a new bulwark to repel this threatening sea. In architecture, sculpture, and painting the arts were marshaled into an instrument that was to overwhelm by its grandeur and persuade by its realism. The miracles of the saints were to be made credible by the very plausibility of the realistic forms and settings in which they were enacted. Art was to appeal to the senses and emotions. If the ultimate realism offered by such an anticlassicist as Caravaggio was unacceptable, the eclectic pastiches of the Carracci and the facilities of the seventeenth-century masters of sentiment were made to order.

If the seventeenth century witnessed a final transformation of the decorous static reticence of the Renaissance into forms of dynamic and theatrical power, this was not the result of artists' questing for new realms of expression but largely the result of the program inaugurated by the Church after the Council of Trent and the formation of the Society of Jesus. There appeared as part of this new drive to convert the unbeliever and to hold the faithful an art directed to provoking a physical realization of belief through the veracity of the portrayal and an appeal to the aesthetic sense through the magisterial bravura of technical execution. In a religion concerned with experiencing divinity and the nature of the miraculous through spiritual exercises heightening sensory perception, art had to be stimulating to the emotions and make an impact on the physical senses. Part of this work of conversion consisted in the violently melodramatic and activated presentation of forms—forms no longer constricted by any arbitrary space but, in sculpture and painting alike, impinging on the space of the beholder in a new, disturbing way. For similar reasons, in architecture and the plastic arts, the grandiose, with all the ostentation of theatrical contrivance, provided a setting for displays of crescendos of emotional stimulation and excitement. It was inevitable that art dedicated to classical rather than religious subjects employed the same style.

Another change that took place in the seventeenth century was the separation of religious and secular themes. Classical mythologies fell into the category of landscapes and still-lifes as attractive to the private patron, and at the same time, as in the allegories of Rubens and Le Brun, never lose their hold as a means for providing the immortalization of the royal patron.

In the Baroque age the battle between classicism and naturalism, already joined in the sixteenth century, continued in aesthetics and artistic performance. More interesting than this pedantic polemic is the antique as a driving force in the work of leading artists. From the comments of men like Rubens and Bernini, it is clear that fundamentally the authority of antiquity was unchallenged as a basis for training, provided the artists observed the precautions necessary to its use. Antiquity, no longer the subject of sedulous imitation and fire of first discovery, remained as a potent source of inspiration in art as it did in literature.

The art of the seventeenth century was determined by many new factors involving the use of space in an explosive fashion, the mastery of realistic representation, and unlimited capacity for expression of emotion. It is fashionable to divide aesthetic opinion and performance in this period between classicism and naturalism. This is a difficult question to resolve because so many artists combined qualities of both movements in their work.

In such an art it would almost seem that any reliance on the antique was outmoded and inappropriate. Antiquity, however, like classical education until the nineteenth century, was a part of every man's training, and so, although it was not employed in an archaeological way, the antique was a source for inspiration both in subject matter and motifs. In the Baroque period the antique was so completely integrated with the style of the individual artist that one feels that these men were not quoting ancient sources but producing fluently in a classical style.

The principal part played by Greek and Roman forms in the Baroque period was in the supplying of themes ranging from the heroic and tragic to the slightest motif in the minor arts. The old mythologies dynamically ennobled by Bernini and Rubens have their literary counterparts in the tragedies of Racine and the operas of Purcell, combinations of passionate feeling and dignified restraint. The fluency in the use of classic metaphor by Poussin was matched by the French tragedians and Pope's writings in the syntax of Horace. Classical allusions were understood and cherished by the ruling class to which artists and writers addressed their creations. Just as genuine classic idioms were part of the fluent vocabulary of Rubens, the ancient literary forms of tragedy, comedy, satire, and oratory lived anew in the literature of the seventeenth century. The effect of the models of Greco-Roman morality provided a restraint for the passions in literature and conduct, just as the nobility and composure of ancient art was at once appropriate for the expression of moral themes, social, political, and religious, and a continued stabilizing norm in even the most dynamic expressions. The danger in the use of classical art as an aesthetic control provided for creation within a discipline so long as this adherence to rules and forms did not become an end in itself. It was inevitable that the restraints and rigid principles imposed by the Academies would lead to petrifaction and sterility in the work of artists unable to see beyond these barriers. The classics in literature as well as in art in the Baroque period provided a unity of the imagination and the intellect that joined all Europe and the Americas in a bond transcending nationality and religion. The universal language of classical art and literature as never before formed a single empire in the minds and tastes of Western men.

The Baroque is sometimes divided into phases: the early stage marked by the passionate exuberance of Bernini and Rubens, and a later chapter marked by a greater sobriety and rational vision that leads into neoclassicism. There was more of an intellectual appeal in terms of balanced harmony of composition and reliance on drawing rather than on color and impasto. The expression of passions in late Baroque painting, like Poussin's, was the language of the contemporary theater in pictorial terms. Artists once more found the attitudes and expressions of the heroic antique completely suited for theatrical effectiveness in art, so that Poussin employed the famous group of the Gaul killing his wife in the Ludovisi Collection for his Massacre of the Innocents, just as later Benjamin West's and David's only more frozen neoclassic dramas were a combination of forms derived from the antique and the repertory of expressions devised by Le Brun.

The antique in every form of expression still provided invariable patterns of perfection without those distortions produced by mere sensory perceptions. In France of the seventeenth and eighteenth centuries reason and logical order prevailed universally: the selective perfection sought by either artists or writers could be obtained by following the rules, the clarification of nature already achieved in antiquity. As Roger de Piles said, "He must regard the antique as a book which one translates into another language, in which it suffices to catch the sense and the spirit without becoming slavishly attached to the words of the original." [1] The knowledge of the works of classical literature that Corneille and Racine received from their Jesuit preceptors, like Poussin's training in the study and copying of Roman antiquities, made it inevitable that these men should express themselves in the classical idiom, not in the interests of duplication but using it as a framework to display the operation of human passions on a grand and heroic scale. Poussin's organization of forces in balanced opposition within the confines of his pictures has its equivalent in Racine's logically ordered conflicts of opposing passions. In both cases it is a matter of order, one based on the shapes of antique art, the other a Baroque psychological adaptation of ancient tragedy that results in the controlled grandiose character of the presentation. The symmetry of Poussin is the same kind of self-imposed law that insures the infallibility of the unities of time, place, and action in the theater of Corneille and Racine. This employment of principles that did not exist in classical times was the result of the Baroque concern to bring control and order into art as into politics and life. Poussin's compositions are invariably more balanced and contrived than any classical prototype, just as Racine's tragedies are more limited than ancient dramas.

— 49 —

Annibale Carracci
and Baroque Classicism

Agostino was discoursing on the great skill of the ancients in statuary; and he paused to celebrate especially the Laocoön . . . He would have wished that Annibale might have said something about the subject: but . . . it almost seemed that he took not the slightest note of his brother's discourse . . . Annibale appeared more and more to turn a deaf ear: and observing his brother even more inspired in his extolling of ancient sculpture and the others more attentive than ever in listening to him, he turned to the wall of the room, and without anyone noticing him, made a drawing of the Laocoön in charcoal, and succeeded so happily that it was as though he had had the original before him to draw the most precise contour from it.
—Agucchi *

THE Carracci brothers of Bologna are generally associated with the idea of eclecticism because the program of their academy is said to have been based upon a judicious adaptation of the manner of the great figures of the High Renaissance. Neither Agostino, Ludovico, nor Annibale completely followed the program outlined in the famous sonnet falsely attributed to Agostino that prescribed the ingredients for achieving perfection in painting by combining Roman drawing, Venetian movement, Lombard coloring, Michelangelo's power, Raphael's symmetry, and so on.

* E discorrendo Agostino, del gran sapere mostrato degli antichi nelle Statue; e fermatosi a celebrare specialmente il Laocoonte . . . ; egli aurebbe voluto, che Annibale ancora alcuna cosa n'hauesse detta: ma . . . pareua quasi, che pochissimo conto egli facesse di quel ragionamento del Fratello; . . . mostraua sempre più Annibale di dargli poco orecchie: e mentre egli vedeua il Fratello più inferuorato nel celebrare quell'antica Scoltura, e gli altri più che mai attenti ad udirlo, si accostò al muro della stanza, e senza che niuno se n'auuedesse, vi disegnò con un carbone la figura del Laocoonte, e gli venne così felicemente espressa, come hauesse hauuto dinanzi à gli occhi l'originale, per farne un'aggiutatissimo contorno.—Giovanni Battista Agucchi, *Trattato della pittura* (1646)

In the beginning of his career Annibale, the most gifted of the three brothers, reflected the manner of Correggio and the Venetians. Later, under the spell of Michelangelo and the antique, he became a completely Roman artist. His diligent return to careful drawing from the model and from the antique, combined with North Italian color, was a deliberate attempt to return to and improve on the manner of the High Renaissance. Annibale's manner was a repudiation of the artificial colors, surface effects, and ambiguities of the Mannerist style in favor of an art both grand and legible. Part of this grandeur led in the direction of the further development of those dynamic effects of space and movement and passionate emotion inaugurated in the High Renaissance and now developed into a properly speaking Baroque form. The seventeenth-century critic, Bellori, refers to Annibale as "ristauratore e principe dell'Arte" (restorer and prince of Art).[1] Annibale Carracci's classicism, however, was something more than a reëstablishment of the Michelangelo and Raphael manners.

The turning point in Annibale's career came with his moving to Rome in 1595, where he became the protégé of Cardinal Odoardo Farnese. In Rome of the seventeenth century the lists were already drawn between the adherents of Caravaggio and his shocking naturalism and the supporters of the classical tradition of the High Renaissance who recognized in Annibale Carracci their greatest champion. This feud was as ardent as the contemporary division between the proponents of abstract expressionism and the followers of realistic art.

Annibale Carracci's greatest commission was the decoration of the gallery of the Farnese Palace for his patron Cardinal Odoardo. Work was begun in 1597. Annibale's adviser for this mythological cycle of paintings was Giovanni Battista Agucchi, author of a tract, *Trattato della Pittura,* which voiced the old contention that imperfect nature must be improved by selecting only the most beautiful and perfect parts in order to realize a nature idealized and embellished. Agucchi took credit for introducing Annibale Carracci to the study of the antique and for his consequent achievement of the supreme *idea della bellezza.* Although the vitality of Annibale's classicism undoubtedly stemmed from his combination of naturalism and the solidity of classical sculpture, he is more a prophet than a renovator in his union of the real and the imaginative. Added to this achievement was the originality of the baroque exuberance of his composing. As Denis Mahon once observed, he achieved "a reinterpretation of the broad elemental formulae of classicism into a living language . . . *en rapport* with the period." [2]

In the decoration of the Farnese Gallery, Annibale Carracci conceived the idea of a picture collection installed on the walls and vaults of an hypaethral gallery. The architectural enframement of this simulated grouping of easel pictures is completely imaginary and painted with the same illusion of recession and foreshortening inaugurated by earlier masters like Correggio and Tibaldi. This is a mixed form of decoration with the framed mythological scenes placed in an illusionistic setting, a scheme ultimately related to Michelangelo's Sistine ceiling. The pictures are surrounded by simulated stucco or marble herms and caryatids and alternate with painted imitations of bronze medallions. Below the architectural figures sit the giant forms of Ignudi, naturalistically painted in flesh tints. At the angles of the room, the cornice seems to break to afford a view of a blue sky with putti clambering on a balustrade. The whole is a kind of grandiose "trompe-l'oeil," a play of real and unreal forms, in which the foreshortened herms and atlantids, the Ignudi contrived as real figures, contrast with the painted pictures which this *schema* supports. This arrangement of easel pictures placed in an imaginary painted architecture was certainly suggested by Michelangelo's Sistine ceiling, and, in its effects of space and foreshortening, by Pellegrino Tibaldi's work in the Palazzo Poggio at Bologna, which had become a kind of little Sistine chapel for the education of Bolognese artists. This scheme is a compromise with those effects of limitless space provided by illusionistic painted architecture that were already finding favor in the Baroque church decoration of Rome, and this compromise was one more feature that led Carracci's admirers to regard him as a true renovator of the ideals of the High Renaissance.

The theme of Annibale's decorations in the Farnese Gallery is the Loves of the Gods or all-conquering love as ennobled in mythological amours. The old obscurity and pedantry of the Mannerists' portrayal of ancient fables and allegories have been replaced by a completely undisguised and joyous pictorial recreation of these ancient stories. How the point of view toward the representation of pagan themes had changed since the period of the Mannerists may be noted in the fact that the allegory of this whole mythological decoration in the Farnese Gallery is only discreetly indicated by the erotes tussling on the balustrade behind the picture of Polyphemus and Acis (figure 174). Their playful struggle (figure 175) informs us that the whole scheme is an emblem of the contest between sacred and profane love. If it were not for this hidden clue, the entire cycle might be a completely straightforward presentation of the ancient myths for their own sake. Their presence in a palace of a prince of the church itself testifies to a relaxation of the moral scruples about paganism promulgated by the Council of Trent. It goes without saying that these pictures were special creations catering to the refined taste of a limited ruling class.

Annibale Carracci, according to a legend reported by Agucchi and Bellori, could draw the Laocoön from memory. At the time that he was working in the gallery, the colossal Farnese Hercules (figure 176) by Glycon stood in the courtyard of the palace. The precise influence of these models can be seen in the artist's panel of Polyphemus hurling stones at Acis, Galatea's lover. In this picture the Farnese Hercules has come alive to impersonate the enraged giant. Not only his immense frame but also the swelling integument of muscles that rings his torso are drawn from this Hellenistic source. The original drawing for Polyphemus shows a model of normal muscular proportions which has been made even more powerful by reference to the titanic anatomy of the Farnese statue. When Sir Joshua Reynolds (Discourse One) mentioned that Annibale's figures were invariably "drawn with all the peculiarities of an individual model," he pinpointed the artist's method for every single figure in the entire Farnese complex. Carracci, perhaps more successfully than any artist since Michelangelo, used the classical sources available to him as a corrective for his drawing from nature.

In this picture the compositional device whereby the fleeing Acis and Galatea—shown as though about to circumambulate the rocky mass that looms behind Polyphemus and obstructs the background—is a purely Baroque one providing an invitation into space, since the spectator is vicariously urged to let his eyes follow the course of the couple racing into the distance. The direction of Polyphemus' cloak repeats their movement and the violently dislocated pose of the giant, himself about to turn and hurl his projectile, dynamically reinforces the concept of recession into the distance.

Turning to the enframement of this panel, it is apparent that for the figures of caryatids Annibale has drawn on his knowledge of the Laocoön. Their statuesque rigidity and pallor are made to contrast with the warm flesh tints of the seated youths which are relaxed versions of Michelangelo's Ignudi. Above the Polyphemus is another simulated framed picture of Ganymede and the Eagle in which the artist has coerced a Praxitelean original, perhaps the Apollo Saurocthonos, into a foreshortened Baroque attitude.

Annibale Carracci's invention of a scheme which, although offering the theatrical illusion of a false architecture and its spatial recession combined with his resuscitation of the massive classic shapes of the High Renaissance, provided a veritable canon for later classical critics and connoisseurs opposed to the naturalistic and spatial effects generally associated with the true Baroque. As Baglione observed,

> And suffice it to say that, as a work of imagination, of decoration, of inventions with nudes, of fables, and histories all variously accomplished, one could not wish for anything more perfect, and everyone who sees it, truly, is forced to speak well of it . . . as one of the finest works that genius has devised and painting expressed in our time.[3]

Although the general impression Carracci sought to create in this vast imaginary stage was the painted illusion of a screen of marble sculpture and architecture as though it were an actual ancient building, the crowded opulence of these grouped caryatids, herms, bronze plaques, and gold frames repeats the restless exciting movement of the mythological scenes. The ingenious deceptions to make the unreal real are as Baroque as his compositions for the individual panels. Like these pictures, the stability of the enframement is assured by the very statuesque solidity of the supporting forms.

Carracci's preceptor, Agucchi, came close to characterizing his style when he observed that Annibale combined "la bellezza del colorito Lombardo" with "il disegno finissimo di Roma." [4] This union of styles does not make the painter an Eclectic in the derogatory sense in which this word was applied to the Carracci in the nineteenth century, any more than Raphael's employment of Umbrian color and classic form justifies the application of this term to him. Although Agucchi and other critics after him tried to make Annibale into a pure classicist and restorer of the High Renaissance ideal, such a classification of his manner is to miss the essentially Baroque qualities of his work: the naturalism and fantasy. Annibale Carracci used classical statues for inspiration and control, but his employment of this idiom was more robust than Raphael's and had nothing to do with the affected grace and surface compositions of the

Mannerists. The vitality of his manner is based on his painstaking modification of classical models by drawing from nature, a method that led directly to the union of Baroque power and classical solidity in Rubens and Poussin.

It was no wonder that the critic Félibien des Avaux, writing in the days of the Grand Monarque and the glories of Versailles, lauded the Galleria Farnese:

There is naught but the grand, the noble, and the well-composed, be it in the arrangement of the bodies in general, in the expression of every part in particular, or in the handling of light and shade. This great work is not one of those in which only the vividness of colors and the brilliance of light first enchant the eyes and startle those who behold it. One sees here a solid beauty which appeals to the mind and the more intelligent will always discover new graces there the more they study it.[5]

— 50 —

Bernini

[Bernini] took no other sustenance in all these days save a little wine and bread, saying that alone the taste of the living lesson of those dead statues filled his body with an indescribable sweetness which was enough to maintain his strength for days on end.
—Domenico Bernini *

GIAN LORENZO BERNINI is an artist who is sometimes described as a painter working with a chisel. His works are dominated by a passion and vivacity of feeling that presents the ultimate in movement and pictorial effects, effects that in their picturesqueness sometimes elude even his capacity to translate into stone. Like so many artists of his time he began his career by the study of the collections of antiquities in the Vatican. His son and biographer, Domenico, tells us how Bernini "applied himself most diligently to those two singular statues of Antinoüs and Apollo, the former wonderful in design, the latter in craftsmanship, and it is usually said that both of these qualities are even more perfectly fused in the famous Laocoön." [1] Like many other great sculptors of the seventeenth century Bernini began his professional work with the study and restoration of antique statues, a line of research which led to such proficiency that many artists became expert in the art of forgery.

Rome of the seventeenth century was the center of the Western world for the collection of ancient fragments. As the biographer of painters, Baglione, relates,

Today in Rome the study of the relics of stone, of bas-reliefs, and of ancient statues following the example of these antiquarians is so widespread and everywhere increasing that the walls of the palaces, the courts, and chambers are filled with them in abundance; and the gardens are as barren of plants as they are rich

* Ne altro refrigerio prendeva in tutti quei giorni, che di poco vino, e cibo dicendo che il solo gusto della viva lezione di quelle morte Statue gli faceva ridondere nel Corpo ancora una non so qual dolcezza, ch'era sufficiente a mantenerlo in forze gl'intieri giorni.—*Vita del cavalier G. L. Bernini, descritta da* Domenico Bernini *suo figlio* (1713)

in works in marble which testify to the whole world and give proof today of the grandeur of that Regent of the Universe.[2]

There were not only the vast accumulations of the Vatican and the Aldobrandini family but many smaller and distinguished collections of classical statuary formed by the Borghese, the Barberini, and the Pamphili. The "gardens of statuary" in the palaces of the Roman nobility were, like the Medici collections in the Quattrocento, the training ground of artists. The seventeenth-century artists to an even greater degree than their forebears adapted pagan themes for Christian usage to such an alarming extent that this practice became a theme for sermons against the use of pagan forms by the General of the Jesuit Order. Although the sculptors of the Seicento adopted the forms and fables of the classical past, they interpreted them in their own way with a new and melting vitality and passion. An artist like Bernini could not forever bend his fantasy to the cold and sterile imitation of classical statuary.

Bernini on more than one occasion cited the famous and ruinous statue known as the Pasquino as the finest antique work, with the Belvedere Torso a close second in his affections. Judging from his own work it appears certain that this preference was affected by the passionate violence of these figures and their relation to the style of Michelangelo, which he fervently admired. A clear idea of Bernini's point of view concerning the antique can be obtained from the journal of his trip in France by the Sieur de Chantelou. On one occasion he reports:

> The Cavalier said that when he was very young he often drew from the antique and that in the first figure he did, when he was not sure of something he went to consult the Antinoüs as his oracle, and he noticed from day to day beauties in this figure which he had never seen and never would have seen had not he himself been working with a chisel. For this reason he always advised his students and all others not to abandon themselves so much to drawing and modeling that they did not work at the same time either in sculpture or painting, combining production and copying, or, so to speak, action and contemplation—from which procedure progress results.[3]

On another occasion, speaking before the assembled French Academy, Bernini observed that:

> in his opinion there should be in the Academy casts of all the beautiful antique statues, bas-reliefs, and busts for the instruction of the young students, who should be required to draw in the antique style in order to form first from these works the idea of beauty which would then serve them all their life. The students would, in his opinion, be ruined if at the beginning they were set to draw from nature, for

nature is almost always feeble and trifling. As a result, their imagination being filled only with the model in nature, they would never be able to produce anything great or beautiful which is not found in nature.[4]

These remarks of Bernini's state firmly the idea that the artist should first study the antique before turning to nature or, better, that the beginning sculptor must study and comprehend the principles underlying works of ancient art in order to achieve perfection on the basis of the imitation of nature. With a foundation in the formal ideality and proportion of antique statues the artists could then use this regulated systematized beauty as a means for correcting the imperfections and accidents of nature's unselected handiwork. Bernini's injunctions to copy the antique were never followed by his pupils; his disciples simply copied him as a model of ultimate perfection, just as the Mannerists had copied Michelangelo and Raphael. It was far easier to imitate the master and the superficial aspects of his technical virtuosity than to prepare for a sculptor's career as Bernini had by copying the antique and then nature. Bernini himself never made any exact copies of antiquity, but all of his great masterpieces, filled as they are with a tempestuous and expansive movement and pictorial manipulation of stone, reveal at the same time the indelible impression of antiquity and the control which it exercised on his performance.

A typical example of Bernini's transformation of the antique is his statue of David in the Villa Borghese (figure 177). There is something completely new in this representation of a transitory movement and in the dynamic tension of the whole figure. Since the whole spiritual focus of the hero is on his unseen opponent in the space where the viewer stands, there is no boundary between the space of the statue and his own. Although the statue is designed for one principal view, there is no longer the slightest suggestion of the figure's being confined to a block or a wall surface as in Renaissance sculpture. The David is based only in a general way on the Borghese Warrior, now in the Louvre (figure 178), and the energy and elasticity of movement in Bernini's work represent the birth of a new realistic style through the discipline and invigorating study of classical antiquity.

The most famous of Bernini's academic mythological groups is his Apollo and Daphne, a work that is a marvelous combination of classicizing idealization and realistic interpretation of the legendary event (figure 179). Although the idea for such a dynamic and activated group may have been suggested to Bernini by the Laocoön (figure 34), this antique composition for all its violence is still confined within the imaginary cubic space enclosed in the contours of the figures that comprised the group so that they do not in any way appear to overflow into the surrounding space. When Michelangelo liberated the image which he described in the rock, the form which emerged was still very much a part of the matrix from which it was freed. Its self-contained mass suggests this, and this stone core gives the impression of an energy pent up in solid material. Michelangelo designed his statues for one commanding point of view. This dominant view prevails for Bernini groups, but they appear to expand into general space. A group like the Apollo and Daphne was meant to be placed against a wall or in a shallow niche, and the figures, although seen from a single point of view, would give the impression of hurtling through space, expanding and moving toward the audience that sees them as though on a stage.

In his group in the Villa Borghese, Bernini has chosen to represent the transitory moment of metamorphosis with a completely nonclassical psychological expression in his portrayal of the horror of Daphne at the touch of her pursuer and the god's amazement at the magical transformation of his quarry. It is apparent at once that the figures are in no way confined to an imaginary block, and the literal explosion of the forms into surrounding space contrives to make the beholder an emotional participant in the spectacle. Indeed, in the Apollo and Daphne an almost centrifugal force impetuously projects the plastic matter beyond the limits of the composition. Part of Bernini's pictorial formula, anticlassical in its realism, is his marvelous description of textures in stone, as in the contrast between skin and bark and the soft and wildly streaming hair of Daphne, which is miraculously transformed into budding laurel leaves.

Turning to the classical aspects of the group, the relation between the Apollo and the famous ancient statue of the Belvedere in the Vatican becomes apparent immediately. It is as though the antique god had been released from the frozen model's pose, which he had held so long, to cavort in this swirling burst of dynamic action. Although the head of Bernini's Apollo (figure 180) follows rather faithfully the classic lineaments of the original (figure 181), the sculptor's tender manipulation of the marble surface to a far greater degree than the Hellenistic original conveys an illusion of the translucent softness and warmth of real flesh. In the same way the treatment of the mass of hair with the dominant *krobylos* suggests the antique model. But under Bernini's chisel Apollo's hair is conceived in more natural and flowing rhythms without division into stiff and waxy individual curls; like Daphne's streaming locks it suggests a coursing fire in the wind.

Whereas the Apollo is a Baroque vivification of the Belvedere statue, the figure of Daphne (figure 182) presents a no less wonderful enlivement of an antique maenad (figure 183). Daphne is an ideation by Bernini from an ancient representation of a Bacchic dancer, such as the one from the Villa of Hadrian, now in the Museo delle Terme. A comparison reveals at once not only a close resemblance in the superficial shapes and contours but in the inner plastic energy that animates the form. Bernini has only intensified the upward spiral movement implied in the classical figure to suggest a form launched rocketlike into space. The clinging robe of the ancient nymph with even more sensually picturesque implications connoted by the naturalism of the textures is adapted for Daphne's enfolding sheath of bark. The sinuous lines of the drapery are transferred to the tree-trunk that envelops Daphne. It is apparent that Bernini was attracted to this antique figure or one like it, because this Hellenistic work already presents the concept of a figure liberated in space with the direction of the body and limbs suggesting a radiating centrifugal movement that was a part of Bernini's pictorial conception of sculpture. As a final touch to this new conception of released form Daphne's wild glance loses itself in infinity, and the cry shaped by her contorted mouth implies a distant echo. Technically the hollowing-out of the pupils of the eyes in Roman fashion stresses the expression of yearning in the mask of Apollo and the frenzy in Daphne's glance. Other aspects of the group, such as the high polish and the supreme technical virtuosity of carving, are further revelations of Bernini's devotion to the antique, not only for the pathos of its subject matter and its dynamic movement, but for its revelation of technical secrets.

Rubens and Classical Antiquity

There are painters for whom the imitation of ancient statues is very useful, and for others dangerous even to the ruination of their art. I conclude nevertheless that in order to achieve final perfection in painting, it is necessary to have an intelligent view of the antique, to be as it were absorbed in it, and it is also necessary to make a judicious use of it, so that one is not conscious of a stony quality in any way.

—Rubens *

THE last of the great Flemish masters, and in many ways the most typical of Baroque artists, was Peter Paul Rubens. Rubens was not only a great painter but a great man of his time. He was once the ambassador to the court of Spain, the companion of kings and courtiers throughout his life. As diplomat and artist, he visited the courts of Italy and England and France. He knew all the European languages and the classic ones as well. His training was acquired largely in copying the Italian masters of the sixteenth and seventeenth centuries. In his art as in his life Rubens was a man of immeasurable vitality, so that his paintings are pervaded with a kind of ecstasy of physical well-being that is conveyed to the spectator both in terms of color and the dynamic arrangement of his compositions. From the technical point of view he was a marvelous performer. In every branch of art he could visualize and transcribe any pose of the human figure in every imaginable condition of lighting. He was by no means imaginative in a poetic sense: what he had was a consummate power of constructing figures in unified groups, and projecting this visualization to the canvas in his own terms. His terms could be described as those of commonplace, Flemish reality raised to a great intensity and perfection by his gift of visual orderliness in terms of color and composi-

* Aliis utilissima, aliis damnosa usque ad exterminium artis. Concludo tamen ad summum ejus perfectionem esse necessariam earum intelligentiam, imo imbibitionem: sed judiciose applicandum earum usum & omnino citra saxum.—Peter Paul Rubens, "De imitatione statuarums" Roger de Piles, *Cours de Peinture par Principes*

tion. There was a combination of calculated order and richness in Rubens's palette that was based on a triad of yellow ocher, burnt sienna, and gray. This simple combination of colors was especially well adapted for expressing in terms of paint the glow and translucence of flesh tints: deep orange in the shadow, opposed to the pearly gray in the half-tones, to suggest both modeling and the blue transparency of the skin.

One of the great critics of the Baroque period, Roger de Piles, noted in one of his essays: "As there are some things in sculpture which are not suitable for painting and since the painter has better means of imitating nature, he must regard antiquity as a book which one translates into another language." [1] In this statement he comes close to paraphrasing the opinions of Rubens on the intelligent use of the antique. In an essay, "De Imitatione Statuarum," Rubens points out that in basing a figure on an antique prototype the artist must paint the flesh in color, not as marble, and notes such pitfalls as the harsh contours, the dark shadows, and the opacity of the stone, which are faults to be avoided in representing the real translucence of skin and flesh, as well as the movement and suppleness of the body's muscular framework. "He who can distinguish all these things with sound judgment can use antique statues scrupulously as a basis for study and creation." [2]

Rubens' creative reworking of classical forms reveals itself in his drawing of the Spinario (figure 184). Although the general confirmation of the famous prototype (figure 185) is there, he translates the bronze into full, glowing flesh, in what has really become a picture of a healthy, undressed Flemish bumpkin. Even in the drawing Rubens' great specialty can be noted: his feeling for transparent shadows and the warm lights on the flesh.

Rubens as a humanist never missed an opportunity to use the innumerable figures and ideas which antiquity furnished him, but he always interpreted rather than copied them, filling them with a suggestion of wonderful vitality, radiant color, and dynamic expansiveness that are of the very essence of his Baroque genius. His art furnishes a supreme example of how, even in an art which seems opposed to classicism, the antique tradition can furnish an ever new and invigorating inspiration.

The most obvious lesson in Rubens' commentary on the uses of antiquity is that the painter must see statues as living models. The stone prototype is not something to be copied literally; it must be enlivened and imaginatively unified in the painter's composition. Probably in railing

263

against the painting of colored statues, rather than figures of flesh and blood, the artist was thinking not only of his immediate predecessors in Flanders but also of Mantegna's icy sculpturesque manner. Such a manner was completely opposed to Rubens' own pictorial style. Furthermore it would have been impossible for an artist of his originality to have been satisfied with a slavish copying of the antique. Whereas earlier artists had depended on an association of line and sculpturesque form of the antique, in Rubens outlines and form disappear in favor of color and a dynamic unity of composition. His painting consists of a rhythm of spatial masses that has replaced the architectonic rhythm of line and form associated with the Italian Renaissance.

A beautiful example of Rubens' creative use of the antique is his painting entitled Venus Frigida, or Venus Chilled (figure 186). The figure of the crouching goddess is quite obviously inspired by an antique original such as the crouching Venus in the Louvre (figure 187). This fragment has been restored by Rubens in his painting. His restoration of the head resting on the right hand is archaeologically credible and generally rather antique in feeling. Rubens is never interested in simply giving a faithful reproduction or translation of an ancient prototype. The antique Venus in this painting has become a figure of flesh and blood, and she is compositionally integrated with the other figures in the setting. The crouching pose of the goddess is echoed in the cowering Amor, and the same motif is repeated by the satyr crouching in the background. The whole conception is united as a mythological fantasy and as a pictorially integrated composition. The figures are joined in their physical movement and poses and in the spiritual relation which links them. Here, as so often in Rubens' paintings, there is a contrast between the breathing vitality and statuesque calm of his wonderfully realized figures, a completely imaginative enlivening transfiguration of ancient myth and form.

— 52 —

The Seventeenth Century
in France

The principal and most important part of Painting, is to find out, and thoroughly understand what Nature has made most Beautiful, and most proper to this Art; and that a Choice of it may be much according to the Taste and Manner of the Ancients.
—Du Fresnoy *

THE development of the arts in seventeenth-century France is invariably associated with Louis XIV and the succession of ministers who advised his prodigal artistic schemes. The palace of Versailles is the symbol of the vast extravagance devoted to support the ideal of royal grandeur, a background for the ritual and pageantry of the court.

During the reign of Louis XIV, Classicism became an instrument of artistic unity reflecting the political centralization of France. One has the feeling that the grandiose schemes in art, not only Versailles itself but also the program of the Academy, were created as a stage set for the sovereign, an artistic confirmation of the monomaniacal will to power of the ruling class. The imposition of such a taste dedicated to the glorification of the monarchy, with all the pompous panoply of allegory invented by Louis' court painter Le Brun and the rigid formulas of the academicians, could produce only a cold and desiccated parody of the ancients and the admired Italians of the High Renaissance. The arts themselves were dedicated to maintaining the propaganda of absolute monarchy, and, with the transference of absolutism to the aesthetic sphere, they were to be governed by the same systematized orderliness that determined the com-

* Praecipua imprimis Artisque potissima pars est,
  Nosse quid in rebus Natura creavit ad Artem
  Pulchrius, idque Modum juxta,
  Mentemque Vetustam.
—C. A. du Fresnoy, *De arte graphica* (1668); translated by John Dryden (1716)

plete rationality and unification of a government centered around the person and will of the monarch. It was with the foundation of the Academy of Painting and Sculpture in 1648 that French art was forced to assume the grandiose official character associated with Louis and his reign. In the arts, standardization was to be achieved by the directors of the Academy. Such a monopolizing of artistic talent to enhance the splendor of courtly life goes back to the enterprises of Francis I at Fontainebleau, but never until the time of Louis XIV was the program pursued with such relentless vigor. The aims of the French Academy were intended to achieve in art something of the same symmetry, dignity, reserve, and clarity that typified the whole tenor of the monarch and his court.

The curriculum of the French Academy, probably borrowed from earlier systems of instruction in Italy, consisted of an arduous routine of copying drawings, drawing from the cast or from the antique, and finally from the life. Even though one might consider such a type of instruction as a veritable brain-washing designed to eradicate all freedom or originality of expression, it was in reality a valuable discipline in which the artist became once and for all the master of his craft, and within which imaginative artists could achieve an extraordinary originality of expression. The Academy dedicated to the perpetuation of a taste suitable to exalt the *roi soleil* and his court was firmly anchored on a classical foundation. The program of study to be administered by the French Academy in Rome had as its basis an indoctrination into the antique and the classicism of the High Renaissance in Italy. Classic, to the arbiters of taste in seventeenth-century France, meant the best, the highest class; and since they found these ideals embodied in the Greco-Roman past, it was inevitable that antiquity should provide the models for the taste of absolutism. The *manière des anciens* not only ensured an aesthetic basis for the training of artists, but it had the added function of providing allegories of the sun king as Apollo or, as military victor, in the role of Alexander the Great. Antiquity provided the unchallenged norm for proportions as well as poses and gestures. The accepted canon was based on the measurements of antique statues, made by Poussin and published by Bellori. To these regulations of proportion and decorum derived from study of the ancients was added the codification of expressions appropriate to the registering of emotions.

Such a program administered by a master decorator and entrepreneur like Charles Le Brun was ideally suited to filling the galleries of Versailles with an overlay of decorations extolling the sublimity of the monarch in the most pompous allegories drawn from mythology and ancient history. Le Brun's program was intended to bestow on the arts the same unity and complete rationality that had raised the economic and military prestige of France to the summit of European power. The foundation of the arts on the classical tradition reveals the supreme official recognition of the authority of the ancients as the ultimate in logic and clarity in the government and its embellishments. Of course, the stultifying demands of the official education offered to selected artists marks the beginning of the confusion of the classic with the Academic, in the worst sense of that term. Only artists like Poussin, Claude Lorrain, and the sculptor Puget, who were able to keep apart from the program sponsored by the government, were able to carry on a creative production in the spirit of the use of the classical tradition by artists of the High Renaissance.

It has often been pointed out that Poussin's compositions, in their architectural solidity and clarity of arrangement, their restrained elegance and restrained formality of expression, approximate the completely controlled emotions and logic of dramatic form and development encountered in the dramas of Corneille and Racine. In the French classic theater of the seventeenth century the most sinister passions, the darkest tragedies and intrigues violent, psychological, and physical, emotions tender and tragic, are all present, but the situations, the speeches, gestures, and manners of the actors are so controlled by the observation of the unities, by the polished correctness and propriety, that a glacial clarity, inevitable logic, and rationality characterized the performance. Historical situations from imperial Rome or from mythology are so ordered and rationalized that the dramatis personae assume a truly heroic, universal stature. They are like Greek tragedies in which the violence and tragic passions of Sophocles and Aeschylus are contained within psychological situations logically and rationally developed with polished correctness, restraint, and propriety. Poussin attains something of this same logic and unity of expression in the classic serenity of his figures and the cool dramatic architecture of his compositions.

— 53 —

Poussin and the Antique

Poussin lived and conversed with the ancient statues so long, that he may be said to have been better acquainted with them, than with the people who were about him. I have often thought that he carried his veneration for them so far as to wish to give his works the air of Ancient Paintings . . . Like Polidoro he studied the ancients so much, that he acquired a habit of thinking in their way, and seemed to know perfectly the actions and gestures they would use on every occasion.

—Reynolds *

THE problem with Poussin, as with every artist of the Baroque period, is that of his special or personal reworking of the antique in the interests of forming his own individual and always Baroque style. Poussin's adaptations are never secondhand copies, but are borrowings made directly from a classical original. They are never complete borrowings, but only a very skillful reuse of the essential motif of the ancient model. A number of early compositions show his close study of antique sarcophagi in such features as the arrangement in shallow planes, the employment of the principle of isocephaly, and a tendency to compose in a series of essentially isolated figures and groups.

Of particular interest to Poussin's reworking of an antique formula is his copy (figure 188) of the famous Roman wall-painting, the so-called Aldobrandini Marriage, now in the Doria Gallery in Rome. This classical wall-painting (figure 189) was discovered in 1606 and represents the preparations for a wedding ceremony. Reading the composition from left to right, we see first the bride and her attendants, then the waiting groom, and at the right two figures performing a sacrifice in honor of the occasion. The composition is that of a long frieze with the figures presented in separate groups against a neutral background. In the classical original the dark band at the top and the dark patch behind the last figure at the right are

* Sir Joshua Reynolds, *Discourses on Art: Discourse Five*, December 10, 1772

268

additions or restorations made at the time of the installation of the wall-painting in the Aldobrandini pavilion in 1620. The composition is painted in light pastel colors without any marked value contrasts, so that the effect is rather that of a low relief.

Poussin in his version of this Greco-Roman original followed his model rather closely, but at the same time made certain alterations that already point to the formation of his own style. There are certain minor changes in the dress and ornaments of the figure and the stage props against which they lean, but the principal alteration is in the format of the picture and in the creation of a quite different spatial conception. Poussin's replica is taller than the original, and the ground has been extended below the row of figures. Poussin has further converted the neutral background into a cloudy sky, and the dark spot at the right has been converted into a vista of a hilly landscape. A comparison will show at a glance that Poussin's version of the Aldobrandini Marriage brings the figures into a quite different relation to space through the heightening of the format. One has the impression of a stage with an infinity of landscape and sky opening in the background. This effective link between foreground and background space by the heightening of the composition is a device that Poussin employed in a number of his early compositions. The colors in Poussin's painting are much stronger, and his emphasis on the contrasts between light and shade makes the figures stand out from the wall in back and the wall itself from the sky. The result is that to a far greater degree than in the classical original we have the illusion of the elements of the composition standing out in a succession of parallel horizontal planes and at the same time set in a convincing spatial organization.

A painting that reveals Poussin's mature transformation of the antique into his own classical style is the superb Triumph of Neptune in the Philadelphia Museum of Art (figure 190). This was one of a group of paintings sent to Cardinal Richelieu in 1639. In its theme as well as certain details this picture is reminiscent of Raphael's Galatea. Raphael, like Poussin, was inspired by the ancient nereid sarcophagi (figure 68), but actually followed an antique model in the putto and foreground and the entwined merman and mermaid at the right. Poussin has made a much closer study of an antique prototype in the composition as a whole and in many of its details. Like his youthful Aldobrandini copy, the horizontal format of the arrangement recalls an ancient relief frieze. Many of the salient motifs in Poussin's Triumph were inspired by a nereid sarcophagus

269

in the Giardino della Pigna (figure 191). The figures of Neptune, Amphitrite, and the nereids appear as a succession of isolated figures, just as they do in the relief; and even the putti hovering in the air have been adapted from this same source. The closed character of the composition is also reminiscent of the unity in the antique sarcophagus. Poussin's painting differs from the antique and differs from Raphael, too, in the spatial depth and the landscape background. The French classicist differs from the Baroque conception of space and action found in the compositions of Rubens. Whereas Rubens' arrangements are animated by a united tempestuous swirl of action, Poussin's composition is more like the balanced separate streams of movement found in antique reliefs. The balance of different groups in Poussin's architecturally composed scene and his building of forms in pyramidal masses firmly establish the static arrangement. Whereas Poussin's ancient models, like the nereid sarcophagi, in reality consist only of laterally balanced groups as accents in a frieze, Poussin's painting in typically Baroque fashion is planned in three dimensions. Not only are the individual figures and groups disposed in diagonals leading into the background, but there are subtleties of arrangement in the position and movement of the forms in foreground and background. So, for example, the outward movement of the pair of seagods at the right is counterbalanced by the beautiful figure of a nymph seen in back view that cuts across them. The essential stabilizing element in Poussin's almost mathematical distribution of forms is to be seen in the great pyramids of deities culminating in the head of Amphitrite. This shape provides an anchor that brings the whole turbulent composition into an ordered static solidity and calm. This play of action against inaction, the balanced order, and the endless suggestion of the shapes moving in space and yet contained within a static framework are what makes for the dynamic excitement of Poussin's creative reordering of the antique.

Poussin also furnishes an illustration of the classic or, as it was described in his day, the heroic style of landscape. His landscapes were not based on classical prototypes, but they can be described as classical in the same way that his figure paintings are, because in them nature is ordered into a system of internal harmonies almost like architecture. Roger de Piles describes this type of painting as follows:

The heroick style is a composition of objects, which, in their kinds, draw, both from art and nature, everything that is great and extraordinary in either. The situations are perfectly agreeable and surprising. The only buildings are temples, pyramids, ancient places of burial, altars consecrated to the divinities, pleasure-houses of regular architecture: and if nature appear not there, as we every day casually see her, she is at least represented as we think she ought to be. This style is an agreeable illusion, and a sort of inchantment, when handled by a man of fine genius, and good understanding, as Poussin was, who has so happily expressed it.[1]

Poussin's painting of St. John on Patmos is a perfect example of this classic recreation of nature (figure 192). The painting appears as a nostalgic recreation of Poussin's memory of an antique land, the great garden of Italy in all its formal splendor. The figure of St. John is only a pretext for a romantic reconstruction of the timeless beauty of the campagna. In the picture the natural elements and the fragments of ruined buildings have been reduced to a classic architectural order of shapes and logical relations. One has the feeling that Poussin literally constructed his landscapes stone by stone and tree by tree, omitting everything superficial or accidental in the achievement of his generalized vision. The composition, almost like a classical building, is stabilized by a series of horizontal planes built up from the broad stylobate of the foreground, and like the opposing diagonals in the Amphitrite the verticals formed by the columned portico and obelisk in the middle distance arrest the sweeping curves of the trees and hills. This mood of almost Virgilian pensive melancholy is frequently encountered in Poussin's idyllic subjects. It is typically Baroque in its truly heroic scale and the symphonic sweep of the architectonic harmonies of which it is built. The balance of shapes is echoed in the harmony of the restricted palette of greens, ochers, and siennas, set off by the deep cobalt of the sky. There is a distant echo of the painting of nature in the ancient period in this kind of sculptural painting of nature in solidly realized shapes, and it is an example of Poussin's classicism in the clarity and order of its structure.

— 54 —

Sculpture in
Seventeenth-Century France

I have fed on great undertakings, I am carried away when I work on them; and
the marble trembles before me, however large the block.   —Puget *

Fʀᴀɴçᴏɪs Gɪʀᴀʀᴅᴏɴ, who worked as a sculptural collaborator of Louis
XIV's artistic director, Le Brun, received his classical training in Rome
from 1645 to 1650. His most famous and ambitious group, ordered
for his royal patron in 1666, was Apollo and the Nymphs (figure 193).
This group, which in the eighteenth century was transferred to a grotto
in the gardens at Versailles, was originally designed for a niche as a
centerpiece for two other groups designed by the sculptor's assistants. It
has rightly been called the most purely classical work in French seventeenth-century sculpture. It takes but a glance to see the Hellenistic inspiration for the types and the handling of the nudes and draperies. In
the course of executing this work Girardon in 1668 paid a special visit
to Rome in order to make a study of antique models for this commission.
The entire group is indeed an anthology of recognizable Hellenistic types.
The Apollo in the center has obviously been inspired by the Apollo Belvedere (figure 31), and the heads of some of the attendant nymphs are
borrowed from the Medici or Capitoline Venus. One of the more active
draped figures in the background is taken from one of the Niobids in the
famous group in the Uffizi Gallery. Beyond the Laocoön and the Farnese
Bull, which were inadequate for Girardon's composition, there were no
extant groups of figures upon which the sculptor could base his arrangement. He seems to have founded his composition on the formula of a
painting by Poussin. This dependence was even more marked when the

* Je me suis nourri aux grands ouvrages, je nage quand j'y travaille; et le marbre
tremble devant moi, pour grosse qui soit la pièce.—Pierre Puget, *Letter to Louvois,* 1685

272

figures were disposed on the shallow stage of the niche originally planned for them. The scheme is not unlike that of Poussin's painting of the Triumph of Amphitrite, with a central frontal figure balanced by symmetrically grouped attendants. Again, as in a Poussin painting, the figures were placed in a succession of planes with the positions of the bodies and the gestures of the foreground figures providing diagonal accents leading to the center of the compositional arrangement. Like Le Brun, whose sculptural counterpart he was, Girardon represents the most academic and in a way rather dead adherence to antique precedent. A more creative phase in the interpretation of the classic belongs to those French sculptors who were able to escape the mortifying influence of the Academy and the court.

Pierre Puget (1620–1694) was a French sculptor who, although nourished in the great Italian Baroque tradition, found an inspiration in the classic style both for his mythology and his form. His training was actually as a painter under the tutelage of Pietro da Cortona during a period of study in Rome and Florence from 1640 to 1643. It is evident that at some time, perhaps during a later visit to Rome, Puget came under the influence of the sculpture of Michelangelo and Bernini. Most of his active life was spent in Marseilles and Toulon, mainly as a furnisher of sculpture and decoration for warships, so that he remained disassociated from the academic tradition of the court.

Perhaps the most typical and certainly the most famous of Puget's works was his colossal group of Milo of Crotona which, begun in 1671, eventually found its way to Versailles in 1683 (figure 194). The group illustrates the agonizing fate of this unfortunate hero who, having caught his hand in the cleft of a stump, was devoured by a lion. The choice of this obscure legend was obviously dictated by the opportunity for the representation of violence and anguish implicit in the subject. We are, of course, reminded of Bernini's selection of the Apollo-and-Daphne and the Pluto-and-Proserpina stories for their possibilities of expressing emotion and action in a psychological as well as physical way. Puget in many respects is the most Baroque French sculptor, and could indeed be said to have invented a French Baroque style.

In Puget's marble we see the unfortunate Milo with his right hand trapped in the stump throwing back his head in anguish, and his left hand endeavoring vainly to fend off the attack of the lion. His feet are braced against the tree as he strains vainly to free himself from the vise. The vio-

273

lence of movement, the twisting of the agonized body, and the naturalism in rendering the tree-stump remind us of similar elements in Italian works like Bernini's Apollo and Daphne (figure 179). At the same time the torment of the giant frame evokes memories of Michelangelo's famous Slaves (figure 144); but Puget's expression of an anguish of mind as well as of body and the sheer tension of the straining form is something far different from the paralyzed movement of Buonarotti.

Puget's expression of emotional intensity, both in the contortion of the facial mask and the violent torsion of the body, is clearly an adaptation from the famous Laocoön group (figure 34). Not only the type of Milo's head, but the detail of the mouth opened in an unuttered scream is taken from the head of the dying priest in the Hellenistic group. At the same time the extraordinarily careful attention paid to the surface texture of the body is reminiscent not only of the Laocoön but of another realistic tour-de-force of the Hellenistic period: The Old Fisherman, sometimes identified as the Dying Seneca. Actually Puget's work is most classic in the self-contained geometric regularity and order of its composition. The group does not burst into surrounding space, like a Bernini composition, but is entirely contained within the framework of straight lines that form its contours. When seen from the side in the photographic view favored in most textbooks, the group is inscribed in a parallelogram, the sides of which are described by leg and left arm and by its body and the tree-stump. The frontal view reveals an equally contained and classical arrangement of two parallel axes formed by the hero's right leg and left arm balanced by the line of his torso and the tree-trunk. It is no wonder that Cézanne, in sketching this group, should have chosen the front view, because this aspect best reveals the blocklike planular character of Puget's classical construction, which appealed to the great Provençal painter for its suggestion of integrated, even cubic, solidity of form. It seems evident, too, that Puget's taste for the colossal was nourished as much by his admiration for classical art as by his acquaintance with the classical work by Michelangelo.

— 55 —

The Rococo in France

His elegance, his daintiness, his sentimental sauciness, his coquetry, his facility, his variety, his brilliance, his rouged pinks, his lewdness, should captivate coxcombs, trifling women, young people, worldly folk, the whole crowd of those who are strangers to good taste, to truth, to good sense, and the discipline of the art.

—Diderot *

THE so-called Rococo style of the eighteenth century in France may be interpreted as a disintegration of the classic Baroque of the seventeenth century into mannered triviality and invention. It was the result in large part of the demands of French society after the close of the reign of Louis XIV. Under Louis XV boredom with the pompous heaviness of the style dictated by Le Brun and the desire for novelty by both aristocratic patrons and the new class of amateur collectors in Paris brought into being a style exactly suited to the new mood of license and novel excitement required by these classes. In the liberalism that replaced the absolutism of the previous century the keynote of art itself was sounded in energy, frivolity, and lightness. In such a climate it was inevitable that the gods themselves enacted the same gallantries as the circle of Madame de Pompadour; a dainty eroticism pervades the Olympus of artists like Boucher and Clodion. In such an art it would seem inevitable that the trammels of classical dogma should be completely discarded. But even in the reign of Louis XV the Rococo was moving inevitably toward the neoclassic. The savage invective of Diderot against the lack of form, discipline, and morality in the work of Rococo artists and the passionate espousal of the antique by the powerful Baron de Caylus inexorably affected a change to a new severity and chastity of design. One should note, too, that as the court moved

* Son élégance, sa mignardise, sa galantine romanesque, sa coquetterie, sa facilité, sa variété, son éclat, ses carnations fardées, sa débauche, doivent captiver les petits maîtres, les petites femmes, les jeunes gens, les gens du monde, la foule de ceux qui sont étrangers au vrai goût, à la vérité, aux idées justes, à la sévérité de l'art.—Denis Diderot, "Salon de 1761," ed. Assezat (1876)

away from Versailles to settle in hôtels and apartments in Paris the demand for smaller, intimate works of art arose. The colossal was replaced by the little. In the new intellectual climate of the eighteenth century, in which philosophical ideas were no longer considered radical, the way was opened to the study of archaeology and the history of art. Freed of the restraints of the academic tyranny of the period of Louis XIV French artists returned to the teachings of nature. The combination of the observation of nature and the studied use of the antique in an artist like Bouchardon was to lead ultimately to the true French classicism of David and Ingres.

The painters of the eighteenth century in France universally display an artificial tone and temper in their performance, a reliance on seductive effects of nacreous color and fluid bravura of brushwork that appear as the very antithesis of the classical tradition. These masters, like Boucher, reflect the taste for the frivolous and trivial that, under Louis XV, developed in response to the boredom of the court and connoisseurs with the endless repetition of the rigid and pompous formulas of the Academy. The painters were quick to cater to the freer modes of life of the early eighteenth century, eager to provide for the new personal taste for luxury that superseded the tyranny of Le Brun. In many ways the painting of the French Rococo was a more vital form of expression: escaping the restraints of tradition and the conventions of the Academy there was a spontaneous return to nature that, with the brush of a Watteau or a Fragonard, returned French painting to the old congenial path of elegance and naturalism.

There are any number of Boucher paintings that would serve to illustrate his treatment of mythological themes. A particularly fine example is the Triumph of Venus which was bought in 1740 by the Comte de Tessin for the King of Sweden and is now in the National Gallery in Stockholm (figure 195). The composition with Venus enthroned above a sporting bevy of nymphs and tritons makes an interesting comparison with earlier marine mythologies from which it is eventually derived. The conception is a shadow of an ancient nereid sarcophagus although it is doubtful if even one of the figures has a specific reference to an antique prototype. There is nothing statuesque about these warm youthful bodies painted in pearly tints and dissolved in cerulean mists and ivory clouds. If we compare the work with Poussin's Triumph of Neptune (figure 190), it becomes obvious at once that the strongly integrated sculptural composition by the seventeenth-century master has completely disintegrated into a vaporous swirl of moving figures rotating about the figure of Venus. Even the floating scarf, which in Poussin's picture served as the culmination of his pyramidal organization, has become a kind of kite blown in the wind and serving as a decorative accessory to enhance the billowing movement of Boucher's scheme and to fill the area of the vacant sky. Boucher was an artist who was able to rely entirely on his memory and the sureness of his hand to dispense with drawing from nature in his creations like this one which are examples of his ability to dissolve his forms in paint and to reduce mythology to a sensuously pleasing erotic ballet.

It is not surprising that even in his lifetime Boucher was disparagingly referred to as a "peintre d'éventail," and that in 1761 Diderot, the scourge of the Rococo court painters, bitterly noted that "from the degradation of taste, of color of composition, of the character of expression, of drawing, there has followed, step by step, the degradation of morals." [1] The charming vanities and frail glories of Boucher's "vulgarité élégante" were for obvious reasons the special target of critics like Diderot and the Baron de Caylus who laid the foundations of neoclassicism in their fervent espousal of an art dedicated to classical principles, based on the solidity and authority of the antique, and also dedicated to expressing in appropriately severe classical terms an edifying morality befitting the generation that made an end to the French monarchy. The triumph of this taste and authority was to be realized in the work of Jacques-Louis David.

Edmé Bouchardon is a sculptor whose work reveals a classical trend that eventually transformed the style of the Rococo into the neoclassic. Bouchardon was a pupil of the great French Baroque master Guillaume Coustou I, and many of his works continue the power and flamboyance of French Baroque monuments of the seventeenth century. His sojourn in Rome from 1723 to 1732 not only won him the widest acclaim in official art circles but filled him with such an admiration for the classical that he produced an almost literal copy of the Barberini Faun, now in the Glyptothek in Munich.

The one work that is most typical of the changing taste of the age is his Cupid in the Louvre (figure 196). Since Cupid is represented carving his bow from the club of Hercules, the subject presented a playful allegory of love's triumph over force. The general inspiration for this work appears to have been the Eros attributed to Lysippus in the Museo Capitolino in Rome. This work was finished in 1750 and evoked a mixed response from contemporary critics. While Voltaire referred to Bouchardon as "notre Phidias," the critic Bachaumont remarked that Bouchardon "imitates the antique and especially nature; but sometimes he imitates them perhaps too exactly." [2] Another writer credited the sculptor with uniting the grace of Correggio and the purity of classic design.[3] Bouchardon conforms to the eighteenth-century taste for the graceful and pretty in the slight, almost feminine, frame of the adolescent Eros. Although the finished statue in marble has an exquisite shining finish on its smooth surfaces, the clay model in the Musée Bonnat at Bayonne reveals an extraordinary naturalism in the representation of the boy's gangling proportions and an interest in texture that are far more in keeping with the tradition of French naturalism than the final version. Bouchardon is reported to have made not only drawings from life but casts of part of the bodies of living models in preparation for his statue. Beyond a suggestion of the poverty of adolescent anatomy the statue as it exists in stone reveals little of this naturalistic foundation, but has something of the cool, icy refinement of the work of Canova. Both the motif and its conception are infinitely lighter and more consciously graceful than true Baroque sculpture. The posturing of the figure in a curve following the line of the bent bow adds an artificial elegance to this playful exercise in the classical vein. The exquisiteness of the conception and polished surfaces are completely typical of the Rococo. Versions of this statue exist in several sizes, but in any scale Bouchardon's Cupid suggests the delicacy and superficial charm more appropriate to the table ornament than to monumental sculpture.

Bouchardon's turn to the conventions of classical art, which in the Cupid anticipate the style of Canova, may be explained in large part by his attachment to the Baron de Caylus. This arrogant antiquary who deprecated the Baroque nobility of so great a sculptor as Guillaume Coustou was both in his collecting of objects of classical art and in his possessive patronage of artists wholly committed to establishing what he considered the infallible taste of antiquity combined with a judicious study of nature. He may be considered one of the first in that line of conservative critics culminating in the writings and opinions of Quatremère de Quincy who were responsible for erecting the structure of neoclassicism in France. In Bouchardon, one of the most talented sculptors produced by the French Academy in Rome, Caylus recognized an instrument to carry out his program of a return to "le beau simple."

The final phase of the Rococo may be illustrated by a single work by Clodion, a sculptor whose career extended from the period of Louis XVI into the first decades of the nineteenth century. Clodion, like all his contemporaries, enjoyed the usual period of study in Rome. It is typical of him and his period that this master's sculpture was no longer regal or monumental, but directed to the tastes not only of the court but of the rising class of amateur collectors in Paris. Its function was to provide enjoyment on an intimate scale.

The fact that Clodion after the Revolution was able to accommodate himself to the frigidity of neoclassicism, as in his reliefs on the Arc du Carrousel, has no bearing on the principal achievement of his career. His contribution to the classical tradition was his vibrant, sensuous translation of Hellenistic themes and techniques into the language of the rococo. In this he was both one of the more original and aesthetically moving sculptors of the period.

Although some marble sculpture by Clodion exists, his most typical and felicitous expression was in small terra-cotta groups that are the modern equivalent of Tanagra figurines. These dainty products of the potters of the late Hellenistic period were not only immensely popular as collectors' items, but also in the world of fashion ladies strove to model their coiffures and costumes on these pretty trifles.

There is no better illustration of how rococo sculptors turned for inspiration to such ancient counterparts than Clodion's Nymph and Satyr (figure 197). It reminds one of the many erotic, often pornographic, subjects that were the specialty of artists in the last centuries of the Hellenistic period (figure 198). Although Clodion could not have seen this particular prototype, the group of a satyr attempting to rape a nymph in the Palazzo dei Conservatori is a perfect example of this taste in ancient times. Doubtless during his years in Italy Clodion had some acquaintance with the kind of Pompeian statuary now secluded in the Gabinetto Segreto of the Museo Nazionale in Naples. Clodion's group is of course not so overt as its predecessor, but the influence of the genre is evident in the emphasis on sexual attraction in terms of subject, form, and texture. As in many of Clodion's groups, the piquancy of the subject is heightened by the contrast between the brutal face of the satyr, burning with the fever of sexual desire, and the mock anxiety of the nymph. Both subject and material are an eighteenth-century reworking of the Tanagra formula. It was a formula sure to please by the delicacy of its execution and the licentiousness of the presentation. The textual intricacy of Clodion's treatment of the accessories surrounding the groups is always amazing and, like the treatment of the forms themselves, is in the tradition of French naturalism. Clodion's differentiation of textures in his little terracotta groups appears as a final restatement in small scale of the genius of Bernini.

The toylike charm and cloying eroticism are as much a *cul de sac* in the classical tradition as the work of his spiritual predecessors in the Hellenistic period was a reduction of the heroic ideal to the superficial attractions of the anecdotal. Clodion is typically rococo in the small scale of his *œuvre,* the ease and grace of movement, and the warm suppleness of the tenderly modeled bodies. It is obvious that the appeal of these groups was directed to the taste of connoisseurs whose interest in such subject matter and style was not entirely intellectual. These groups are so wildly alive that they suggest indecent *tableaux vivants.* Their extraordinary movement, fervid expression, and daintiness of execution are completely rococo in the reduction of the statuesque to action and texture.

— 56 —

The Neoclassic Period

One observes among all the countries of Europe a community of instruction and
knowledge, an equality of taste, learning, and talent. It could truly be said that
there is less difference between them than between the provinces of a single empire.

—Quatremère de Quincy *

I N the last decades of the eighteenth century all Europe had become Roman and all eyes turned to Rome as the capital of the arts. This was the
height of the neoclassic period when as never before the passion for Roman antiquity burned in the breasts of connoisseurs and artists of every
nation. Rome was the mecca for artists from every country of Europe,
and, even before the American Revolution, Benjamin West and John
Singleton Copley had responded to the beckoning invitation of Italy. Rome
in this period was not only as it always had been—the rendezvous of
Christianity filled with the pious establishments of all nations—but the
seat of artistic establishments, the Academies, dedicated to instructing
students to paint in the grand manner. This was a time when the community of classical education turned men to Italy. Mythology was a symbolism common to all, and the study of Latin and ancient history fired
every man with visions of the Rome of Caesar and Augustus. As part of
this bond in the greatness and authority of the classic past was the study
of Roman law and morality. Men like Washington and Jefferson saw
their policies reflected in the mirror of Roman history. There was a new
fervor and excitement in the great discoveries that were reshaping and
enlarging Western man's view of his classic past. The *scavi* of Pompeii and

* On observe entre toutes les contrées de l'Europe une communauté d'instruction et
de connaissance, une certaine égalité de goût, de savoir et de talent: on peut dire avec
vérité qu'il se trouve entre elles beaucoup moins de différences qu'on n'en rencontre
quelquefois entre les provinces d'un seule empire.—A. C. Quatremère de Quincy, *Lettres
sur les monuments de l'Italie* (1798)

Herculaneum kindled excitement as much as the adventures of Cagliostro and the flights of Montgolfière.

The last half of the eighteenth century produced a new archaeological classicism with a far more antiquarian approach to the great tradition than that of any previous age. This phenomenon, which came to be known as the neoclassic movement, is to be explained partly by the excitement provided by great archaeological discoveries in the Near East, Greece, and above all, the uncovering of Herculaneum and Pompeii. This new and intensive revival is also to be interpreted in the light of certain political and social factors. The simplicity and austerity of the classical ideal appealed to the revolutionary generation in France of the late eighteenth century which revolted against the sensuality, insincerity, and sophistication of the court art of the so-called Rococo period. The forms of classical art completely suited this puritanical idealism by its purity, harmony, and satisfying regularity of line and mass.

The imitation of classical art became fashionable in every form of expression. Systematic archaeological research began at the same moment that the experience of archaeology became the subject for a romantic artistic treatment of Roman ruins by the famous etcher and engraver, Piranesi.

The prophet of this resurgence of Hellenism was an obscure German professor, Joachim Winckelmann (1717–1768). The son of an impoverished cobbler, he was as a boy attracted to the beauties of Greek literature and managed to obtain a training in the classics in Germany. For some time he was attached to the court of Saxony where his attention wandered from the Baroque sculpture of the gardens to the copies of classic sculpture crated up in the cellars of the palace. By a miracle of divination rather than knowledge he was able to evoke the essential qualities of classic art, first expounded in 1755 in his *Thoughts on the Imitation of Greek Works in Painting and Sculpture*. When he finally went to Rome to become attached as curator to the household of Cardinal Albani, he was able to study actual examples of ancient sculpture and to elicit from them the fundamental principles of Greek art. He summarized these qualities and presented art as part of the growth of the human race and as a manifestation of the societies that produced it.

Winckelmann proclaimed that the imitation of sensuous beauty in nature and in spiritual beauty in man, the combination of beauty and sublime nobility, could be attained only by studying and imitating the

Greeks. "The noble simplicity and serene greatness of Greek statues is the true characteristic of Greek literature of the best period . . . Perhaps the draughtsmanship of the earliest Greek painters resembled the style of their first fine tragic poet." [1] This statement is the motto of neo-classicism and the first reconciliation of art and literature as manifestations of a single ideal.

Winckelmann's influence descended on Gotthold Ephraim Lessing, famed for his essay on the Laocoön.[2] This work was admired for its technical mastery, its superb anatomy. Today we can admire it for the masterful pattern and balance of the intricate arrangement. Lessing claimed to see in it a revelation of dignity and restraint (because Laocoön is not screaming with his mouth wide open). He was wrong in treating it as an example of classical ideals, which have nothing to do with tension or Baroque agitation. Actually the Laocoön appealed to Lessing because it had something of the same pathos and exaggerated feeling that he and all his generation were familiar with in the religious art of the Baroque period, so that the Laocoön really approximated the taste of this dying age.

Beyond his definition of the qualities to be discerned in Greek art, Winckelmann's real contribution was that he made people look with enthusiasm and love at classical art, now for the first time ordered in truly scientific fashion. Perhaps the principal artistic exponent of his ideas was the painter Anton Rafael Mengs, one of the first to be influenced by the newly discovered paintings of Herculaneum.

Goethe, a spiritual descendant of Winckelmann, believed that within a few years he could rediscover the lost tradition of the Greek artist and reduce it to a system that could be handed down from master to pupil. Following Winckelmann, he held that the different ideal characters of the gods in ancient art were portrayed by differences in the ideal forms of their faces and bodies. He believed that this lost vision of the ideal could be rediscovered by making the most exact and correlated measurements of many perfect statues and thereby found the Hellenic tradition anew. For Goethe these ancient canons for the gods and heroes were really the form of the Urmensch, the original man in the perfection of his golden day. For the Sage of Weimar man was the perfected microcosm of the universe and the key to the knowledge of God. Art as something representing men like gods was to be refounded to fulfill its highest mission as in ancient Hellas.

The neoclassic period was officially established in 1785. This year marked the exhibition of David's Oath of the Horatii, the one picture that really launched this new turn to the austerity of antiquity. By this time the Doric order, lately discovered in the temples of Paestum and Sicily, was accepted as appropriate to the new and severe ideals. By 1785 the royal porcelain factory in Naples was turning out classical designs for distribution to all the courts of Europe, and Pichler, the lapidary, was at the height of his fame for the carving of gems in a classical manner.

The origins of this movement are so multiple and complex that it is impossible to give more than a survey of a phenomenon that was changing the artistic face of Europe. The excavations undertaken in Italy publicly and privately by the middle of the eighteenth century were adding a vast population in marble to the museums of Rome and to the galleries of princely collectors in all of Europe. The discovery of the antiquities of Herculaneum and Pompeii, although for decades a closely guarded secret by the Bourbon kings of Naples, excited the imagination of the whole continent. The taste for the antique was fostered not only by the presence of this resurrection of its artistic treasures but by the first scholarly writings on antique art by historians, philosophers, and the more articulate collectors like the Baron de Caylus. For artists from all over Europe Rome became a new center of devotion, not for her Christian saints but for her images of pagan gods and goddesses.

The Academies maintained by various nations in the Eternal City emphasized as never before the value of turning to the antique for inspiration and instruction in attaining the *beau idéal* in art. The copying of ancient statuary from life-sized facsimiles to table ornaments in marble, bronze, and ceramics gratified the requirements of every purse and served to spread the doctrine to the ends of Europe. In architecture this new wave of enthusiasm for the classic standard brought into being the vast collection of prints of the monuments of Rome by Piranesi and the same etcher's collection of ancient ornaments suitable for contemporary use. Finally, this was an age of new explorations, not in space but in time, that revealed for the first time the hidden treasures of Greek art, first in Italy at Paestum, and then, through the travels and publications of Stuart and Revett and Wood, the hitherto unknown marvels of Greek art in Athens and the Near East.

Now, not classical art but the styles of the Baroque and Rococo belonged to the ancient past in the newness and fashionable appropriateness attached to anything Greek or Roman. Even in the eighteenth century artists and connoisseurs were still under the delusion that what they saw in the cold galleries of the Vatican was the purest Greek art. It is no wonder that when the first genuine works reflecting Greek archaic art appeared in the bronzes of Herculaneum they were not understood, and that the first discoveries of the severe grandeur of Doric architecture seemed completely at variance with accepted standards of the classic forms as determined by knowledge of the more elaborate Roman orders.

Whereas in the Renaissance classical art was the foundation of the ideology of the humanists and the antischolastic and anticlerical ideas of the intelligentsia, the art of the seventeenth century interpreted the world of Greece and Rome as a reflection of the aristocratic image of man and the ideals of the court of the absolute monarchs who liked to think of themselves as Olympians. In the eighteenth century classical art takes on a truly political character, when the French Revolutionaries chose the classical past as their ideal for its outlook and its example of Roman civic virtues, Spartan stoicism, and hardiness. This ideal had already been realized in some of the paintings exhibited by Jacques-Louis David even before the fateful year of 1789. When classical art becomes accepted as the embodiment of French revolutionary ideals, art becomes part of the social structure, an instrument for teaching and improvement, inspiring and setting an example in Republican virtues. At the same time that the arts of Greece and Rome recommended themselves as symbols of revolutionary protest, the writings of Seneca and Cicero supported the idea that sovereignty resides in the people.

The virtues and morality of the republics and democracies of the ancient world were a mirage guiding Frenchmen in their justification of the moral and philosophical ideals of their own world. The struggle for the establishment of a French state was in reality the dramatic interpretation of an antique image. Indeed, the pattern followed ancient history so closely that the Empire succeeded the Directory. It was not for nothing that Napoleon's portraitists stressed his resemblance to Augustus or that Bonaparte himself requested that the Brutus of the Capitoline, looted from Rome, be placed in his office in the Tuileries.

The great figure in French neoclassic art is the painter Jacques-Louis David. His immense authority in art was partly due to the fact that his particular conception of art was most in harmony with the political aims both of the Consulate and Napoleon's revival of the Roman Imperium.

Napoleon himself looms as the very keystone of this political classicism. He was fond of pointing out as his models Alexander and Caesar, noting that as Alexander traversed Asia and Caesar crossed the Rubicon, so he traversed the Alps and the Mediterranean to some of his greatest triumphs. Napoleon simply inherited the popular classical vocabulary in both oratory and art already established in the revolutionary period. He used classicism as an instrument to awaken national ambitions. This policy was embodied partly in the looting of masterpieces of classical art in Italy for export to France, literally a new sack of Rome with the advice of art experts, which brought all of the famous masterpieces of antiquity, such as the Apollo Belvedere and the Laocoön, to grace Napoleon's triumphs.

A statue of Napoleon as emperor is the famous likeness by the great Italian neoclassic sculptor Canova, the original of which appropriately found its way into the collection of the Duke of Wellington. Canova chose to represent Napoleon as completely nude in the pose and proportions of a Polyclitan athlete. When Napoleon protested feebly at this revealing portrayal, Canova lectured him: "We, like the poets, have our own language. If a poet introduces into tragedy phrases and idioms used habitually by the lower classes in the public streets, he would be rightly reprimanded by everyone. In like manner we sculptors cannot clothe our statues in modern costumes without deserving a similar reproach." [3]

The neoclassic style is reflected in the mirrors of Tsarskoye Selo and in the faded drawing-rooms of Adam's Dublin mansions. Ultimately it reached the forests of the New World in the architecture of Latrobe and Jefferson. One of its last manifestations was in the chill statuary that Hiram Powers provided for Victorian parlors. The neoclassic was a universal style, international in extent. It was responsible not only for solemn and elegant architecture on two continents, for monuments of painting and sculpture often poetic as well as heroic, but also for Empire furniture and the cameolike beauty of Wedgwood pottery.

In the later eighteenth and early nineteenth centuries, the imitation of classical antiquity became an end in itself; its study and collection, a cult for collectors and connoisseurs. The Society of Dilettanti founded in 1733 was only one of many such bodies formed to encourage the cultivation of antique tastes. Under the patronage of this group, Stuart and Revett published in 1762 their great contribution to the study of Hellenic art, *The Antiquities of Athens*.[4] A conversation piece by Zoffany shows Charles

Townley surrounded by his treasures of Greek and Roman sculpture.[5] This collection which formed the basis of the classical collection of the British Museum was only one of many assembled by private individuals. The partisans of the neoclassic style were not all of them frozen in classic decorum: we need only think of Catherine of Russia and the seductress, Paolina Borghese.

During this period there began what can be described only as a romantic cult of the ancient past with the idea of antiquity as the springtime of our culture. This notion, propagated by Winckelmann and Goethe, that the ancient world was the source for the renewal of great art and literature is not very different from the nostalgic philosophy based on the Middle Ages as set forth by Rousseau. Part of this romantic passion for antiquity was Keats' "Ode on a Grecian Urn." One thinks of Shelley writing "Prometheus Unbound" on the dizzy summits of the ruined Baths of Caracalla. Byron, too, in his praise of the "marble wilderness" of Rome and its treasures and in his passionate support of the cause of Hellenic freedom was more romantic than classic. In the final analysis the neoclassic movement and its exponents were as much romantic as classic. The *Zeitgeist* of the period is as elusive as it is contradictory, if only because the quest for the Greek ideal was a part of the nostalgia for the past and admiration for chivalric ages that typify the romantic movement.

What exactly were the neoclassic artists striving for? They were interested not so much in the exact imitation of classical models as in the creative use of antiquity for the renovation of art for contemporary needs. The younger artists of 1750 and later were weary of the meaningless decorative manner of the Rococo. As the decades rolled inexorably toward the debacle of 1789, there was, with the rise of Republican sentiments, a feeling for the appropriateness of the austerity and simplicity of ancient sculpture and architecture to express the revolutionary ideals of the new society that was to replace the decadent pageant of aristocracy. The artists of this time were as much moved by their experience in Greco-Roman art as painters and sculptors of the twentieth century were profoundly affected by their discovery of the moving expressiveness of form in primitive art that in their case provided an effective blade against the academic tradition.

Critics and artists alike varied in their opinions on how far it was desirable to go in the imitation of antique models. Goethe believed that it would be possible to rediscover the lost tradition of Greek art and to reduce this knowledge to an infallible system based on exact measurements and norms of representation in antique statuary. In this way art could be refounded as an ancient Hellas. Again, although a superficial reading of critics, like Count de Caylus and Quatremère de Quincy, might lead one to suppose that the strictest adherence to ancient prototypes was the ultimate aim of art, this was by no means the case in actual artistic practice. The degree of imitation of classical originals varied greatly with the personality of different artists. In general it was the artist's aim to use these models intelligently as a new way of seeing nature, particularly the human nude, in a reordered purified form. Classical marbles were by no means the unique precedent for artists reared in a variety of traditions. Canova remained faithful to the Baroque, and David's acquaintance with Roman architectural and sculptural forms was tempered by his admiration for the earlier French classicism of Poussin. Ingres owed as much to Raphael as to Phidias, and his art was inevitably filled with overtones of the romantic.

— 57 —

Anton Raphael Mengs

His heavenly forms have as little human about them as they possibly could . . .
From this stems that sublime ideal beauty which distinguishes his works . . .
Mr. Mengs's ceiling astounds all who see it: it is regarded as a magic creation.

—Winckelmann *

ANTON RAPHAEL MENGS was one of the first artists to be identified
with the neoclassic movement; at the same time his painting provides an
illustration of the contradictions that existed within his style. At the age of
thirteen he began his artistic education in Rome, following the eclectic
system then in vogue by copying Raphael and drawing from the nude and
the antique. In 1745 he was appointed painter to the court of Saxony, and
at this period of his career he was turning out portraits in the accepted
Rococo style. The model, invariably painted in soft blended colors with
careful attention to the textures of dress and accessories, is at the same
time made to look the part of a thoughtful and elegant man of the world.
This manner was at once a prelude and at the same time a foundation
for the type of painting style which Mengs set out to develop when he
returned to Rome in 1746. He continued to base himself upon Raphael,
but the turning point of his career came in 1755 when Joachim Winckelmann moved into the Mengs household. This association lasted for many
years until an unsavory liaison between Winckelmann and Frau Mengs
led to a break between the two men. Winckelmann certainly regarded
Mengs as his artistic protégé and was certainly largely responsible for
turning the artist to a calculated exploitation of the antique. Another
powerful factor contributing to the classical elements in Mengs's style
was the discoveries at Herculaneum and Pompeii.

* Seine himmlischen Gestalten haben der Menschlichen so wenig als sie nur haben
können . . . daher ensteht jene erhabene idealische Schönheit die seine Werke aus-
zeichnete . . . Der Plafond des Herrn Mengs setzt alle, die ihn sehen, in Erstaunen: man
hält ihn für Schöpfung der Zauberkunst.—J. J. Winckelmann, Ein Brief an Wille, June 14,
1760

The story of these excavations which had begun with accidental discoveries as early as 1738 need not be repeated here. The results of these diggings were for many years kept a closely guarded secret by the Bourbon rulers of Naples who, for reasons of jealousy and prestige, strictly forbade the sketching of the extraordinary objects collected in the museum at Portici. For nearly two decades before the Neapolitan government finally began the publication of its official catalogue, the only information that leaked out to the learned and artistic worlds was based on verbal descriptions and inadequate sketches made from memory by the few visitors privileged to view the vast treasure of wall-paintings and bronzes. Only in 1757 did the first of the folio volumes devoted to the finds at Pompeii and Herculaneum make its appearance, illustrated like the remaining seven volumes with engravings after drawings by reasonably competent artists. These books were not for sale, but were capriciously distributed by the monarch. It was not for many years that the publication of a catalogue for general distribution and the lifting of the restrictions on visitors made this vast corpus of ancient material available to all. However, even before the publication of the first volumes by the Museo Borbonico, forgeries of the Pompeian wall-paintings had been palmed off on English milords making the grand tour.

In certain respects the discoveries of Pompeii and Herculaneum came as a confirmation of an existing taste and not as a discovery of a completely new world. Many of the themes popular in Pompeian mural decoration—the playful genii and romps of putti—had been known since the Renaissance from Hellenistic and Roman reliefs and had continued in popularity with the sculptors and painters of the Rococo. The subjects of the Pompeian wall-paintings like Perseus and Andromeda, the Rape of Europa, and the Fall of Icarus had been favorites with painters since the fifteenth century. More than anything else, the discoveries of this vast treasure of classical art provided a new impulse for the exploration of ancient themes and styles. Although in the middle eighteenth century the new and strenuous imitation of the antique may have been regarded as a magic formula for laying the ghosts of the Baroque and Rococo styles, these spirits were not to be so easily exorcised and they continued to haunt both the art of Mengs and that of the great neoclassic sculptor Canova.

Even Mengs's mentor, Winckelmann, inevitably revealed the taste of his time in his fervent espousal of such examples of the antique rococo as the Apollo Belvedere (figure 31). How far Mengs was able to satisfy this taste is illustrated ironically by his painting a forgery of an antique Jupiter and Ganymede, which Winckelmann was happy to describe as one of the greatest surviving examples of classical painting. Winckelmann's writing on the necessity for modern artists to imbue their works with "Grace," a quality which the critic discerned everywhere in the art of the ancients, clearly demonstrates that antique art only provided him with a confirmation of his own contemporary taste.

Mengs established his reputation as an exponent of the new antique taste by his ceiling painting of Apollo on Parnassus for the stronghold of classical studies, the Villa Albani (figure 199). The picture represented a complete break from the Baroque–Rococo style of decoration: instead of the usual illusionistic architectural painting of painters like Pietro da Cortona and Tiepolo, painted in elaborate foreshortening in order to give an illusion of the composition's extension into an infinity of space, Mengs's ceiling decoration is an easel picture with the composition in normal view and with no suggestion of an extension into imaginary space. This was in a sense a return to a type of decoration that had not been used since Annibale Carracci's scheme for the vault of the Farnese Palace. This allusion to Carracci is not inappropriate in another respect, because Mengs was in reality an eighteenth-century eclectic. In this decoration done for the Villa Albani in 1761 the figure of Apollo is a facile transformation of the Apollo Belvedere (figure 31), and the dancers at the left just as certainly stem from Herculaneum.

Even more indicative of Mengs's performance in "le style Winckelmann" is his conception of Perseus and Andromeda (figure 200). The artist must have had access to Plate VII in Volume IV of the Bourbon catalogue, and he also referred to a mosaic representing the Deliverance of Hesione in the collection of the Villa Albani (figure 201). Mengs has slightly modified the figures in this source material in complete conformity with contemporary taste, the playful artificiality of the late Baroque or Rococo. Andromeda's pose is certainly close to the heroine of the mosaic, but Mengs's figure displays the coy grace and condescending hauteur of a Boucher or a Fragonard. His figure of Perseus, although based on the Pompeian prototype, has been somewhat refashioned on the more imposing impression of elegance of the Apollo Belvedere; the trunk and legs of Mengs's hero are a mirror image of this famous source of inspiration that had already served the artist for his Parnassus. Such copying was intended to present a novelty, appealing to connoisseurs and artists alike in these borrowings from the very latest fashionable source of antique inspiration: the scavi of Herculaneum.

This seemingly more archaeological approach of Mengs did not really inaugurate a new art, although his fidelity to the antique seems to herald the beginning of modern archaeology. The effect of the whole painting is more late Baroque than Pompeian. Mengs paints in a twilight tonality with a soft Correggiesque light and shade; and the aliveness and sensuosity of both the palette and the handling of paint are thoroughly rococo. It was hard to discard these graces. Perhaps the only novelty that Mengs presents within this framework is something of the quiet and serenity defined as "Greek" by the learned archaeologists. With Mengs one feels this quality was conditioned as much by his acquaintance with Raphael as by his studies of the antiquities of Campania. It remained for more imaginative artists like David, Canova, and Ingres to produce a new art form based on the antique and molded by the fervor of the discovery of new worlds in the political and social, as well as archaeological, spheres.

— 58 —

Canova

Ah, so highly honored will be his name to make
The revered ashes of Polyclitus, Alcamenes, and Phidias
Shake in their urns with envy
Since God inspired Canova in sculpture;
So may Pallas on him smile, that standing by his marbles
She may o'ercome the ravages of time.

—Tadini *

THE most famous and successful exponent of the neoclassic style was the sculptor Antonio Canova. He was an artist of universal renown who in his lifetime knew greater glory than perhaps any personage in the history of art. He enjoyed the patronage of the Pope and Napoleon and dominated the sculptural taste of the entire Western world. "Such as the great of yore, Canova is today," wrote Byron, and this is only one of innumerable poetic tributes laid at the feet of the master.[1] Cicognara regarded him as the climax of sculpture and the Phidias of his time.

Canova was born at Possagno in the Veneto in 1757. He studied under a Venetian follower of Bernini, Giuseppe Tavetti. His birth into a family of stonecutters endowed him with a lifelong feeling for the nature of the blocks of marble quarried from the bowels of the earth. Essentially, Canova was a belated Baroque artist with all the technical facility of a Bernini, who set out to master the style of the ancients. His feeling for texture and his dynamic Italian creativeness combined to impart an aliveness to works which in the hands of less gifted sculptors resulted only in a

* Ah pur levato al Ciel suo nome, e invidia
  Fia scuota in l'urne il cenere onorato
  Di Policleto, d'Alcamene, e Fidia
  Della scultura di Dio Canova inspira;
  Palla gli arride, onde a' suoi marmi a lato
  Vinca de' tempi le vicende e l'ira.

—Luigi Tadini

293

dry repetition of a Grecian mold. It is believed that his attention was first attracted to the antique by the counsel of his friends among the English connoisseurs in Rome. It was not long before he became an instrument for realizing the dreams of the theoreticians of classicism. His spirit and chisel seemed a perfect response to Winckelmann's theory of "noble simplicity and quiet grandeur." At the same time his sureness and sensibility for the material and the tools of his craft enabled him to retain the elegance and sensuality of Baroque form rather than the external appearance of studied classicism. This exact and sober sense of his metier and the function of sculpture enabled Canova to transcend the taste of his time. He was always an artist in love with marble.

It is difficult to select any one work to represent an artist so universally inspired by the antique. For stylistic as well as symbolic reasons one might select the famous Perseus (figure 202) which was commissioned in 1799 as a substitute for the Apollo Belvedere (figure 31) which, together with so many famous works of classical antiquity, had been sent to Paris by Napoleon. It is known that Canova had a cast of the Apollo in his studio. The pose of the Perseus, the neck, the torso, and the left arm are all derived from the famous classical original. Apollo's lightness of stance is missing; his weight rests on his left leg, and instead of the tree-trunk Canova has used the hero's chlamys as a support. The head of Medusa which Perseus holds is adapted from the famous Medusa Rondanini. Compared with the classical original Canova's hero has a Baroque vitality and *élan* that have led some to compare it to an Italian tenor singing a bravura aria. Like many of Canova's works it has more picturesque delicacy than sculptural mass and robustness. It also demonstrates Canova's rather warm pictorial technique in giving a different tactile value to the drapery, flesh, and hair. Canova's Venetian lightness and sensuousness reveal themselves in this pictorial chiaroscuro and delicate manipulation of the material. Canova had the serenity of Goethe in his cult of the antique. He was able to achieve at once classical idealization and the transformation of a real image into a plausible and tangible mythology.

Canova, in essaying the Perseus to fill the vacant niche of the Apollo Belvedere, was accused of attempting to surpass one of the entrenched models of antique perfection. Edward Everett, in reviewing the famous work on Canova by the Contessa Albrizzi, remarked that the Apollo and the Venus are placed by the nature of their subjects beyond the possibility of rivalry. He goes on to say that "the Apollo Belvedere and the Venus dei Medici will probably be regarded for ever as the *ne plus ultra* of statuary." He remarks on their "perfection of execution, which renders it nearly impossible that they can ever be surpassed or even equalled." [2] Many of Canova's Italian champions, like the Contessa Albrizzi herself and the critic, Cicognara, were quite sure that Canova had equaled if not surpassed the ancients. The Contessa remarks on the wonderful fusion of the divine and human in the Perseus, and Cicognara lauds the sculptor's invention of an ideal at once warlike, heroic, and Apollonian.

Canova's contemporary critics and even twentieth-century writers on his work seem for the most part to hold to the fixed idea that Canova was deliberately trying to produce substitutes for antique works of art. In actuality, here in the Perseus as in all his works, he was always true to his own style. Canova's realistic articulation of the body and the textural embellishments of his carving are all Canova's heritage from the Baroque rather than the antique. These are the very qualities of his technique that enliven the performance in contrast to the more accurate and also more dead derivations from the antique in the work of Thorwaldsen and the American neoclassicists.

In every one of Canova's works, although his style seems made to order to realize the dreams of the exponents of classicism, his delicate eighteenth-century sensitivity and his feeling for his metier as a sculptor in marble enabled him to retain a freshness and integrity rather than the external appearance of studied classicism. Like no other works, the originals of his famous Cupid and Psyche (figure 203), debased in countless mechanical copies, have a lightness and warmth that belong to the late Baroque tradition. The complicated rhythms of the composition of this group are like the movement of Tiepolo transformed into marble. The harmony of forms rises in intertwining curves, culminating in the circle of arms interlaced about the joined faces. The figure of Psyche may perhaps be recognized as a nereid, and Cupid's dreaming head framed in its crisply carved, waxy ringlets is an adaptation of the Centocelle Eros by Praxiteles (figure 204), of which Canova on one occasion had made a plaster copy. The ancient source of Canova's composition for the classic love story is not difficult to find. Among the ancient marbles collected by the Grimani family and brought to Venice as early as 1586 is a panel on a Roman candelabrum representing the embrace of Cupid and his love (figure 205). The style of the carving with its flat low relief and plain background may be described as neo-Attic. The fundamental arrangement of Canova's group is there, together with the wistful sentiment of later Greek art. It only remained for Canova to reimagine the figures in the round and to imbue them with the lightness and pervasive sensuality of the Venetian tradition. Canova's group presents a combination of an unmistakable rococo eroticism and the approved dependence on the antique that completely fulfilled the taste of the time. Although these fragile forms in iridescent Carrara marble give a superficial impression of the lightness of a poised dragonfly, the equilibrium of the static composition is combined with Canova's sense of the weightiness of the stone to produce a completely integrated and stable sculptural conception.*

* A painting of Cupid and Psyche by Canova in the Museo Correr in Venice was obviously done from his own completed marble. Like other examples of Canova's work in oil, it is in the style of the Venetian Renaissance masters. The view chosen by the artist with Cupid head-on to the beholder must have been Canova's favorite for his creation.

— 59 —

Classicism and Republican Ideals:
Jacques-Louis David

I want to work in a pure Greek style. I feed my eyes on antique statues, I even have the intention of imitating some of them. The Greeks had no scruples about copying a composition, a gesture, a type that had already been accepted and used. They put all their attention and all their art on perfecting an idea that had been already conceived. They thought, and they were right, that in the arts the way in which an idea is rendered, and the manner in which it is expressed, is much more important than the idea itself. To give a body and a perfect form to one's thought, this—and only this—is to be an artist.

—David *

Jacques-Louis David was an artist who, like Canova, emerged from the eighteenth-century Rococo tradition. His earliest work, under the court painter Boucher, is hardly to be distinguished from the indifferent pastiches turned out by the French school under Louis XVI. David's Contest of Minerva and Mars is made up of the same panoply of boudoir fripperies: pretty colors and violent highlights in the bravura manner, which were the stock in trade of the fashionable painters of the early eighteenth century. When it was first suggested that he go to Rome, David casually remarked, "the antique will not seduce me; it lacks warmth and is not moving." [1]

This airy disdain of the classic tradition was soon forgotten when David found his way to the Eternal City as a pensionnaire at the French

---

* Je veux faire du *grec pur;* je me nourris les yeux de statues antiques, j'ai l'intention même d'en imiter quelques-unes. Les Grecs ne faisaient nullement scrupule de reproduire une composition, un mouvement, un type, déjà reçus et employés. Ils mettaient tous leurs soins, tout leur art, à perfectionner une idée que l'on avait eue avant eux. Ils pensaient, et ils avaient raison, que l'idée dans les arts est bien plus dans la manière dont on la rend, dont on l'exprime, que dans l'idée elle-même. Donner une apparence, une forme parfaite à sa pensée, c'est être un artiste; on ne l'est que par là.—E. J. Delécluze, *Louis David;* p. 62; translated by Goldwater and Treves

Academy under the tutelage of Vien. This painter in his rather coquettish adaptations of the style of Pompeian paintings was one of the forerunners of the neoclassical movement. It was not long before David became an enthusiastic admirer of the antique. As he himself was soon to admit, the scales dropped from his eyes at the sight of the great monuments of the classical past. His days were spent in sketching in the famous collections in the Villa Medici, at the Capitol, or in the palaces of the Giustiniani and Farnese families. At this moment the stage was set for the final triumph of antiquity; the museums were populated as never before with a great host of marble statues unearthed all over the Latin world. The theories of Winckelmann were universally established and admired; the affectations of the Rococo were fading into the past. In the Academies the emphasis was universally placed on draftsmanship, expression, and the nude. The moment was ripe for the appearance of an artist who could perfectly embody the new ideal of rationality and severity, based on the antique. The world of artists and connoisseurs did not have long to wait. In 1785 David unveiled his canvas of The Oath of the Horatii, a picture that was to shake the world, as Picasso's Guernica affected his contemporaries in the twentieth century.

For all of its impressiveness the Oath of the Horatii (figure 206) was in reality a continuation of the homely naturalism of Greuze accoutred in fashionable Roman dress. This essentially sentimental bombastic drama was different only from Greuze's homely scenes of domestic crises in being raised to a heroic level. The combination of naturalism and classical format was bound to appeal to the taste of the middle class, just as the patriotic theme, hinting of revolutionary change, could not have come at a more opportune moment. It is only surprising that subjects like this were acceptable to the monarchy, since in spirit at least they were directed against the rule of the very king who patronized them. Probably in these last years of his demoralized rule Louis XVI was happy to condone such inflammatory propaganda as a token of that benevolence and liberality toward the bourgeoisie which he hoped would save the throne. David repaid this indulgence by voting for the king's execution. But, since he had set himself up as an exemplar of the unflinching Roman virtue personified by Brutus, he could not have done otherwise.

There is no question that the first inspiration for the Oath of the Horatii came from Corneille's play, which was being presented in Paris in 1784. David, as a matter of fact, remarked, "If I owe my subject to Corneille, I owe my picture to Poussin." [2] This indebtedness to the great classicist of the seventeenth century is evident not only in this but in many other canvases by David. Poussin's Death of Germanicus seems to have influenced the general arrangement of the figures against the closed background, and the individual forms, both of the heroes themselves and of the mourning women at the right, are modifications of his figures. Again the main compositional element of a triangle culminating in the apex of the raised swords is a favorite of David's predecessor.

David strove to create an appropriately Etruscan setting for his drama in the arcade of robust, but inelegant, Doric in the background. The artist, as a matter of fact, was criticized in some quarters for introducing the motif of arches resting on columns, which presumably only came into use late in the Imperial period. Actually this type of building was not an invention of David's. There are a number of instances of the employment of rugged Doric pillars in conjunction with arches in designs paralleling David's picture. It can be seen today in the rue des Colonnes.

David's Oath of the Horatii, upon its unveiling, was the manifesto of the new school based on the fervent study of the antique. It fulfilled the hopes of some twenty years of theorizing in subject, expression, and style. This moral tragedy met the highest requirements of the history painter in its dramatic combination of figures expressing greatness of soul, love of country, and filial love. It satisfied the current admiration of Roman virtue in this victory in the struggle of duty and passion. It was at once philosophical, tragic, and antique. Many of the individual details of the painting were of course taken from appropriate classical sources. The head of the father is borrowed from a portrait of Marcus Aurelius, and the mourning women are modeled on Roman matrons. At the same time the severity of the atrium in which the scene is set announces the simple times prophesied by the revolutionaries. If the figures in this composition, as in others by the artist, do not suggest the frozen coldness of marble, it is because David invariably worked from the living model and had a sense for the enlivening touch of the brush. At the same time the color and dramatic chiaroscuro owe something to the palette of Caravaggio, which David studied in order to imbue his picture, as he said, with the properly masculine strength.

The Death of Socrates (figure 207) was commissioned in 1787, only a few years after the artist first won renown with his famous Oath of the Horatii. This canvas was another example of David's formula for Stoic

Republican painting, a testament at once of verile will and action and an emblem of the patriotic self-sacrifice and moral stability completely satisfying to the ferment of liberal thought in the years before the Revolution. When he was commissioned for this work, David, who had been only an indifferent student in the classical curriculum at the Collège des Quatre-Nations, felt impelled to consult a specialist for the recreation of such an important episode from the past. He consulted a lay member of the Pères de l'Oratoire, one Jean Félicissime Aday, who counseled him to study the representations of sorrow in antiquity, particularly a relief of the Death of Meleager (figure 208), illustrated in the famous encyclopedia of ancient art by Montfaucon. At the same time he was enjoined to study surviving portraits of Socrates and Plato. Legend has it that David's friend, the poet André Chénier, persuaded the artist to have Socrates reaching for the cup of hemlock and not actually drinking it.

In the canvas Socrates is seated on a bed reaching for the cup which a dramatically grief-stricken executioner hands him. Grouped around the philosopher are his disciples in varied attitudes of consternation and grief. At the foot of the bed sits Plato, seemingly paralyzed with grief. The group is set off against the blank wall of the dungeon, and at the left, through an archway, is a view of two figures moving up the stairway. Both the conception of the individual figures and the arrangement of the picture as a whole are typical of David's method of procedure. Not only had he made precise inquiries regarding the exact age and temperament of each of the personages to be portrayed, but he also intended each figure to be a separate unit registering the characteristics and state of mind of these heroes of antiquity. The expressions, gestures, and postures served to join the participants into a united frieze of action. The figures are combined in the manner of a relief, set off by the enclosing wall of the background. This type of composition was not original with David. He may even have been influenced by the version of the same subject by his student companion in Rome, Jean-François Peyron. Here, as in so many other compositions, David was indebted to the compositional arrangements of Poussin. Not only the arrangement in planes and the pyramidal central group are suggestive of the great seventeenth-century classicist, but also the enclosing wall itself takes the place of the screens of trees or architecture that project the figures to the foreground in paintings by Poussin. However, unlike Poussin, David strove for a purified simplicity both in content and composition through the elimination of all extraneous

details. This pictorial frugality and the artist's reliance on statuesque prototypes for both heads and figures result in an effect of far greater hardness and coldness. The simple primary colors, here as always, are entirely
subordinate to the precise draftsmanship and sculpturesque modeling.
The strong contrasts of light and dark which enhance this sculpturesque
quality are the evident result of the artist's adaptation of the *tenebroso* of
Caravaggio. As in his famous Oath of the Horatii, the unadorned simplicity of the setting echoes the democratic sobriety of the utilitarian architecture that in these same years replaced the frivolity of the Rococo
style.

David was accused of committing an anachronism in representing
Plato as an old man. In the interests of making himself completely explicit
he chose to use the accepted antique likeness of Plato, just as in our own
day Grant Wood put Stuart's head on the boy Washington in his playful
evocation of Parson Weems's fable.

A decade after the painting of these panels of antique Republican
virtue David repudiated the work of this Roman period in favor of something more specifically Greek. In speaking of his projected painting of
The Sabines (figure 209) he declared, "This will be a picture more in the
Greek style." [3] The subject from Plutarch depicting the Sabines come to
avenge the abduction of their women by the Romans was certainly intended to have a reference to the internecine conflict between political
factions in contemporary France. But as usual the allusion to the struggle
was in appropriate classical terms.

A single figure from this complex picture will illustrate the Greek trend
of David's classicism (figure 210). This is the repetition of the figure of
Romulus in the Detroit Institute of Arts. One can well understand how,
in looking at this frozen model, Bonaparte naively exclaimed, "Vos per-
sonnages ne bougent pas." [4] Legend has it that, as was the custom of the
studio, one of David's pupils, Bayard, posed for the nude of the Roman
hero. It is interesting to see how David was moved to repeat this single
figure from one of his favorite compositions in 1824, only a year before
his death. That the figure can stand as an isolated composition perhaps
demonstrates how isolated the figures are in the original composition.
Although the svelte proportions may remind us more of Canova than of
the antique, David certainly had some ancient prototype in mind. Actually the figure seems to have been suggested by the rigid martial pose of
the goddess Athena as she appears with spear and aegis on any number of

panathenaic amphorae (figure 211). It was only necessary to undress the prototype and change the sex in order to achieve the pose of the Romulus. As has already been noted, when David was painting the Sabines, he decried the Roman qualities of earlier canvases like the Horatii. What exactly is Greek about this figure in contrast to the Roman classicism of 1785? The pose is an alteration of a Greek attitude, and the emphasis on contour, which reduces the figure almost to a silhouette, is the result of the attention David was now paying to the linear technique of the Greek vases. The nudity is another Greek quality, which David explained was invariable for the representation of gods and heroes in antiquity.

Not all of David's protestations about recapturing the spirit of Greek art, nor his drawing from the living model, could save this canvas and its details from being a lifeless pageant of artificial heroic attitudes. The artist was incapable of realizing the impossible ideal of purified art for which he stood. It is interesting to observe that David's pupils were perhaps his severest critics. The master was accused of being too embroiled in politics to carry out the artistic reform he had promised. Some said he was too vacillating in character and lacking any breadth of scope in his ideas. It was even remarked that the painting of the Sabines was not linear enough to be Greek. One particular group of students, who styled themselves "les primitifs," maintained that David was not successful in evoking the spirit of Greek art because he had not drunk at the real fountainhead of Hellenism in the work of Phidias and his predecessors. When some of David's critics derisively referred to The Sabines as rococo, they were probably offended by one of its redeeming qualities: the freedom of brushwork, and certain other qualities that are perhaps better called romantic. Among these elements are the completely medieval bastions of the city in the background. Even the painting of the atmospheric distance is more romantic than classical. Actually, the crowded baroque character of the painting may be explained by the fact that its arrangement was certainly derived in part from an earlier version of this rare subject by David's contemporary, André Vincent.[5] This confusion of the ideals of classicism and romanticism is not unusual in the work of artists of this period. It demonstrates the folly of attempting to confine the work of any period strictly within a prefabricated *Zeitgeist*. In the work of David's pupil, Ingres, the intrusion of exotic romantic elements is even more apparent.

— 60 —

The Nineteenth Century

And marble statues stand and gaze at me:
What have they done to you, poor child?
—Goethe *

THE opening decades of the nineteenth century were still in the thrall of the classic revival; some of the most distinguished monuments of neo-classicism date from this period. Certain architects of genius, like Schinkel, were able to raise the classic idiom to a functional, rather than an archae-ological, level. In sculpture, however, there was a steady deterioration into a quasi-sentimental, quasi-archaistic mode, in which the classical prototypes are reworked into brittle pastiches characterized by a machine-made hardness.

The nineteenth century ushers in the final chapter in the history of the classical tradition. The complexities of the period—social, economic, and political—contribute both to florescence and eclipse of the authority of the antique. To a certain extent the Greek War of Independence pro-moted the persistence of the Hellenic ideal. Although this struggle was mainly a theme for romantic painters like Delacroix and the poetry of Byron and Bryant, one of the few results of its influence on sculpture was Hiram Powers' Greek Slave.

It seems both tragic and ironic that, once they were rescued from the crumbling Acropolis, the great marbles of the Parthenon and the Erechtheum should have exercised so little influence. Canova in his old age exclaimed wistfully that he had been born too early to model his style on these true examples of Greek art. So had the whole generation of neo-classic sculptors who were reared on the standard fare of Hellenistic and

* Und Marmorbilder stehn und sehn mich an:
Was hat man dir, du armes Kind, getan?
—Goethe (1778)

Greco-Roman statues revered for so many centuries as the perfection of Hellenic art. Although the tragic painter Haydon and his friend Keats were overcome with emotion at the beauty of the Elgin marbles, Byron regarded the famous figures from the Parthenon as "bruisers." * Nothing more than Inwood's playful adaptation of the Erechtheum caryatids for St. Pancras' church and Decimus Burton's screen at Hyde Park Corner testify to any kind of direct influence of this Phidian sculpture. Only later a Rodin and a Maillol could discern the heroic plasticity of this genuine Greek art as a foundation on which to raise a new form and a new spirit in sculpture.

The early nineteenth century witnessed the twilight of paganism, this time a final Götterdämmerung in the invocations of the mad Hölderlin and Schiller's passionate espousal of the Hellenic. Part of the paraphernalia of neoclassicism in literature is the espousal of the Hellenic gods as an avowal of the liberty and license denied by the tenets of Christianity. So, in *Die Götterlehre* of 1791, Karl Philip Moritz became the evangelist of a new religion based on the pagan tradition which Christianity had destroyed. In a way these evocations of the classic shades were only the respectable variations of the cults of satanism which flourished in grottoes and hidden rooms from Sicily to Scotland. All were a form of romantic escapism, and even the gods whom Goethe evokes in his Walpurgisnacht perform on a tenebrous romantic stage. For Goethe, as for Hölderlin and Schiller, the phantom of the Greek ideal vanished into Teutonic mists as Faust's Helena faded into invisibility at his embrace. During the romantic interlude and the succeeding decades of the nineteenth century there was no longer that intellectual absorption in antiquity that had made for the greatness of the neoclassic movement in the eighteenth century.

With a rising necessity for scientific education in the last century and our own, the study of Greek and Latin came to be regarded as expendable, to be regarded as the hallmark of a class educated to idleness. The study of the classics gradually disappeared from a curriculum that once required them, not as a luxurious reward of leisure, but as a valuable discipline. The result has been that knowledge of the classical tradition is no

* "The Curse of Minerva," one of Byron's many attacks on Lord Elgin, II, 179–182:

> Be all the Bruisers called from all St. Giles',
> That Art and Nature may compare their styles;
> While brawny brutes in stupid wonder stare,
> And marvel at his Lordship's "stone shop" there.

See also Larrabee, *English Bards and Grecian Marbles*, p. 155.

longer as it once was, a part of the public domain. The fact remains, however, that our old common heritage, in spite of its seeming eclipse in the standard educational program, continued as a source of inspiration for poets, dramatists, and artists in its eternal themes and in its forms.

In the nineteenth century the imitation of Greek art scarcely kept pace with the adventures in archaeology. This is a century marked by a systematic exploration of the literature, history, and art of the classical period. The triumphs of archaeological restoration at Olympia and Pergamum were part of the advance in every branch of science in the nineteenth century. This was something quite different from the fervent but haphazard treasure-hunting that had gone on for so long. The tradition of learning from the antique was left behind in this century of exploration of other more immediate fields. The romantic tendencies, of which the nostalgia for the classic past was a part, reached out to other bourns of experience partly as a revolt against the academic rigor imposed by the classical canon, partly as a reflection of the awakening to other facets of human experience. The romantics' pursuit of the wild, the marvelous, and the terrible was succeeded by the impressionists' search for the mystery of light. Even the great romantic artist, Delacroix, had occasionally drawn his subject matter from classic themes, and Gustave Moreau, like a pictorial counterpart of Pierre Louys drowning in the erotic perfume of ancient loves, drew his own satanic conception of the old legends in colors of smoldering fire and icy jewels. In spite of these anticlassical movements the authority of the classic did not disappear. It was being investigated in a new way to meet new needs. There appeared in the middle decades of the nineteenth century a study of the Hellenic achievement for its principles rather than its outward form. Horatio Greenough said, "American builders by a truly philosophic investigation of ancient art will learn of the Greeks to be American." [1] Or, as Rodin put it, "The schools copied Greek works, but what is important is to rediscover their methods," [2] in other words, by a return to the laws governing great statues.

Part of the typically romantic evocation of antiquity is the theme of *Sic transit gloria mundi*. For artists like John Martin and Thomas Cole the catastrophic destruction of great civilizations was a constantly repeated subject. Such reconstructions and destructions of ancient cities on canvas involved a partly archaeological, partly fantastic, interpretation of ancient architecture. The source for this favorite romantic concept is found in Volney's *Les Ruines ou Méditations sur les Révolutions des Em-*

pires, a work dedicated to philosophic speculation on the rise and fall of the great empires of the past.[3] The treatment of such themes in the violence of action and sulphuric illumination has little to do with the classic in the true sense of the word, even though the backgrounds of these lurid canvases are often filled with temples and pavilions reconstructed from the plates of Piranesi and Stuart and Revett.

If we take the survival of the classical tradition to mean the reliance on antique forms to the extent of using these models as a point of departure for original creation, the history of art in the later nineteenth century is marked by a disappearance of this approach. Although subjects from mythology and ancient history continued as the stock in trade of painters in every country of Europe, their presentation had little to do with the antique in form or content. The work of the French academicians like Gérome and Bouguereau, although often classical in subject matter, consisted of a reconstruction of episodes from the ancient period painted from the model, not from antique statues, and executed in a hard, enamellike technique in which the figures stand out with the clarity of objects in a diorama. In the same way the always sentimental, sometimes mystical or humorous, mythologies of the German Böcklin are painted in the veristic technique of the genre masters of the time. Not only are they classical in theme, but also the best of Böcklin's canvases display a haunting nostalgia for antiquity, a romantic return to Arcady. This disappearance of the antique as a guide for painters, except as students drawing from casts in the routine of academic painting, is counterbalanced by the continued intelligent discovery of ancient art by sculptors like Rodin and his successors into the twentieth century. Regardless of whether they derived their forms from the ancient marble or bronze images of the gods, artists like Hans von Marees sought to create at once a new classic myth and a new classic canon. His contribution, however modest, prepared the way for the more imaginative artists who resuscitated the classic idiom in the twentieth century. In a similar manner the German sculptor, Hildebrand, was one of the later nineteenth-century masters who turned away from the current vogue for pictorial baroque sculpture. His concentration on the nude, in what amounted to an approximation of the rugged, thoroughly glyptic, style of Polyclitus, embodied the serenity and stability of Greek art, and in its reduction of form to the essentials of plastic expression anticipated the work of Maillol.

— 61 —

Classicism and Romanticism: Ingres

Phidias, his Olympian Jupiter completed, asks the god if he is satisfied with his image and to give him a sign. The god makes his thunder roll.　　　—Ingres *

Of all the artists who emerged from the studio of David, the one painter who most truly carried on the tradition of revived classicism and raised it to a far more personal and creative form of expression was Jean-Auguste-Dominique Ingres. As a mature painter Ingres was far more than a faithful follower of David and exemplar of the teaching of the French Academy at Rome. His own tastes were far more varied and included the then neglected painting of the Italian Quattrocento and even aspects of Oriental art. It is not surprising that Ingres was attracted by Greek or, as they were then called, Etruscan vases. The Greek vase painter's statement in intrinsic purity of linear definition was the foundation of his own draftsmanship. To these artistic qualities was added a note of ecstatic sensuality which was always completely absent in the frigid classic anatomies by David.

Like few other painters Ingres remained preoccupied with certain themes throughout his long life, so that on many occasions he repeated or returned to a subject done as a youth, when he was still active as an octogenarian. One of these canvases to which he returned in later years, as in a drawing of 1848,[1] was his composition of Jupiter and Thetis (figure 212), first conceived when he was a student in Rome in 1807 and sent to Paris for exhibition in 1811. As early as 1806 Ingres had written of his vision of the Father of the Gods: "He would have such a beautiful countenance, that all, even the mad dogs who would bite me, would have to be touched by it. I have almost composed it in my mind and I visualize

---

* Phidias, son Jupiter Olympien fini, lui demande s'il est content de son image, et qu'il lui donne un signe. Le dieu fait gronder son tonnerre.—Jean-August-Dominique Ingres, *Cahiers*

it." [2] The picture is ostensibly an illustration of the episode from the Iliad, when the nymph Thetis pleads with Jupiter on behalf of her son, Achilles. There are indications that Ingres, in composing this picture, was concerned with something more than an illustration of the Homeric myth. Like Botticelli in his recreation of the lost masterpieces of Apelles, Ingres was haunted by dreams of the Olympian Zeus of Phidias, so that the form of his Zeus is an attempt to recapture the supernal majesty of the most famous ancient portrayal of the chief of the Olympians. Ingres was a life-long Bonapartist, and it is not unlikely that this picture, painted in the greatest days of the Empire, was a veiled symbolic tribute to Napoleon. On other occasions Ingres had painted Napoleon in a pose not dissimilar to that of Jupiter, seated in Augustan splendor as the very personification of the world ruler.

In the picture itself the ruler of Olympus is seated in imperturbable majesty on an adamantine throne above the clouds. His right hand raises the scepter of divine authority. Behind the throne at the right sits an eagle, the agent of the god's divine commands. The nymph Thetis kneels at his feet, embracing his knees with her left hand and raising her right to caress his chin in entreaty. Half hidden in the cloud in the tempestuous sky behind the throne of Olympus one can make out the spying form of Juno. In the painting we are struck by the wonderful contrast between the massive imperturbable figure of Zeus and the slight and pliant figure of the beseeching nereid. Although Ingres was probably concerned with the ambrosial locks that made great Olympus quake, the face of the Olympian in a sense is more romantic than classic; it is filled with an infinite sadness, the eyes haunted by mysterious tragedy. It is obvious that more than twenty centuries of time separate Phidias from Ingres. The ominous lead-blue sky with its phosphorescent cloud phantoms presents a mood of ominous and awful mystery that in a way is a negation of the classic framework of the artist's mighty conception.

For an understanding of the classical bias of Ingres's art one must remember that his name is linked with that of the great neoclassic critic, Quatremère de Quincy, who evolved a theory of the final perfection of art as a suprareal beauty beyond the accidental foibles of nature, to be achieved by learning those principles which enabled Phidias to "correct nature through herself," [3] to realize that type of "superior beauty, upon which Phidias fixed his attention and by which he directed his art and his hand." [4] For Quatremère de Quincy the classical tradition was the exclusive source of artistic procedure; nature herself should have been a pupil of Phidias. For this critic ideal beauty was created once and for all in the ancient period: art was revealed to Greece by God, as religion to the chosen people. Ingres deviated from the teachings of this master in that he regarded nature as the final source for the *beau idéal*. For him the contemplation of the masterpieces of the classical period only served to facilitate the study of nature. Although to the end he admitted the authority of the classical, the beautiful for Ingres was the splendor of truth drawn from nature. Like so many artists of his period, Ingres was attracted to the great font of inspiration in the classical past because, being an artist of somewhat limited imaginative powers, he needed a visible object as a point of departure.

As Ingres himself observed, "Greek statues surpass nature only because they assemble so many beautiful parts, which nature has never, or indeed rarely, joined together in a single object. The artist who proceeds in this way is admitted to the sanctuary of nature." [5] Admission to this sanctuary is to be gained by approaching nature through the predetermined perfection of the antique. Ingres in his selective imitation of nature did not entirely accept Quatremère de Quincy's idea of an ideal beauty above nature. Ingres' ideal was always a combining of the imitation of the antique and living reality to realize the myth in epic flesh and blood. In its following of the antique his painting was a kind of ideal imitation: "Je pense que je saurai être original en imitant." [6] The artist's method can well be illustrated by an analysis of the famous Jupiter and Thetis. It is apparent the whole conception is in large part an heroic magnification of Flaxman's drawings for the Iliad. [7] The figure of Jupiter himself, which was intended to vie with the grandeur of the Olympian Zeus by Phidias, was probably inspired by one of a number of available reflections of this famous Greek original (figure 213). The head of the titanic figure is Ingres' romantic reworking of the Zeus of Otricoli. The figure of Thetis, again suggested by Flaxman's drawing (figure 214), might also suggest some of the undulating shapes of nereids in Roman sarcophagi. But there the resemblance to the antique ends. This haunting figure of the imploring goddess is characteristic of Ingres' almost Oriental distortion to achieve an effect of breathtaking seductiveness and allure. The female nude was the supreme instrument of his artistic expression, an expression that, for all his protestations of creating like the Greeks, was as sensual, even provocative, as the most carnally abandoned figures in Indian sculpture. Although Ingres' line is derived from the flowing contours of Greek vase painting, it has an un-dulating, moving quality that is like the lyric, sensual drawing of Rajput painting. The very distortions that he employs here—the heavy thighs contrasting with the tiny breasts, the swelling neck and cameo head—are distillations of his erotic ideal, a straining expression of aching love for the female body that possessed him like a demon to the end.

Although it is unlikely that any Greek artist would have produced such a literal presentation of this minor myth and although the sensuous and romantic overtones are completely anticlassical, the picture does succeed in some mysterious way in conveying a sense of the Greek heroic ideal, at once Homeric and Phidian. This is conveyed in part by the very gigantic dimensions of Zeus enthroned in the realm of storms and clouds above the earth, his head towering to the top of the firmament. There is at the same time a kind of architectural order about this great body; the massive base of the feet and knees support the snow-white column of the massive trunk. This human order is completed by the vast entablature of the arms and shoulders. In creating this figure, Ingres must have had in mind what he himself wrote of the greatest of Greek sculptors: "Phidias was the first, so to speak, to achieve divine majesty and to add a new concept for the veneration of the people in making perceptible for them what they had adored." [8]

— 62 —

Neoclassicism in America

And why need we copy the Doric or the Gothic model? Beauty, convenience, grandeur of thought and quaint expression are as near to us as to any, and if the American artist will study with hope and love the precise thing to be done by him, considering the climate, the soil, the length of the day, the wants of the people, the habit and form of the government, he will create a house in which all these will find themselves fitted, and taste and sentiment will be satisfied also.   —Emerson *

A SEPARATE chapter in the history of the neoclassic era is the spread of this style to the United States. It is not at all surprising that its adaptation in North America should reveal the same employment of classical forms as a kind of backdrop appropriate for extolling and embodying the republican virtues of ancient democracies that had in many ways made for its popularity in Europe. Even before 1800 the Italian adventurer Ceracchi had come to America especially to take the likeness of George Washington, in a style that was a travesty of the great Canova. The architecture provided for the first capitol building by Latrobe was an example of the functional simplified use of ancient forms employed by Sir John Soane. Jefferson's passionate enthusiasm for the beauty and enthusiasm of what he called the "cubic" Roman architecture as he knew it through his visits to Provence and his volumes of Palladio had its profound effect in making neoclassic a national style. The spread of temple-type banks, churches, and houses to every part of the country from Maine to Mississippi may be accounted for not only by the taste of professional architects but also by the dissemination of countless editions of builders' manuals which facilitated the erection of structures with orders correctly described so as to be constructed easily by any village carpenter.

Although neoclassic architecture found a ready acceptance both for patriotic reasons and because it reflected the accepted taste of the old

* Ralph Waldo Emerson, "Self-Reliance"

world, the history of the style in American sculpture and painting was a different story. In the first decades of the American republic one of the refinements adopted from neoclassic Europe to provide a material symbolism for liberty was sculpture. Beginning with Ceracchi's likeness of Washington the marble effigies of the founding fathers appeared in greater and greater numbers, veritable emblems in their antique style of the ancient democracies of Greece and Rome. The notion was also current that, since the republics of the ancient world had produced some of the greatest sculpture the world had ever seen, the democracy of the New World could not fail to create sculpture in every way the equal of the ancients. Although a few native-born sculptors like William Rush and John Frazee of Philadelphia produced a kind of indigenous version of the neoclassic style, the wave of patriotism which followed the War of 1812 produced an even greater demand for heroic public sculpture, and it is not at all surprising that in 1821 the great Canova received a commission to carve a statue of Washington for the capitol of North Carolina. Jefferson had been responsible for this commission, and he was only the official spokesman for the taste that regarded Canova as the sculptor perfectly fitted for the expression of popular republican ideals.

Just as earlier American painters had journeyed to Rome in search of the grand manner of painting, so in the twenties and thirties of the nineteenth century American sculptors began a descent upon Italy, eager to equal the renown of Canova. There they found the second generation of neoclassic artists at the height of their fame: Thorvaldsen, Gibson, and Bartolini. The Americans had no difficulty in acquiring the superficial mannerisms of neoclassicism—the cold and artificial style, the smooth and elegant finish, the fluent lines and facile rhetoric—qualities which were invariably fatal to whatever indigenous talent they might have possessed.

The most famous name among the American neoclassicists was that of Hiram Powers, a self-taught carver who, thanks to the renown he achieved from a bust of President Jackson, was able to embark for Italy in search of fame and fortune. He lost no time in acquiring both. In Florence, where Powers settled down for the rest of his life, he set to work to acquire a facile and fashionable neoclassic manner based on the style and technique of Thorvaldsen and Bartolini. Powers was first and foremost a businessman, and his business was the production of statues and busts; these were especially directed to the taste of the American tourists who in ever greater numbers were coming to Europe in search of culture with little knowledge to guide their appreciation of art.

Powers' sculptural procedure was typical of his generation. The sculptor executed a model in plaster, leaving the task of transferring it to marble to workmen specializing in this mechanical operation. Generally the sculptor himself would enliven the stone with a few final touches of his chisel. Powers boasted of having invented a machine for reproducing the "porosities" of the skin in marble. He rejoiced in the sobriquet of "the ingenious Yankee mechanic," a title which unfortunately was more descriptive of the mechanical nature of his work than any true inventive genius in sculpture.[1]

A characteristic work which illustrates Powers' style and, indeed, the general character of the American neoclassicists is The Greek Slave (figure 215). This statue, slightly less than life size, was intended to play upon the sympathies of his customers, European and American, for the Greek struggle for independence. From a stylistic point of view it is a rather obvious and lifeless derivation from a classical original, most likely the Venus dei Medici (figure 30), an interesting borrowing, since Powers never tired of extolling the superiority of his own work over the classical original. To be sure, Powers' work has a certain rococo delicacy that superficially recalls the touch of Canova, but the arms, the legs, and the torso are reduced to a tubular smoothness that displays all too well the sculptural rather than the human quality of the model filled with wistful sentiment, carved with superficial technical perfection, and lacking in any kind of sensual attraction. This statue was completely suited to American taste in the nineteenth century.

In Powers' statue the white Carrara marble, so cherished for its snowy luster, has been tooled with such satiny smoothness in its unbroken tubular surfaces that the viewer is conscious only of this slick finish and no really convincing connotation of form or mass or weight remains in the slight figure. One has the impression of a clever but slight performance in wax or even sugar without suggestion of plastic quality or bodily warmth. A false demureness of expression successfully cloaks the hidden erotic charm. This sentimentalized chastity is what Powers' American clients felt they could safely admire without straining their moral sensibilities.

The sculpture of Powers does not render the real beautiful. He is rather the sculptor of sentimental prettiness, a dainty workman in marble, as incapable of realizing high ideal motives by his conventional treatment as he is of rendering genuine naturalism. . . . Powers' idea [in the Greek Slave] was to make an effigy of a terror-stricken girl, whose purest instincts and holiest affections are about to be tramped into the dust by a mercenary wretch. Under no conditions could maidenly modesty and innocence appear more pathetically to the sympathies of spectators before whose compassionate look pure girlhood must instinctively shrink. What have we? A feebly conceived, languid, romantic miss, under no delusion as to the quality and value of her fresh charms viewed by the carnal eye. . . . We need have no pitying pang; the bought and the buyer will soon be on speaking terms, for a coquette at heart always has her price. The failure to attain high art out of an exalted motive is caused by mistaking the outside pretty for the interior beautiful.[2]

This criticism of Powers' sentimental marble trifle by the distinguished American pioneer of art history, James Jackson Jarves, could be applied to a whole marble host of such marble maidens that once graced Victorian parlors. They represent the final sentimentalization and one can safely say mechanization of the classic formula to the level of the sweet and boneless, quasi-erotic pastiches popularized by such degraders of Canova's mastery as Gibson.

A far more serious and gifted sculptor than Powers was Horatio Greenough of Boston. He began his sculptural career as a boy copying the intaglios and cameos in the collection of the Boston Athenaeum. It was only after his journey to Italy that he came to have any remote idea of what sculpture really was. In the United States of Greenough's day, there were neither schools of sculpture nor examples upon which a student could base his technique and training. Here and there—and usually kept under lock and key for reasons of prudery—were plaster casts of the Apollo Belvedere and the Venus dei Medici; a marble replica of the latter now in the Boston Athenaeum found its way to the Harvard Medical School in 1819.

In Italy, following the neoclassic program of artistic education, Greenough studied the antique and sought the counsel of the leading practitioner of neoclassicism, Thorvaldsen. For a time he studied at the Accademia in Florence under Bartolini, an artist whose work in its somewhat more naturalistic character provided a slight variation from the general frozen neoclassic norm.

Greenough's most famous work was his colossal marble effigy of George Washington (figure 216). This statue, commissioned by Congress in 1832, was an American version of the portrait by Canova destroyed in the burning of the capitol at Raleigh. It comes as no surprise that Greenough's conception was entirely neoclassic. Washington is represented seated on a massive throne as a kind of Phidian Zeus: his right hand is raised in an imperious gesture; in his left, he holds the sword as symbol of his command of the army of the revolution; he is draped in a toga, nude from the waist up. Like some of Bartolini's portrait statues, Washington is represented as a distinguished Roman personage, both in the pose and the device of the drapery covering one shoulder and the lower part of the body. It lacks, however, the strong bodily structure so notable in monuments by his teacher. Greenough also lacked completely the ability to caress, so to speak, the flesh and animate it in marble.

What we have is an attempt to produce an heroic patriotic ideal. This effect was based on the grandiose scale, the symbolical accessories, and the authority of the neoclassic style. The statue has all the defects of the neoclassic—the rigidity, hardness, the smooth cylindrical surfaces of a shape copied from antique models and not from a living and breathing human body. Many of the faults of Greenough's Washington, as in the case of Powers, result from the practice of entrusting the actual carving to professional stone cutters who transferred the original plaster model to marble.

The statue of Washington was the failure and tragedy of Greenough's sculptural career. It proved too heavy for the rotunda of the capitol for which it had been planned, so that it was moved first to an ignoble position out-of-doors and finally to the dark recesses of the Smithsonian Institution. The general outcry against such a semi-nude, classical portrayal of the Father of his Country was completely in line with current American ideas of prudery and taste.

Greenough's Washington was an attempt to combine the virtues of Houdon's or Stuart's great portraits with the associations of neoclassic symbolical paraphernalia and technique. The result was a magnification rather than a truly monumental statue. The attempt to portray a real personage in the allegorical accouterments of an Olympian appeared rather ridiculous even to the classically minded connoisseurs of 1832. In this rhetorical presentation of Washington as Zeus, Greenough lacked the imagination that enabled Canova to ennoble Napoleon as a Polyclitan athlete. It marked the sad end of a fashion that had begun in the eighteenth century for representing the great in the timeless dress or undress of the ancients as a patent of their inheritance of the nobility and virtue of the heroes of the classical republics.

Greenough's grasp of the qualities of sculpture far transcended the facility of Powers and his followers in the massiveness of the form that undoubtedly has a borrowed Olympian grandeur, but Greenough, like all the sculptors of his period, lacked the ability to create a statue as an animate object and to imbue it with a suggestion of the inner structure and life of a real body. Since the sculptor left the actual carving to the insensitive reproductive skill of professional marble cutters, the finished image could hardly be expected to reveal the enlivening touch of the chisel that distinguished the work of Canova. The neoclassic sculptors of the middle nineteenth century were among the first to suffer from the results of mass production, a process of duplication which they accepted as a token of progress in a world that more and more was fixing its attention on mechanized convenience rather than craftsmanship.

Greenough himself amid the ruin of his career as a sculptor was able to recognize the inappropriateness of his rhetorical approach and, in the last years of his life, became a man of ideas: "The translation of rhetoric into stone [is] a feat often fatal to the rhetoric, always fatal to the stone." [3] His mind in its search for the functional in art and architecture proved far sharper than his chisel in the penetration of the problem of developing an art both useful and appropriate to its time and place. Greenough never more eloquently embodied the classical tradition than when he said, "We should learn of the Greeks to be American."

Although earlier American painters like Benjamin West and Washington Allston had worked in the neoclassic manner, the only artist in the United States to follow in the tradition of David was John Vanderlyn who has the distinction of being the one American of the early nineteenth century who studied in Paris rather than in London or Rome. He was trained in the studio of the Davidian artist André Vincent; on one occasion he copied a painting by Ingres; and so it is not surprising that the few classical subjects he attempted should bear the strongest resemblance to the style of David and his pupils.

One of Vanderlyn's first original essays in the neoclassic manner was his painting of the Death of Jane McCrea (figure 217). This picture was originally painted in 1804 as one of a series of proposed illustrations for Joel Barlow's epic *The Columbiad*. Vanderlyn was not commissioned to complete this series, and the painting remains as his one venture into American subject matter. The presentation of this famous legend of a young girl slain by Indians on the way to her betrothal is interesting from

316

a number of viewpoints. It represents a picture of the red man as brutal and untrustworthy in opposition to the current ideas of the Noble Savage. Except for an earlier sketch of this popular legend by John Trumbull, famed for his painting of events from the Revolution, this is the earliest presentation of an Indian theme by an American artist. Vanderlyn's treatment of the subject is as could be expected an adaptation of the David formula. The dependence on a prototype such as David's Oath of the Horatii is apparent at once. The figures of the two Indians although not recognizable as borrowings from any specific ancient statues are completely sculptural in conception. The victim of their onslaught is a kind of American Niobid. She resembles two statues of a crouching Venus that were among the treasures looted from Rome by Napoleon and, during Vanderlyn's years in Paris, displayed in the Louvre—and the Mohawks may owe something to two statues of fauns in the same collection. The picture is the David manner in American dress.

The American aspects of the painting beyond the subject may be discerned in the anecdotal quality and in the heroic sentimentalizing of this minor tragedy and in the intermixture of romantic details of the setting. Like so many neoclassic pictures, the aim of a painting of this sort was not only to realize the beautiful in the accepted classical idiom but to impart an edifying moral lesson to the beholder. The subject is presented mainly in terms of drawing and the smooth textureless finish of the European neoclassicists. Only the background in its hazy luminosity is suggestive of the coloristic brilliance typical of Vanderlyn's romantic contemporary Washington Allston.

Edgar Richardson has noted, "Unfortunately, for Vanderlyn, he had absorbed along with the technique of French neoclassicism its grandiose ambitions, which he was neither able to carry out by his own unaided strength nor to find a foundation for in American society." [4] In America there was no Louvre and no Salon to instruct taste and to confer prestige on the arts. There was no noble patronage and no monumental architecture to house great historical canvases. The sorry end of the neoclassic tradition in America may also be explained by the very absence of the antique models on which such an art was nourished. Theoretically there should have been great promise for such a style in a society like that of post-Revolutionary America that identified itself with the virtues and valor of the ancients, but even Vanderlyn's Death of Jane McCrae was only a single desultory effort. As Horatio Greenough must have realized, too, although there were many men in public life full of respect for classical literature and jurisprudence, the connoisseur who could appreciate the aesthetic qualities of a Canova or a David did not exist in America of the early nineteenth century. Only the overtly sentimental transformation of the neoclassic style by Hiram Powers could appeal to a society that mistook the pretty for the beautiful and saw all art through a veil of literary association.

— 63 —

Rodin

Yet sculpture was never more radiant than when it was inspired by this narrow order. It was because that calm beauty could find entire expression in the serenity of transparent marbles; it was because there was perfect accord between the thought and the matter that it animated. The modern spirit, on the contrary, upsets and breaks all forms in which it takes body. —Rodin *

THE importance of Rodin for a study of the classical tradition rests on the fact that he was the first of modern sculptors to turn to the principles of Greek art rather than its superficial imitation or adaptation. "While among the ancients the generalization of lines is a totalization, a result made up of all the details, the academies' simplification is an impoverishment, an empty bombastry." [1]

For Rodin the modern sculptor's aim was the rediscovery of the methods of antiquity. He probably had a more intimate, penetrating knowledge of the inner principles of Greek sculpture than any of the neoclassicists. He was conscious of the animating effect of the subtle variations in the multiple planes of Greek sculpture in suggesting the breathing warmth of the human frame. His study of casts and copies of Polyclitan originals filled him with admiration for the distribution of balance and movement enlivening the serenely composed body. Rodin's feeling for Polyclitus and Phidias was tempered by his overwhelming interest in the dynamic energy and passion of Michelangelo. Although the general effect of a typical Rodin statue is of the pictorial treatment of the chiaroscuro that envelops it and the superficial suggestion of fleshly texture in the variegated surfaces of marble or bronze, the underlying form has a solidity and integrity of construction in solid masses and simple enclosing planes that reveals the master working in a classic manner; that is, working from the inside and not from the outward imitation of shapes.

* Auguste Rodin, *Art,* pp. 217–218

Rodin's Half-figure of a Woman, dated 1910, illustrates his preoccupation with the antique within the essentially realistic framework of his approach (figure 218). The bronze has the soft Praxitelean modeling he admired.[2] If compared with an actual Praxitelean original (figure 50), it becomes evident immediately that Rodin was concerned with a far more impressionistic textural suggestion of the skin enclosing the body and a really unidealized presentation of the breasts and belly. The head, as often in Rodin's work, is reminiscent of the veiled dreaming beauty of Praxiteles, here intensified by the impressionistic, fluid handling of the medium. This fluidity and impressionistic abbreviation, as in the cloth over the head, transcends anything seen in the antique.

This statue is an example of what has been called the "cult of the fragment." The deliberate lopping off of arms and legs, as in a mutilated ancient statue, concentrates attention on the torso as an isolated pure form without the distraction of the movement and position of the limbs in a complete image. In Rodin's case it is a deliberate attempt to preserve something of the freshness and incompleteness of the sketch in a finished work. Although Rodin has been accused of an overemphasis on sensuality, of destroying form in favor of superficial texture, it remains that he was a great innovator, not only in his impressionistic experiments but in returning sculpture to nature and to the aims of ancient art. The artist believed that his real contribution resided in his return to the laws of the great statues of antiquity, not in mere innovation.

— 64 —

The Twentieth Century

The true relation between the modern world and the classical world is the same, on a larger scale, as the relation between Greece and Rome . . . Rome grew powerful through her military and political genius; and then, from Greece, she learnt to live the life of the mind . . . The real duty of man is not to extend his power or multiply his wealth beyond his needs, but to enrich and enjoy his own imperishable possession: his soul.
                                                                        —Highet *

Amid the complexity of the artistic movements of the twentieth century the classical tradition seemingly has been eclipsed by the search for other realms of expression. Although it no longer commands the immense authority imposed by academic training in earlier periods, the vitality of classical art as one of many sources of technical and symbolical inspiration can be seen in the work of many artists who turned to this inexhaustible reservoir of creative ideation. The architecture of Le Corbusier is an eloquent illustration of the transformation of the simplicity and adequacy of the temple and its place in landscape to modern design. The beckoning gods in Arcadia, where their rule has never been challenged, continue to lure artists in quest of the eternal poetry which they teach until our own time. Even the employment of classical shapes for the expression of the world of the psyche by artists like de Chirico, Dali, and Delvaux is addressed to presenting one of the greatest boons of humans: the evocation of mystery.

The appeal of classical art, especially in its archaic phases, has provided a point of departure for sculptors like Maillol and Henry Moore in their search for the intrinsic plastic basis of the art. The cult of the incomplete, the presentation of decapitated and limbless torsos, is a part of the modern sculptor's concentrating attention on pure form of body as

* Gilbert Highet, *The Classical Tradition*, pp. 548–549

321

suggested by the similar fragmentary aesthetic sensation in the works of antiquity.

Although Gauguin is said to have remarked that the Greek tradition was the bane of art, even this explorer of the magic power and form of the primitive on occasion availed himself intuitively of the remembered finality of ancient shapes. Picasso, an artist trained in the academic tradition, has over and over again displayed his poetic reverence for the antique. The sensuous curvatures of the flowing line of Greek vase painting have stimulated him to an austere but erotic line drawing, in which the antique subjects are handled as playful and symbolical themes, and under his pencil the veiled symbolism of the ancient myths takes on a new life. If the classical serves only as a romantic metaphor for artists like Peter Blume and Edwin Dickinson, this is not to deny the continuing strength of its magnetic attraction. It provides, as it always has in post-classical ages, only a different possibility of interpretation in tune with the world the artist lives in.

The gods and heroes remain as eternal themes, just as their shapes remain eternal in ancient marble and bronze as subjects for the modern artists' more inward, romantic exploration and reshaping in a modern idiom. The haunting presence of classical shapes in the minds of modern artists who reformed them for purely personal psychic ends is only one illustration of the intuitive recognition of the inescapable finality of these ancient creations. This is no more plagiarism than drawing from a natural form. Jackson Pollock used the Roman wolf as the core of one of his early ventures into action painting, and Ben Shahn derives something from this same monument in his Allegory. "I had always found it disconcerting the familiar sculpture of Romulus and Remus being suckled by the She-Wolf. Now I found that, whether by coincidence or not I am unable to say, the stance of my imaginary beast was just that of the great Roman wolf." [1]

Many writers and many artists believe that the classical tradition as an active force is dead. Even the founder of the Warburg Institute, lamenting the passing of ancient myths and ritual as a source of security and imaginative creation, wrote a meaningful paragraph that has a bearing on the survival of the classical heritage in art.

Electricity enslaved, the lightning held captive in the wire, has produced a civilization which has no use for heathen poetry. But what does it put in its place? The forces of nature are no longer seen in anthropomorphic shapes; they are conceived in an endless succession of waves, obedient to the touch of a man's hand. With these waves the civilization of the mechanical age is destroying what natural science, itself emerging out of myth, had won with such vast effort—the sanctuary of devotion, the remoteness needed for contemplation. The modern Prometheus, Franklin and the Wright brothers, are those fateful destroyers of our sense of distance who threaten to lead the world back into chaos.[2]

Although Impressionism and all that followed have in an artistic parallel to the disintegration wrought by science destroyed the old imaginative idiom of the classical heritage, dehumanized art is only an interlude. Only the ruthless skepticism of a scientific age and the frenetic search for variety and untrammeled freedom of expression in art could finally discard the certainties of myths and symbols and the humanism of the Mediterranean tradition. Human need for reliance and dreams made real in human terms may seek them out again when men lose faith in the comfortable and meaningless world that science and the pursuit of the meaningless have built.

— 65 —

Maillol

I prefer the still primitive art of Olympia to that of the Parthenon. It is the most beautiful I have seen, more beautiful than anything else in the world. It is an art of synthesis, an art superior to our modern art which seeks to represent human flesh.

—Maillol *

ARISTIDE MAILLOL was one of the first modern sculptors to react against the impressionistic emphasis on texture that characterized the work of Rodin. His reaction took the form of a return to a more solid plastic feeling for sculpture in its purest sense. In 1908 his point of view and his style were vindicated by a trip to Greece, which he regarded as a journey to the land of his true artistic ancestors. His view of the sculpture of the pre-Phidian period provided a confirmation of his own ideas and feelings. The story that Maillol had to be restrained from embracing one of the caryatids of the Erechtheum is a symbol of his passionate infatuation with the monumental form of Greek art. His true love was the sculpture of Olympia. When he said, "It is an art of synthesis, a higher art than ours today, which seeks to represent human flesh," [1] he was thinking primarily of Rodin. Maillol was concerned first and foremost with solid plastic harmonies and intensity of expression, with an elimination of everything unessential and artificial. The equilibrium of masses in sculpture seemed to him as important as the abstract balance of shapes in architecture. His figures have an impressive monumentality and dignity, and their blocklike solidity seems to confirm the artist's observation that he always began with a geometric figure—a cube, a lozenge, or a triangle. Whereas the construction of Greek sculpture develops from the organic unity of the human body and the order of its articulation, Maillol, start-

* Je préfère l'art encore primitif d'Olympie à celui du Parthénon. C'est ce que j'ai vu de plus beau, ce qu'il y a de plus beau dans le monde. C'est un art de synthèse, un art supérieur à ce travail de chair que nous, modernes, nous cherchons.—Aristide Maillol, Letter to Count Kessler in Cladel, *Maillol,* p. 97

ing from a conception of the body as an architectural, rhythmic organization of the whole body and its parts, builds a representation of the human form in terms of solid abstract masses.

Maillol's La Méditerranée (figure 219) is typical of his work under Olympian inspiration. It affords a ready comparison with one of the crouching figures from the west pediment at Olympia (figure 220). The pose has been slightly altered, but only to make the form even more self-contained. La Méditerranée was created in the years 1902 to 1905 for his patron, Baron Kessler. Even though this statue was conceived before his voyage to Greece, Maillol was well-acquainted with the principles of pre-Phidian Greek art in the Louvre and presumably knew the Olympia sculpture in photographic reproductions. He has eliminated any kind of description of the surfaces of the body, reducing them to volumes of moving simplicity. The compactness of the composition goes beyond the sculptor of Olympia in suggesting the emergence of a form from the material. Maillol declared that he wished his figures to be without motion or expression in order to emphasize the glyptic nature and weight of the material. He returned to sculpture its proper sense of weight and impenetrable substance. Movement and life were to be implied rather than described; the massive relaxed figure seems to wake from a deep slumber congealed in stone. If, in Maillol's art, the volumes are simplified almost to the point of resembling a collection of spheres, cones, and cylinders, he never loses the sense of an inner organic life, of a real body, alive and breathing. His uninterrupted surfaces suggest something of the Greek sculptor's feeling for the intrinsic beauty of the marble.

— 66 —

Picasso

[Picasso] was continually fascinated by classicism, in spite of his various disparaging remarks about the antique; for example, the statement (1935): "The beauties of the Parthenon, the Venuses, the nymphs, the Narcissi are all so many lies." . . . His classical works . . . always include a retrospective element, combined with mischievous double meanings and touches of parody: half of these works give the impression that the artist wishes to make fun of Mannerism and the surfeit of the classical Mediterranean tradition from which he springs and which alternately draws his hate and love.　　　　　　　　　　　　　　　—Richardson *

Picasso in his long career is an artist who has revealed a greater capacity for creative ideation in every vein of expression than any other single painter since the great age of the Baroque. In the variety of his experiments he is unique. Part of this experience in more than sixty years of painting has been the intelligent exploitation of past modes of artistic expression, which in Picasso's case has persistently included the antique. It was probably in part Picasso's training in the academic tradition of drawing from casts and models that led to his lifelong attachment to the formal beauty of Greek art.

Picasso is never a neoclassicist, but an explorer in antique realms that have opened to him the possibilities of new forms of expression. Whether or not this is only a part of the artist's endless quest for novelty is beside the point; it is everywhere apparent that Greek sculpture showed him the way toward the reduction of human figures to shapes of massive sim-

* Im übrigen dürfen wir nicht vergessen, dass [Picasso] sets vom Klassizismus fasciniert war, ungeachtet seiner verschiedentlichen herabsetzenden Bemerkung über die Antike, wie zum Beispiel die Behauptung (1935): "Les beautés du Parthenon, les Vénus, les Nymphes, les Narcisses sont autant de mensonges." . . . Seine klassizischen Arbeiten . . . enthalten immer ein rückschauendes Element, verbunden mit boshaften und doppelsinnig parodistischen Zügen: die Hälfte dieser Werke erweckt den Eindruck, der Künstler wolle sich über den Manierismus und die Uberladenheit der klassischen Mittelmeer Tradition lustig machen, der er entstammt und der abwechselnd sein Hass und seine Liebe gilt.—John Richardson, *Pablo Picasso*, pp. 14–16

plicity that radiate a kind of fecund power in forms that are simplified presentations of the intrinsic glyptic bulk of statuary. Again, the clarity and probity of draftsmanship of Greek vases and Etruscan mirrors offered a point of departure for the most fluent and activated drawing in an endless variety of mythological subjects. Sometimes these contain symbolical meanings; sometimes they are lyric and playful improvisations in the mode of line or line and flat tone. The painter displays a caressing touch in the exploitation of the erotic beauty of the female nude, which far surpasses in its provocative appeal the tender and chaste forms outlined on Attic lekythoi.

The treatment of classic subjects in Picasso's classic vein is marked by his superb cursive draftsmanship and his feeling for the poetry of the motif. In his dynamic experimentation there are no rules; any distortion is permissible. Mythological themes have appealed to Picasso not for their authority but because they have offered him the opportunity to project the inexhaustible fertility of his imagination to new levels of vision. The approach is sensuous both in the presentation of the subject and a suggestive visual manipulation of the medium.

In the poignancy of the artist's touch in brushing the curves of the nude body there is more erotic attraction than in the most finished academic painting by a Raphael or a Botticelli, artists whose forms remain enclosed in an inviolable envelope of chastity. The repertory of Picasso's classical performances has been inexhaustible. From his so-called Blue Period to the Ovidian lithographs of his later years any one would be worthy of analysis, and any one would reveal a true classicism in the purity of linear definition or in the establishment of an intrinsic plastic integrity derived from the mighty simplified forms of classical sculpture.

A typical and beautiful example of Picasso's poetic derivation from the antique is his painting of a Boy Leading a Horse which dates from 1905 (figure 221). The subject of man's triumph and mastery of the wild energies and massive strength of the beast is an immemorial theme. It stands as a symbol of young manhood and virile beauty both rational and erotic. Although one is ultimately reminded of the pensive boys in the Parthenon frieze (figure 18) there is something romantic in the thoughtful expression of this sad and serious youth. Although in Picasso there is only a vague suggestion of a classical form, the painting in a way recaptures the classic mood in its serenity and in the austerity of the form and moving probity of the linear drawing. Again, in a classic way this youth who masters the wild steed radiates a kind of divine energy as a modern reincarnation of one of the Heavenly Twins. In the balance and *élan* of his creation, Picasso creates his own classical world.

The Classic Head in the Worcester Art Museum is one of Picasso's many experiments in evoking a voluminous sculptural form in painting (figure 222). The classic prototype, whichever it may have been, was of no archaeological interest to the artist. It only provided him with a point of departure for the realization of an almost repressively heavy form, in which he has reduced the features to a mask even more simplified than the Greek original. Picasso's head does not suggest marble or flesh or, in fact, any material except that of the pigment itself. It is without personality or sentimental overtones. Like Maillol's sculpture, this stage in Picasso's artistic journey found him fascinated with the possibilities of realizing a sense of pneumatically expansive volume that projects itself to the spectator with great tactile force. The head is superficially classic in the imperturbable serenity of the expressionless mask.

If this head appears as ugly because of its lumpy features and chalky color, this is because Picasso in all of his many modes of expression has deliberately bypassed any kind of externally pleasing beauty in order to project more forcefully his concern with a more permanent beauty in the simplicity of the forms and the inherent solidity of matter presented in volumes of calculated rude strength.

Although the monumental form appears classical, the discarding of all incidental reality and surface is probably as much the result of other forces acting on the artist's performance. This painting and others like it were done in the years after Picasso had already investigated the power of primitive art and had passed through the period of his adventures in the realm of cubism. It was most likely painted at some time after his visit to Rome in 1917 aroused anew his admiration for classical subjects. It represents an interval of calm between his cubist discoveries and the violence and disintegration of form that marks the disillusionment of the artist in the period between the two World Wars.

Picasso's drawing of L'amour masqué, or Venus and Cupid, is a typical example of his exercise in a Greek key (figure 223). The figure of the crouching nude can well be compared to the decisive line drawings of the Greek vases, especially the outlined figures on the funeral lekythoi (figure 224). The contours of the image are drawn with the greatest rapidity and fluency. In Picasso's drawing, of course, the anatomical distortion of the figure is realistically impossible. Multiple profiles and facets of the body are shown simultaneously: the torso is in front view, the buttocks in three-quarters, the legs in profile. This is a kind of composite snapshot of all the desirable parts of the anatomy seen all at once and each in its most provocative aspect. Picasso's pliancy of line is far different from the careful definition of form in a Greek vase, but the total impression is of the same lyric grace of pose and silhouette found in the prototype. The distortion of the parts of the body seems to suggest the figure's moving and twisting, posturing in a rapid sequence of provocative attitudes, all of which occurred to the artist in the tremendously pregnant seconds of his execution. This is the Greek line revised in a completely modern manner. Picasso's hand recorded and combined with lightning response the various emblems of the aspects of a body consecutively remembered as being most appealing from a certain point of view. This is only an exaggeration of the conceptual presentation already noted in the Diana of the Fontainebleau school (figure 169). For all the explosive qualities of technique and the outrageous distortion, the figure in an unbelievable way evokes the poetry of Greek myth and form.

— 67 —

Henry Moore

This is not an imitation of its Greek prototype; it is a new icon expressing a modern consciousness of the Greek mystery, of the human rooted in the chthonic, of the sublime struggling to expression in a pagan death.   —Read *

Henry Moore is a modern sculptor who is completely aware of the inherent possibilities of earlier art forms to aid him in the solution of his own problems. His particular response to classical art stems from a visit to Greece in 1950 when, as Sir Herbert Read has put it, seeing Greek sculpture in an Attic landscape, he saw it for the first time as something coming vibrantly to life.[1] A series of reclining draped figures, among them a colossal bronze, now in the Neue Pinakothek in Munich (figure 225), most clearly reveal the sculptor's use of this new source of inspiration.

This massive figure swathed in drapery from neck to knees seems to stir into wakefulness as from a deep slumber. The mountainous proportions of the form enveloped in a web of moving wavelike drapery are immediately suggestive of the great seated images of the Parthenon pediment (figure 14). But this is not in any sense a literal translation of the classical model. It is a calculated adoption of the very elements in Phidian sculpture that command bigness and superhuman weight and dignity. Henry Moore was powerfully affected by the inert massiveness of the archaic figures from Chalcidae in the British Museum which he describes as "female figures, seated in easy, still naturalness, grand and full like Handel's music." [2] Here he found those suggestions of dignity and heroic impassivity that were the aim of his own work. He was aware of the mountainous convolutions of the Phidian drapery, like a pliant crust containing the full, breathing bodies beneath, and reinforcing the sense of

---

* Sir Herbert Read, *Henry Moore,* II, xi

their expansive warmth and fullness. The sculptor himself explains his personal adaptation of the Phidian drapery formula:

Drapery can emphasize the tension of a figure, for where the form pulses outward, such as on the shoulders, the thighs, the breasts, etc., it can be pulled tight across the form (almost like a bandage), and by contrast with the crumpled slackness of the drapery which lies between the salient points, the pressure from inside is intensified. Also in my mind was to connect the contrast of the sizes of folds, here small, fine and delicate, in other places big and heavy, with the form of mountains, which are the crinkled skin of the earth. Although static this figure is not meant to be in slack repose, but, as it were, alerted.[3]

In studying this regally composed figure one is struck by the great beauty of his handling of textural surfaces and his differentiation in the handling of folds, alternately high and low, thick and thin, to create a web of moving light over the surface of the image. The ponderous earthbound mass of the body is relieved by the stirring flow of the drapery that engulfs the figure like another Anadyomene. The voluminous body is revealed through this drapery that flows over it in waves ordered in a rhythmic design that is a reshaping of the factors determining the heroic forms of Phidias. Fecund and earthy, the figure clings to the ground, solid and weighty as a glacial boulder. In the figures of this classical phase of his work Moore retains the negation of identity through the small, doll-like head. This archaic head has a certain elegance through the simplicity of the modeling: its qualities of anonymity and simplicity set off the richness of the treatment of the bodily form. One feels that in this classic phase of his work the sculptor's forms have taken on a humanism and grandeur evoked by the vision of archaic and Phidian antiquity. The present figure, designed for an open-air setting, seems to expand and accommodate itself to surrounding air and space, and at the same time the mass of this mother goddess almost overwhelms the spectator by its pregnant volume.

Henry Moore is an artist who, perhaps more in his work than in his words, has displayed a deep awareness and understanding of the true principles of Greek art. His powerful volume and impenetrable solidity are a translation into modern terms of the underlying quality of sculpture from the Archaic through the Great Period. His heroic female forms, the magnificent "earth mothers," recapture the sense of physical power and breathing life of the Parthenon marbles. Some of his essays in bronze are Moore's recapturing of the magic geometry of the Greek helmet.

His gigantic reclining forms in an abstract idiom, sometimes pierced by tunnel-like holes, are a modern rebirth of the chthonian strength and titanic glyptic mass of the earliest forms of Greek art. In his own language, he combines the moving beauty of material, fluid bronze or rigid stone, and the sense of overpowering massiveness of ancient forms.

— 68 —

De Chirico

The sense of the Hellenic which continually returns to the most refined archaism, to the most abstruse myth, to the fabulous Homeric grandeur, through a sensibility exquisitely modern and cultivated, which cannot be divorced from the reaction of irony and sometimes sarcasm, resolves itself, then, in de Chirico into a kind of refined Hellenism.

—Pica *

THE last stage in the development of the classical tradition is marked by the retreat of the old gods and the marbled vestiges of ruined Hellas to the interior world of the artist's mind. Giorgio de Chirico is the artist who has best worked this transformation of the mysterious tragic grandeur of antique fragments into a new reality of mystery and incongruity. In this he invented his own myths imbued with strange memories of the magic and the supernatural.

De Chirico was born of Italian parents in the Thessalian town of Volo in 1888. His youth was spent in Greece and he received his first artistic training at the Polytechnic Institute in Athens. There he progressed through the rigid discipline of the typical nineteenth-century instruction, beginning with drawing from still life and the cast, and then moving on to painting from the nude, and finally to the use of color. In 1905, De Chirico and his family removed to Munich, where the young artist was enrolled in the Academy of Fine Arts for two years. More important than his attendance of art classes in the Bavarian capital was De Chirico's discovery of Arnold Böcklin. He became enchanted with Böcklin's strange, metaphysical power and his ability to make the real unreal, the unreal real, to give fantasy the credibility of everyday happening. There was also

* Il senso della grecità che continuamente si rivolge al più alto arcaismo, al mito più astruso, alla favolosa grandezza omerica, attraverso una sensibilità squisitamente moderna e culta che non sa sottrarsi al reagente dell' ironia e talvolta del sarcasmo, si risolve poi in de Chirico in una sorta di raffinato ellenismo.—Agnoldomenico Pica, *12 Opere di Giorgio de Chirico* (Milan, 1952), p. x

the element of surprise in Böcklin, such as the incongruous appearance of mythical creatures in modern surroundings, that fed De Chirico's own evocation of a disquieting world of dreams. De Chirico's youthful poetic memory was filled with the marble classicism of Greece and the pathetic nobility and mystery of her ruins. He recognized in Böcklin a kindred sense of the tragic aspects of sculpture and it was not surprising that he responded with quickened imaginative excitement to his discovery of Schopenhauer's ideas on the phantomlike power of statuary. To these stimuli may be added the impression made on the painter by Nietzsche's exhortation to the artist to create a symbolical dream picture as a transfiguration of unbearable reality.

Throughout his career Giorgio de Chirico has shown a visionary longing for the historical past, which he transforms into haunting emblems of an interior world presented in terms of dazzling clarity of focus and disquieting infinite space. Part of his nostalgia or the recognition of an inner longing in the artist's psyche was his discovery of Italy and Italian art. The art of the Quattrocento provided him with a sharp crystalline definition of a super-reality, elusive even in its precision.

Of primary interest is the part played in De Chirico's art by the classical tradition in its material relics and its spirit. There is no need to investigate his creation of what is called "metaphysical painting" or his prophecies of surrealism, except for the part played by these integral elements of his artistic personality in relation to the classic aspects of his style. As early as the twenties De Chirico repudiated his youthful adventures in the wonderful hidden realms of his own creating. He seems more and more to have found himself congenial with the exploitation of his marvelous technical virtuosity in a type of classical painting that echoes at once his passionate attachment to the intrinsic beauties of the antique, the metallic clarity of the Quattrocento, and the metaphysical realism of Böcklin. In part this repudiation of youthful invention seems to have been affected by De Chirico's almost obsessive concern with his métier. It was as though he regarded himself as a champion called to defend the crumbling citadel of painting. He wrote in 1922 to the surrealist Breton, "Terrible things go on today in painting and . . . if the painters continue on this route we are approaching the end." [1] Although this return to tradition has led his artistic colleagues and critics to abandon him as a turncoat *retardataire,* it remains that few artists have given such a poetic vision, such a truly supernatural intensity of expression based on the form and mystery of the classic, a poetic vision of Nietzsche's Apollonian dream image.

An illustration of Giorgio de Chirico's metaphysical transformation of classical memories is his painting of 1913, The Joys and Enigmas of a Strange Hour (figure 226). In a vast space demarcated by an arcade, a tower, and a buttressed wall, a statue of Ariadne dominates the empty foreground. An ancient locomotive puffs behind the wall, and in the infinite sunlit distance two lonely figures cast their long penciled shadows across the empty street.

The statue in this picture is only one of many paintings he made of the famous Ariadne in the Vatican (figure 33). The image has its place here not only as an emblem of classical Greece and the past, but as a marble personification of the human being lost in the world of dreams. As in so many of De Chirico's paintings, this sculpture has a strange life of its own. He once wrote, in describing just such a picture as this, "In everlasting happiness the statue immerses its soul in the contemplation of its shadow." [2] This painting is an illustration of De Chirico's creation of a kind of inhabitable dream filled with silence and inertia and strangely foreboding in its quiet and desolation. The two tiny figures, like their companion, the Ariadne, are engulfed in the blaze of the Mediterranean sunlight. The very emptiness and stillness enclosed by the architectural enframement that seems to mark the limits of the world create an air of somnolence and stupefying immobility. This type of picture in its quality of mystery and enigma and the suggestion of the clarified and yet incongruous vision of dreams was on the threshold of surrealism. Its classicism resides not only in the artist's personification of the marmoreal eternity of Hellas in the statue of Ariadne, but in his creation of a cold and precise clarified reality evocative of the perspective and the emotive power of geometric forms of the great Renaissance scientists Uccello and Piero della Francesca.

In paintings like this the vast endless perspectives enclose a world of silent sunlight, in which all motion, sound, and time appear suspended as in a dream, a vision haunted by the dreaming image of the ancient heroine fixed in marble. The artist induces a mood of infinite serenity and deathly stillness in this abandoned place, a memory at once of the marble eternity of the ancient statue and the haunting sense of infinity connoted by the Roman arcades. These arcades were symbols that filled De Chirico's mind with an aching nostalgia for the Latin past and the connotation of the quiet shelter of the world of dreams. He said, "There is nothing like the enigma of the *Arcade*—invented by the Romans . . . The Roman arcade is a fatality. Its voice speaks in enigmas filled with a strangely Roman poetry; shadows on old walls and a curious music, profoundly blue, having something of an afternoon at the seaside." [3] Here, as on so many other occasions, De Chirico was fascinated by the evocation of a strange melancholy pathos that fills Italian piazzas with a palpable sense of silence and eternity.

The Roman Villa (figure 227) belongs to a period when De Chirico had happily returned to the enfolding serenity and warmth of the womb of the past. Two massive Renaissance buildings that might be on the Aventine, at Tivoli, or Sutri are outlined against a curtain of rocks. On the balustrades of their terraces stand a group of famous classical statues including Polyclitus' Amazon, the Meleager (figure 24), and the Antinoüs of the Vatican (figure 47). Tiny figures move about on the roof and recline on the shadowed balcony. In the dark windows loom other dim shapes of the human inhabitants of this marble world. In the sky a melancholy Pan floats on a cloud above the strangely incongruous lozenge of a flying kite. The picture is painted in the hard, meticulously finished technique of the North Italian masters whom De Chirico had come to admire extravagantly. He returns here as a revenant to an ancient land.

One is again in a dream world, made, if anything, more poetic and mysterious by the precision of the mode. The manner and its romantic overtones resemble Böcklin. This is again De Chirico's domain of fantasms in which the ivory forms of the statues are as strangely alive as the figures who move among them. In this realistic, classic phase of his art, he still creates a strange mood of suspense and apprehension, not only in the enigma of incongruously combined elements, but also in the visionary clarity of definition and the strangely somnambulent aspect of the statues and their shadowy human counterparts. Here, in their final role of apparitions in a haunted world, the ancient images are once again evoked to play their parts in this subjective romantic creation. Even in this phantom guise, they are painted *con amore,* with a beauty and accuracy of definition surpassing any neoclassic artist.

A final exemplar of De Chirico's absorption in his classical world is his Self Portrait of 1924 (figure 228). Behind the bust of the painter appears a marble statue of Apollo with his lyre. The picture is painted with that virtuoso *bravura* of precise definition that is De Chirico's recapturing of the Renaissance technique and that echoes the magic realism of Böcklin. The painting is built on both striking technical contrasts and inner psychological ties. Notable are the powerful distinctions in the painting of the two heads: the warm, excited, passionate head of the painter and the icy marble pallor of the god, counterbalanced in a cool, limpid, spatial ambient. As though entranced, the artist's hands repeat the gestures of the god as though in response to a ritual command. There is, as in De Chirico's earlier metaphysical experiments, the implied presence of another reality and the atmosphere of the dream.

One wonders, if both in pose and theme, De Chirico was thinking of Böcklin's famous self-portrait in which the artist pauses, brush in hand, to listen, as though transfixed in a dream, to the music of Death's violin (figure 229). In De Chirico's self-portrait, the statue of Apollo has replaced the skeleton of Böcklin's *memento mori*. The artist is haunted by the unheard sounds of Apollo's lyre, the music that has called him, like so many poets and dreamers—not to death but to mysterious life—into the classical land, the eternal inner world where the gods are.

— 69 —

Epilogue

Such dim-conceived glories of the brain
Bring round the heart an undescribable feud;
So do these wonders a most dizzy pain,
That mingles Grecian grandeur with the rude
Wasting of old Time—with a billowy main—
A sun—a shadow of a magnitude.
　　　　　—Keats, "On Seeing the Elgin Marbles
　　　　　　　　　　for the First Time"

IN following the transformations that the classical ideal has undergone in many different places and times we can gain an insight into the abstract order that governs art in a universal sense; we can come to identify certain qualities that made this standard of perfection an inevitable choice and an irresistible attraction. In this identification, it is hoped, the reader can begin to discern a norm of judgment that is applicable to works of art of all periods.

The classical ideal is like a dark pool, a mirror that in its magic depths has always revealed in different reflections, clouded or clear, dependent on the capacity of the viewer, the same beckoning mask of beauty set there in the ancient period. The bias of the seeker for this treasure in the depths and the bias of his times change the form he descries there and the image he withdraws from these shapes fixed for eternity. In part, the reflection will be his own.

Why have I written a book on the survival of the classical tradition? It is because I see that tradition as a golden thread running through the whole fabric of Western civilization and its study as a means of seeing our past and our present as one living, organic cultural unity—something that is as much a part of us as our bodies, our speech, and our air, an inheritance on which our spiritual culture and its understanding depend. Perhaps I have always been a *classiciste manqué,* or perhaps classical art is so much a part of me, of my personal as well as racial mythology and tradition, that I feel obliged to return to it, like Antaeus to his earth— perhaps more than all, because the study of classical Greco-Roman art as it began, as it affected all our yesterdays, and as it molds our present, seems a happy home-coming, a casting anchor at last.

Bibliography

General

W. R. Agard, *The Greek Tradition in Sculpture*. Baltimore: Johns Hopkins, 1930.

K. Clark, *The Nude*. New York: Bollingen, 1956.

G. Highet, *The Classical Tradition in Western Literature*. New York: Galaxy, 1957.

H. Ladendorf, *Antikenstudium und Antikenkopie*. Berlin: Akademie, 1958.

—— "The Influence of Greek Ideas and Art in the Western World," Berlin: Akademie, 1958. *The Connoisseur*, 150:44–50 (May 1962).

E. Panofsky, *Renaissance and Renascences in Western Art*. Stockholm: Almquist & Wiksell, 1960.

C. R. Post, *History of European and American Sculpture*. 2 vols., Cambridge, Mass.: Harvard, 1922.

E. Relonge and B. Cichy, *Masterpieces of Figure Painting*. New York: Viking, 1959.

J. Seznec, *The Survival of the Pagan Gods*. New York: Bollingen, 1953.

F. H. Taylor, *The Taste of Angels*. Boston: Little, Brown, 1948.

Chapters 1–2

D. von Bothmer, "The Classical Contribution to Western Civilization," *Bulletin, Metropolitan Museum of Art*, 7:209–215 (1949).

R. Carpenter, *The Esthetic Basis of Greek Art of the Fifth and Fourth Centuries* B.C. Bloomington: Indiana, 1959.

E. Hamilton, *The Greek Way*. New York: W. W. Norton, 1930.

H. Mayor, *The Classical Contribution to Western Civilization*. (Exhibition Catalogue Metropolitan Museum and Art Gallery of Toronto), 1949.

H. J. Muller, *The Uses of the Past*. New York: Oxford, 1952.

The Present-day Vitality of the Classical Tradition. Bloomington: Indiana, 1958.

C. E. Robinson, *Hellas*. Boston: Beacon, 1955.

J. J. Winckelmann, *Gedanken über die Nachahmung der griechische Werke in der Malerei und Bildhauer Kunst*. Dresden, 1755.

—— *Geschichte der Kunst des Altertums*. Dresden, 1764.

—— *History of Ancient Art*. 4 vols., Boston, 1850.

Chapters 3–6

P. E. Corbett, *The Sculpture of the Parthenon*. Harmondsworth: Penguin, 1959.

E. A. Gardner, *A Handbook of Greek Sculpture*. London: Macmillan, 1929.

W. Hege and G. Rodenwaldt, *The Acropolis*. Oxford: B. H. Blackwell, 1957.

W. Hege and G. Rodenwaldt, *Olympia*. New York: B. Westerman, 1936.

F. P. Johnson, *Lysippus*. Durham, N.C.: Duke, 1927.

H. S. Jones, *Select Passages from the Ancient Writers Illustrative of the History of Greek Sculpture*. London and New York: Macmillan, 1895.

G. Karo, *Greek Personality in Archaic Sculpture*. Cambridge, Mass.: Harvard, 1948.

A. W. Lawrence, *Classical Sculpture*. London: J. Cape, 1929.

R. Lullies and M. Hirmer, *Greek Sculpture*. New York: Abrams, 1957.

G. M. A. Richter, *Kouroi, Archaic Greek Youths*. London: Phaidon, 1960.

G. Rodenwaldt, *Die Kunst der Antike, Propylaean-Kunstgeschichte,* vol. III. Berlin: Propylaean, 1927.

N. Yalouris, *Classical Greece. The Elgin Marbles of the Parthenon*. Greenwich, Conn.: New York Graphic Society, 1960.

Chapters 7–8

G. W. Batsford and C. A. Robinson, *Hellenic History*. New York: Macmillan, 1939.

M. Bieber, *Laocoön: The Influence of the Group since its Rediscovery*. New York: Columbia, 1942.

—— *The Sculpture of the Hellenistic Age*. New York: Columbia, 1954.

E. Hamilton, *The Echo of Greece*. New York: W. W. Norton, 1957.

E. Langenskiöld, "Torso Belvedere," *Acta Archaeologica,* 1:121–146 (1930).

A. W. Lawrence, *Later Greek Sculpture*. New York: Harcourt, Brace, 1934.

E. Löwy, "Zur Geschichte des Torso von Belvedere," *Zeitschrift für bildende Kunst,* 23:21–84 (1888).

A. Michaelis, "Die älteste Kunde von der Mediceischen Venus," *Zeitschrift für bildende Kunst,* 25:287–301 (1889–90).

W. Muller, "Zur schlafenden Ariadne des Vaticans," Deutsches Archäologisches Institut, *Römische Mitteilungen,* Rome, 53:164–174 (1938).

H. E. Stier, *Aus der Welt des Pergamonaltars*. Berlin: Heinrick Keller, 1932.

Chapter 9

A. Maiuri, *Roman Painting*. New York: Skira, 1953.

E. Pfuhl, *Masterpieces of Greek Drawing and Painting*. London: Chatto and Windus, 1955.

M. Swindler, *Ancient Painting*. New Haven: Yale, 1929.

Chapter 10

R. H. Barrow, *The Romans*. Harmondsworth: Penguin, 1949.

Curtius-Nawrath, *Das Antike Rom*. 3rd ed., Vienna and Munich: Anton Schroll, 1957.

E. Gibbon, *The Decline and Fall of the Roman Empire*. 6 vols., New York: Harper, n.d.

L. Goldscheider, *Roman Portraits*. New York: Phaidon, 1940.

M. Hadas, *A History of Rome*. New York: Anchor, 1956.

E. Hamilton, *The Roman Way*. New York: W. W. Norton, 1932.

H. B. Walters, *The Art of the Romans*. London: Methuen, 1928.

Chapters 11–13

Augustan Art. New York: Metropolitan Museum of Art, 1938.

A. Kühler, *Die Augustusstatue von Primaporta*. Cologne, 1959.

G. Marchetti-Longhi, *La Memoria di Augusto e dei suoi monumenti nel Medioevo*. Rome: Instituto di studi romani, 1939.

I. Montini, *Il ritratto di Augusto, mostra augustea della romanita*. Rome, 1938.

G. Rodenwaldt, *Kunst um Augustus*. Berlin: W. deGruyter, 1945.

D. E. Strong, *Roman Imperial Art*. London: Tiranti, 1961.

E. Strong, *Roman Sculpture from Augustus to Constantine*. New York: Scribner's, 1907.

J. M. Toynbee, *The Hadrianic School*. Cambridge: Cambridge, 1934.

Chapters 14–17

D. V. Ainalov, *The Hellenistic Origins of Byzantine Art*. New Brunswick, N.J.: Rutgers, 1961.

B. Berenson, *The Arch of Constantine or the Decline of Form*. New York: Macmillan, 1954.

H. Buchthal, *The Miniatures of the Paris Psalter*. London: Warburg Institute, 1938.

J. Burckhardt, *The Age of Constantine the Great*. New York: Anchor, 1956.

R. Delbrück, *Die Consulardiptychen und verwandte Dekmäler*. Berlin and Leipzig: W. deGruyter, 1929.

—— *Denkmäler spätantiker Kunst*. Berlin: Archäologisches Institut, 1931.

—— *Spätantike Kaiserporträts von Constantius Magnus bis zum Ende des Westreiches*. Berlin and Leipzig: W. deGruyter, 1933.

F. Gerke, *Christus in der spätantiken Plastik*. Berlin: F. Kupferberg, 1940.

J. Kollwitz, *Oströmische Plastik der Theodosianischen Zeit*. Berlin: W. deGruyter, 1941.

P. Muratoff, *La pittura bizantina*. Rome: Casa Editrice d'arte "Valori Plastici," n.d.

H. P. L'Orange, *Apotheosis in Ancient Portraiture*. Cambridge, Mass.: Harvard, 1947.

H. Peirce and R. Tyler, *L'Art byzantin*, vol. I. Paris: Librairie de France, 1932.

D. T. Rice, *Byzantine Art*. Harmondsworth: Penguin, 1954.

—— *The Great Palace of the Byzantine Emperors*, 2nd report. Edinburgh: University, 1958.

—— and M. Hirmer, *The Art of Byzantium*. London: Abrams, 1959.

A. Sambon, "L'Hercule Anteportanus de la Basilique de Saint-Marc à Venise," *Le Musée*, 8 (1925–32).

O. G. von Simson, *Sacred Fortress*. Chicago: Chicago, 1948.

W. F. Volbach, *Early Christian Art*. New York: Abrams, 1962.

K. Weitzmann, *Greek Mythology in Byzantine Art*. Princeton: Princeton, 1931.

Chapters 18–20

A. Freeman, "Theodulf of Orléans and the Libri Carolini," *Speculum,* 32:663 (October 1957).

A. Goldschmidt, *Die Elfenbeinskulpturen,* vols. I–IV. Berlin: B. Cassirer, 1914–1926.

A. E. G. Haseloff, *Pre-Romanesque Sculpture in Italy.* New York: Harcourt, Brace, 1931.

W. J. Heckscher, "Relics of Pagan Antiquity in Christian Settings," *Journal of the Warburg and Courtauld Institutes,* 1:204 (1937).

R. Hinks, *Carolingian Art.* London: Sidgwick & Jackson, 1935.

E. Kitzinger, *Early Medieval Art.* London: British Museum, 1940.

W. R. W. Koehler, *Die Karolingischen Miniaturen.* 3 vols., Berlin: B. Cassirer, 1930–1960.

W. Oakeshott, *Classical Inspiration in Medieval Art.* London: Chapman & Hall. 1959.

E. Panofsky, "Renaissance and Renascences," *Meaning in the Visual Arts.* Garden City, N.Y.: Anchor, 1955.

G. B. Parks, *The English Travellers in Italy.* Stanford: Stanford, 1954.

E. Patzelt, *Die Karolingische Renaissance.* Vienna: Österreicher Schulbücher, 1924.

G. M. Rushforth, "Magister Gregorius De Mirabilibus Urbis Romae," *Journal of Roman Studies,* 9:14–58 (1919).

Chapters 21–22

J. Adhémar, *Influences antiques dans l'art du moyen âge français.* London: Warburg Institute, 1939.

E. Battisti, "Simbolo e classicismo," *Umanesimo e simbolismo, Atti del IV convegno internazionale di studi umanestici.* Padua, 1958.

F. von Bezold, *Die Fortleben der antiken Götter im mittelalterlichen Humanismus.* Bonn and Leipzig: K. Schroeder, 1922.

A. Goldschmidt, "Das Nachleben der antiken Formen im Mittelalter," *Vorträge der Bibliothek-Warburg, 1921–22.* Leipzig and Berlin, 1923, pp. 40–50.

H. R. Hahnloser, *Villard de Honnecourt.* Vienna: A. Schroll, 1935.

R. Hamann, *Die Abteikirche von Saint-Gilles.* Berlin: Akademie, 1955.

R. H. L. Hamann-Mac-Lean, "Antiken Studium in der Kunst des Mittelalters," *Marburger Jahrbuch fur Kunstwissenschaft,* 5:157–250 (1949–50).

R. Jullian, *L'éveil de la sculpture italienne.* Paris: Van Oest, 1945.

—— "Les survivances antiques dans la sculpture Lombarde," *Études Italiennes.* 1932, pp. 131–140.

Chapter 23

E. Kantorowicz, *Frederick the Second.* New York: Ungar, 1957.

G. von Kaschnitz-Weinberg, "Bildnisse Friedrichs II von Hohenstaufen, 1, Der

Kolossalkopf aus Lanuvium," Deutsches Archäologisches Institut, *Römische Mitteilungen*, Rome, 60–61:2–21 (1955).

G. Masson, *Frederick II of Hohenstaufen*. London: Secker & Warburg, 1957.

C. A. Willemsen, *Kaiser Friedrich II Triumphtor zu Capua*. Wiesbaden: Insel, 1953.

Chapters 24–25

A. Bush-Brown, "Giotto: Two Problems in the Origin of his Style," *The Art Bulletin*, 34:42 (March 1952).

E. Cecchi, *The Sienese Painters of the Trecento*. New York and London: Frederick Warne, 1931.

G. H. and E. R. Crichton, *Nicola Pisano*. Cambridge: Cambridge, 1938.

G. N. Fasola, *Nicola Pisano*. Rome: Filli Palombi, 1941.

F. J. Mather, *A History of Italian Painting*. New York: Henry Holt. 1923.

J. Pope-Hennessy, *Italian Gothic Sculpture*. London: Victoria & Albert Museum, 1955.

N. Rubenstein, "Political Ideas in Sienese Art," *Journal of the Warburg and Courtauld Institutes*, 21:179–207 (1958).

G. Swarzenski, *Nicola Pisano*. Frankfurt: Iris, 1926.

Chapters 26–33

J. Burckhardt, *The Civilization of the Renaissance in Italy*. 2 vols., New York: Harper, 1958.

K. Clark, *Piero della Francesca*. New York: Phaidon, 1951.

B. Degenhart and A. Schmitt, "Gentile da Fabriano in Rom und die Anfänge des Antikens Studium," *Münchener Jahrbuch der bildender Kunst,* third series, 11:59–151 (1960).

L. Ghiberti, *I Commentarii*, ed. J. von Schlosser. Berlin: J. Bard, 1912.

E. M. Gombrich, "Botticelli's Mythology," *Journal of the Warburg and Courtauld Institutes*, 8:7–60 (1945).

P. G. Hübner, "Studien über die Benutzung der Antike in der Renaissance," *Monatshefte für Kunstgeschichte*, 2:6 (1909).

H. W. Janson, *The Sculpture of Donatello*. Princeton: Princeton, 1957.

R. Krautheimer and T. Krautheimer-Hess, *Lorenzo Ghiberti*. Princeton: Princeton, 1956.

J. Mesnil, "Masaccio and the Antique," *Burlington Magazine*, 48:91–98 (1926).

L. Planiscig, *Die Italienischen Bronzestatuetten der Renaissance*. Vienna: Anton Schroll, 1925.

J. Pope-Hennessy, *Italian Renaissance Sculpture*. London: Phaidon, 1958.

A. von Salis, *Antike und Renaissance*. Erlenbach-Zurich: Eugen Rentsch, 1947.

P. Saxl, *Classical Antiquity in Renaissance Painting*. London: National Gallery, 1938.

M. Simon, *Hercule et le Christianisme*. Strasbourg: University, 1955.

A. Warburg, *Sandro Botticellis Geburt der Venus und Frühling*. Hamburg, 1892.

E. Wind. *Pagan Mysteries in the Renaissance*. New Haven: Yale, 1958.

Chapters 34–38

O. J. Brendel, "Borrowings from Ancient Art in Titian," *The Art Bulletin,* 37:113–125 (1955).

R. J. Clements, *Michelangelo's Theory of Art.* New York: New York University, 1961.

L. Dolce, *Dialogo della pittura intitolato l'Aretino.* Venice, 1557.

O. Fischel, *Raphael.* 2 vols., London: Kegan Paul, 1948.

S. J. Freedberg, *Painting of the High Renaissance in Rome and Florence.* 2 vols., Cambridge, Mass.: Harvard, 1961.

L. Goldscheider, *The Paintings of Michelangelo.* New York: Phaidon, 1940.

—— *The Sculptures of Michelangelo.* New York: Phaidon, 1940.

P. G. Hübner, "Raffael und die Sammlung Grimani," *Monatshefte für Kunstwissenschaft,* 2:273–280 (1909).

G. Kleiner, *Die Begegnungen Michelangelos mit der Antike.* Berlin: Gebr. Mann, 1950.

K. Lanckoronska, "Antike Elemente im Bacchus Michelangelos und in Seiner Darstellungen des David," *Dawne Sztuka Rocznik,* Lwow, 1:3 (1938).

R. Lomazzo, *Trattato dell'arte della pittura scultura ed architertura.* Rome, 1844.

A. Pope, *Titian's Rape of Europa.* Cambridge, Mass.: Harvard, 1960.

W. E. Suida, *Raphael.* New York: Phaidon, 1941.

J. A. Symonds, *The Life of Michelangelo Buonarroti.* 2 vols., New York: Scribner's, 1925.

C. de Tolnay, *Michelangelo.* 5 vols., Princeton: Princeton, 1943–1960.

H. Weizsäcker, "Der David Michelangelos in seinen Beziehungen zur Antike," *Jahrbuch der Preussischen Kunstsammlungen,* 61:163–172 (1940).

—— "Raphaels Galatea im Lichte der antiken Uberlieferung," *Die Antike,* 14:231–242 (1938).

Chapters 39–44

G. B. Armenini, *De' veri precetti della pittura.* Ravenna, 1586.

A. Blunt, *Artistic Theory in Italy, 1450–1600.* Oxford: Clarendon, 1940.

P. B. Bober, *Drawings after the Antique by Amico Aspertini.* London: Warburg Institute, 1957.

G. Briganti, *Il manierismo e Pellegrine Tibaldi.* Rome: Cosmopolita, 1945.

—— *La Maniera italiana.* Rome: Riuniti, 1962.

E. Camesasca, *Tutta l'opera del Cellini.* Milan: Rizzoti, 1955.

B. Cellini, *The Autobiography of Benvenuto Cellini,* tr. J. A. Symonds. New York: Modern Library, 1927.

A. Emiliani, *Il Bronzino.* Busto Arsizio, 1960.

S. J. Freedberg, *Parmigianino.* Cambridge, Mass.: Harvard, 1950.

C. Huelsa, *Das Speculum Romanae Magnificentiae des Antonio Lafreri.* Munich, 1921.

F. Kriegbaum, "Marmi di Benvenuto Cellini ritrovati," *L'Arte,* n.s. 11:3–25 (January 1940).

L. Megugliani, *L'Hypnos ed il Cellini.* Milan, 1955.

B. Schweitzer, "Zum Antikenstudium des Angelo Bronzino," Deutsches Archäologisches Institut, *Römische Mitteilungen,* Rome, 33:45–63 (1918).

E. Tormo y Monzo, *Os Desenhos das Antiqualhas que vio Francisco d'Ollanda, pintor portuguès.* Madrid, 1940.

Chapters 45–55

G. Baglione, *Le vite de' pittori, scultori, architteti, ed intagliatori.* Naples, 1733.

G. P. Bellori, *Le vite de' pittori, scultori, ed architett i moderni.* Rome, 1642.

A. Blunt, *Art and Architecture in France, 1500 to 1700.* Harmondsworth: Pelican, 1953.

S. F. Emmerling, *Antiken verwendung und Antiken Studium bei Nikolas Poussin.* Würzburg: Triltsch, 1939.

P. Francastel, *Girardon.* Paris: Beaux-arts, 1928.

C. A. du Fresnoy, *De arte graphica. The Art of Painting.* London, 1695.

E. Keiser, "Antikes im Werke des Rubens," *Münchener Jahrbuch der Bildende Kunst,* n.s. 10:110–137 (1933).

K. Lankheit, "Eine Serie barocker Antiken—Nachbildungen des Messimiliano Soldani," Deutsches Archäologisches Institut, *Römische Mitteilungen,* Rome, 65:186–198 (1958).

R. Lee, "Ut Pictura Poesis: The Humanistic Theory of Painting," *The Art Bulletin,* 22:205 (1940).

G. P. Lomazzo, *Trattato dell'arte de la pittura.* Milan, 1584.

D. Mahon, *Studies in Seicento Art and Theory.* London: Warburg Institute, 1947.

A. Muñez, "La scultura barocca e l'antico," *L'Arte,* 19:129–160 (August 1916).

E. Panofsky, "Et in Arcadia Ego," *Meaning in the Visual Arts.* New York: Anchor, 1955, pp. 295–320.

R. de Piles, *The Art of Painting and the Lives of the Painters.* London, 1706.

—— *Cours de Peinture par Principes.* Paris, 1708.

Fr. G. von Ravensburg, *Rubens und die Antike.* Jena, 1882.

J. Reynolds, *Discourses on Art.* New York: Collier, 1961.

A. Roserot, *Edmé Bouchardon.* Paris: E. Lévy, 1910.

H. Tietze, "Annibale Carracis Galerie im Palazzo Farnese," *Jahrbuch der Kunstsammlungen, Wien,* 26:49–182 (1906–7).

R. Wittkower, *Art and Architecture in Italy, 1600–1750.* Harmondsworth: Pelican, 1958.

Chapters 56–60

Contessa I. Albrizzi, *The Works of Antonio Canova.* 3 vols., London, 1849.

Conte L. Cicognara, *Biographia di Antonio Canova.* Venice, 1823.

E. J. Delécluze, *Louis David, son école et son temps.* Paris, 1855.

E. Everett, "Canova and his Work," *The North American Review*, n.s. 27:372–386 (April 1820).

L. Hautecoeur, *Louis David*. Paris: Table ronde, 1954.

—— *Rome et la Renaissance de l'Antiquité à la fin du 18e Siècle*. Paris: Fontemoing, 1912.

H. Honour, "Bronze Statuettes by Giacomo and Giovanni Zoffoli," *The Connoisseur*, pp. 198–205 (November 1961).

S. Larrabee, *English Bards and Grecian Marbles*. New York: Columbia, 1943.

H. T. Parker, *The Cult of Antiquity and the French Revolutionaries*. Chicago: Chicago, 1957.

M. Praz, *Gusto neoclassico*. 2nd ed., Naples: Scientifiche italiane, n.d.

—— "Herculaneum and European Taste," *Magazine of Art*, 32:684–693 (1939).

R. Rosenblum, "A New Source for David's Sabines," *Burlington Magazine*, pp. 158ff. (April 1962).

—— "Gavin Hamilton's 'Brutus' and its aftermath," *Burlington Magazine*, pp. 15ff. (January 1961).

R. Schapire, "Der Apoll von Belvedere und seine Nachbildungen im 19 Jahrhundert," *Monatsberichte fur Kunstwissenschaft und Kunsthandel*, 2:323–326 (1902).

Chapters 61–69

B. d'Agen, *Ingres, dessinateur des antiques*. Paris: Delagrave, 1926.

A. H. Barr, Jr., *Picasso: Forty Years of his Art*. New York: Museum of Modern Art, 1939.

E. M. Butler, *The Tyranny of Greece over Germany*. Boston: Beacon, 1958.

J. Cassou, *Picasso*. New York: Hyperion, 1940.

J. Cladel, *Aristide Maillol*. Paris: H. Grosset, 1937.

"Classical Order for Today's Chaos," *Art News*, 48:17–24 (December 1948).

A. T. Gardner, *Yankee Stonecutters*. New York: Columbia, 1945.

W. Grohmann, *Henry Moore*. Berlin: Rembrandt, 1960.

B. Hackelsberger, *Aristide Maillol: la Méditerranée*. Stuttgart: Philipp Reclam Jun., 1960.

O. Larkin, *Art and Life in America*. New York: Holt, Rinehart and Winston, 1960.

S. Larrabee, *Hellas Observed. The American Experience in Greece*. New York: New York University, 1957.

A. Mongan, "Ingres and the Antique," *Journal of the Warburg and Courtauld Institutes*, 10:8–9 (1947).

A. Pica, *Dodici opere di Giorgio de Chirico*. Milan: Milione, 1947.

A. C. Quatremère de Quincy, *An Essay on the Nature and Means of Imitation in the Fine Arts*, trans. C. Kent. London, 1837.

—— *Le Jupiter olympien*. Paris, 1815.

H. Read, *Henry Moore*. 2 vols., London: Lund, Humphries, 1949–1955.

J. Rewald, *Maillol*. New York: Hyperion, 1939.

BIBLIOGRAPHY

J. Richardson, *Pablo Picasso*. Basel: Holbein, 1956.

A. Rodin, *Art*. Boston: Small, Maynard, 1912.

―――― *Venus*. New York: B. W. Huebsch, 1912.

A. von Salis, "Arnold Bocklin und die Antike," *Basler Jahrbuch*, 83–119 (1935).

N. Schlenoff, *Ingres: Ses Sources littéraires*. Paris: Presses Universitaires, 1956.

M. Schoonmaker, *John Vanderlyn*. Kingston, N.Y.: Senate House Association, 1950.

J. T. Soby, *Giorgio de Chirico*. New York: Museum of Modern Art, 1955.

H. Trevelyan, *Goethe and the Greeks*. Cambridge: Cambridge, 1941.

W. Wegener, *Goethes Anschauung antiker Kunst*. Berlin: Gebrüder Mann, 1944.

Notes

Chapter 1. Introduction

1. Johann J. Winckelmann, "Thoughts on the Imitation of Greek Art in Painting and Sculpture" (1755) in E. G. Holt, *Literary Sources of Art History* (Princeton, 1947), p. 524.
2. John Keats, "On Seeing the Elgin Marbles for the First Time," l. 14.
3. Winckelmann, "Imitation of Greek Art," p. 523.
4. *Ibid.,* p. 532.

Chapter 2. The Greek Ideal

1. Anaxagoras, Fragment 6.
2. Sophocles, *Antigone* in Gilbert Murray, *Ten Greek Plays* (New York, 1929), p. 61.
3. Heraclitus of Ephesus, Fragment 8.
4. Homer, *Iliad,* XVIII. 478 ff.

Chapter 3. The Archaic Period

1. Diodorus of Sicily, I. 98. 5–9.
2. G. Karo, *Greek Personality in Archaic Sculpture* (Cambridge, Mass., 1948), p. 104.

Chapter 5. The Great Period

1. "Il y a eu sur le globe un petit coin de terre qui s'appelait la Grèce, où, sous le plus beau ciel . . . les lettres et les beaux arts ont repandu sur les choses de la nature comme une seconde lumière, pour tous les peuples et pour toûtes les générations à venir." P. Courthion, ed., *Ingres, Pensées et écrits du peintre* (Vésenaz-Geneva, 1947), p. 85.
2. For an explanation of Polyclitus' canon as an application of the Golden Section, see Donald Edward Gordon and Francis de L. Cunningham, "Polykleitos' 'Diadoumenos': Measurement and Animation," *The Art Quarterly,* 25:128 ff. (Summer 1962).
3. Galen, *De placitis Hippocratis et Platonis,* 5.
4. Strabo, *Geography,* VIII. 353.
5. Pausanias, X. 12. 10.
6. Benjamin Robert Haydon, *Autobiography and Memoir,* ed. Tom Taylor, 2 vols. (New York, n.d.), I, 66–67.

Chapter 6. The Fourth Century: Praxiteles, Lysippus, Scopas

1. *The Greek Anthology* was originally a collection of fugitive, epigrammatic poetry compiled by Meleager of Gadara in 60 B.C. In its final form it came to

include many later additions collected by one Constantinus Cephalus in the tenth century.

2. Diodorus, XXVI.
3. Sappho, 71.
4. Sappho, 2.

Chapter 8. A Gallery of Masterpieces

1. G. N. G. Byron, *Childe Harold,* Canto 4, xlix, 1–2; liii, 8–9.
2. Qual arte estrema il cielo in te constrinse
   Scultor fra tutti gli altri 'l più perfetto
   E con quel bel color tua destra tinse
   Questo corpo, ch'abbaglia ogni intelletto?
   Et de quel lembo 'l ciel tua membra cinse,
   Che sei d'ogni sua gratia ampio ricetto?
   Ch'io so costretto da lo stil tuo divo,
   Questo lodar, come se fusse vivo?
      Devrialo d'Ascoli, *Sopra la statua di Laocoönte, di Venere, et d'Apollo* (Rome, 1539).
3. Johann J. Winckelmann, *The History of Ancient Art,* 2 vols. (Boston, 1856), II, 212.
4. "Io non ho mai ritrovato che alcuno che abbia seguito l'orma o l'esempio d'un altro, lo abbia potuto agguagliare, non che avvanzare. Michelangelo ne fa fede, il quale non è mai potuto aggiungere alla bellezza del torso di Ercole (di) Apollonio ateniese che si trova in Belvedere in Roma, che fu da lui continuamente seguitato." G. P. Lomazzo, *Trattato dell'arte della pittura, scoltura, et architettura* (Milan, 1585), II, ch. 1.
5. Philostratus, *Imagines,* I. 15.
6. "Laocoonte qui est in Titi imperatoris domo, opus omnibus et picturae et statuariae artis preferendum. Ex uno lapide eum ac draconumque mirabiles nexus . . . fecere summi artifices Agesander et Polydorus et Athenodorus Rhodii." Pliny, *Natural History,* XXIV. 37.

Chapter 9. Painting in the Ancient World

1. Ernest Pfuhl, *Masterpieces of Greek Drawing and Painting* (New York, 1926), pp. 106–107.
2. Philostratus, *Imagines,* I. 15.
3. Pliny, *Natural History,* XXXV. 120.

Chapter 10. Rome and Roman Art

1. Quoted by H. J. Muller, *The Uses of the Past* (New York, 1957), p. 205.
2. "Tot aquarum pyramides videlicet otiosas compares aut certa inertia set fame celebrata opera Graecorum." Sextius Julius Frontinus, *De Aquis Urbis Romae,* I, 16.
3. Quoted by Muller, *Uses of the Past,* p. 210.

Chapter 11. Augustus

1. *Res Gestae Divi Augusti,* tr. and ed. F. W. Shipley (New York and London, 1924), p. 365.

Chapter 13. Originals and Roman Copies

1. Gisela M. Richter, *Sculpture and Sculptors of the Greeks* (New Haven, 1930), figs. 394–396.

Chapter 14. The Late Antique Period

1. Palladas of Alexandria in *The Greek Anthology.*

Chapter 18. The Barbarian Period

1. Paulus Diaconus, *Historia gentis Langobardorum,* II, 31.

Chapter 19. The Carolingian Renaissance

1. Bishop Theodulf of Orléans, *Ad Iudices.* Cf. Ann Freeman, "Theodulf of Orléans and the *Libri Carolini,*" *Speculum,* 32:695–697 (October 1957).
2. Erwin Panofsky and Fritz Saxl, "Classical Mythology in Mediaeval Art," *Metropolitan Museum Studies* (New York, 1932–33), IV, 274. See also Erwin Panofsky, "Renaissance and Renascences," *The Kenyon Review,* 6:212; *Meaning in the Visual Arts* (New York, 1955), pp. 49–50.

Chapter 20. The Late Middle Ages and Classical Antiquity

1. F. M. Nichols, ed., *Mirabilia Urbis Romae (The Marvels of Rome)* (London, 1889).
2. *Ibid.,* p. 117.
3. G. B. Parks, *The English Traveler in Italy* (Stanford, 1954), p. 261. See also G. M. Rushforth, "Magister Gregorius de Mirabilibus urbis Romae," *Journal of Roman Studies,* 9:14–58 (1919).
4. His superum formas superi mirantur et ipsi
   Et cupiunt fictis vultibus esse pares.
   Non potuit natura deos hoc ore creare
   Quo miranda deum signa creavit homo,
   Vultus adest his numinibus, potius coluntur
   Artificum studio quam deitate sua.

   B. Hauréau, *Les Mélanges poétiques d'Hildebert de Lavardin* (Paris, 1882), p. 61.
5. *Ibid.*

Chapter 21. Classical Forms in the Romanesque Period

1. M. Collignon, *Histoire de la Sculpture Grecque* (Paris, 1892), fig. 119.
2. See Figure 67.
3. Erwin Panofsky, *Renaissance and Renascences in Western Art* (Stockholm, 1960), pp. 94–95.

Chapter 24. Nicola Pisano

1. Dante Alighieri, *The Inferno,* IX, 97.

Chapter 25. Classical Forms in Fourteenth-Century Italy

1. Alcuin, *The Marvels of Ancient Rome,* trans. M. Scherer (New York, 1955), p. 3.
2. Fazio degli Uberti, "Dittamondo," in Scherer, *Marvels of Ancient Rome,* p. 6.
3. Canto I, l. 85.
4. E sol ad una immagine m'attegno, / Che fe' non Zeusi, Prasitele o Fidia, / Ma miglior mastro e di più alto ingegno. (Petrarch, Sonnet C.)
5. Mantua Virgilium qui talia carmina finxit / Sena tulit Symonem digito qui talia pinxit.
6. L. Ghiberti, *I Commentarii,* ed. Julius Schlosser (Berlin, 1912), III, 4.

Chapter 26. The Renaissance in Italy

1. Cf. R. Krautheimer, *Lorenzo Ghiberti* (Princeton, 1956), pp. 293–296.
2. Muller, *Uses of the Past,* p. 266.
3. See Chapter 20, note 3.
4. Krautheimer, *Ghiberti,* p. 303.

Chapter 28. Venus Reborn

1. B. Berenson, *The Florentine Painters of the Renaissance,* rev. ed. (New York, 1909), p. 27.
2. Giorgio Vasari, *The Lives of the Most Eminent Painters, Sculptors, and Architects* tr. and ed. J. Foster (London, 1851), I, 402. "Egli desse principio alle belle attitudini, movenze, fierezza, e vivacità, ed un certo rilievo veramente proprio e naturale . . . le cose fatte innanzi a lui si possano chiamar dipinte, e le sue vive, veraci, e naturali, allato a quelle state fatte dagli altri." Vasari, *Le Vite* (Florence, 1878), II, 288.

Chapter 31. Donatello

1. Vasari, *Lives,* I, 477.

Chapter 32. The Labors of Hercules

1. "Toute pechié vainquit et toute vice, tout errour et toute malice." *Ovidius Moralizatus,* IX, ll. 989 f. in C. de Boer, *"Ovide Moralisé," Verkandelugen der Köninklike Akademie van Wetenschaffen,* new series, 30.

Chapter 33. Mantegna

1. Vasari, *Lives,* II, 265. ". . . che non erano cosa buona, perchè aveva nel farle imitato le cose di marmo antiche, dalle quali non si può imparare la pittura perfettamente; perciocchè i sassi hanno sempre la durezza con esso loro, e non mai quella tenera dolcezza che hanno le carni e le cose naturali, che si piegano e fanno diversi movimenti; aggiugnendo che Andrea avrebbe fatto molto meglio

quelle figure, e sarebbono state più perfette, se avesse fattole di color di marmo, e non di que'tanti colori; perciocchè non avevano quelle pitture somiglianza di vivi, ma di statue antiche di marmo." Vasari, *Le Vite*, III, 389.

2. Vasari, *Lives*, II, 266. ". . . la quale di rado in un corpo solo accozza ed accompagna insieme tutta la bellezza; onde è necessario pigliarne da uno una parte e da altro un'altra: ed oltre a questo, gli parevano le statue più terminate e più tocche in su' muscoli, vene, nervi ed altre particelle, le quali il naturale, coprendo con la tenerezza e morbidezza della carne certe crudezze, mostra talvolta meno." Vasari, *Le Vite*, III, 290.

Chapter 35. Raphael's Galatea

1. Raphael painted the Galatea in 1514 for the Sienese merchant Agostino Chigi. It is part of a mythological cycle designed by Raphael but executed largely by his pupils Giulio Romano, Giovanni Francesco Penni, and Giovanni da Udine.
2. Jakob Burckhardt, *Der Cicerone*, 10th ed. (Leipzig, 1910), III, 877.
3. He could have seen a small version of this statue in the Grimani Collection now in the Museo Archaeologico, Venice. For Raphael and his relation to the Grimani marbles, see P. G. Hübner, "Raffael und die Sammlung Grimani," *Monatshefte für Kunstwissenschafft*, 2:273–280 (1909).
4. There are so many possible sources available to Raphael that it is unwise to try to pin the concept to a single literary source. Philostratus' description may have served him, and there are suggestions of the playful Thiasos depicted by Colonna in the *Hypnerotomachia*. Raphael's treatment of Galatea's hair as a compact mass rather than as individual strands may be as much an illustration of the High Renaissance sculptural mode of expression as a translation of Philostratus' description: "Her hair is not tossed by the breeze, for it is so moist that it is proof against the wind." Philostratus the Elder, *Imagines*, Loeb ed. (London and New York, 1931), II, 215.
5. "Per dipingere una bella mi bisognerebbe vedere più belle, ma per essere carestia di belle donne, io mi seruo di una certa Idea, che mi viene in Mente." Translated by Holt, *Literary Sources*, p. 322, n. 6.
6. "Idea del pittore e dello scultore è quel perfetto ed eccellente esempio della mente, alla 'cui immaginata forma imitando, si rassomigliano le cose, che cadono sotto la vista." G. P. Bellori, *Vite dei pittori, scultori, ed architetti moderni* (Pisa, 1821), I, 8.
7. *Ibid.*, p. 16; translated by Holt, *Literary Sources*, p. 327.
8. L. Dolce, *Dialogo della pittura intitolato l'Aretino* (Florence, 1735), p. 190; first published in Venice in 1557.

Chapter 36. Francesco Penni and the Statuary Style

1. The sixteenth-century painter Federigo Zuccaro explains *disegno interno* as "the concept formed in our mind which enables us to apprehend any object and to do practical work in accordance with this concept." It is an a priori concept in the mind which, in the process of transferring it to paint or marble, is

to be clarified by reference to models in the world of reality, which would include the antique. Cf. Holt, *Literary Sources*, p. 270.

Chapter 37. Michelangelo

1. "According to the general rule which teacheth; that so much of that parte must be added, as is lost by the distance of the place; that so the picture may come to the eie in his due proportion. Which rule Phidias and Praxiteles observed, in those statues in Monte Cavallo in Rome, which Michael Angelo measuring, found their faces to be so much bigger, as they lost by standing in so high a place: from whence the eie judgeth of them as most proportionable." Jo. Paul Lomatius, *A Tracte containing the Artes of Curious Paintinge Caruing Building.* Englished by R(ichard). H(aycocke). (Oxford, 1958), p. 22.

    "Perchè la regola generale è che tanto s'habbia d'aggiungere a quelle parte, quanto gli toglie la distanza del luogo che così la figura viene poi proporionata a l'occhio. Il che si vede ch'osservarono Prasitele e Fidia in quelle statue che sono a Montecavallo in Roma lequali misurò Michel Angelo, & trouò che le faccie loro sono tanto più grandi quanto perdono per essere in luogo così alto, & per questo appaiono a l'occhio proportionassime." Lomazzo, *Trattato dell'arte,* I, 29–30.

2. Charles de Tolnay, *Michelangelo: The Sistine Ceiling* (Princeton, 1945), II, 63–64, 65.

3. M. Bieber, *Sculpture of the Hellenistic Age* (New York, 1955), figure 260.

4. J. A. Symonds, *The Life of Michelangelo Buonarroti* (New York, 1893), II. 36.

Chapter 38. Titian

1. R. Goldwater and M. Treves, *Artists on Art* (New York, 1945), p. 127.

2. Alexander Gilchrist, *Life of William Blake* (London, 1863), II, 149.

3. I am indebted to the excellent article on Titian and the antique by Dr. Otto J. Brendel. The reader is referred to this source for further information and bibliography: "Borrowings from ancient art by Titian," *The Art Bulletin*, 37:235–238 (June 1955).

Chapter 39. Mannerism

1. Baldassare Castiglione, *The Book of the Courtier,* Done into English by Sir Thomas Hoby, 1561 (London and New York: Everyman's Library, n.d.), p. 43.

2. Vasari, *Lives*, II, 360–361.

3. Lomazzo, *Trattato dell'arte* in Holt, *Literary Sources*, p. 260.

Chapter 41. Bronzino's Allegory of Luxury

1. "E parte si debbono imitar le belle figure di marmo o di bronzo antichi. La mirabile perfezione delle quale chi gusterà e possederà a pieno, potrà sicuramente corregger molti difetti di essa natura, e far le sue pitture riguardevoli e grate a ciascuno: perciocchè le cose antiche contengono tutta la perfetion

dell'arte, e possono essere esemplari di tutto il bello." L. Dolce, *Dialogo delle Pittura intitolato l'Aretino* (Florence, 1735), p. 190.

2. "Che i pittori cavino spesso le loro invenzioni dai poeti, ed i poeti dai pittori." L. Dolce, *Dialogo delle Pittura intitolato l'Aretino* (Milan, 1863), p. 53.

3. Vasari explains that this picture was presented by Duke Cosimo dei Medici to Francis I (*Vite,* VII, 598).

4. John Donne, "Elegy XIX."

Chapter 42. Benvenuto Cellini's Narcissus

1. Prior to its discovery some years ago, this statue stood weathered and broken in the Boboli Gardens. Fr. Kriegbaum, "Marmi di Benvenuto Cellini ritrovati," *L'Arte,* n.s. 11 (January 1940).

Chapter 43. Replicas in Bronze

1. A drawing by G. A. da Brescia, dated about 1515, shows the Torso with both legs and the chest still intact. H. Ladendorf, *Antikenstudium und Antikenkopie* (Berlin, 1958), XX, 74.

2. Winckelmann, *History,* II, 265.

3. Andrea Emiliani, *Il Bronzino* (Busto Arsizio, 1960), plates 73, 77.

4. ". . . serie di Figure fatte e da farsi dell'altezza di un palmo e mezzo bono Romano." Hugh Honour, "Bronze Statuettes by Giacomo and Giovanni Zoffoli," *The Connoisseur* (November 1961), p. 202.

Chapter 44. Montecavallo

1. Antonio Lafreri (or Antoine Lafréry), 1512–1577, was the head of a workshop of engravers and etchers that turned out scores of prints illustrating the famous monuments of Rome. Lafreri himself signed many of these plates as early as the 1540's. Others, sometimes with the plate completely reworked, have the signatures of later managers such as Ducheti with dates in the eighties of the Cinquecento. Although a few supposedly complete copies of Lafreri's work exist, no two are alike in content. The general title is *Speculum Romanae Magnificentiae.* The best of the drawings for the prints were done by Nicolaus Beatrizet between 1548 and 1553.

Chapter 45. The Renaissance in France

1. E. and D. Panofsky, "Iconography of the Galerie François Premier at Fontainebleau," *Gazette des Beaux-Arts* (September 1958), p. 160.

Chapter 46. Albrecht Dürer

1. Erwin Panofsky, "Albrecht Dürer and Classical Art," *Meaning in the Visual Arts* (New York, 1955), pp. 237 ff.

Chapter 48. The Baroque

1. "Il faut qu'il regarde L'Antique comme un Livre qu'on traduit dans une autre langue, dans laquelle il suffit de bien rapporter le sens et l'esprit, sans s'attacher

servilement aux paroles de l'original." Roger de Piles, *Abrégé de la vie des peintres* (Paris, 1715), pp. 26–27.

Chapter 49. Annibale Carracci and Baroque Classicism

1. Bellori, *Vite dei pittori, scultori, ed architetti moderni,* p. 89.
2. Denis Mahon, *Studies in Seicento Art and Theory* (London: Warburg, 1947), p. 199.
3. "E basti solo dire, che per opera d'invenzione, d'ornamento, di capricci con nudi, di favole, e d'istorie diversamente condotte, non si può sperar cosa più perfetta; e chiunque la vede, della verità, è sforzato a dirne bene . . . per esser questi delle più belle opere, che a nostri tempi abbia inventate l'ingegno, ed espresse la pittura." G. Baglione, *Le vite de' pittori, scultori, architetti, ed intagliatori* (Naples, 1737), p. 101.
4. Mahon, *Studies in Seicento Art and Theory,* p. 252.
5. "Il n'y a rien que de grand, de noble et de bien entendu, soit dans l'ordonnance de tous les corps en général, soit dans l'expression de toutes les parties en particulier, soit dans la conduite des lumières et des ombres. Tout ce grand ouvrage n'est pas de ce dont la seule vivacité de couleurs et le brillant de lumière charment d'abord les yeux et surprennent ceux qui le regardent. On voit dans celui-çi une beauté solide qui frappe l'esprit et les plus intelligents y découvrent toujours des grâces nouvelles à mesure qu'ils les considèrent." André Félibien des Avaux, *Entretiens* (Paris, 1679), II, 67.

Chapter 50. Bernini

1. *Vita del cavalier G. L. Bernini, descritta da* Domenico Bernini *suo figlio* (Rome, 1713), p. 12.
2. "Hoggi in Roma, lo studio delle memorie di pietre, di bassorilievi, e delle statue antiche ad esempio et emulatione di questi antiquarii si e cosi fortemente disteso, e de per tutto accresciuto, che le muraglie dei palazzi, i cortilli, e le stanze ne sono piene, e dovitiose: ed i giardini come son vaghi d'ordini di piante, così sono ricchi d'opere di marmi; e co'l loro testimonio al mondo fanno anch'oggi fede della grandezza di questa Reggia dell'Universo." G. Baglione, *Vite de' pittori* (Rome, 1642), p. 74.
3. "Il a dit après qu'étant encore fort jeune, il dessinait souvent l'antique, et que, dans la première figure, qu'il fit, lorsq'il doutait de quelque chose, il s'en allait consulter l'Antin comme son oracle, et a dit qu'il remarquait alors de jour à autre, dans cette figure, des beautés qu'il n'avait pas encore vues et n'eût jamais vues, s'il n'eût point manié le ciseau pour opérer, à raison de quoi il conseillait toujours à ses élèves et à tous les autres de ne s'abandonner pas tant à dessiner et à modeler qu'ils ne se mettent aussi presqu'en même temps à travailler, soit de sculpture, soit de peinture entremêlant la production et l'imitation, l'une avec l'autre et, pour ainsi dire, l'action et le contemplation, dont résulte un grand et merveilleux progrès." Chantelou, *Journal,* quoted in A. Muñoz, "La Scultura barocca e l'antico," *L'Arte,* 19:151 (1916).

4. "Après, s'étant tenu debout au milieu de la salle, environné de tous ceux de l'Académie, il dit que son sentiment était que l'on eût dans l'Académie des plâtres de toutes les belles statues bas reliefs et bustes antiques pour l'instruction des jeunes gens, les faisant dessiner d'après ces manières antiques, afin de leur former d'abord l'idée sur le beau, ce que leur sert après toute leur vie; que c'est les perdre que de les mettre à dessiner au commencement d'après nature, laquelle presque toujours est faible et mesquine." *Ibid.*

Chapter 51. Rubens and Classical Antiquity

1. De Piles, *Abrégé de la vie des peintres,* pp. 26–27.
2. Roger de Piles, *Cours de Peinture par Principes* (Amsterdam and Leipzig, 1766), p. 127.

Chapter 53. Poussin and the Antique

1. Holt, *Literary Sources,* p. 406.

Chapter 55. The Rococo in France

1. "De la dégradation du goût, du coleur, de la composition, des caractères, de l'expression, du dessin, a suivi, pas à pas, la dégradation des mœurs." Quoted in Lady Dilke, *French Painters of the XVIIIth Century* (London, 1899), p. 56.
2. "Imite le bel antique et surtout la nature; mais quelquefois il l'imite peut-être trop exactement." Quoted in Lady Dilke, *French Architects and Sculptors of the XVIIIth Century* (London, 1900), p. 77.
3. *Ibid.,* p. 74.

Chapter 56. The Neoclassic Period

1. Winckelmann, in Holt, *Literary Sources,* pp. 532, 534.
2. Gotthold Ephraim Lessing, *Laocoön, oder über die Grenze der Malerei und Poesie* (Berlin, 1766).
3. Goldwater and Treves, *Artists on Art,* p. 196.
4. The architects James "Athenian" Stuart and his companion Nicholas Revett undertook a journey to Greece and the Greek isles in 1751–1753. Their book with its magnificent plates and measured drawings introduced to Western Europe the beauties of Greek architecture which for centuries had been hidden behind the "Iron Curtain" of Turkish domination of the Near East. *The Antiquities of Athens* was published in five volumes in London between 1762 and 1830.
5. Johann Zoffany (1733–1810) was a painter renowned for his portrait groups, not only in England but in Italy and India as well. He was a foundation member of the Royal Academy. The painting of Mr. Townley and his friends is reproduced in Francis Henry Taylor, *The Taste of Angels* (Boston, 1948), pp. 448–449.

Chapter 58. Canova

1. Byron, *Childe Harold's Pilgrimage,* Canto 4, LV, 9.
2. Edward Everett, "Life and Works of Canova," *The North American Review,* 29:441–478 (April 1829).

Chapter 59. Classicism and Republican Ideals: Jacques-Louis David

1. "L'antique ne me séduira pas; il manque d'entrain et ne remue pas." Conversation with Nicholas Cochin, quoted in Charles Saunier, *Louis David* (Paris, 1909), p. 12.
2. "Si c'est à Corneille que je dois mon sujet, c'est à Poussin que je dois mon tableau." Quoted by L. Hautecœur, *Louis David* (Paris, 1954), pp. 71–72, as a likely remark for David to have made. Actually, the motif of the father administering the oath to his sons does not occur in Corneille's *Horaces;* it appears likely—as Robert Rosenblum has pointed out in *Burlington Magazine* (January 1961), p. 15—that David was inspired by an engraving of Gavin Hamilton's canvas of The Oath of Brutus of 1764.
3. "Ca sera un tableau plus grec." M. E. J. Delécluze, *Louis David: son école et son temps* (Paris, 1855), p. 179.
4. Richard Cantinelli, *Jacques-Louis David* (Paris, 1930), p. 59.
5. R. Rosenblum, "A New Source for David's 'Sabines,' " *Burlington Magazine* (April 1962), pp. 158 ff.

Chapter 60. The Nineteenth Century

1. *Form and Function, Remarks on Art by Horatio Greenough,* ed. H. A. Small, (Los Angeles and Berkeley, 1947), p. 67.
2. *Rodin,* ed. Sommerville Story (Oxford and New York, 1939), p. 14.
3. First published in Paris, 1791.

Chapter 61. Classicism and Romanticism: Ingres

1. Norman Schlenoff, *Ingres, Ses sources littéraires* (Paris, 1956), pl. XV.
2. "Il aurait une telle physionomie de beauté que tout le monde, même les chiens enragés qui veulent me mordre, en devraient être touchés. Je l'ai presque composé dans ma tête et je le vois." Henry Lapauze, "Le Roman d'amour de M. Ingres," *Revue de Deux Mondes* (May 1910), p. 173; Schlenoff, pp. 122–123.
3. "Phidias parvint au sublime en corrigeant la nature avec elle-même." P. Courthion, ed., *Ingres: Pensées et écrits du Peintre* (Vésenez-Geneva, 1947), p. 44.
4. A. C. Quatremère de Quincy, *An Essay on the Nature and Means of Imitation in the Fine Arts,* trans. C. Kent (London, 1837), p. 275.
5. "Les statues grecques ne surpassent la nature que parce qu'on y a rassemblé toutes les belles parties que la nature réunit bien rarement dans un même sujet." Henri Delaborde, *Ingres: sa vie, ses travaux, sa doctrine* (Paris, 1870), p. 113.
6. Courthion, *Ingres,* p. 23.
7. Agnes Mongan, "Ingres and the Antique," *Journal of the Warburg and Courtauld Institutes,* 10:8–9 (1947).
8. "Phidias fut le premier qui atteignit, pour ainsi dire, la majesté divine et sut ajouter un nouveau motif au respect des peuples en leur rendant sensible ce qu'ils avaient adoré." Schlenoff, *Ingres,* p. 132.

Chapter 62. Neoclassicism in America

1. Albert Ten-Eyck Gardner, *Yankee Stonecutters* (New York, 1945), p. 31.
2. James Jackson Jarves, *The Art-Idea,* ed. B. Rowland, Jr. (Cambridge, Mass., 1960), p. 215.
3. Greenough, *Form and Function,* p. 19.
4. E. P. Richardson, *Painting in America* (New York, 1956), pp. 91–92.

Chapter 63. Rodin

1. Auguste Rodin, *Art* (Boston, 1912), p. 57.
2. See epigraph; *ibid.,* p. 8.

Chapter 64. The Twentieth Century

1. Ben Shahn, *The Shape of Content* (Cambridge, Mass., 1957), pp. 32–33.
2. Aby Warburg, "A Lecture on Serpent Ritual," *Journal of the Warburg Institute,* 2:292 (1938–1939).

Chapter 65. Maillol

1. Aristide Maillol, Letter to Count Kessler, from J. Cladel, *Maillol* (Paris, 1937), p. 97.

Chapter 67. Henry Moore

1. Sir Herbert Read, *Henry Moore* (London, 1955), II, xi.
2. *Ibid.,* p. xvi.
3. *Ibid.*

Chapter 68. De Chirico

1. James Thrall Soby, *Giorgio de Chirico* (New York: The Museum of Modern Art, 1955), p. 158.
2. *Ibid.,* p. 253.
3. *Ibid.,* p. 247.

Register of Places

363

Index

Aachen, Palace of Charlemagne, 101; Palatine Chapel, 102
Abelard, Peter, 122
Abraham, Prophet, 143, 157
Academy of Painting and Sculpture, 266, 297–298
Achilles, Shield of, 10
Adam: by Federighi, 177–178; by Ghiberti, 159; by Masaccio, 163–165; by Michelangelo, 201–202
Adam, Robert, 52, 286
Aday, Jean Félicissime, 300
Adonis, Sarcophagus of, 159
Aeneas, 60, 61, 137, 141
Aeschylus: and Greek sculpture, 9; mentioned, 36, 267
Agesandros of Rhodes, 46
Agucchi, Giovanni Battista: *Trattato della Pittura*, on Annibale Carracci, 251–252, 255; on imitation of nature, 252
Albani, on Titian and Correggio, 207, 209
Alberti, G. B.: architecture, 167, 177; *de Statua*, 165, 185; on proportion, 165–166, 185; mentioned, 147, 150, 154
Albrizzi, Contessa, on Canova, 294–295
Alcuin, and ruins of Rome, 136
Aldobrandini Marriage: ancient painting (Vatican), 50; copied by Poussin, 269
Alexander the Great, portrait of (Boston): and portrait of Constantine, 82; mentioned, 35, 36, 42n, 43, 82, 266, 286
Alexandria, 37, 96
Allegory of Luxury, by Bronzino, 219–221
Allston, Washington, 316–317
AMADEO, Giovanni Antonio (1447–1522), and German art, 179
    Labors of Hercules, Bergamo, Colleoni Chapel, 178–179
Amazon, 209; by Phidias, 67; by Polyclitus, 67, 69
Ampelius, Lucius, *Liber Memorialis*, 35
Amphitrite, by Poussin, 269–270
Anaxagoras, 8
Andrei Ungari, *Descriptio Victoriae Karolo Provinciae Comité Reportatae*, 128
Anima razionale, 200

ANTELAMI, Benedetto (1177–1233), 118–121
    Archangel (Parma, Baptistery), 120–121
    Victory, Arch of Constantine, 120
Antigone. See Sophocles
Antinoüs: portrait of, 67–68; and De Chirico, 336; and Michelangelo, 198; and Phidias, 67; and Polyclitus, 67; and Zoffoli, 229–230
Apelles, Greek painter, and Botticelli, 170, 308; mentioned, 49, 183
Aphrodite, 26n, 31–32, 141, 169, 190
    Crouching (Paris), 203
    Greco-Roman head (Paris), 70
    Kaufmann head (Paris), 221
    See also Bartlett Head; Capitoline Venus; Venus dei Medici
Apollo, 3, 9, 12–14, 15, 57, 75, 107; and Christ, 85–86, 204–205, 240–241; and Louis XIV, 266
Apollo (Kouros), statue of (New York), 13–14
Apollo, statue of (Olympia), 26; by Dürer, 241–242
Apollo and Daphne, by Bernini, 259–261
Apollo Belvedere (Vatican), 43–44; and Bernini, 257, 260–261; and Canova, 294–295; and Dürer, 240–241; and Girardon, 272; and Mengs, 291; and Michelangelo, 204–205, 241; mentioned, 41, 185, 204–205, 228, 236, 286, 314
Apollodorus of Athens, 42
Apollonius of Athens, 44. See also *Belvedere Torso*
Apoxyomenos, by Lysippus, 32–33
Apuleius, *The Golden Ass,* 217
Aquinas, St. Thomas, and art, 122–123, 142
Ara Pacis, Rome, 61–63; and Byzantine mosaics, 91–92; and Parthenon, 60–61; and Theodulf's vase, 102
Aratus MS (Leyden), 105
Arcadius, Emperor, column of, 76
Archangels, by Guglielmo, 115–116, 121
Architecture, Roman, 58, 114
Arete, 27

Quartremère de Quincy, *Lettres,* 281; on Greek art, 308–309; mentioned, 279, 288

Quirinale, Piazza del. *See* Montecavallo

RAPHAEL (1483–1520), 186–187, 189–190; and Botticelli, 186–187, 190; and Castiglione, 191; and Giulio Romano, 193, 355; and Ingres, 288; and Mengs, 289; and Michelangelo, 114; and Parmigianino, 215; and Penni, 192; and Perugino, 186; and Philostratus, 355; and Picasso, 187; and Poussin, 269–270; and *Venus of Capua,* 189, 355; and *Montecavallo,* 189; and Phidian sculpture, 188; and Pompeian painting, 189–190; *Idea,* 190; mentioned, 45, 50, 52, 193, 215, 234, 255, 259, 288, 327

    Galatea (Rome), 189–190, 234, 269, 355

    Knight's Dream (London), 187

    School of Athens (Vatican), 184

    Three Graces (Chantilly), 186–187, 189

Read, Sir Herbert, on Henry Moore, 330

Reims, Scriptorium of, 103

Renovatio, 102–103, 112

Revett. *See* Stuart and Revett

Reynolds, Sir Joshua, *Discourses:* on Annibale Carracci, 254; on Poussin, 268

Richardson, Edgar, on Vanderlyn, 317

Richardson, John, on Picasso, 326

Richelieu, Cardinal, 269

Rienzi, Coladi, 109

RODIN, Auguste (1840–1917): and Michelangelo, 319; and Phidias, 319; and Polyclitus, 319; and Praxiteles, 320; *Art,* 319; on Greek sculpture, 319; mentioned, 304, 306, 324

    Half-Figure of a Woman (Paris), 320

Rome, Marvels of. See *Mirabilia Urbis Romae*

Rome: ruins of, 98, 109, 147; and Alcuin, 136; and Hildebert of Lavardin, 106, 108, 112; and Petrarch, 108, 111, 147; and Giulio Romano, 45; and Parmigianino, 45, 216; and Piranesi, 56

Rosso, Il, 236–237

RUBENS, Peter Paul (1577–1640): and Poussin, 270; and *Spinario,* 263; and *Crouching Venus,* 264; *De Imitatione Statuarum,* 262–263; on imitating ancient statues, 262–264; palette, 263; mentioned, 249–256

Spinario (London), 263

Venus Frigida (Antwerp), 264

Rush, William, 312

Rutilius Namatianus, 108; *Itinerarii,* 56

Sabines, by David, 301–302

Sadoletus, Jacobus, *De Laocoöntis Statua,* 243

St. Gilles, and Roman architecture, 117

St. Sebastian, by Mantegna, 181, 182

Salutati, on Labors of Hercules, 152, 158

Samson, 77, 107, 134, 161

Sappho, and Greek sculpture, 31–32, 34

Sarcophagi: Early Christian, 114, 117–118; Late Antique, 117; Roman, 99, 119, 133–135, 142, 151, 159, 177, 197, 208, 213, 238, 269, 276, 309

Savonarola, 196

Schatzkammer Gospels (Vienna), 103–104; and Reims sculpture, 103; and Pompeian painting, 103

Schiller, 304

Schopenhauer, 334

Scipio Africanus, 187

SCOPAS (fourth century B.C.): and Praxiteles, 33; and Phidias, 33

    Maenad (Dresden), 34

    Meleager (Cambridge, Mass.), 33–34

    Thiasos, 189

Seurat, 166

Shahn, Ben: *Allegory,* 322; and Roman wolf, 322

Shelley, 2; "Prometheus Unbound," 12, 287; on Montecavallo, 231

Soane, Sir John, 311

Socrates, Death of, by David, 299–300

Sol Invictus, Christ as, 204, 241

Soldani, Massimiliano, 229

Sophocles, 9, 267; and Greek sculpture, 9, 27; *Antigone,* 9; statue of (Lateran), 86, 143

Speculum Romanae Magnificentiae, 234, 357

Spinario, statue of (Rome), 174, 227, 263; drawing of by Rubens, 263

Squarcione, 180–181

Stuart and Revett, *The Antiquities of Athens,* 284, 286, 306, 359

Suetonius, on Augustus, 64

Suger, Abbot, 98

Symmachii, ivory plaque of (London), 78–79

Symmachus, Q. Aurelius, 78–79, 97

Symonds, John Addington, *The Renaissance in Italy,* 146

ILLUSTRATIONS

2. *Pericles. London, British Museum*

1. *Zeus of Artemision. Athens, National Museum*

3. *Temple of the Olympian Zeus with the Acropolis. Athens*

4. *The Parthenon. Athens*

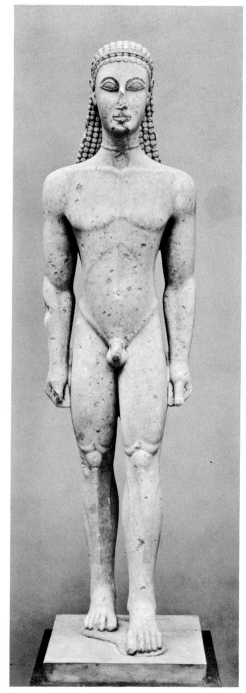

5b. *Apollo or Kouros. Detail of head*

5a. *Apollo or Kouros. New York,*
Metropolitan Museum of Art,
Fletcher Fund, 1922

6. Apollo. Olympia, Museum

7. Apollo. Detail of Head. Olympia, Museum

8. The Chatsworth Head. London, British Museum

9. *Discobolos of Myron. Rome, Museo
Nazionale Archeologico*

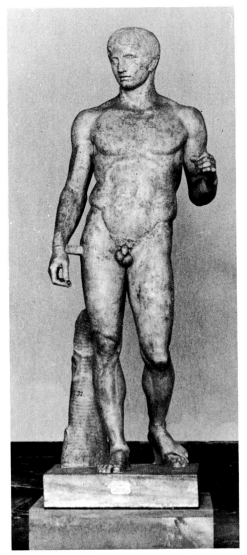

10. *Doryphoros of Polyclitus. Naples,
Museo Nazionale Archeologico*

11. Head of Zeus after Phidias. Boston,
Museum of Fine Arts

12. Head of Lemnian Athena after Phidias.
Bologna, Museo Civico

13. Theseus or Olympus from the Parthenon. London, British Museum

14. Aphrodite in the lap of Dione from the Parthenon. London, British Museum

15. Centaur and Lapith from the Parthenon. London, British Museum

16. Centaur and Lapith from the Parthenon. London, British Museum

17. Detail from the Parthenon frieze. London, British Museum

18. Detail from the Parthenon frieze. London, British Museum

19. Hermes of Praxiteles. Olympia, Museum

20. Hermes of Praxiteles. Detail of head. Olympia, Museum

21. Head of Aphrodite by Praxiteles. Boston, Museum of Fine Arts

22. Greco-Roman copy of Aphrodite of Praxiteles. Paris, Louvre

23. *Apoxyomenos of Lysippus. Rome, Vatican*

24. *Meleager of Scopas. Cambridge, Massachusetts, Fogg Art Museum*

25. *Maenad of Scopas. Dresden, Albertinum*

26. Detail of Frieze of the Pergamum Altar. Berlin, Staatliche Museen

27. Detail of Frieze of the Pergamum Altar. Berlin,
Staatliche Museen

28. *Detail of Frieze of the Pergamum Altar. Berlin,
Staatliche Museen*

29. *Iris from the Parthenon. London, British Museum*

*30. Venus dei Medici. Florence,
Uffizi*

31. Apollo Belvedere. Rome, Vatican Museum

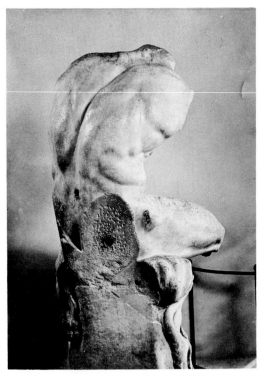

*32a. The Belvedere Torso. Rome,
Vatican Museum*

*32b. The Belvedere Torso. Rome,
Vatican Museum*

33. Ariadne. Rome, Vatican Museum

34. Laocoön. Rome, Vatican Museum

35. *Theseus Triumphant over the Minotaur. Naples, Museo Nazionale Archeologico*

36. *Perseus and Andromeda. Naples, Museo Nazionale Archeologico*

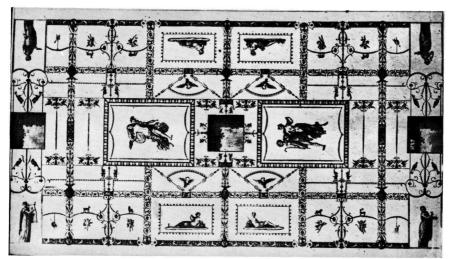

37. *Grotteschi. Rome, Baths of Titus*

*38. Hercules and Telephus. Naples, Museo Nazionale
Archeologico*

39. Odyssey Landscape. Rome, Vatican Museum

40. *The Ara Pacis. Rome*

41. *Frieze of Ara Pacis. Rome*

42. Augustus of Prima Porta. Rome, Vatican Museum

43. Reflecting Pool. Tivoli, Hadrian's Villa

44. Caryatids by reflecting pool. Tivoli,
Hadrian's Villa

45. *Caryatid from Tivoli.*
    Hadrian's Villa

46. *Caryatid. Athens, The Erectheum*

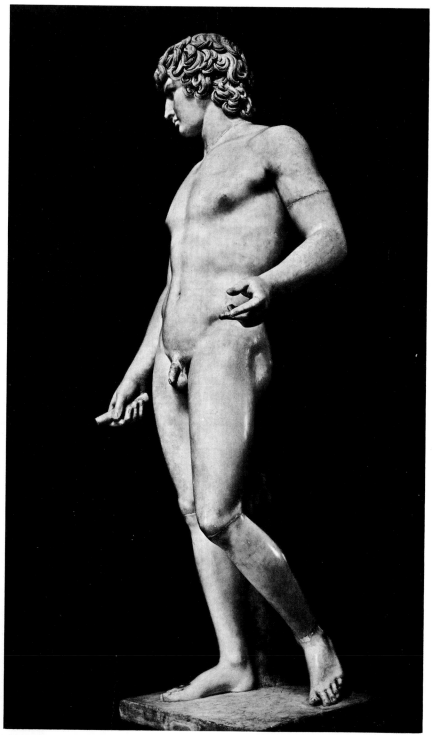

47. Antinoüs. Naples, Museo Nazionale Archeologico

*48. Boy from the Bay of Marathon.
Athens, National Museum*

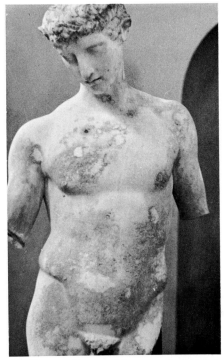

49. Hermes. Boston, Museum of Fine Arts

50. *Boy from the Bay of Marathon. Detail of head. Athens, National Museum*

51. *Hermes. Detail of head. Boston, Museum of Fine Arts*

52. *Poseidon from the Parthenon. London,
British Museum*

53. *Horse-tamer. Rome, Piazza del Quirinale*

54. *Hercules and the Erymanthian Boar. Venice, San Marco*

55. *Nike. Istanbul, Archaeological Museum*

56. *Nike from the Parthenon. London, British Museum*

57. Diptych of the Symmachii. London, Victoria and Albert Museum

58. Illustration from the Vatican Virgil. Rome, Vatican Museum

59. *Head of Alexander the Great. Boston, Museum of Fine Arts*

60. *Head of Constantine. Rome, Palazzo dei Conservatori*

61. Sarcophagus from Psamatia. Berlin, Staatliche Museen

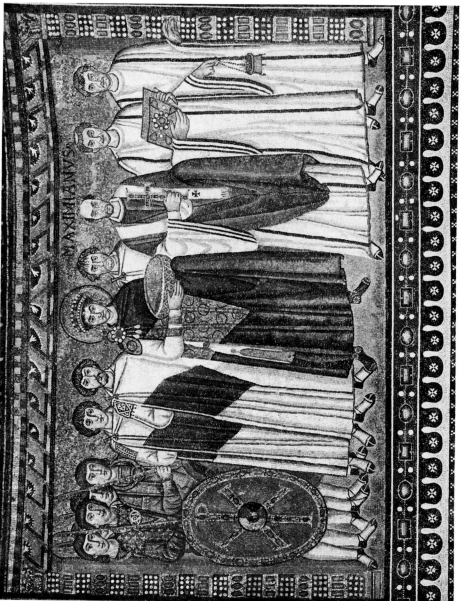

62. *Justinian and his Retinue. Ravenna, San Vitale*

63. *Moses before the Burning Bush. Ravenna, San Vitale*

64. *Nike tying her Sandal. Athens, Acropolis*

65. *Illustration from the Paris Psalter. Paris, Bibliothèque Nationale*

66. *Sarcophagus of Selene and Endymion. Rome, Palazzo dei Conservatori*

67. *Fragment of Sarcophagus. Calvi, Cathedral*

68. *Nereid Sarcophagus. Detail. Rome, Museo Nazionale Archeologico*

69. Gospels of Lothair. Paris,
Bibliothèque Nationale

70. Missorium of the Emperor Theodosius. Madrid, Museo de la
Academia de la Historia

71. *Evangelist. Schatzkammer Gospels. Vienna,
Kunsthistorisches Museum*

72. *Evangelist. Gospels of Ebbo. Epernay,
Bibliothèque de la ville*

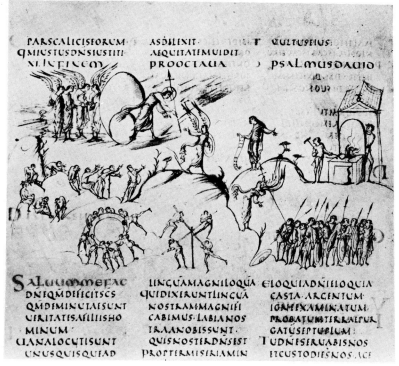

73. *Illustration from the Utrecht Psalter. Utrecht, University Library*

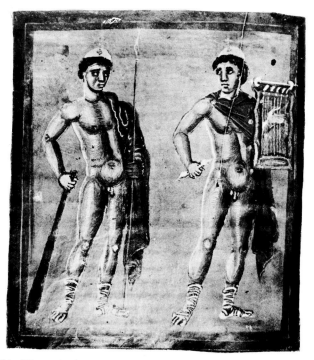

74. *Dioscuri. Aratus Manuscript. Leyden, University Library*

75. *Claudio Coello. House of Crescentius, Rome. Vienna, Albertina*

76. *Francisco de Hollanda.*
Venus. Escorial, Library

77. *Apostles. Arles, St. Trophîme*

78. *St. James the Great. St. Gilles*

79a. Hercules. Arles, St. Trophîme

79b. Hercules and the Cecrops. Arles, St. Trophîme

80. Master Guglielmo. Genius with Torch. Modena, Cathedral

81. Genius with Torch. Fragment of Sarcophagus.
Rome, Museo Nazionale Archeologico

82. *Antelami. Archangel. Parma, Baptistry*

83. *Victory. Rome, Arch of Constantine*

84. Villard d'Honnecourt. Drawings of Statues. Paris, Bibliothèque Nationale

85. Villard d'Honnecourt. Drawing of Two Saints.
Paris, Bibliothèque Nationale

86. The Visitation. Reims, Cathedral

87. *Torso of a draped figure. Avignon, Musée Calvet*

88. *Statue of a Vestal. Rome, Museo Nazionale*
Archeologico

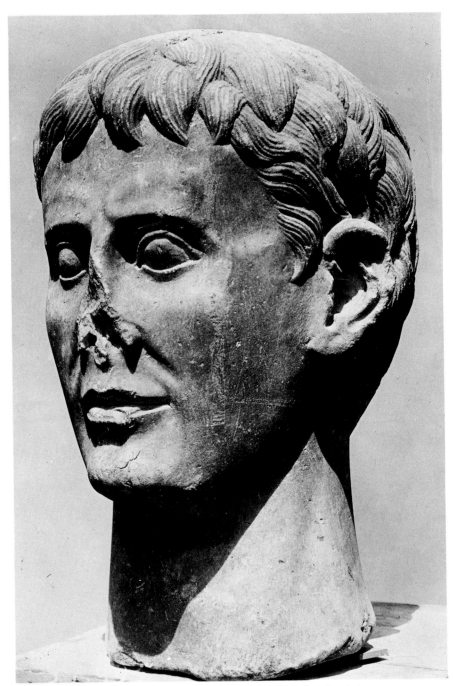

89. *Head of Frederick II. Rome, Deutsches Archäologisches Institut*

90. *Augustus of Prima Porta. Detail of head. Rome, Vatican Museum*

91. *Augustales of Frederick II. Naples, Museo Nazionale
Archeologico*

92. *Nicola Pisano. Fortitude. Pisa, Baptistry*

93. *Sarcophagus of Phaedra and Hippolytus.*
Detail of Hippolytus. Pisa, Campo Santo

94. *Hercules Sarcophagus. Detail. Rome, Museo*
Nazionale Archeologico

95. Nicola Pisano. Adoration of the Magi. Pisa, Baptistry

96. Sarcophagus of Phaedra and Hippolytus. Detail
of Phaedra. Pisa, Campo Santo

97. *Duccio. The Three Marys at the Tomb. Siena, Opera del Duomo*

98. *Simone Martini. Illustration for Virgil Codex. Milan, Ambrosiana*

99. *Ambrogio Lorenzetti. Allegory of Good Government. Detail of Peace. Siena, Palazzo Pubblico*

100. *Fragment of Phaedra Sarcophagus. Girgenti, Cathedral*

101. Sacrifice of Isaac. Assisi, San Francesco

102. Sophocles of the Lateran. Rome,
Lateran Museum

103. *Jacob's Offering. Detail of head of Isaac. Assisi, San Francesco*

104. Giotto. Pietà. Padua, Arena Chapel

105. Sarcophagus with Death of Meleager. Location unknown

106. *Ghiberti. Sacrifice of Isaac. Florence, Museo Nazionale*

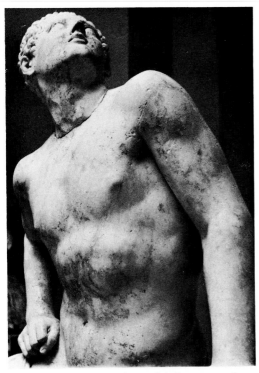

107. *Niobid. Rome, Palazzo dei Conservatori*

108. *Torso of a Faun. Florence, Uffizi*

109. *Hercules. Porta della Mandorla. Florence, Cathedral*

110. *Sarcophagus with Legend of Adonis. Detail. Rome, Casino Rospigliosi*

111. Ghiberti. Genesis. Florence, Baptistry

113. Masaccio. The Expulsion from Eden. Florence, Santa Maria del Carmine

112. Giovanni Pisano. Prudence. Pisa, Cathedral

114. *Piero della Francesca. Hercules. Boston, Isabella*
Stewart Gardner Museum

115. *Hercules. Los Angeles, Getty Museum*

116. *Botticelli. La Primavera. Florence, Uffizi*

117. *The Three Graces. Siena, Opera
del Duomo*

118. *Maenad. Rome, Palazzo dei
Conservatori*

119. *Botticelli. The Birth of Venus. Florence, Uffizi*

120. *Masolino. Baptism. Castiglione d'Olona, Baptistry*

121. Donatello. David.
Florence, Museo
Nazionale

122. Mercury. Florence, Uffizi

123. *Donatello. Gattamelata Padua, Piazza del Santo*

124. Marcus Aurelius. Rome, Campidoglio

125. Bronze Horses. Venice, San Marco

126. *Federighi. Hercules and the Lion. Siena, Cathedral*

127. Hercules and the Stag. Rome, Villa Borghese

128. Amadeo. Labors of Hercules. Bergamo, Colleoni Chapel

129. *Mantegna. St. Sebastian. Paris,*
Louvre

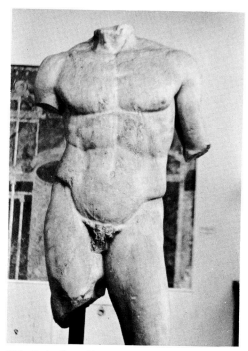

130. *Polyclitan Torso of an Athlete. Boston,*
Museum of Fine Arts

131. Raphael. The Three Graces. Chantilly, Musée Condé

132. The Three Graces. Naples, Museo Nazionale

133. *Raphael. Galatea. Rome, Villa Farnesina*

134. Venus of Capua. Naples, Museo Nazionale Archeologico

135. *Penni. Council of the Gods. Rome, Villa Farnesina*

136. Michelangelo. Battle of the Centaurs. Florence, Casa Buonarroti

137. Sarcophagus with Battle of Romans and Barbarians. Rome,
Museo Nazionale Archeologico

138. Michelangelo. David. Florence, Accademia

139. Head of Horse-tamer.
Rome, Piazza del Quirinale

141. Head of Antinoüs. Rome, Museo
Nazionale Archeologico

140. Michelangelo. David. Detail of head.
Florence, Accademia

142. *Michelangelo. Ignudo. Rome, Vatican,*
Sistine ceiling

143. *Michelangelo. Creation of Adam. Rome, Vatican, Sistine ceiling*

144. Michelangelo. Bound Slave.
Paris, Louvre

145. Michelangelo. Giuliano dei Medici. Florence,
San Lorenzo Sacristy

146. *Michelangelo. Night. Florence, San Lorenzo Sacristy*

147. Michelangelo. Last Judgment. Rome, Vatican, Sistine Chapel

*148. Michelangelo. Last Judgment. Detail of head of Christ. Rome, Vatican,
Sistine Chapel*

149. Titian. Bacchus and Ariadne. London, National Gallery

150. Sarcophagus with Legend of Orestes. Rome, Lateran Museum

151. Falling Gaul. Venice, Museo Archeologico

152. Titian. Rape of Europa. Boston, Isabella Stewart Gardner Museum

153. *Parmigianino. Madonna della Rosa. Dresden, Gallery*

154. Parmigianino. Amor.
Dresden, Gallery

155. Cupid after Lysippus. Venice,
Museo Archeologico

156. *Bronzino. Allegory of Luxury. London, National Gallery*

157. *Kaufmann. Head of Aphrodite.*
Paris, Louvre

158. *Bronzino. Martyrdom of St. Lawrence.*
Detail. Florence, San Lorenzo

159b. Cellini. Narcissus. Detail of head. Florence,
Museo Nazionale

159a. Cellini. Narcissus. Florence,
Museo Nazionale

160. *Reclining Faun. Naples, Museo Nazionale*
Archeologico

161. *Cellini. Ganymede. Florence,*
Museo Nazionale

162. *Torso. London, Victoria and Albert Museum*

163. *Zoffoli. Antinoüs. Cambridge, Massachusetts, Rowland Collection*

164. *Horse-tamer. Rome, Piazza del Quirinale*

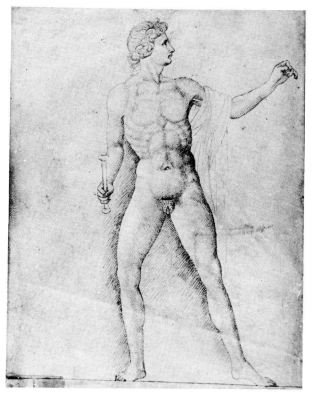

165. Pisanello. Horse-tamer. Milan, Ambrosiana

166. Horse-tamers of Montecavallo. Cambridge, Massachusetts, Rowland Collection

167. *Lafreri. Horse-tamers of Montecavallo* (from *Speculum Romanae Magnificentiae*)

168. *Horse-tamer. London, Wallace Collection*

169. *Diana the Huntress. Paris, Louvre*

170. *Diana of Versailles. Paris, Louvre*

171. Goujon. Nymphs. Paris, Fontaine des Innocents

172. Dürer. Apollo. London, British Museum

173. El Greco. Laocoön. Washington, National Gallery

174. Carracci. Polyphemus. Rome, Palazzo Farnese

175. Carracci. Detail of ceiling. Rome, Palazzo Farnese

176. Farnese Hercules. Naples,
Museo Nazionale Archeologico

177. Bernini. David. Rome, Villa Borghese

178. Borghese Warrior. Paris, Louvre

179. Bernini. Apollo and Daphne. Rome, Villa Borghese

*180. Bernini. Apollo and Daphne. Detail of head of
Apollo. Rome, Villa Borghese*

*181. Apollo Belvedere. Detail of head. Rome,
Vatican Museum*

183. Maenad. Rome, Museo
Nazionale Archeologico

182. Bernini. Apollo and Daphne.
Rome, Villa Borghese

184. Rubens. Drawing of Spinario. London, British Museum

185. Spinario. Rome, Museo Capitolino

186. Rubens. Venus Chilled. Antwerp, Museum

187. Crouching Venus. Paris, Louvre

188. *Poussin. Copy of the Aldobrandini Marriage. Rome, Doria Gallery*

189. *Aldobrandini Marriage. Rome, Vatican Museum*

190. Poussin. Triumph of Neptune and Amphitrite. Philadelphia Museum of Art

191. Sarcophagus with Marine Deities. Rome, Vatican, Giardino della Pigna

192. Poussin. St. John on Patmos. Chicago, Art Institute

193. Girardon. Apollo and the Nymphs. Versailles

194. Puget. Milo of Croton. Paris, Louvre

195. Boucher. Triumph of Venus. Stockholm, National Gallery

196. Bouchardon. Cupid. Paris, Louvre

197. Clodion. Nymph and Satyr. New York,
Metropolitan Museum of Art, Altman Bequest, 1913

198. Nymph and Satyr. Rome, Palazzo dei Conservatori

199. Mengs. Parnassus. Rome, Villa Albani

200. Mengs. Perseus and Andromeda. Leningrad,
Hermitage

201. Freeing of Hesione. Rome, Villa Albani

202. *Canova. Perseus. Rome, Vatican Museum*

203. Canova. Cupid and Psyche. Lago di Como, Villa Carlotta

204. Eros of Centocelle. Rome, Vatican Museum

205. Cupid and Psyche. Venice, Museo
Archeologico

206. *David. Oath of the Horatii. Paris, Louvre*

207. *David. Death of Socrates. New York, Metropolitan Museum of Art*

208. *Sarcophagus with Death of Meleager.* Engraving (from Bernard de Montfaucon,
L'Antiquité Expliqué)

209. David. The Sabines. Paris, Louvre

210. David. Warrior. Detroit Institute of Arts

211. Athena from Panathenaic Amphora.
Location unknown

212. *Ingres. Jupiter and Thetis. Aix-en-Provence, Museum*

213. Zeus Enthroned. Engraving (from
Museo Real Borbonico)

214. Flaxman. Thetis before Jupiter. Engraving (from John Flaxman,
The Iliad of Homer)

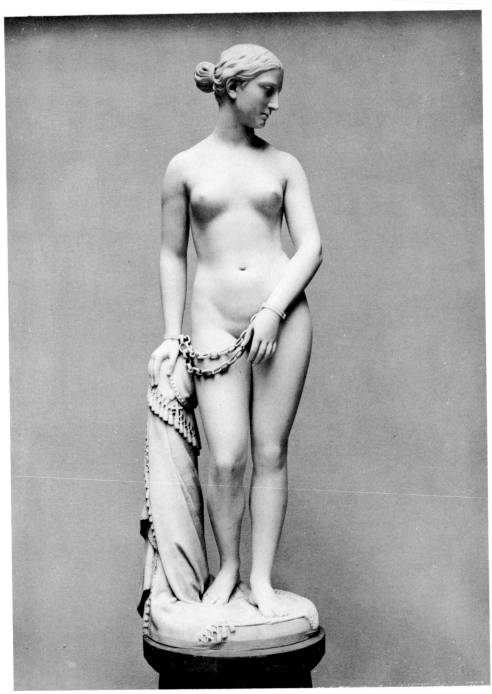

215. Powers. The Greek Slave. Washington, Corcoran Gallery

216. *Greenough. Washington. Washington, Smithsonian Institute*

217. *Vanderlyn. Death of Jane McCrea. Hartford, Wadsworth Atheneum*

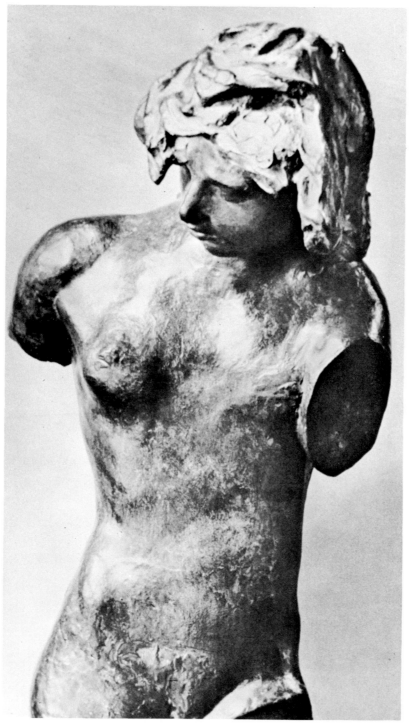

218. *Rodin. Half-figure of a Woman. Paris, Musée Rodin*

219. Maillol. La Méditerranée. Winterthur,
Dr. Oskar Reinhart Collection

220. Crouching Youth. Olympia, Museum

221. *Picasso. Boy Leading a Horse. New York, Paley Collection*

222. *Picasso. Classic Head. Worcester, Art Museum*

223. *Picasso. L'Amour Masqué. Paris, Galerie Leiris*

224. *White-figured Lekythos. Athens, National Museum*

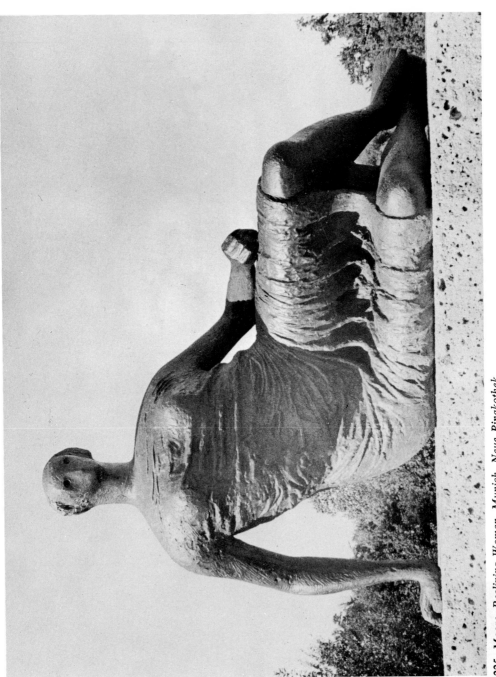

225. Moore. *Reclining Woman. Munich, Neue Pinakothek*

226. De Chirico. Joys and Enigmas of a Strange Hour. Santa Barbara, Ludington Collection

227. *De Chirico. Roman Villa. Mexico City, Pagliai Collection*

228. De Chirico. Self-portrait. Location unknown

229. Böcklin. Self-portrait. Berlin, National Galerie